Microsoft® Access 2000

Illustrated Second Course

Microsoft® Access 2000 Illustrated Second Course

Lisa Friedrichsen

COURSE TECHNOLOGY
Thomson Learning™

ONE MAIN STREET, CAMBRIDGE, MA 02142

Australia • Canada • Denmark • Japan • Mexico • New Zealand • Philippines
Puerto Rico • Singapore • South Africa • Spain • United Kingdom • United States

Microsoft Access 2000—Illustrated Second Course is published by Course Technology

Senior Product Manager:	Kathryn Schooling
Product Manager:	Rebecca VanEsselstine
Associate Product Manager:	Emily Heberlein
Contributing Author:	Elizabeth Eisner Reding
Production Editor:	Elena Montillo
Developmental Editor:	Rachel Biheller Bunin
Marketing Manager:	Karen Bartlett
Editorial Assistant:	Stacie Parillo
Composition House:	GEX, Inc.
QA Manuscript Reviewer:	Jeff Schwartz, Alex White, Matt Carroll, Jonathan Greacen, John Freitas
Text Designer:	Joseph Lee, Joseph Lee Designs
Cover Designer:	Doug Goodman, Doug Goodman Designs

Trademarks

Course Technology and the Open Book logo are registered trademarks of Course Technology.

Illustrated Projects and the Illustrated Series are trademarks of Course Technology.

Some of the product names and company names used in this book have been used for identification purposes only and may be trademarks or registered trademarks of their respective manufacturers and sellers.

Microsoft and the Microsoft Office User Specialist Logo are registered trademarks of Microsoft Corporation in the United States and other countries. Course Technology is an independent entity from Microsoft Corporation, and not affiliated with Microsoft Corporation in any manner. This publication may be used in assisting students to prepare for a Microsoft Office User Specialist Exam. Neither Microsoft Corporation, its designated review company, nor Course Technology warrants that use of this publication will ensure passing the relevant Exam.

Use of the Microsoft Office User Specialist Approved Courseware Logo on this product signifies that it has been independently reviewed and approved in complying with the following standards:

Acceptable coverage of all content related to the Microsoft Office Exam entitled Microsoft Access 2000 and sufficient performance-based exercises that relate closely to all required content, based on sampling of text.

For more information contact:

Course Technology
One Main Street
Cambridge, MA 02142

or find us on the World Wide Web at: www.course.com

Disclaimer

Course Technology reserves the right to revise this publication and make changes from time to time in its content without notice.

ISBN 0-7600-6071-1

Printed in the United States of America

1 2 3 4 5 6 7 8 9 BM 04 03 02 01 00

The Illustrated Series Offers the Entire Package for your Microsoft Office 2000 Needs

Office 2000 MOUS Certification Coverage

The Illustrated Series offers a growing number of Microsoft-approved titles that cover the objectives required to pass the Office 2000 MOUS exams. After studying with any of the approved Illustrated titles (see list on inside cover), you will have mastered the Core and Expert skills necessary to pass any Office 2000 MOUS exam with flying colors. In addition, **Access 2000 MOUS Certification Objectives** at the end of the book map to where specific MOUS skills can be found in each lesson and where students can find additional practice.

Helpful New Features

The Illustrated Series responded to Customer Feedback by adding a **Project Files list** at the back of the book for easy reference, Changing the red font in the Steps to green for easier reading, and Adding New Conceptual lessons to units to give students the extra information they need when learning Office 2000.

New Exciting Case and Innovative On-Line Companion

There is an exciting new case study used throughout our textbooks, a fictitious company called MediaLoft, designed to be "real-world" in nature by introducing the kinds of activities that students will encounter when working with Microsoft Office 2000. The **MediaLoft Web site**, available at www.course.com/illustrated/medialoft, is an innovative Student Online Companion which enhances and augments the printed page by bringing students onto the Web for a dynamic and continually updated learning experience. The MediaLoft site mirrors the case study used throughout the book, creating a real-world intranet site for this chain of bookstore cafés. This Companion is used to complete the WebWorks exercise in each unit of this book, and to allow students to become familiar with the business application of an intranet site.

Enhance Any Illustrated Text with these Exciting Products!

Course CBT

Enhance your students' Office 2000 classroom learning experience with self-paced computer-based training on CD-ROM. Course CBT engages students with interactive multimedia and hands-on simulations that reinforce and complement the concepts and skills covered in the textbook. All the content is aligned with the MOUS (Microsoft Office User Specialist) program, making it a great preparation tool for the certification exams. Course CBT also includes extensive pre- and post-assessments that test students' mastery of skills.

SAM 2000

How well do your students *really* know Microsoft Office? SAM 2000 is a performance-based testing program that measures students' proficiency in Microsoft Office 2000. SAM 2000 is available for Office 2000 in either a live or simulated environment. You can use SAM 2000 to place students into or out of courses, monitor their performance throughout a course, and help prepare them for the MOUS certification exams.

Create Your Ideal Course Package with CourseKits™

If one book doesn't offer all the coverage you need, create a course package that does. With Course Technology's CourseKits—our mix-and-match approach to selecting texts—you have the freedom to combine products from more than one series. When you choose any two or more Course Technology products for one course, we'll discount the price and package them together so your students can pick up one convenient bundle at the bookstore.

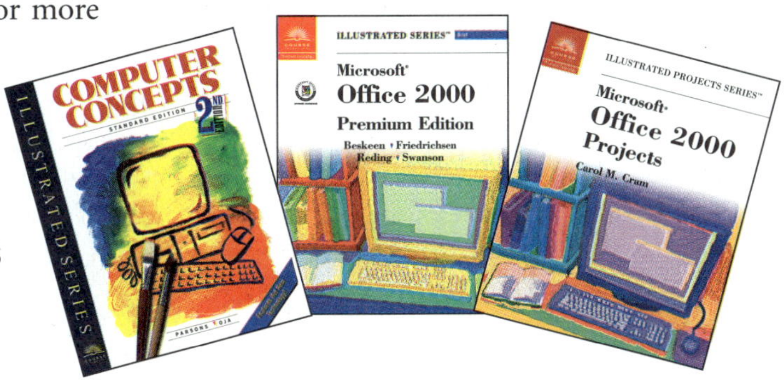

For more information about any of these offerings or other Course Technology products, contact your sales representative or visit our web site at:

www.course.com

Preface

Welcome to *Microsoft Access 2000—Illustrated Second Course.* This highly visual book is a continuation of *Microsoft Access 2000—Illustrated Introductory*, and is designed for people who want even more hands-on coverage of Access 2000 skills.

► Organization and Coverage

This text contains eight units that cover advanced Access skills. In these units, students learn how to share information with other Office programs, create data access pages, create advanced forms and reports, manage database objects, create macros and modules, and maintain relational databases.

► About this Approach

What makes the Illustrated approach so effective at teaching software skills? It's quite simple. Each skill is presented on two facing pages, with the step-by-step instructions on the left page, and large screen illustrations on the right. Students can focus on a single skill without having to turn the page. This unique design makes information extremely accessible and easy to absorb, and provides a great reference for after the course is over. This hands-on approach also makes it ideal for both self-paced or instructor-led classes.

Each lesson, or "information display," contains the following elements:

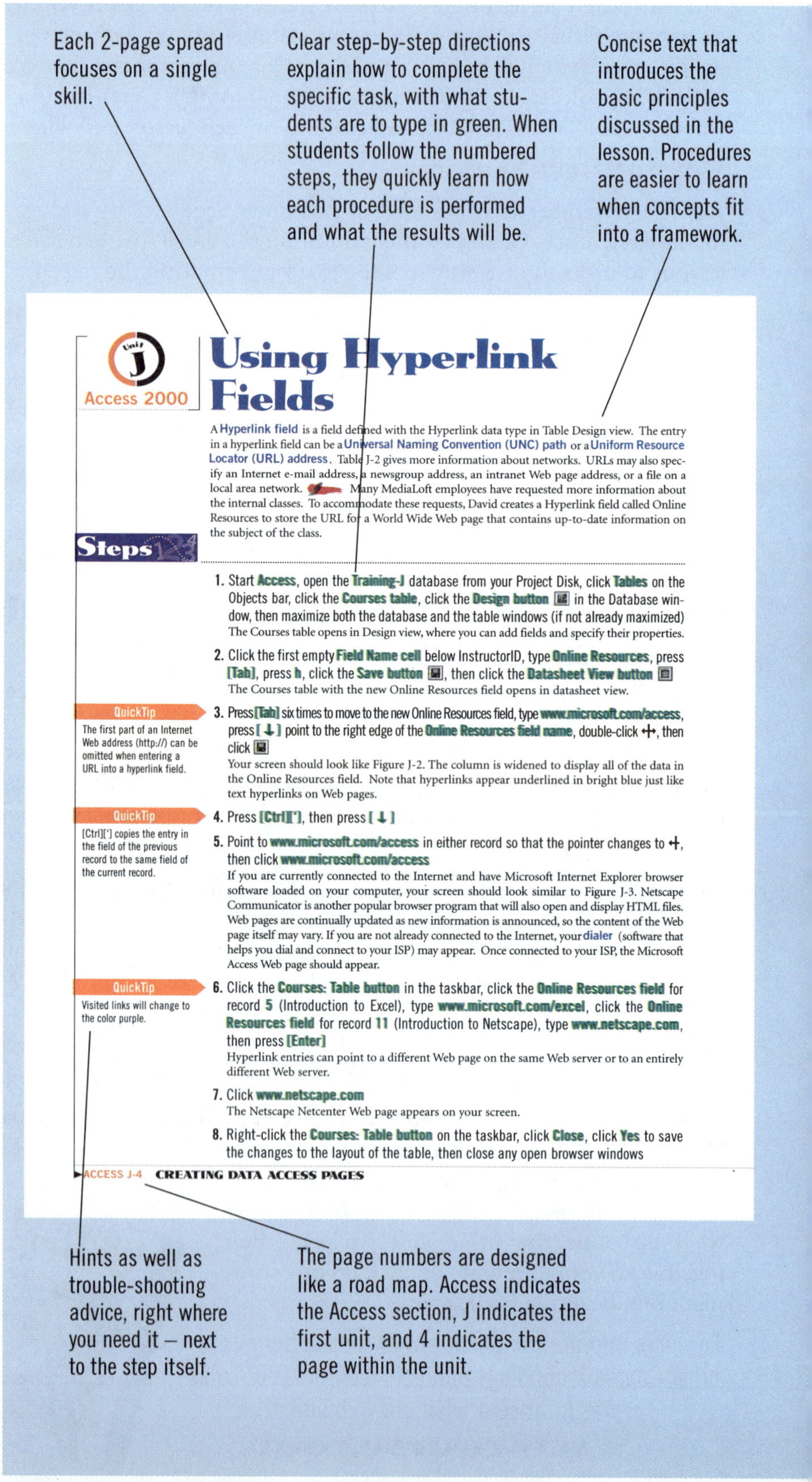

Unit J Access 2000

Using Hyperlink Fields

A Hyperlink field is a field defined with the Hyperlink data type in Table Design view. The entry in a hyperlink field can be a Universal Naming Convention (UNC) path or a Uniform Resource Locator (URL) address. Table J-2 gives more information about networks. URLs may also specify an Internet e-mail address, a newsgroup address, an intranet Web page address, or a file on a local area network. Many MediaLoft employees have requested more information about the internal classes. To accommodate these requests, David creates a Hyperlink field called Online Resources to store the URL for a World Wide Web page that contains up-to-date information on the subject of the class.

Steps

1. Start Access, open the Training-J database from your Project Disk, click Tables on the Objects bar, click the Courses table, click the Design button in the Database window, then maximize both the database and the table windows (if not already maximized)
   The Courses table opens in Design view, where you can add fields and specify their properties.
2. Click the first empty Field Name cell below InstructorID, type Online Resources, press [Tab], press h, click the Save button, then click the Datasheet View button
   The Courses table with the new Online Resources field opens in datasheet view.
3. Press [Tab] six times to move to the new Online Resources field, type www.microsoft.com/access, press [↓] point to the right edge of the Online Resources field name, double-click, then click
   Your screen should look like Figure J-2. The column is widened to display all of the data in the Online Resources field. Note that hyperlinks appear underlined in bright blue just like text hyperlinks on Web pages.
4. Press [Ctrl]['], then press [↓]
5. Point to www.microsoft.com/access in either record so that the pointer changes to, then click www.microsoft.com/access
   If you are currently connected to the Internet and have Microsoft Internet Explorer browser software loaded on your computer, your screen should look similar to Figure J-3. Netscape Communicator is another popular browser program that will also open and display HTML files. Web pages are continually updated as new information is announced, so the content of the Web page itself may vary. If you are not already connected to the Internet, your dialer (software that helps you dial and connect to your ISP) may appear. Once connected to your ISP, the Microsoft Access Web page should appear.
6. Click the Courses: Table button in the taskbar, click the Online Resources field for record 5 (Introduction to Excel), type www.microsoft.com/excel, click the Online Resources field for record 11 (Introduction to Netscape), type www.netscape.com, then press [Enter]
   Hyperlink entries can point to a different Web page on the same Web server or to an entirely different Web server.
7. Click www.netscape.com
   The Netscape Netcenter Web page appears on your screen.
8. Right-click the Courses: Table button on the taskbar, click Close, click Yes to save the changes to the layout of the table, then close any open browser windows

QuickTip: The first part of an Internet Web address (http://) can be omitted when entering a URL into a hyperlink field.

QuickTip: [Ctrl]['] copies the entry in the field of the previous record to the same field of the current record.

QuickTip: Visited links will change to the color purple.

ACCESS J-4 CREATING DATA ACCESS PAGES

Other Features

The two-page lesson format featured in this book provides the new user with a powerful learning experience. Additionally, this book contains the following features:

Every lesson features large-size, full-color representations of what the students' screen should look like after completing the numbered steps.

FIGURE J-2: A hyperlink entry

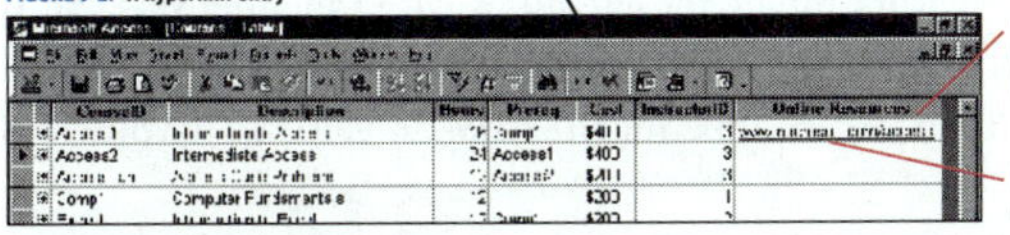

FIGURE J-3: www.microsoft.com/access Web page

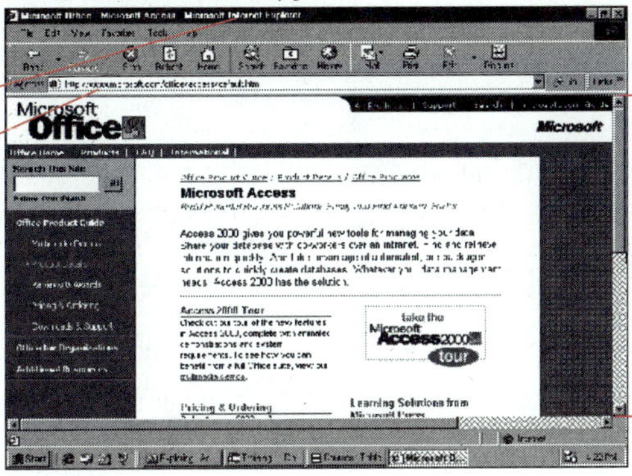

Access 2000

TABLE J-2: Types of networks

type of network	description
LAN (local area network)	Connects local resources such as file servers, user computers, and printers by a direct cable. LANs do not cross a public thoroughfare such as a street because of distance and legal restrictions on how far and where cables can be pulled.
WAN (wide area network)	Created when a LAN is connected to an existing telecommunications network, such as the phone system, to reach resources across public thoroughfares such as streets and rivers
Internet	Largest WAN in the world, spanning the entire globe and connecting many diverse computer architectures
Intranet	WANs that support the same services as the Internet (i.e., e-mail, Web pages, and file transfer) and are built with the same technologies (e.g., TCP/IP communications protocol, HTML Web pages, and browser software), but are designed and secured for the internal purposes of a business. To secure intranet information and resources from outsiders, passwords and data encryption techniques are used.

CLUES TO USE

Understanding the Universal Naming Convention (UNC)

Universal Naming Convention (UNC) is another naming convention (in addition to URL) to locate a file on a network. The structure of a UNC is \\server\sharedfoldername\filename. UNCs are used for local resources, such as a file stored on a local area network. URL addresses are used for Web pages on the Internet or a company intranet.

CREATING DATA ACCESS PAGES ACCESS J-5

Quickly accessible summaries of key terms, toolbar buttons, or keyboard alternatives connected with the lesson material. Students can refer easily to this information when working on their own projects at a later time.

Clues to Use boxes provide concise information that either expands on one component of the major lesson skill or describes an independent task that is in some way related to the major lesson skill.

► MOUS Certification Coverage

Each unit opener has a MOUS next to it to indicate where Microsoft Office User Specialist (MOUS) skills are covered. In addition, there is a MOUS appendix which contains a grid that maps to where specific skills can be found in each lesson and where students can find additional practice. Complete coverage of both Expert and Core MOUS skills can be found in *Microsoft Access—Illustrated Complete, 0-7600-6072-X.*

► Real-World Case

The case study used throughout the textbook, a fictitious company called MediaLoft, is designed to be "'real-world" in nature and introduces the kinds of activities that students will encounter when working with Microsoft Access 2000. With a real-world case, the process of solving problems will be more meaningful to students.

Students can also enhance their skills by completing the Web Works exercises in each unit by going to the innovative Student Online Companion, available at **www.course.com/illustrated/medialoft**. The MediaLoft site mirrors the case study by acting as the company's intranet site, further allowing students to become familiar with applicable business scenarios.

► End of Unit Material

Each unit concludes with a Concepts Review that tests students' understanding of what they learned in the unit. The Concepts Review is followed by a Skills Review, which provides students with additional hands-on practice of the skills. The Skills Review is followed by Independent Challenges, which pose case problems for students to solve. At least one Independent Challenge in each unit asks students to use the World Wide Web to solve the problem as indicated by a Web Work icon. The Visual Workshops that follow the Independent Challenges help students develop critical thinking skills. Students are shown completed Web pages or screens and are asked to re-create them from scratch.

Instructor's Resource Kit

The Instructor's Resource Kit is Course Technology's way of putting the resources and information needed to teach and learn effectively into your hands. With an integrated array of teaching and learning tools that offers you and your students a broad range of technology-based instructional options, we believe this kit represents the highest quality and most cutting edge resources available to instructors today. Many of these resources are available at www.course.com. The resources available with this book are:

MediaLoft Web site Available at **www.course.com/illustrated/medialoft**, this innovative Student Online Companion enhances and augments the printed page by bringing students onto the Web for a dynamic and continually updated learning experience. The MediaLoft site mirrors the case study used throughout the book, creating a real-world intranet site for this fictitious company, a national chain of bookstore cafés. This Companion is used to complete the WebWorks exercise in each unit of this book, and to allow students to become familiar with the business application of an intranet site.

Instructor's Manual Available as an electronic file, the Instructor's Manual is quality-assurance tested and includes unit overviews, detailed lecture topics for each unit with teaching tips, an Upgrader's Guide, solutions to all lessons and end-of-unit material, and extra Independent Challenges. The Instructor's Manual is available on the Instructor's Resource Kit CD-ROM, or you can download it from **www.course.com**.

Course Faculty Online Companion You can browse this textbook's password-protected site to obtain the Instructor's Manual, Solution Files, Project Files, and any updates to the text. Contact your Customer Service Representative for the site address and password.

Project Files Project Files contain all of the data that students will use to complete the lessons and end-of-unit material. A Readme file includes instructions for using the files. Adopters of this text are granted the right to install the Project Files on any standalone computer or network. The Project Files are available on the Instructor's Resource Kit CD-ROM, the Review Pack, and can also be downloaded from www.course.com.

Solution Files Solution Files contain every file students are asked to create or modify in the lessons and end-of-unit material. A Help file on the Instructor's Resource Kit includes information for using the Solution Files.

CyberClass CyberClass is a web-based tool designed for on-campus or distance learning. Use it to enhance how you currently run your class by posting assignments and your course syllabus or holding online office hours. Or, use it for your distance learning course, and offer mini-lectures, conduct online discussion groups, or give your mid-term exam. For more information, visit our Web site at: **www.course.com/products/cyberclass/index.html**.

WebCT WebCT is a tool used to create Web-based educational environments and also uses WWW browsers as the interface for the course-building environment. The site is hosted on your school campus, allowing complete control over the information. WebCT has its own internal communication system, offering internal e-mail, a Bulletin Board, and a Chat room.

Course Technology offers pre-existing supplemental information to help in your WebCT class creation, such as a suggested Syllabus, Lecture Notes, Figures in the Book / Course Presenter, Student Downloads, and Test Banks in which you can schedule an exam, create reports, and more.

Brief Contents

Contents

Access 2000

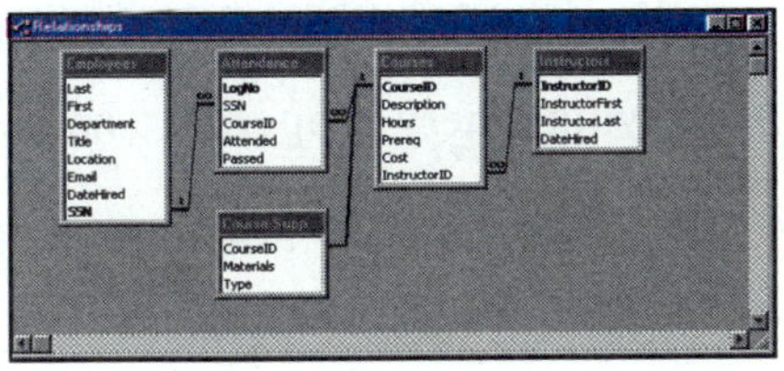

Contents

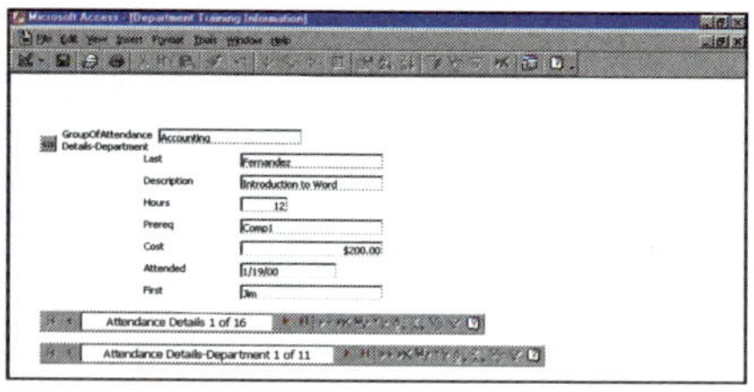

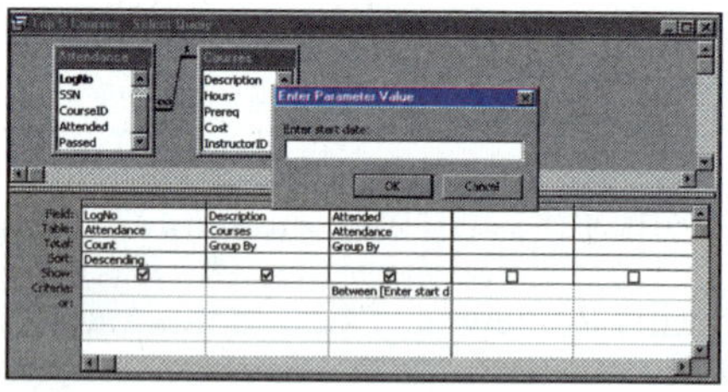

Creating Advanced Forms and Reports

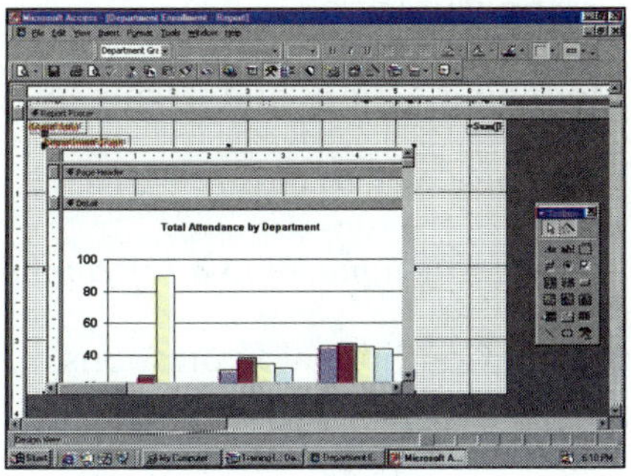

Managing Database Objects

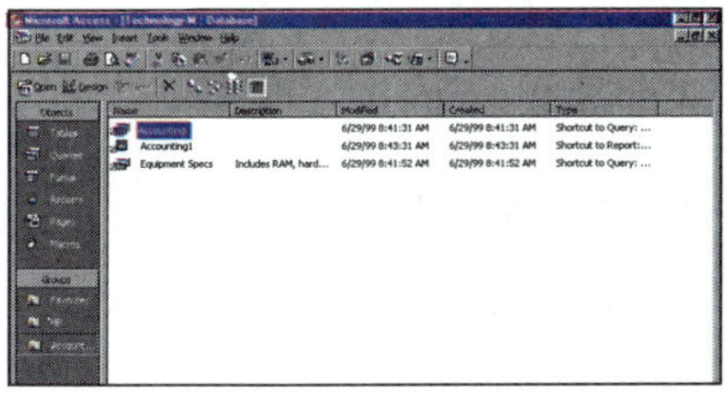

Contents

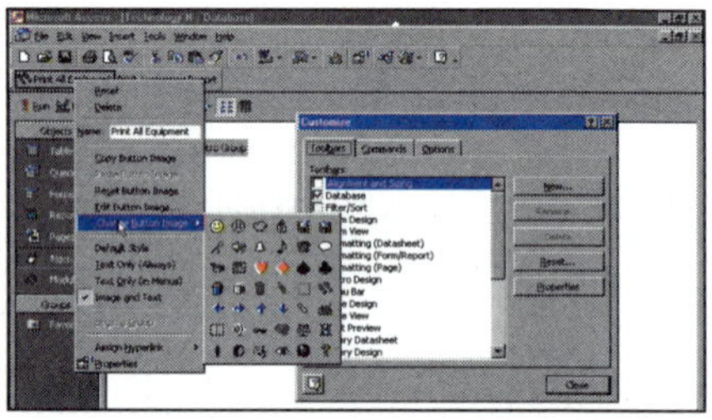

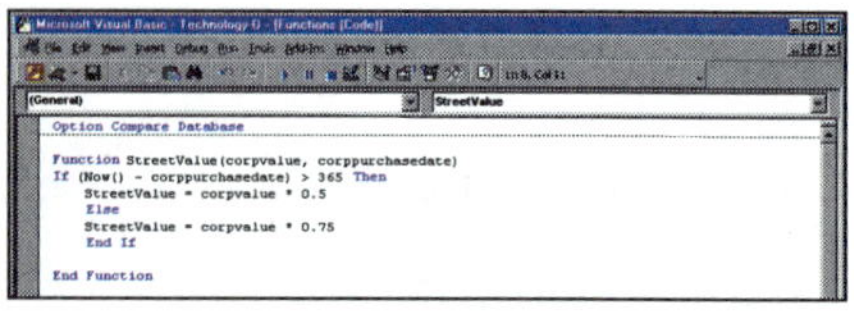

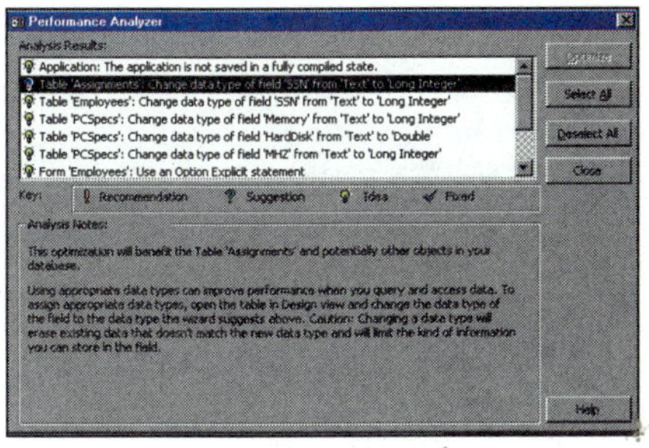

Performance Analyzer
Analysis Results:
Application: The application is not saved in a fully compiled state.
Table 'Employees': Change data type of field 'SSN' from 'Text' to 'Long Integer'
Table 'PCSpecs': Change data type of field 'Memory' from 'Text' to 'Long Integer'
Table 'PCSpecs': Change data type of field 'HardDisk' from 'Text' to 'Double'
Table 'PCSpecs': Change data type of field 'MHZ' from 'Text' to 'Long Integer'
Form 'Employees': Use an Option Explicit statement
Select All
Deselect All
Close
Help

Access 2000

Unit I

Sharing

Access Information with Other Office Programs

Objectives

- Examine Access Objects
- MOUS Examine Relationships Between Tables
- Importing Data from Excel
- MOUS Link Data to an Excel worksheet
- MOUS Create Hyperlinks
- MOUS Analyze Data with Excel
- Copy Records to Word
- MOUS Export Data to Excel

Access is a powerful relational database program that can share data with many other application Microsoft Office 2000 software products. Choosing the right tool for each task is important because you often need to use features from one program and data stored in another type of file. For example, you might want to use financial data in an Excel spreadsheet as part of an Access database. Or, you might want to copy records from an Access query into a Word document that will be published to the Internet. Before you copy or link Access data to another program, however, you should determine if the capability exists within Access. David Dumont, director of training at MediaLoft, has developed an Access database that tracks courses, employees, and course attendance for the internal education provided by MediaLoft. David will share Access data with other software applications to provide each MediaLoft department the data they have requested in a format they can use.

Examining Access Objects

In order to become proficient with Access, it is important for you to understand the capabilities of the seven Access objects. David reviews key Access terminology and the seven Access objects.

Details

A **database** is a collection of data associated with a topic (for example, the training each employee at MediaLoft has received). The smallest piece of information in a database is called a **field**, or category of information such as the employee's name, e-mail address, or department. A **key field** is a field that contains unique information for each record such as an employee's Social Security number. A group of related fields, such as all descriptive information for one employee, is called a **record**. A collection of records for a single subject, such as all of the employee records, is called a **table.** When a table object is opened, the fields and records are displayed as a **datasheet**, as shown in Figure I-1.

Tables are the most important **objects** within an Access database because they contain all of the data within the database. An Access database also may contain six other object types that serve to enhance the usability and value of the data. The objects in an Access database are **tables**, **queries**, **forms**, **reports**, **pages**, **macros**, and **modules**, and are summarized in Table I-1.

Query objects are based on tables; and form, page, and report objects can be based on either tables or queries. Data can be entered and edited in four of the objects—tables, queries, pages, and forms—but is always stored in tables. These relationships are shown in Figure I-2. The macro and module objects are used to provide additional database productivity and automation features such as **GUI** (**graphical user interface**) screens and buttons, which surround and mask the complexity of the underlying objects. All of the objects are stored in one database file.

TABLE I-1 Access objects

object	purpose
Table	Contains all of the raw data within the database in a spreadsheet-like view; can be linked with a common field to share information and therefore minimize data redundancy
Query	Provides a spreadsheet-like view of the data that is similar to tables, but can display a subset of fields and/or records from one or more tables; created when a user has a "question" about the data in the database
Form	Provides an easy-to-use data entry screen that generally shows only one record at a time
Report	Provides a professional printout of data that may contain enhancements such as headers, footers, and calculations on groups of records; mailing labels can also be created from report objects
Page	Creates Web pages from Access objects as well as Web page connectivity features to an Access database
Macro	Stores a collection of keystrokes or commands such as printing several reports in a row or displaying a toolbar when a form opens
Module	Stores Visual Basic programming code that extends the functions and automated processes of Access

FIGURE I-1: Table datasheet

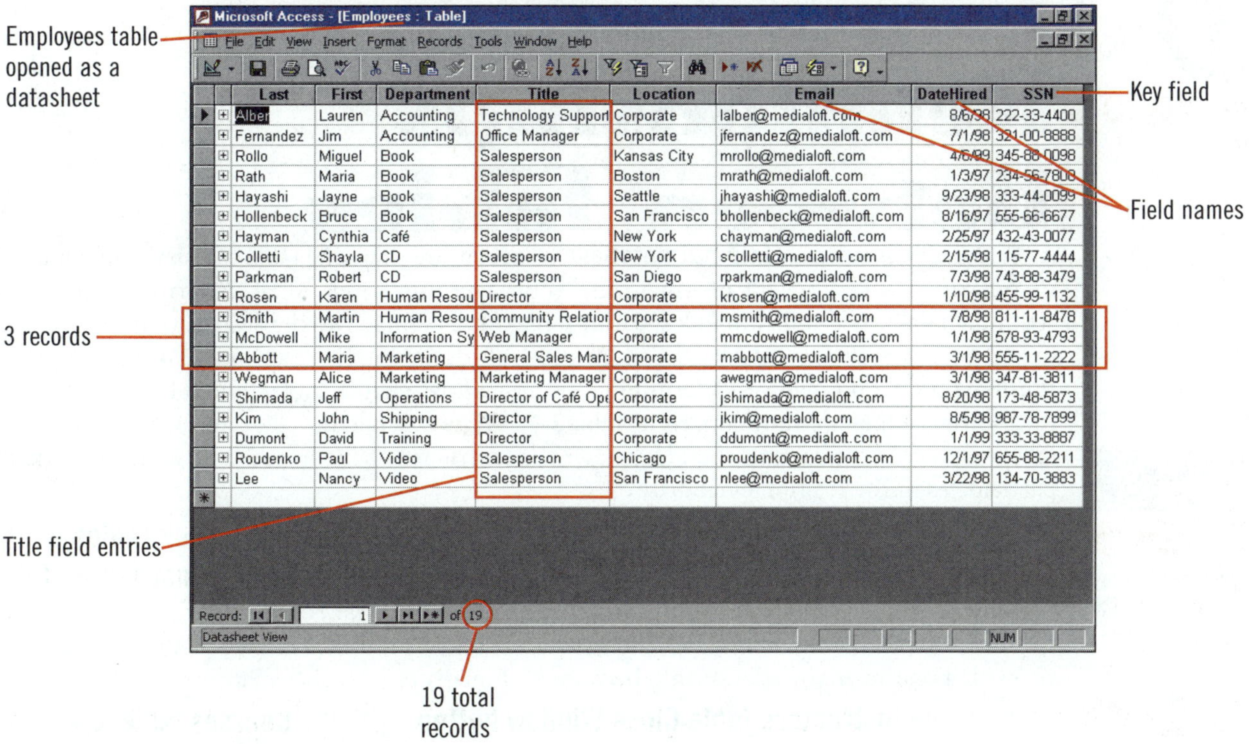

Last	First	Department	Title	Location	Email	DateHired	SSN
Alber	Lauren	Accounting	Technology Support	Corporate	lalber@medialoft.com	8/6/98	222-33-4400
Fernandez	Jim	Accounting	Office Manager	Corporate	jfernandez@medialoft.com	7/1/98	321-00-8888
Rollo	Miguel	Book	Salesperson	Kansas City	mrollo@medialoft.com	4/6/99	345-88-0098
Rath	Maria	Book	Salesperson	Boston	mrath@medialoft.com	1/3/97	234-56-7800
Hayashi	Jayne	Book	Salesperson	Seattle	jhayashi@medialoft.com	9/23/98	333-44-0099
Hollenbeck	Bruce	Book	Salesperson	San Francisco	bhollenbeck@medialoft.com	8/16/97	555-66-6677
Hayman	Cynthia	Café	Salesperson	New York	chayman@medialoft.com	2/25/97	432-43-0077
Colletti	Shayla	CD	Salesperson	New York	scolletti@medialoft.com	2/15/98	115-77-4444
Parkman	Robert	CD	Salesperson	San Diego	rparkman@medialoft.com	7/3/98	743-88-3479
Rosen	Karen	Human Resou	Director	Corporate	krosen@medialoft.com	1/10/98	455-99-1132
Smith	Martin	Human Resou	Community Relatior	Corporate	msmith@medialoft.com	7/8/98	811-11-8478
McDowell	Mike	Information Sy	Web Manager	Corporate	mmcdowell@medialoft.com	1/1/98	578-93-4793
Abbott	Maria	Marketing	General Sales Man:	Corporate	mabbott@medialoft.com	3/1/98	555-11-2222
Wegman	Alice	Marketing	Marketing Manager	Corporate	awegman@medialoft.com	3/1/98	347-81-3811
Shimada	Jeff	Operations	Director of Café Ope	Corporate	jshimada@medialoft.com	8/20/98	173-48-5873
Kim	John	Shipping	Director	Corporate	jkim@medialoft.com	8/5/98	987-78-7899
Dumont	David	Training	Director	Corporate	ddumont@medialoft.com	1/1/99	333-33-8887
Roudenko	Paul	Video	Salesperson	Chicago	proudenko@medialoft.com	12/1/97	655-88-2211
Lee	Nancy	Video	Salesperson	San Francisco	nlee@medialoft.com	3/22/98	134-70-3883

FIGURE I-2: Objects of an Access database

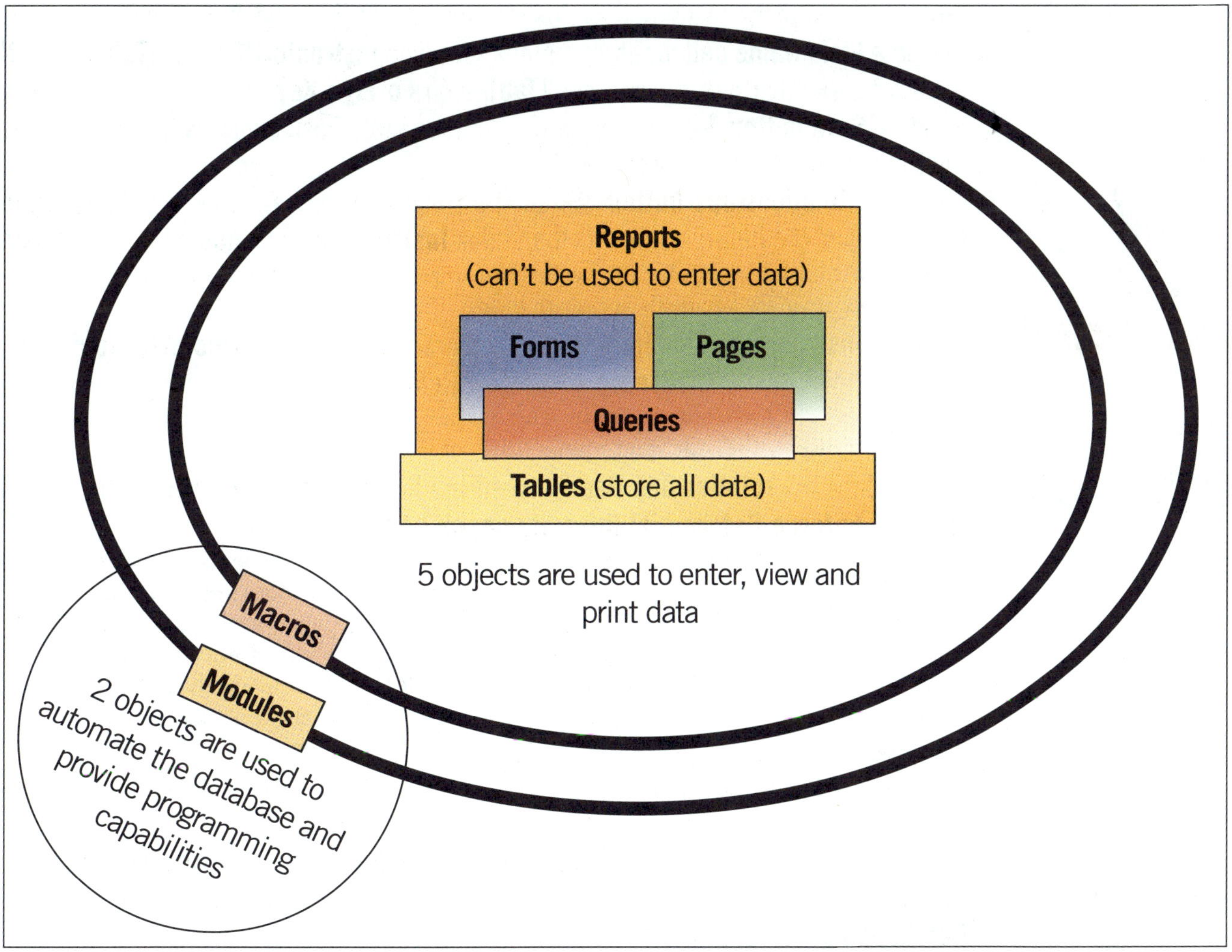

Unit I

Access 2000

Examining Relationships Between Tables

An Access database is a **relational database** in that more than one table can share information, or "relate." The key benefit of organizing your data into a relational database is minimized redundant data. The ability to link separate tables of data improves the accuracy, speed, and flexibility of a relational database. The process of designing a relational database is called **normalization**, and involves determining the appropriate fields, tables, and table relationships. Relationship types are summarized in Table I-2. David develops an Instructors table to store one record for each teacher. He relates the Instructors table to the Courses table so that it participates in the relational database.

Steps

QuickTip

The primary key field always acts as the "one" side of a one-to-many relationship.

QuickTip

For clarity, give the primary and foreign key fields of two linking tables the same name.

QuickTip

To display all the fields in a table, drag ↘ on a corner of the table until the scroll bars are no longer visible.

Trouble?

Double-click the middle part of the linking line to edit the relationship.

1. Start Access, open the **Training-I** database on your Project Disk, click **Tables** on the Objects bar, maximize the database window, then double-click the **Instructors table**

   The InstructorID field serves as the **primary key field** so it contains unique data for each record in the Instructors table. The Instructors table should be related to the Courses table with a one-to-many relationship because each instructor teaches many courses.

2. Click the **Instructors Table Close Window button**, click the **Courses table**, then click the **Design button** in the database window

   A matching field, often called the **foreign key field**, must be added to the table on the "many" side of a one-to-many relationship to link with the primary key field of the "one" table.

3. Click the **Field Name cell** in the first blank row, type **InstructorID**, press **[Tab]**, press **N** to select a Number data type, press **[Tab]**, type **Foreign Key** as shown in Figure I-3, click the **Save button**, then close the Courses table Design view window

   The linking field for both tables is created.

4. Click the **Relationships button** on the Database toolbar, click the **Show Table button** on the Relationships toolbar, click **Instructors**, click **Add**, then click **Close**

   The Instructors table appears in the Relationships window without any relationships to other tables. Primary key fields appear in bold.

5. Drag the **InstructorID field** from the Instructors table to the **InstructorID field** in the Courses table, then click **Create** in the Edit Relationships dialog box

   The link between the Courses and Instructors tables has been established, but the linking line doesn't display the "one" and "many" sides of the relationship.

6. Double-click the **relationship line** between the Instructors and Courses tables, then click the **Enforce Referential Integrity check box**, see Figure I-4

   The **Enforce Referential Integrity** option does not allow values to be entered in the foreign key field that are not first entered in the primary key field. It also does not allow records to be deleted in the "one" table if related records exist in the "many" table. **Cascade Update Related Fields** automatically updates the data in the foreign key field when the matching primary key field is changed. **Cascade Delete Related Records** automatically deletes all records in the "many" table if the record with the matching key field in the "one" table is deleted.

7. Click **OK** in the Edit Relationships dialog box

   Printing the Relationships window shown in Figure I-5 creates a valuable report that helps you remember what fields are in which tables.

8. Click **File** on the menu bar, click **Print Relationships**, click the **Print button** on the Print Preview toolbar, click **Close**, click , accept the default report name **Relationships for Training-I**, then close the Relationships window

FIGURE I-3: Adding the foreign key field to the Courses table in Design view

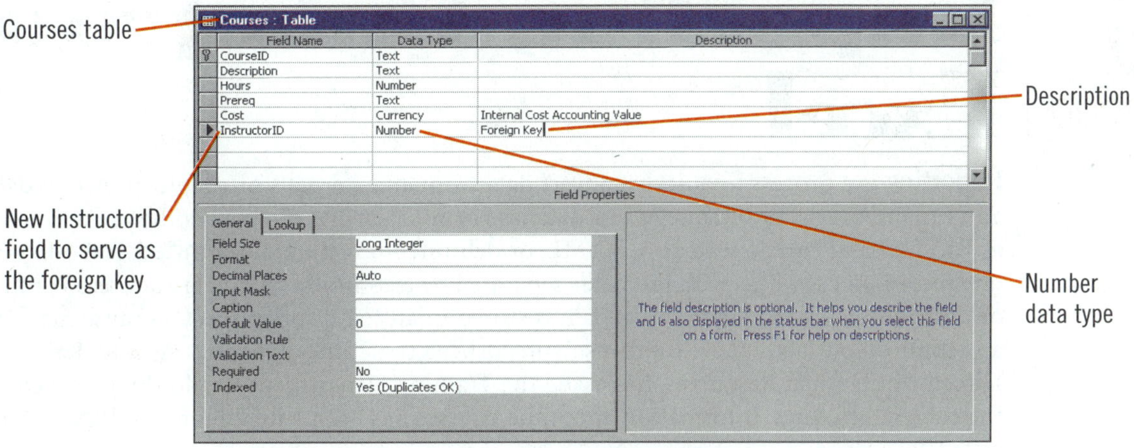

FIGURE I-4: Edit Relationships dialog box

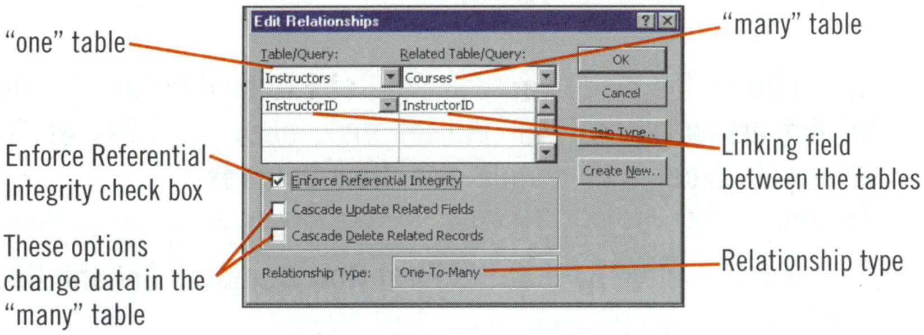

FIGURE I-5: Relationships window

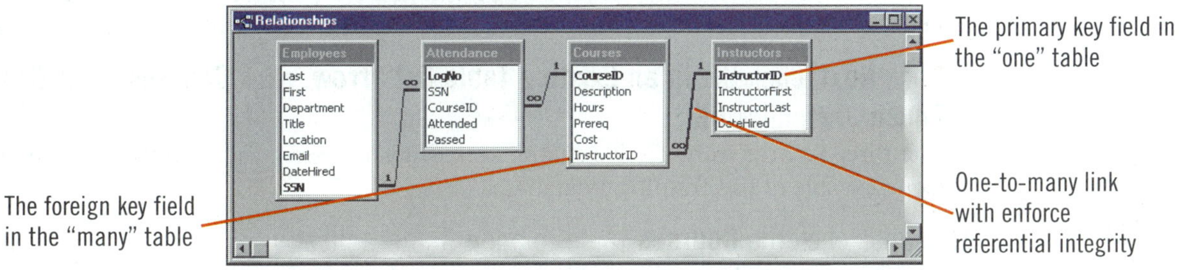

TABLE I-2: Relationship types

relationship	description	example	notes
One-to-One	A record in Table X has no more than one matching record in Table Y.	A student table would have no more than one matching record in a graduation table that tracks the student's graduation date and major.	Not common, because all fields related this way could be stored in one table; sometimes used to separate rarely used fields from a table to improve the overall performance of the database
One-to-Many	A single record in Table X has many records in Table Y.	One product can be sold many times, one customer can make many purchases, one teacher can teach many courses, and one student can take many courses.	Most common type of relationship
Many-to-Many	A record in Table X has many records in Table Y, and a record in Table Y has many records in Table X .	One employee can take several courses, and the same course can be taken by several employees. (In the MediaLoft database, the Attendance table serves as the junction table between the Courses and Employees tables.)	It is impossible to directly create many-to-many relationships in Access. Instead, a third table, called a junction table, must be established between the original tables. The junction table contains foreign key fields that link to the primary key fields of each of the original tables and establishes separate one-to-many relationships with them. The junction table serves as the "many" side of each relationship.

Unit I
Access 2000

Importing Data from Excel

Importing is a process to quickly convert data from an external source into an Access database. You can import data from one Access database to another, or from many other data sources such as Excel, dBase, Paradox, FoxPro, HTML, or delimited text files. A **delimited text file** contains one record on each line, with the fields separated by a common character such as a comma, tab, or dash. Often, external numerical data is stored in an Excel spreadsheet, because many people are comfortable with the easy-to-use spreadsheet structure of Excel. Karen Rosen, Director of Human Resources, has asked the Training Department to add three new courses to the current offerings. Information about the courses has been entered into an Excel spreadsheet called New Courses.

Steps

QuickTip

The Files of type list displays the data file formats that can be imported into Access.

1. Click **File** on the menu bar, point to **Get External Data**, click **Import**, click the **Look in: list arrow**, locate your Project Disk, click the **Files of Type list arrow**, click **Microsoft Excel**, then double-click **New Courses**
   The Import Spreadsheet Wizard dialog box opens, as shown in Figure I-6.
2. Click **Next**, then verify that the **First Row Contains Column Headings check box** is checked
   The second dialog box of the Import Spreadsheet Wizard, shown in Figure I-7, is extremely important. In order to successfully import data from an Excel spreadsheet to an existing table, the spreadsheet fields (columns) must be consistent with the fields of the Access table.
3. Click **Next**, click the **In an Existing Table list arrow**, click **Courses**, click **Next**, click **Finish**, then click **OK**
   The three records from the New Courses spreadsheet were successfully imported into the Courses table of the Training-I database.
4. Double-click the **Courses** table to open its datasheet
   The Courses datasheet, with the three new records, is displayed in Figure I-8. By default, the records in the Courses table sort by the primary key field, CourseID. Note that the new records do not have any values in the Prereq field, but they do have entries in the InstructorID field. Even if the field is **null** (contains nothing), the number and type of fields in the Excel spreadsheet must be consistent with the Access table to successfully import the Excel data. If you import an Excel spreadsheet into a new table, Access will choose an appropriate data type and field name for each field in the new table.
5. Close the **Courses** datasheet
   Now that the Excel data has been imported into the Access Training-I database, it can link to many other tables of data to create valuable queries, forms, and reports, and therefore it can serve the varied needs of simultaneous users.

FIGURE I-6: Import Spreadsheet Wizard's first dialog box

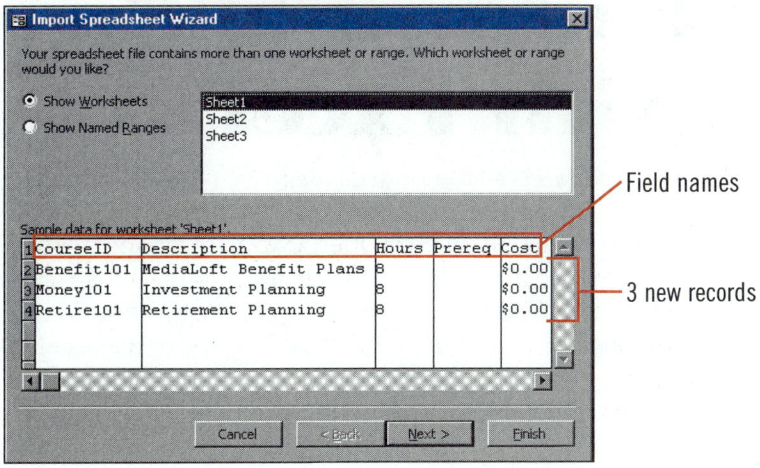

FIGURE I-7: Import Spreadsheet Wizard's second dialog box

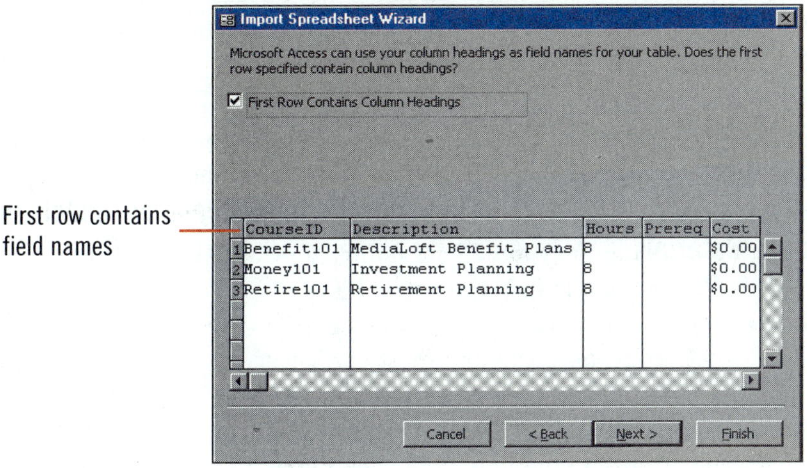

FIGURE I-8: Courses table with three new imported records

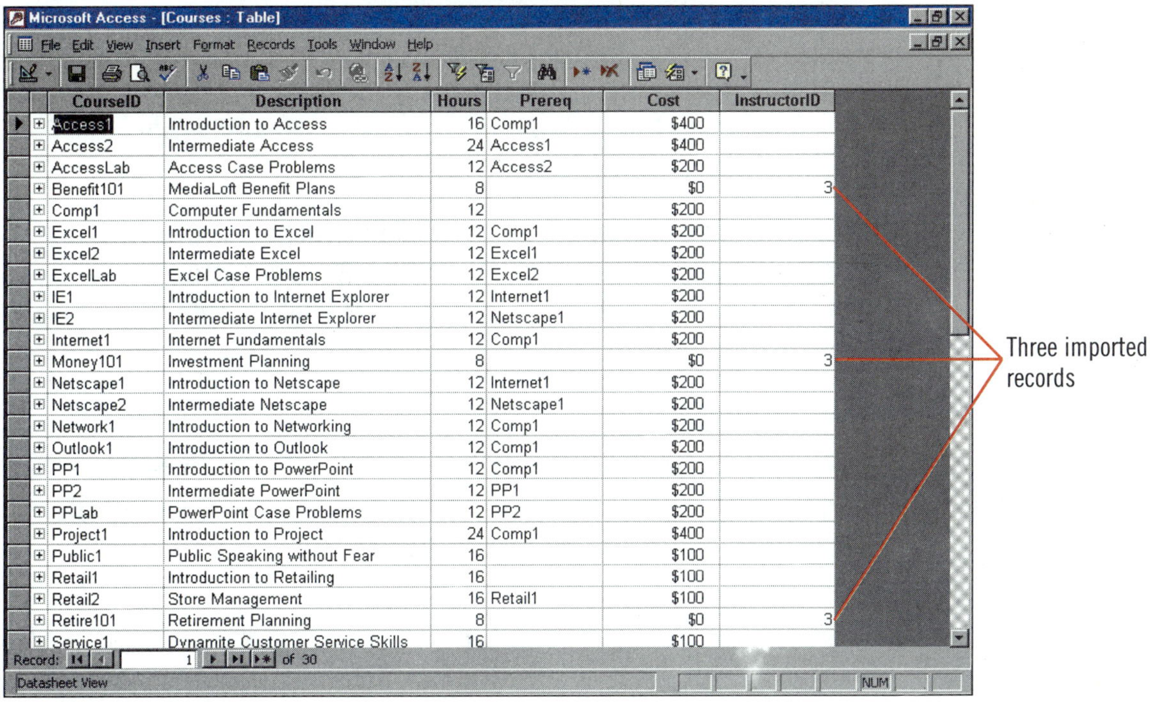

Unit I

Access 2000

Linking Data with Excel

Linking connects an Access database to data in an external file such as another Access, dBase, or Paradox database; an Excel or Lotus 1-2-3 spreadsheet; a text file; an HTML file; and other data sources that support **ODBC** (**Open Database Connectivity**) standards. If you link, data can be entered or edited in either the original file or the Access database even though the data is only stored in the original file. Changes to data in either location are automatically made in the other. **Importing**, in contrast, makes a duplicate copy of the data in the Access database, so changes to either the original data source or the imported Access copy have no affect on the other. David asked the new instructors to make a list of all of their class materials. They created this list in an Excel spreadsheet, and wish to maintain it there. David creates a link to this data from within the Training database.

Steps

1. Click **File** on the menu bar, point to **Get External Data**, then click **Link Tables**
   The Link dialog box opens, listing Access files in the current folder.
2. Click the **Files of Type list arrow**, click **Microsoft Excel**, click **Course Materials** in the files list, then click **Link**
   The Link Spreadsheet Wizard appears, as shown in Figure I-9. Data can be linked from different parts of the Excel spreadsheet. The data you want is on Sheet 1.
3. Click **Next**, click the **First Row Contains Column Headings check box** to specify **CourseID**, **Materials**, and **Type** as field names, click **Next**, type **Course Supplies** as the Linked Table Name, click **Finish**, then click **OK**
   The Course Supplies table appears in the database window with a linking Excel icon, as shown in Figure I-10. A linked table can and must participate in a one-to-many relationship with another table if it is to share data with the rest of the tables of the database.
4. Click the **Relationships button** on the Database toolbar, click the **Show Table button**, double-click **Course Supplies**, then click **Close**
   Rearranging the tables in the Relationships window can improve the clarity of the relationships.
5. Drag the **Course Supplies table title bar** to a position under the Attendance table, drag the **CourseID field** in the Courses table to the **CourseID field** in the Course Supplies table, then click **Create** in the Edit Relationships dialog box
   A one-to-many relationship is established between the Courses and Course Supplies tables. You cannot establish referential integrity when one of the tables is a linked table, but the table can now participate in queries, forms, pages, and reports that use fields from multiple tables. Your screen should look like Figure I-11.
6. Click the **Save button**, close the **Relationships window**, double-click the **Course Supplies table** to open it, click the **New Record button** on the Table Datasheet toolbar, type **Access1**, press **[Tab]**, type **MediaLoft.mdb**, press **[Tab]**, then type **File**
   You added a new record. When first creating a linked table, you should check the original data source, the Course Materials Excel file, to make sure that the data was automatically updated there.
7. Close the **Course Supplies table**, right-click the **Start button** in the taskbar, click **Explore**, locate your Project Disk, double-click the **Course Materials Excel file** to open it in Excel, then press **[Page Down]**
   The new Access1 record should be visible in row 40 of the Excel spreadsheet.
8. Click **File** on the menu bar, click **Exit** to close the worksheet and exit Excel, then close Explorer

Trouble?

If your Project Disk files do not display in the Link dialog box, click the Look in: list arrow to locate your Project Disk.

QuickTip

If you update data in a linked table, it will update the original source.

FIGURE I-9: Link Spreadsheet Wizard dialog box

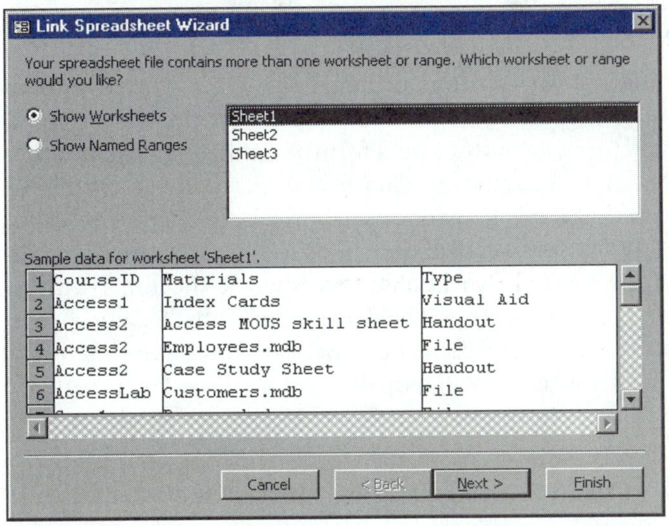

FIGURE I-10: Course Supplies table is linked from Excel

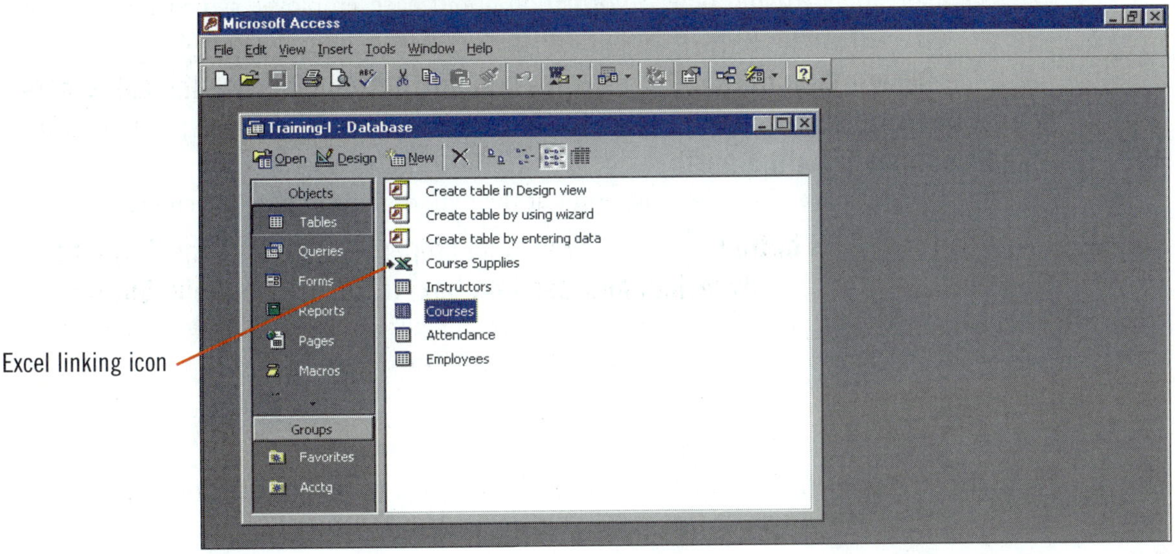

FIGURE I-11: Relationships window with Course Supplies table

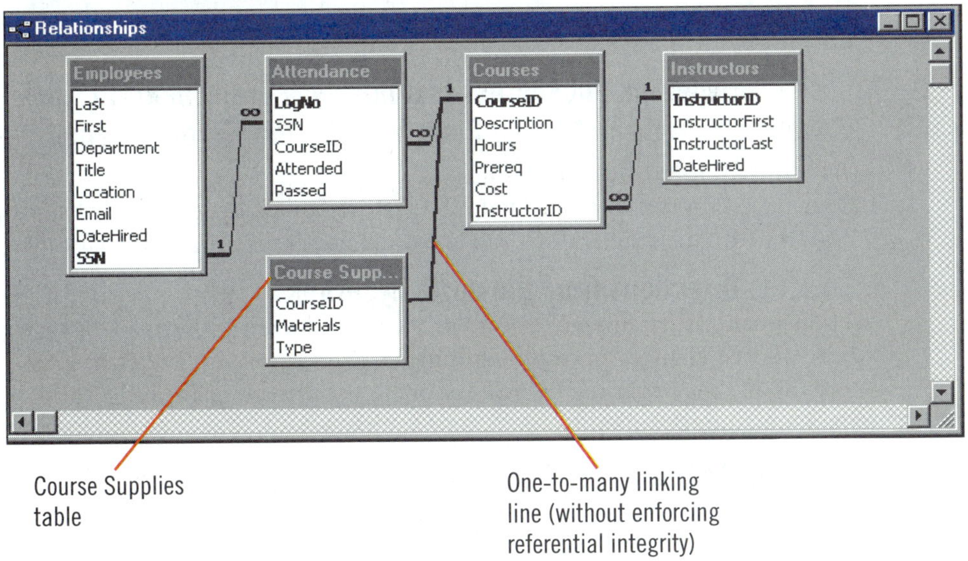

Access 2000

Creating Hyperlinks

A **hyperlink** is a label, button, or image that when clicked automatically opens another object, document or graphic file, e-mail message, or World Wide Web page. Hyperlinks can be added as labels, pictures, or buttons on a form. A field with a **hyperlink data type** can be defined in a table's Design view so that the datasheet displays and stores different hyperlink information for each record. David created a Word document called "Directions to MediaLoft Corporate" that gives detailed directions to the San Francisco training facility. Within the Word document he created two **bookmarks**, specific locations within the document marked by a bookmark code, called "fromTheNorth" and "fromTheSouth" that identify the beginning of the paragraph that describes each route. Because employees often ask for detailed directions to the training facility when they sign up for a course, David will create hyperlinks to these instructions from the Courses form.

Steps 1 2 3 4

1. Click **Forms** on the Objects bar, then double-click the **Courses form** to open it in Form view
   The Courses form displays course information in the main form, whereas the subform logs the SSN, date attended, and other information about each employee signed up for each course. Create hyperlinks from the Courses form to the Directions document.
2. Click the **Design View button**, click the **Toolbox button**, click the **Label button** on the Toolbox, click +A in the **Detail section** of the form at the 5" mark, then type **Directions from the north**
   Any label on a form can become a hyperlink if the hyperlink properties are entered.
3. Click the **Properties button** to open the label property sheet, click the **Format tab** (if necessary), click the **Hyperlink Address text box**, then click the **Build button**
   The Insert Hyperlink dialog box appears, as shown in Figure I-12. This dialog box helps you link to a file, Web page, database object, or e-mail address.
4. Click **File**
   The Link to File dialog box opens.
5. Locate your Project Disk, then double-click **Directions to MediaLoft Corporate**
   The filename appears in the Type the file or Web page name text box.
6. Click **OK**
   The entry for the Hyperlink Address property appears in the label's property sheet. Use the Hyperlink SubAddress property to specify the bookmark name within the Directions document to link to a specific paragraph within the document.
7. Click the **Hyperlink SubAddress text box**, type **FromTheNorth**, click to close the property sheet, then click the **Form View button** on the Form Design toolbar to view the updated Courses form
   Your screen should look like Figure I-13. By default, a hyperlink label appears in blue and is underlined. This style is similar to the way hyperlinks usually appear on Web pages.
8. Click the **Directions from the north hyperlink**
   The Directions document appears in Word, as shown in Figure I-14. A hyperlink that has been clicked changes from blue to purple, similar to Web hyperlinks. You can copy, paste, and modify the hyperlink to create a link to the directions from the south bookmark within the Directions document.
9. Close the Word window, then save and close the Courses form

QuickTip

The mouse pointer changes to a pointing hand when pointing to a hyperlink.

QuickTip

Bookmarks cannot have any spaces in them. The name of the bookmark in the document must exactly match the Hyperlink SubAddress.

FIGURE I-12: Insert Hyperlink dialog box

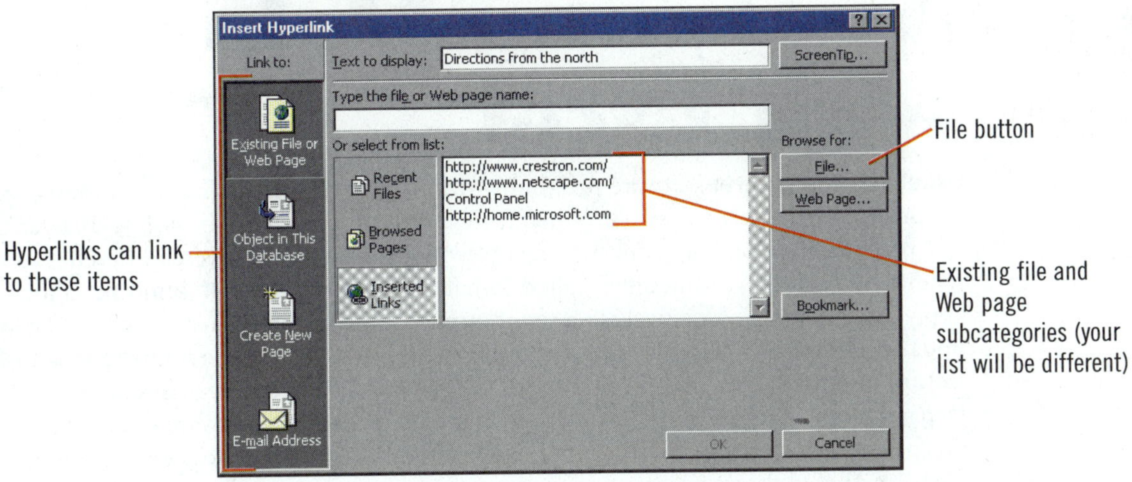

FIGURE I-13: Hyperlink label displayed in Form view

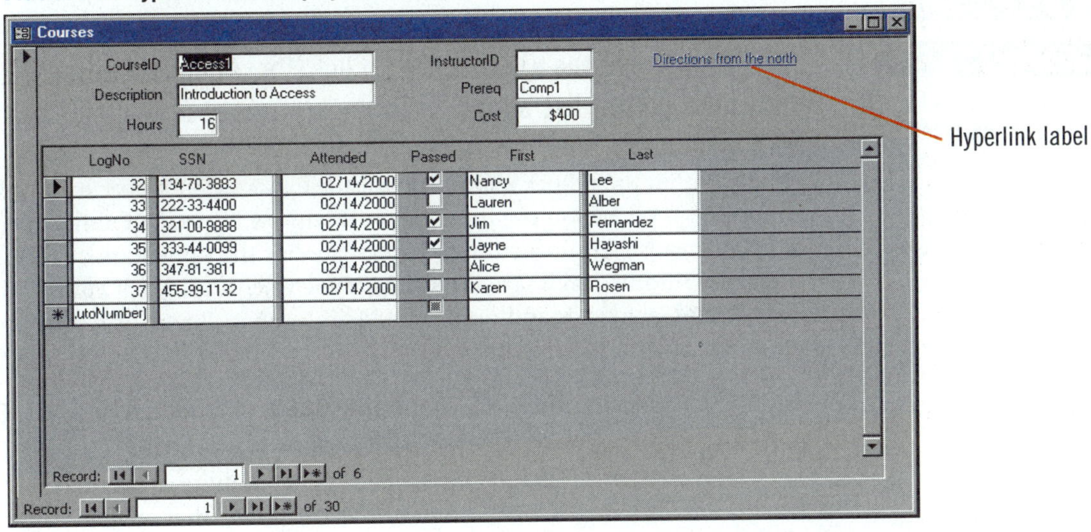

FIGURE I-14: Directions to the Media Loft Corporate Word document with bookmark highlighted

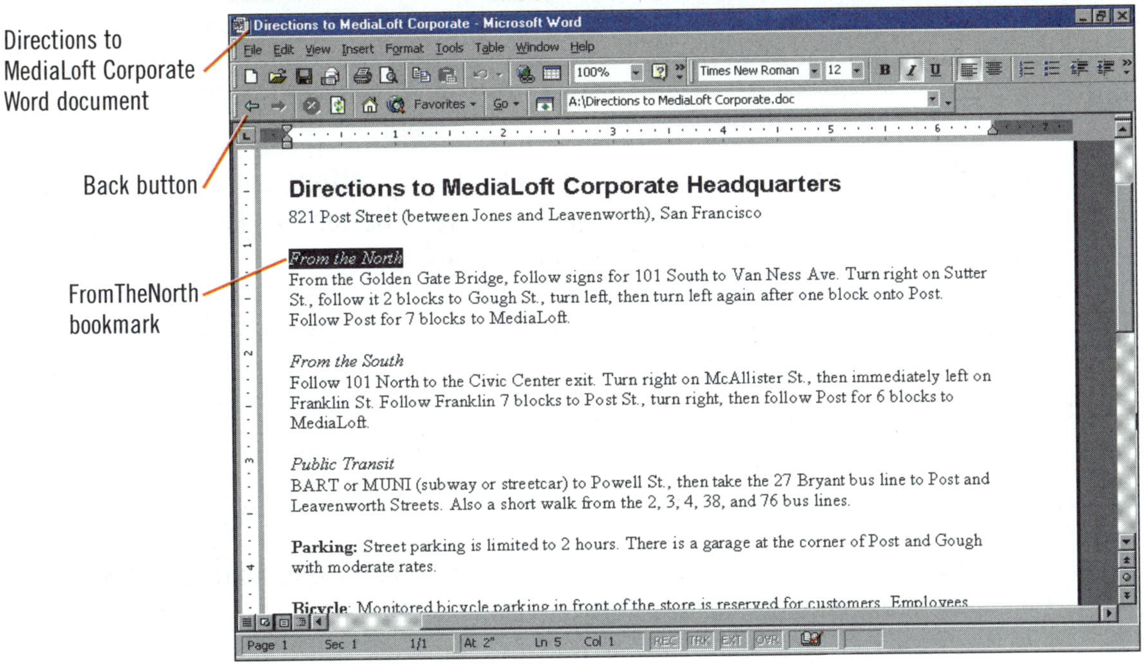

Unit I

Access 2000

Analyzing Data with Excel

Excel, the spreadsheet software program within the Microsoft Office Suite, is an excellent tool for projecting numeric trends into the future. For example, you may wish to analyze the impact of a price increase on budget or income projections by applying several different numbers. This reiterative analysis is sometimes called "what-if" analysis. **What-if analysis** allows a user to apply assumptions interactively to a set of numbers and watch the resulting calculated formulas update instantly. This is a very popular use for Excel. You can use the **Analyze It with MS Excel** feature to quickly copy Access data to Excel. David has been asked by the Accounting Department to provide some Access data in an Excel spreadsheet so they can analyze how various percentage increases in the cost of the Access classes would affect each of the departments. He has gathered the raw data into a report, called Access Courses Report, and will use the power of Excel to analyze the impact of increased costs.

Steps 1 2 3 4

Trouble?

It takes several seconds for Access to export and create the .xls file. If a dialog box opens indicating that the file already exists, click Yes to replace the existing file.

1. Click **Reports** on the Objects bar, click the **Access Courses Report**, click the **OfficeLinks button list arrow** on the Database toolbar, then click **Analyze It with MS Excel**

   The data within the report was automatically exported into an Excel spreadsheet, as shown in Figure I-15. When you use the Analyze It with MS Excel or Publish It with MS Word buttons, the spreadsheet or document you create has the same name as the Access object, and it is usually automatically saved in the My Documents folder of your C: drive. You can send the **recordset** (the fields and records) of a table, query, form, or report object to Excel using the Analyze It with MS Excel button.

2. Click cell **G1** (column G, row 1), type **Increase**, click cell **A16**, type **Increase %**, click cell **A17** (column A, row 17), type **10%**, then press **[Enter]**

   Cell G2 will contain a formula that calculates the additional increase in cost (in column E) for the Access classes. Cell A17 stores an "assumption" that will be used in the formula, the 10% growth factor.

3. Click cell **G2**, type **=E2*A17**, then press **[Enter]**

   Your screen should look like Figure I-16. All formulas in Excel begin with an equal sign. This formula multiplies the cost value in cell E3 by 10% to calculate the $20.00 increase for the Introduction to Access class. The Accounting Department completed this Excel spreadsheet analysis in another spreadsheet file.

4. Click **File** on the Excel menu bar, click **Close** to close the **Attendance Log Report file**, click **No** if prompted to save changes, click the **Open button**, locate your Project Disk, then double-click the **Final Attendance Log Report**

   The Final Attendance Log Report has subtotaled and graphed the increased cost for Access classes for each department, as shown in Figure I-17. The 10% cost increase assumption in cell A22 is shaded bright yellow.

5. Click cell **A22**, type **12%**, then press **[Enter]**

   By changing assumption values, Excel automatically updates all dependent formulas and graphs. You can enter any number in cell A22 to see "what if" the percentage increased by different amounts.

6. Click **File** on the Excel menu bar, click Exit to close **Final Attendance Log Report**, then click **Yes** if prompted to save the changes

FIGURE I-15: Attendance Log Report spreadsheet

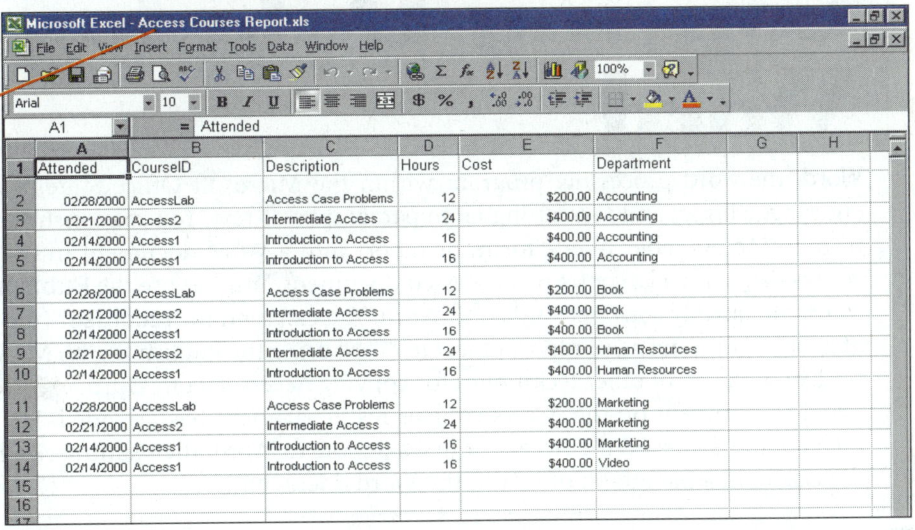

	A	B	C	D	E	F
1	Attended	CourseID	Description	Hours	Cost	Department
2	02/28/2000	AccessLab	Access Case Problems	12	$200.00	Accounting
3	02/21/2000	Access2	Intermediate Access	24	$400.00	Accounting
4	02/14/2000	Access1	Introduction to Access	16	$400.00	Accounting
5	02/14/2000	Access1	Introduction to Access	16	$400.00	Accounting
6	02/28/2000	AccessLab	Access Case Problems	12	$200.00	Book
7	02/21/2000	Access2	Intermediate Access	24	$400.00	Book
8	02/14/2000	Access1	Introduction to Access	16	$400.00	Book
9	02/21/2000	Access2	Intermediate Access	24	$400.00	Human Resources
10	02/14/2000	Access1	Introduction to Access	16	$400.00	Human Resources
11	02/28/2000	AccessLab	Access Case Problems	12	$200.00	Marketing
12	02/21/2000	Access2	Intermediate Access	24	$400.00	Marketing
13	02/14/2000	Access1	Introduction to Access	16	$400.00	Marketing
14	02/14/2000	Access1	Introduction to Access	16	$400.00	Video

FIGURE I-16: Entering assumptions and formulas in an Excel spreadsheet

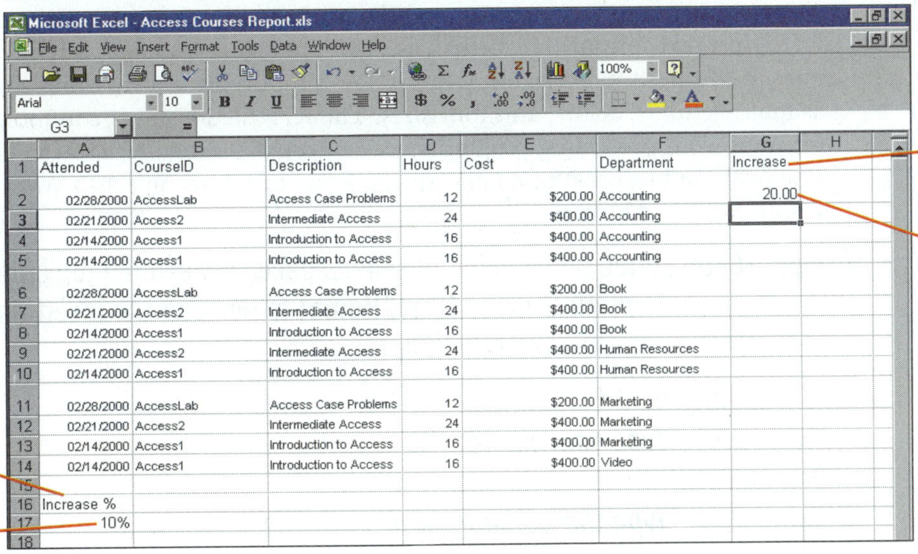

	A	B	C	D	E	F	G
1	Attended	CourseID	Description	Hours	Cost	Department	Increase
2	02/28/2000	AccessLab	Access Case Problems	12	$200.00	Accounting	20.00
3	02/21/2000	Access2	Intermediate Access	24	$400.00	Accounting	
4	02/14/2000	Access1	Introduction to Access	16	$400.00	Accounting	
5	02/14/2000	Access1	Introduction to Access	16	$400.00	Accounting	
6	02/28/2000	AccessLab	Access Case Problems	12	$200.00	Book	
7	02/21/2000	Access2	Intermediate Access	24	$400.00	Book	
8	02/14/2000	Access1	Introduction to Access	16	$400.00	Book	
9	02/21/2000	Access2	Intermediate Access	24	$400.00	Human Resources	
10	02/14/2000	Access1	Introduction to Access	16	$400.00	Human Resources	
11	02/28/2000	AccessLab	Access Case Problems	12	$200.00	Marketing	
12	02/21/2000	Access2	Intermediate Access	24	$400.00	Marketing	
13	02/14/2000	Access1	Introduction to Access	16	$400.00	Marketing	
14	02/14/2000	Access1	Introduction to Access	16	$400.00	Video	
16	Increase %						
17	10%						

FIGURE I-17: Performing "what-if" analysis

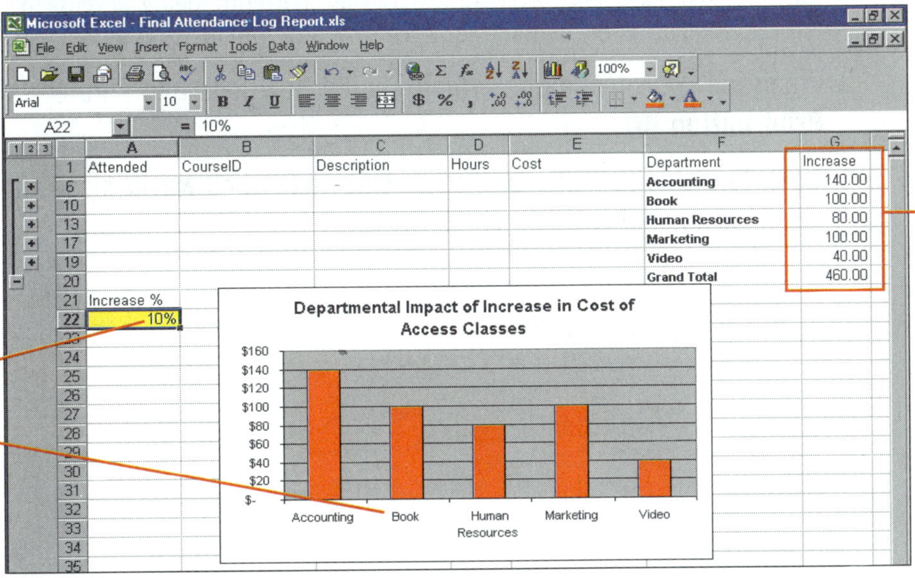

	A	B	C	D	E	F	G
1	Attended	CourseID	Description	Hours	Cost	Department	Increase
6						Accounting	140.00
10						Book	100.00
13						Human Resources	80.00
17						Marketing	100.00
19						Video	40.00
20						Grand Total	460.00
21	Increase %						
22	10%						

Copying Data to Word

Word, the word processing program within the Microsoft Office Suite, is a premier tool for entering, editing, and formatting large paragraphs of text. You may wish to copy the recordset from an Access table, query, form, or report into a Word document in order to integrate the Access data with a larger word-processed document. You can use the **Publish it with MS Word** feature to quickly copy Access data to Word. You can send the **recordset** (the fields and records) of a table, query, form, or report object to Word using the Publish It with MS Word button. Table I-3 lists a variety of other techniques for copying Access data to Word. David has been asked to comment on the Access courses his department has provided. He will use the Office Links buttons to send the Access Courses Report to Word, then summarize his thoughts about the classes in a paragraph of text in the Word document.

Steps

Trouble?

If a dialog box appears indicating that the file already exists, click Yes to replace the existing file.

1. Click **Access Courses Report**, click the **OfficeLinks button list arrow** on the Database toolbar, then click **Publish It with MS Word**

   The records from the Access Courses Report object appear in a Word document with an **RTF (rich text format)** file format, as shown in Figure I-18. The RTF format does not support all advanced Word features, but it does support basic formatting embellishments such as multiple fonts, colors, and font sizes. The RTF file format is commonly used when two different word processing programs need to use the same file. You can send the **recordset** (the fields and records) of a table, query, form, or report object to Word using the Publish It with MS Word button.

2. Press **[Enter]** three times to increase the space between the top of the document and the Access information, press **[Ctrl][Home]** to position the insertion point at the top of the document, then type the following:

   To: Management Committee
   From: [***type your name***]
   Re: Analysis of Access Courses
   Date: [***type the current date***]

   The following information shows the recent demand for Access training. The information is sorted by department, and shows that the Accounting Department has had the greatest demand for Access courses. Since Access databases are currently being developed in many MediaLoft areas, I predict that the demand for Access training will increase in the near future.

3. Proofread your document, which should now look like Figure I-19, then click the **Print button**

4. Click **File** on the menu bar, click **Exit**, then click **No** to close the Access Courses Report document without saving it

FIGURE I-18: Publishing an Access report to Word

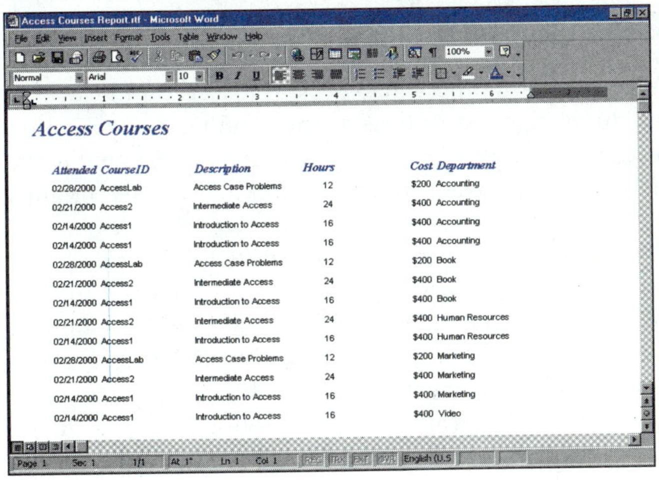

FIGURE I-19: Using Word to enter text

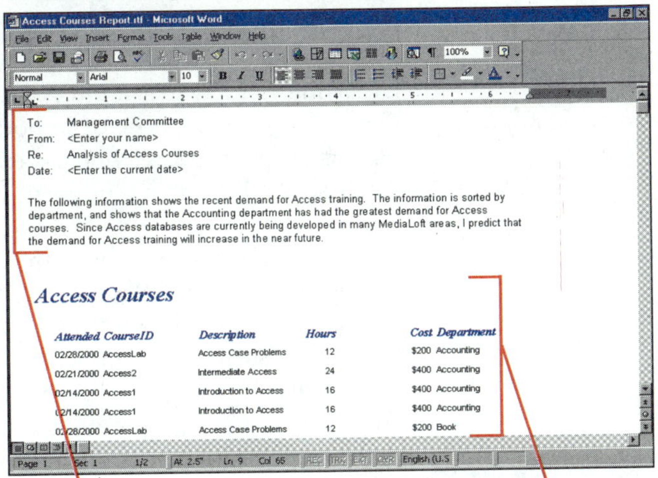

TABLE I-3: Techniques to copy Access data to other applications

technique	button or menu option	description
OfficeLinks buttons		Sends selected data to Excel or Word
	Analyze It with MS Excel	Sends a selected table, query, form, or report object's records to Excel
	Publish It with MS Word	Sends a selected table, query, form, or report object's records to Word
	Merge It with MS Word	Helps merge the selected table or query recordset with a Word document
Office Clipboard	Copy and Paste	Copies selected fields and records in a datasheet or a record in a form to the Clipboard. Open a Word document or Excel spreadsheet, click where you want to paste the data, then click the Paste button. The copied data remains on the Office Clipboard until you close all open Office applications in case you want to paste it again.
Exporting	File on the menu bar, then Export	Copies information from an Access object into a different file format
Drag and drop	Right-click an empty space on the taskbar, then choose the Tile Windows Horizontally or Tile Windows Vertically option	With the windows tiled, drag the Access table, query, form, or report object icon from the Access window to the target (Excel or Word) window. You cannot drag an object icon from one window to the next if the windows are maximized.

CLUES TO USE

Creating form letters with Merge It to MS Word

You can merge the information in a table or query with a Word document to create form letters by clicking the object, then clicking the Merge It to MS Word button. Word will start and load a blank document that will serve as the form letter. Type the standard text into the document, then use the Insert Merge Field button on the Mail Merge toolbar to position the table or query fields in the appropriate positions in the letter. Merge the Access data into the form letter by clicking the Merge to New Document button also on the Mail Merge toolbar within Word.

Unit I

Access 2000

Exporting Data

Exporting is a way to send Access information to another database, spreadsheet, or file format. Exporting is the opposite of importing. Importing is a process to copy and paste information *into* an Access database, whereas exporting is a process used to copy and paste data *out of* the database. Unlike linking, importing and exporting retain no connection between the original source of data. Therefore, when exporting data, changes in either the original Access database or the exported copy do not affect the other. Table I-4 shows the data formats that Microsoft Access can export data to. Jim Fernandez, Office Manager of the MediaLoft Accounting Department, has requested that David export the first six months of training activity into an Excel spreadsheet. Jim wants to use his Excel skills to further analyze the historical training activity data using Excel formulas and graphing tools. David gathered the fields that Jim requested into a query called Accounting Data. David also will provide Jim with a list of the courses offered by the MediaLoft Training Department. David never misses an opportunity to take advantage of the power of Access.

Steps

QuickTip

You can also right-click an object in the database window and click Export from the shortcut menu.

1. Click **Queries** on the Objects bar, click **Accounting Data**, click **File** on the menu bar, then click **Export**
   The Export Query 'Accounting Data' To... dialog box opens, requesting information on the location and format for the exported information.
2. Locate your Project Disk, click the **Save as type list arrow**, click **Microsoft Excel 97-2000**, then click **Save**
   The fields and records in the Accounting Data query have been exported to an Excel file.
3. Right-click the **Start button** in the taskbar, click **Explore**, locate your Project Disk, then double-click the **Accounting Data** Excel file to open it, right-click the **Exploring button** on the task bar, then click **Close**
   Your screen should look like Figure I-20. Each field became a column and each record a row of data within Excel. A common reason to export Access information to Excel is to use Excel's extensive graphing (charting) capabilities. Yet another way to export Access information to Excel is the **drag-and-drop** method.
4. Click **File** on the menu bar, click **Close** to close the **Accounting Data** file (but leave Excel open), click the **New button** on the Excel Standard toolbar to open a new workbook, right-click an empty space on the **taskbar**, then click **Tile Windows Vertically**
   Depending upon how many programs you have open, you may have several windows tiled on the screen. If they are too small to work with, close or minimize the windows you do not need and retile the windows. Your screens should look like figure I-21.
5. Click **Tables** on the Objects bar in the Access window, click **Courses** in the Training-I Database window, then drag the **Courses table icon** to cell **A1** in the Excel window
   Your screen should look like Figure I-22. You can drag any table or query object from an Access database window to an Excel window. This action copies the recordset from the Access object to the Excel spreadsheet just as export or copy and paste does.
6. Close the Excel window without saving the changes, then close the **Training-I** database
7. Exit Access

FIGURE I-20: Excel Accounting Data file

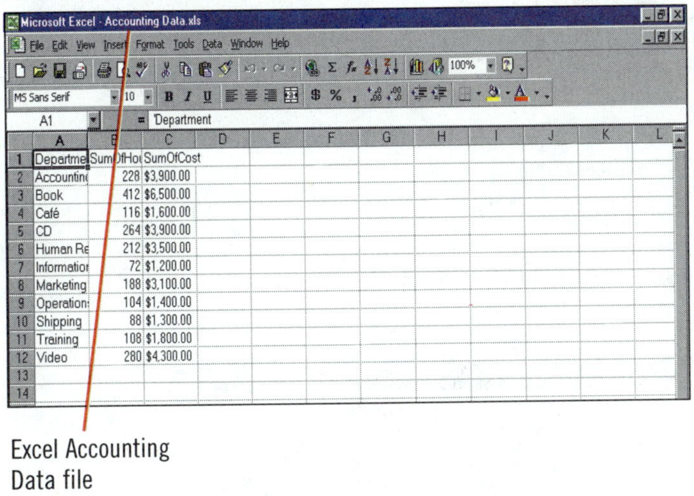

FIGURE I-21: Tiling Windows

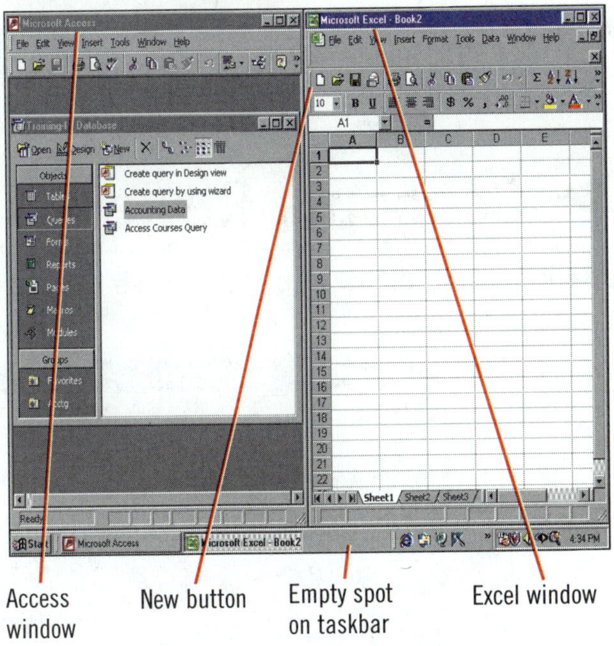

FIGURE I-22: Drag-and-Drop to Excel

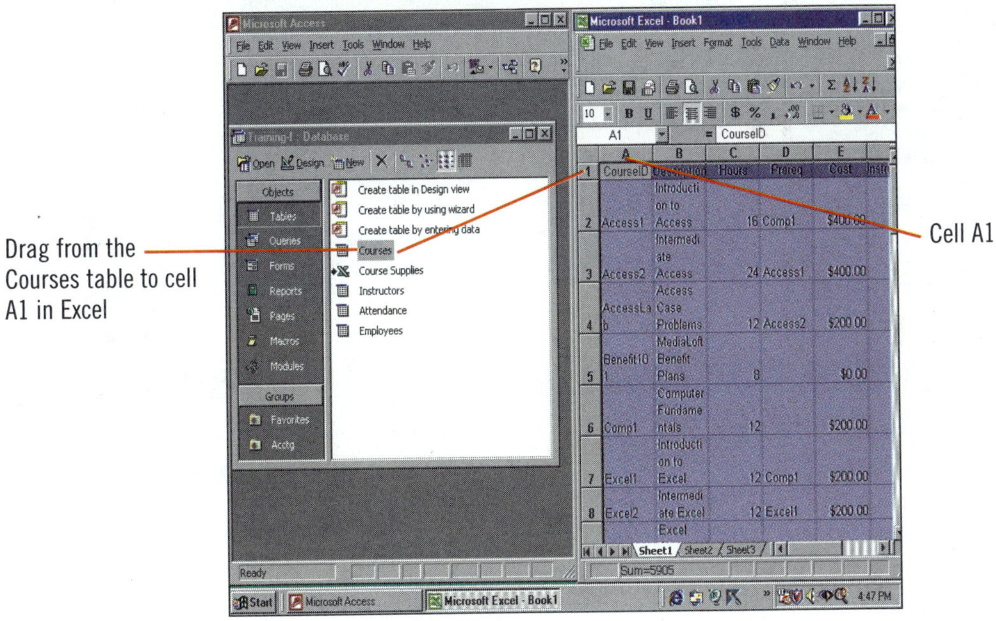

TABLE I-4: Data formats Microsoft Access can export

application	version or format supported	application	version or format supported
Microsoft Access database	2.0, 7.0/95, 8.0/97, 9.0/2000	**Lotus 1-2-3**	.wk1 and .wk3
Microsoft Access project	9.0/2000	**Delimited text files**	All character sets
dBASE	III, III+, IV, and 5	**Fixed-width text files**	All character sets
Paradox, Paradox for Windows	3.x, 4.x, and 5.0	**HTML**	1.0 (if a list) 2.0, 3.x (if a table or list)
Microsoft Excel	3.0, 4.0, 5.0, 7.0/95, 8.0/97, 9.0/2000	**SQL tables, Microsoft Visual Foxpro, and other data sources that support ODBC protocol**	Visual FoxPro 3.0, 5.0, and 6.x

Practice

► Concepts Review

Identify each element of the form's Design view shown in Figure I-23.

FIGURE I-23

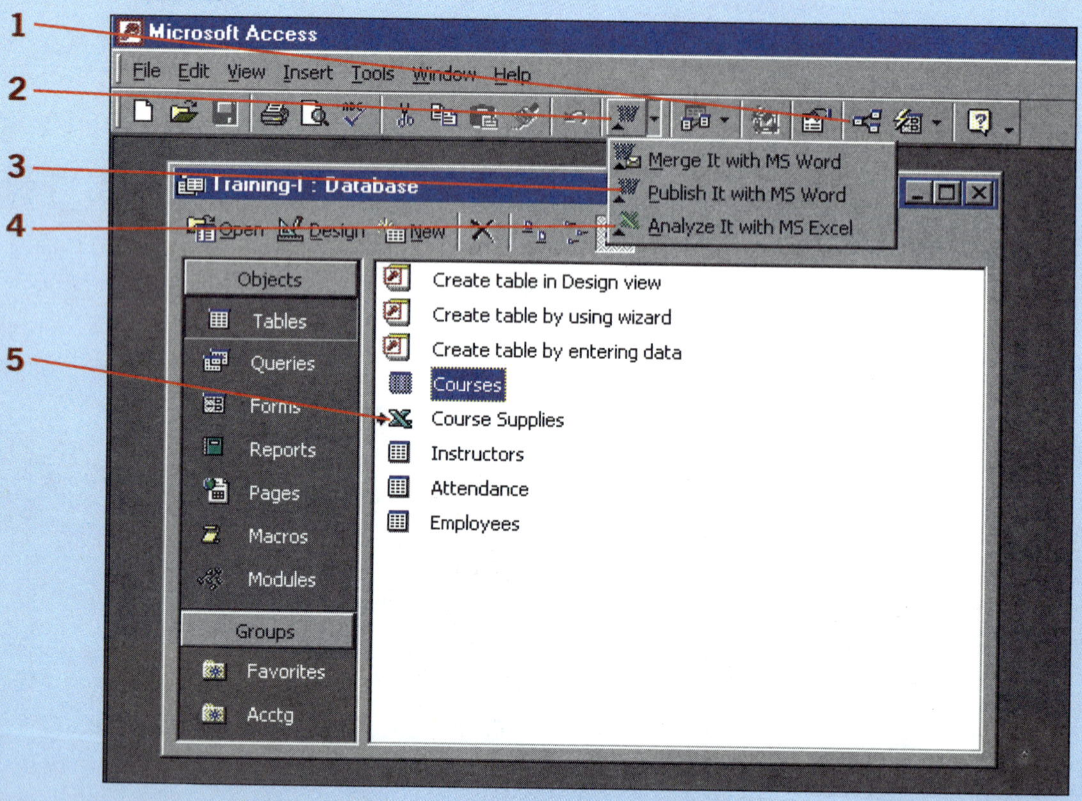

Match each term with the statement that describes its function.

6. **hyperlink**
7. **junction table**
8. **linking**
9. **what-if analysis**
10. **key field**
11. **normalization**

a. A field that contains unique information for each record
b. Testing different assumptions in a spreadsheet
c. Contains foreign key fields that link to the primary key fields of each of two other tables
d. The process of determining the appropriate fields, records, and tables when designing a relational database
e. A way to connect to data in an external source without copying it
f. A label, button, or image placed on a form that when clicked automatically opens another object, file, e-mail message, or Web address

Select the best answer from the list of choices.

12. Which of the following is NOT an Access object?
- **a.** Spreadsheet
- **b.** Report
- **c.** Table
- **d.** Query

13. Which of the following is NOT part of the normalization process?
- **a.** Determining the appropriate fields for the database
- **b.** Identifying the correct number of tables within the database
- **c.** Establishing table relationships
- **d.** Creating database hyperlinks

14. Which of the following is NOT true about linking?
- **a.** Linking does not duplicate data
- **b.** Changes to linked data will be updated in the original data source
- **c.** Changes to the original data source will be displayed in the linked data
- **d.** Linking is the same thing as copying and pasting

15. Which of the following software products would most likely be used to analyze and graph the effect of several potential price increases?
- **a.** Word
- **b.** Excel
- **c.** Access
- **d.** PowerPoint

16. Which of the following is NOT an OfficeLinks button?
- **a.** Analyze it with MS Excel
- **b.** Publish it with MS Word
- **c.** Present it with MS PowerPoint
- **d.** Merge it with MS Word

Skills Review

1. Examine Access Objects.
- **a.** Start Access, then open the Machinery-I database from your Project Disk.
- **b.** On a separate piece of paper, list the seven Access objects and the number of each type that exist in the Machinery-I database.
- **c.** List each Access table name, then use the table's Datasheet and Design views to write down the number of records and fields within each table.

2. Examine Relationships.
- **a.** Click the Relationships button on the Database toolbar.
- **b.** Drag the ProductID field from the Products table to the ProductID field of the Inventory Transactions table to create a one-to-many relationship between those tables.
- **c.** Click Enforce Referential Integrity in the Edit Relationships dialog box, then click Create.

d. Drag the PurchaseOrderID field from the Purchase Orders table to the PurchaseOrderID field of the Inventory Transactions table to create a one-to-many relationship between those tables.
e. Click Enforce Referential Integrity in the Edit Relationships dialog box, then click Create.
f. Print the Relationships, then save and close the Relationships window.

3. **Importing Data from Excel.**
   a. Click File on the menu bar, point to the Get External Data option, then click Import.
   b. In the Import dialog box, change the Files of type list to Microsoft Excel, then import the Machinery Employees Excel file on your Project Disk.
   c. In the Import Spreadsheet Wizard, be sure to specify that the first row contains column headings and that five data records are imported in a new table.
   d. Do not make any changes to fields you are importing, and be sure to select the EmpNo field as the table's primary key.
   e. Name the new table "Employees".
   f. Click the Relationships button on the Database toolbar.
   g. Drag the EmpNo field from the Employees table to the EmployeeID field of the Purchase Orders table.
   h. Click Enforce Referential Integrity in the Edit Relationships dialog box, then click Create.
   i. Save and close the Relationships window.

4. **Link Data to Excel.**
   a. Click File on the menu bar, point to the Get External Data option, then click Link Tables.
   b. In the Link dialog box, change the Files of type list to Microsoft Excel, then link to the Machinery Vendors Excel file on your Project Disk.
   c. In the Link Spreadsheet Wizard, be sure to specify that the first row contains column headings and that five data records are linked.
   d. Name the new table "Vendors".
   e. Open the Relationships window.
   f. Click the Show Table button on the Relationship toolbar.
   g. Double-click the Vendors table in the Show Table dialog box to add it to the Relationships window, then close the Show Table dialog box.
   h. Drag the VendorNo field from the Vendors table to the SupplierID field of the Purchase Orders table.
   i. Drag the title bars of the field lists in the Relationships window to more clearly present the relationships between the tables.
   j. Save and close the Relationships window.

5. **Create Hyperlinks.**
   a. Open the Product Entry Form in Design view.
   b. Add a label with the caption "Product Contacts" to the right side of the form.
   c. In the Hyperlink Address property of the Product Contacts label, click the Build button, then browse for the Product Contacts file (it is a Word document) on your Project Disk.
   d. Close the new label's property sheet, and display the Product Entry Form in Form view.
   e. Click the Product Contacts hyperlink, which will open the Product Contacts Word document, then print and close the Product Contacts Word document.
   f. Save and then close the Product Entry Form.

6. Analyze Data with Excel.

a. Click the Reports button on the Object bar, click the Every Product We Lease report, click the Office Links List arrow, then click the Analyze It with MS Excel button to send the information to Excel.

b. Press [Tab] seven times to move to column H, type "Tax" in cell H1, then press [Enter] to move to cell H2.

c. In cell H2, type =6%*D2, the formula to calculate tax that is 6% of the Unit Price, then press [Enter].

d. Print the Excel spreadsheet, then close the Every Product We Lease spreadsheet without saving the changes. Don't exit Excel.

7. Copy Data to Word.

a. Click the Machinery-I Database button on the taskbar to open the window on your screen.

b. Click the Reports button on the Objects bar, click the Every Product We Lease report, click the Office Links list arrow, then click the Publish It with MS Word button to send the information to Word.

c. Click to the right of the "We" in the title and type "Lease".

d. Press [Ctrl][Home] to go to the top of the document, press the [Enter] key twice, then press [Ctrl][Home] to return to the top of the document.

e. Type the following at the top of the document:

INTERNAL MEMO
From: [*Your Name*]
To: Sales Staff
Date: [*Today's Date*]
When quoting prices to customers over the phone, do not forget to mention the long lead times on the Back Hoe and Thatcher products. We usually do not keep these expensive items in stock.

f. Proofread the document, then print it.

g. Close the document without saving changes, then exit Word.

8. Export Data.

a. Right-click an empty space on the taskbar, then choose Tile Windows Vertically.

b. Click Tables on the Objects bar in the Access window, click the New button on the Excel standard toolbar, then drag the Products table icon to cell A1 in the Excel window.

c. Maximize the Excel window, click cell A9, and type your name.

d. Print the Excel spreadsheet, then close the Excel window without saving the Excel spreadsheet.

e. Maximize the Access window, then click the Employees table.

f. Choose File from the menu bar, then Export.

g. Locate your Project Disk, choose Microsoft Excel 97-2000 as the option in the Save as type list, and save the spreadsheet with the name "Employees".

h. Close the Machinery-I database and exit Access.

Independent Challenges

1. As the manager of a college women's basketball team, you have created a database called Basketball-I that tracks the players, games, and player statistics. You need to complete the table relationships as well as import some of the statistics that were created in an Excel file.

To complete this independent challenge:

a. Start Access and open the database Basketball-I.

b. Click the Relationships button and create a one-to-many relationship using the GameNo field between the Games table and the Stats table. Enforce referential integrity.

c. Similarly, create a one-to-many relationship using the PlayerNo field between the Players and Stats table. Note that the Stats table should be the "many" side of both relationships.
d. Close the Relationships window.
e. Click the File menu, point to Get External Data, click Import, locate your Project Disk and display Excel files in the Import dialog box, then Import the BB Stats spreadsheet.
f. Make sure that the first row contains column headings, and store the data in the existing Stats table.
g. Open the Stats table and press [Page Down] several times to make sure that the records for PlayerNo 30 and 35 were successfully imported, then close the Stats table.
h. Enter one new record in the Players table with your own information, using a PlayerNo of 99, then close the Players table.
i. Open the Players Query in Design view, double-click the link line between the Players and Stats tables to open the Join Properties dialog box, click option 2 to include all records from 'Players' and only those records from 'Stats' where the joined fields are equal, then click OK.
j. Open the Players Query in datasheet view, then print it. Jamie Johnson and your name should be the last two records. Because neither you nor Jamie has played in a game yet, you do not have any corresponding statistics.
k. Close the Basketball-I database and exit Access.

2. As the manager of a women's college basketball team, you have created a database called Basketball-I that tracks the players, games, and player statistics. You wish to link to an Excel file that contains information on the player's course load and create a hyperlink on a form to a Word document that gives more detailed information about each player.
To complete this independent challenge:

a. Start Access and open the database Basketball-I.
b. Click the File menu, point to Get External Data, click Link Tables, locate your Project Disk and display Microsoft Excel files in the Import dialog box, then Link the Course Load spreadsheet.
c. Make sure that the first row contains column headings, and link the data to a new table called "Course Load".
d. If you have not already done so, enter one new record in the Players table with your own information, using a PlayerNo of 99, then close the Players table.
e. Open the Course Load table from within Access, enter two more new records for PlayerNo 99 (you) with your own ClassNo (try to think of unique ClassNos that will differentiate your printout from that of the other students) and Grade information, print the datasheet, then close the table.
f. Click the Relationships button, click the Show Table button, then double-click the Course Load table to add it to the Relationships window.
g. Close the Show Table dialog box, then drag the PlayerNo field from the Players table to the PlayerNo field of the Course Load table and create a one-to-many relationship between the tables.
h. Save and close the Relationships window.
i. Open the Player Information Form in Design view, then add a label to the right side of the form with the caption "Player Profiles".
j. In the Hyperlink Address property of the new label, browse for the file BB Player Information Word document.
k. Close the property sheet of the new label, save the form, view it in Form view, display the last record for PlayerNo 99 (your record), then use the Selected Record option from the Print dialog box (choose File, then Print from the menu system) to print only that record.
l. Click the Player Profiles hyperlink to display the BB Player Information document, create a blank line at the top of the document and enter your name there, print the document, then close the document.
m. Close the Basketball-I database and exit Access.

3. As the manager of a women's college basketball team, you have created a database called Basketball-I that tracks the players, games, and player statistics. You wish to copy and export some of the information in the Basketball-I database to other applications such as Excel and Word.

To complete this independent challenge:

a. Start Access and open the database Basketball-I.

b. Click the Games table, then choose the Analyze It with MS Excel option from the OfficeLinks button on the Database toolbar. (If a dialog box indicating that the file already exists appears, click Yes to replace the existing file.)

c. Click cell H1, type "Margin", then click cell H2 and type the following Excel formula: =E2-F2

d. Scroll and click cell A25 and type your name, change the print settings (use the Page Setup option on the File menu) to a landscape orientation, then print the spreadsheet.

e. Close the spreadsheet without saving the changes.

f. Return to the Basketball-I database, click Reports on the Objects bar, click the Player Statistics report, then click the Publish It with MS Word option from the OfficeLinks button on the Database toolbar. (If a dialog box opens indicating that the file already exists, click Yes to replace the existing file.)

g. Enter two blank lines at the top of the document, then add the following text there:
Name: [*Your Name*]
Date: [*Today's Date*]
Subject: Offensive Statistics
The following statistics show the number of field goals, three-point completions, and field goals completed for selected players and games.

h. Print the first page of the document. (Use the Print option from the File menu and choose the Current Page option.)

i. Close the document without saving changes.

j. Close the Basketball-I database and exit Access.

WEB WORK

4. MediaLoft has developed a Web site that provides internal information to its employees. In this independent challenge, you'll add a hyperlink to a form in the Training-I database that allows the user to link to this Web page.

To complete this independent challenge:

a. Start Access, open the Training-I database, click the Forms on the Objects bar, then open the Employees form in Design view.

b. Add a label to the right side of the form with the caption "MediaLoft Home Page".

c. In the Hyperlink Address property of the new label, enter the following WorldWide Web address: http://www.course.com/illustrated/MediaLoft/ (*Hint*: You do not need to use the Builder button to enter this address.)

d. Close the properties sheet, save the Employees form, and open it in Form view.

e. Connect on to the Internet (if necessary).

f. Return to the Employees form and click the MediaLoft Home Page hyperlink label.

g. Print the MediaLoft Web page.

h. Return to the Employees form, view the form in Design view, and add a label with your name to the lower-right corner of the form.

i. Save the Employees form, display it in Form view, then print the first record.

j. Close the Employees form, then exit the Training-I database.

► Visual Workshop

Use any technique you wish (drag-and-drop, export, Analyze It with MS Excel, or copy and paste) to copy the Field Goal Stats query to an Excel spreadsheet shown in Figure I-24. Enter the formula =B2/C2 in cell D2 to determine the field goal percentage. Enter your name in cell F2, then print the first page of the spreadsheet.

FIGURE I-24

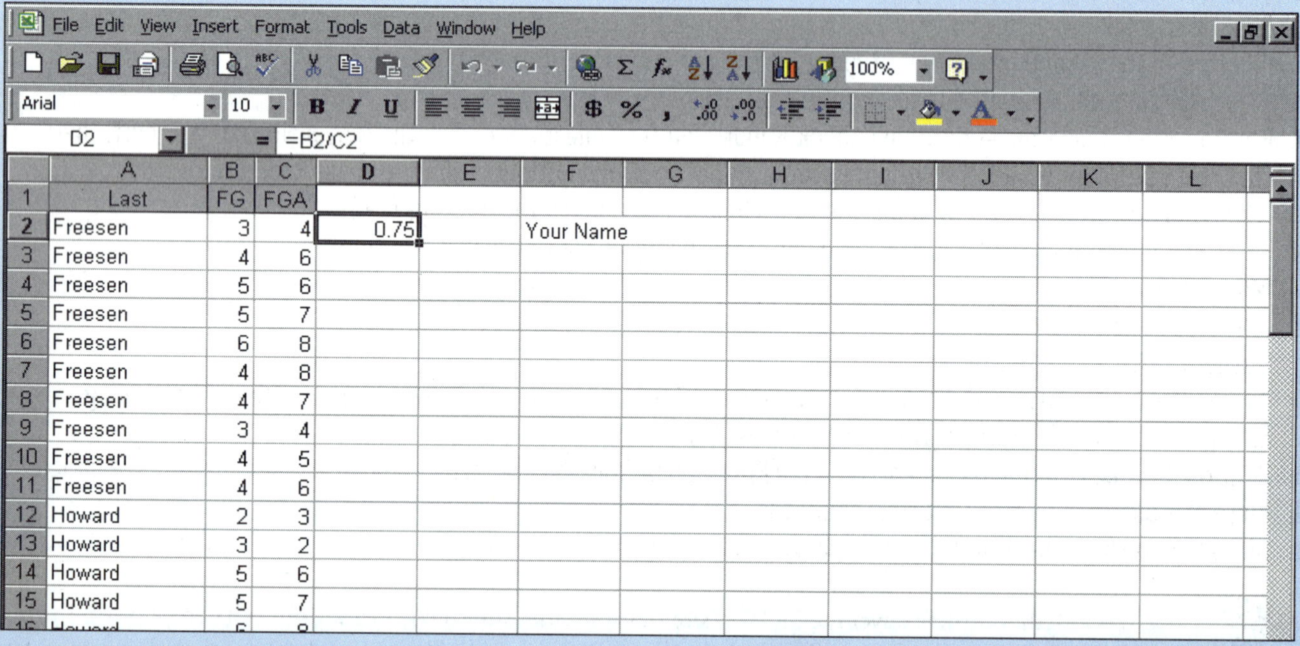

Access 2000

Unit J

Creating

Data Access Pages

Objectives

- Understand the World Wide Web
- MOUS Use hyperlink fields
- MOUS Create pages for interactive reporting
- Create pages for data entry
- Create pages for data analysis
- Work in Page Design view
- Insert hyperlinks to other pages
- Publish Web pages to Web servers

The Internet has an enormous wealth of information, unlimited potential for business opportunity, and ability for instant global communication. A tremendous amount of energy is being focused on how to connect **World Wide Web pages**, which are hyperlinked documents that make the Internet easy to navigate, directly to underlying databases. Linked pages enable employees, customers, or vendors to view, find, enter, edit, analyze, and order products via an Internet connection rather than having direct access to the database file. Access 2000 provides a connection between Web pages and an Access database through the **page** object. MediaLoft employees are located throughout the United States, and David Dumont would like to give them the ability to access the Training-J database via the Internet.

Unit J

Access 2000

Understanding the World Wide Web

Creating Web pages that dynamically interact with an Access database is an exciting process that involves many underlying technologies. Understanding how the Internet, the World Wide Web, and Web pages interact is extremely important in order to successfully connect a Web page to an underlying Access database. David reviews some of the history and key terminology of the Internet and World Wide Web to better prepare himself for the task of connecting a Web page to an Access database.

Details

The **Internet** is a worldwide network of computer networks that sends and receives information through a common **protocol** (set of rules) called **TCP/IP** (Transmission Control Protocol/Internet Protocol).

The Internet supports many services including:

- **E-Mail:** electronic mail
- **File Transfer:** uploading and downloading files
- **Newsgroups:** similar to e-mail, but messages are posted in a "public mailbox" that is available to any subscriber rather than sent to one individual
- **World Wide Web (WWW):** a vast number of linked documents stored on thousands of different Web servers

The Internet has experienced tremendous growth in the past decade partly because of the following three major factors:

- In the early 1990s, the U.S. government lifted restrictions on commercial Internet traffic, causing explosive growth in electronic commerce activities.
- Technological innovations resulted in breakthroughs in hardware such as faster computer processors and storage devices, and in networking media such as fiber-optics and satellite transmission.
- Less expensive and easier-to-use Internet systems and program software were developed for both **clients** (your computer) and **servers** (the computer that "serves" the information to you from the Internet).

Behind all of these innovations are many amazing people. Of special note is the scientist who saw the need to easily share real-time information with colleagues. This scientific initiative grew into today's World Wide Web. Table J-1 introduces more Internet and World Wide Web terminology. Figure J-1 shows how hyperlinks work on a Web page.

FIGURE J-1: Hyperlinks on a Web page

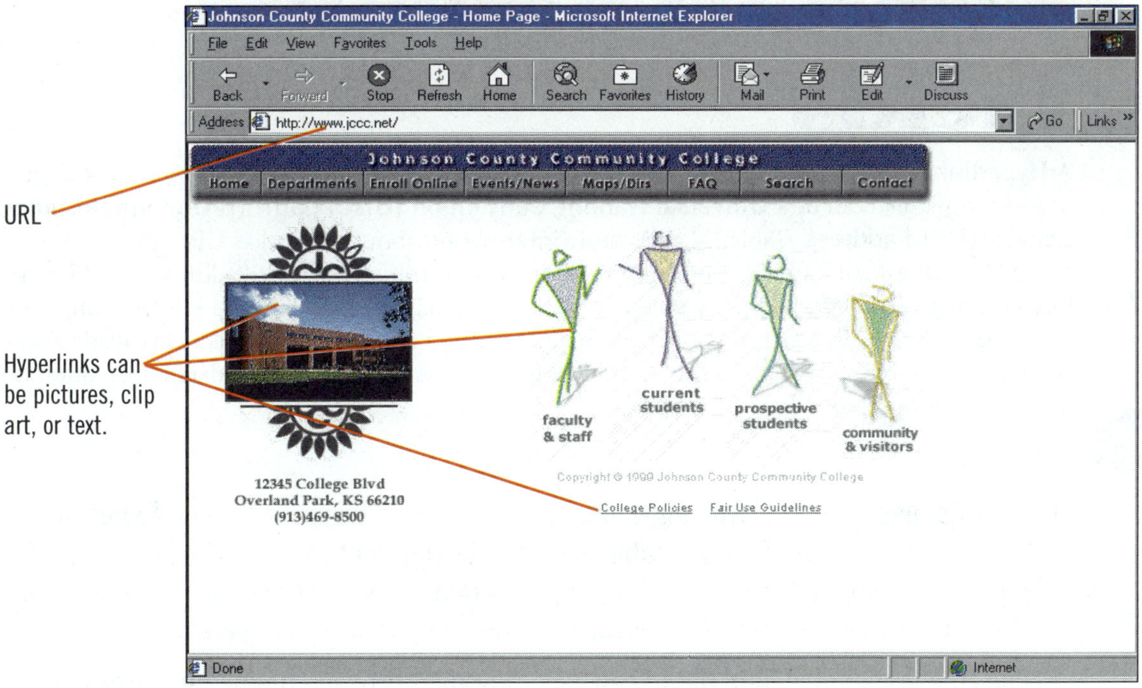

TABLE J-1: Internet and World Wide Web terminology

term	definition
Web page	A special type of file created with HTML code that contains hyperlinks to other files
Web server	A computer that stores Web pages
Hyperlink	Text (usually underlined), an image, or an icon on a Web page that when clicked, presents another Web page. Hyperlinks can jump to another part of the same Web page, a different page on the same Web server, or to a different Web server in another part of the world.
HTML	Hypertext Markup Language. HTML is a special programming language used to create Web pages. An HTML programmer writes HTML code to create a Web page. Nonprogrammers create HTML Web pages using FrontPage or by converting files such as Word, Excel, and PowerPoint files into HTML Web pages using menu options within those programs.
Browser	Software such as Microsoft's Internet Explorer (IE) or Netscape Navigator used to find and display Web pages. HTML files created through the Access Page object are best displayed with IE version 5 or later.
ISP	Internet Service Provider. To access the Internet from a home computer, your computer first must dial an ISP that connects your computer with the Internet. National ISPs include America Online, The Microsoft Network, and Sprint's Earthlink Internet. Hundreds of regional and local ISPs exist as well.
Modem	Short for *mod*ulate-*dem*odulate. A modem is hardware (usually located inside the computer) that converts digital computer signals to analog telephone signals to allow a computer to send and receive information across ordinary telephone lines.
URL	Uniform Resource Locator. Each resource on the Internet (including Web pages) has an address so that other computers can accurately and consistently locate and view it. http://www.course.com/products/ is the URL for the Web page that displays information about Course Technology, Inc. (the publisher of this textbook.) There is never a space in a URL.
Domain name	The middle part of a URL, such as www.course.com. The middle part of the domain name is often either the company's name or words that describe the information you will find at that site. The last part of the domain name indicates the type of site, such as commercial (com), educational (edu), military (mil), organizational (org), or governmental (gov).
Home page	The first page displayed on a Web server.

Unit J

Access 2000

Using Hyperlink Fields

A **Hyperlink field** is a field defined with the Hyperlink data type in Table Design view. The entry in a hyperlink field can be a **Universal Naming Convention (UNC) path** or a **Uniform Resource Locator (URL) address**. Table J-2 gives more information about networks. URLs may also specify an Internet e-mail address, a newsgroup address, an intranet Web page address, or a file on a local area network. Many MediaLoft employees have requested more information about the internal classes. To accommodate these requests, David creates a Hyperlink field called Online Resources to store the URL for a World Wide Web page that contains up-to-date information on the subject of the class.

Steps

1. Start **Access**, open the **Training-J** database from your Project Disk, click **Tables** on the Objects bar, click the **Courses table**, click the **Design button** in the Database window, then maximize both the database and the table windows (if not already maximized)
   The Courses table opens in Design view, where you can add fields and specify their properties.

2. Click the first empty **Field Name cell** below InstructorID, type **Online Resources**, press **[Tab]**, press **h**, click the **Save button**, then click the **Datasheet View button**
   The Courses table with the new Online Resources field opens in datasheet view.

3. Press **[Tab]** six times to move to the new Online Resources field, type **www.microsoft.com/access**, press **[↓]** point to the right edge of the **Online Resources field name**, double-click ✛, then click
   Your screen should look like Figure J-2. The column is widened to display all of the data in the Online Resources field. Note that hyperlinks appear underlined in bright blue just like text hyperlinks on Web pages.

> **QuickTip**
> The first part of an Internet Web address (http://) can be omitted when entering a URL into a hyperlink field.

4. Press **[Ctrl][']**, then press **[↓]**

> **QuickTip**
> [Ctrl]['] copies the entry in the field of the previous record to the same field of the current record.

5. Point to **www.microsoft.com/access** in either record so that the pointer changes to , then click **www.microsoft.com/access**
   If you are currently connected to the Internet and have Microsoft Internet Explorer browser software loaded on your computer, your screen should look similar to Figure J-3. Netscape Communicator is another popular browser program that will also open and display HTML files. Web pages are continually updated as new information is announced, so the content of the Web page itself may vary. If you are not already connected to the Internet, your **dialer** (software that helps you dial and connect to your ISP) may appear. Once connected to your ISP, the Microsoft Access Web page should appear.

6. Click the **Courses: Table button** in the taskbar, click the **Online Resources field** for record **5** (Introduction to Excel), type **www.microsoft.com/excel**, click the **Online Resources field** for record **11** (Introduction to Netscape), type **www.netscape.com**, then press **[Enter]**
   Hyperlink entries can point to a different Web page on the same Web server or to an entirely different Web server.

> **QuickTip**
> Visited links will change to the color purple.

7. Click **www.netscape.com**
   The Netscape Netcenter Web page appears on your screen.

8. Right-click the **Courses: Table button** on the taskbar, click **Close**, click **Yes** to save the changes to the layout of the table, then close any open browser windows

FIGURE J-2: A hyperlink entry

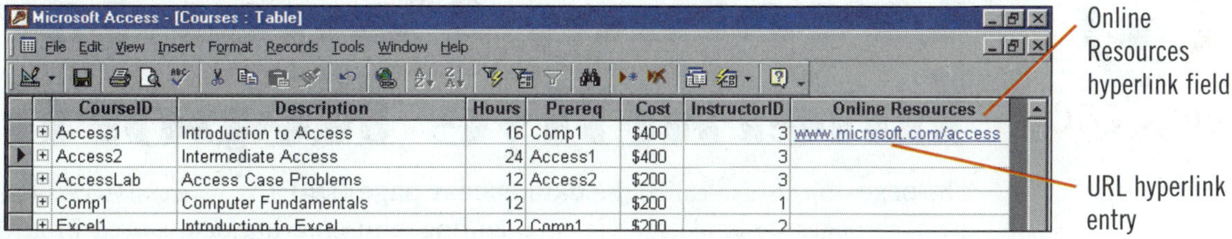

FIGURE J-3: www.microsoft.com/access Web page

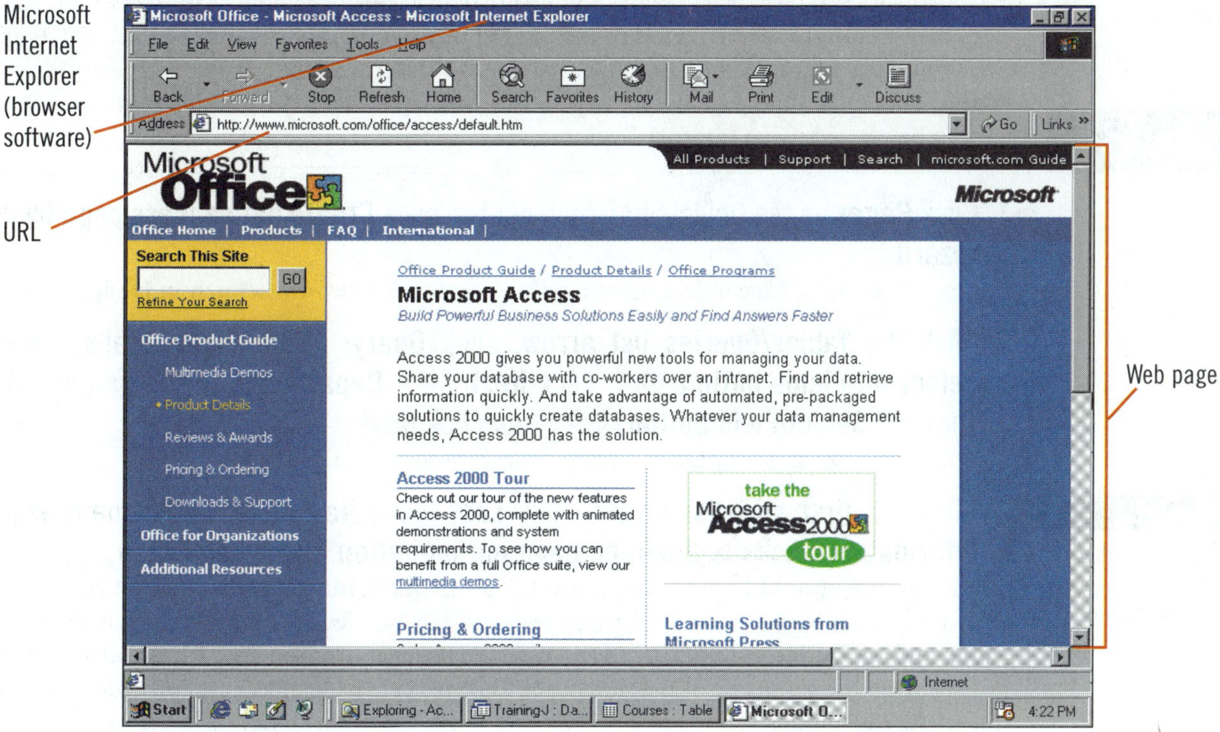

TABLE J-2: Types of networks

type of network	description
LAN (local area network)	Connects local resources such as file servers, user computers, and printers by a direct cable. LANs do not cross a public thoroughfare such as a street because of distance and legal restrictions on how far and where cables can be pulled.
WAN (wide area network)	Created when a LAN is connected to an existing telecommunications network, such as the phone system, to reach resources across public thoroughfares such as streets and rivers
Internet	Largest WAN in the world, spanning the entire globe and connecting many diverse computer architectures
Intranet	WANs that support the same services as the Internet (i.e., e-mail, Web pages, and file transfer) and are built with the same technologies (e.g., TCP/IP communications protocol, HTML Web pages, and browser software), but are designed and secured for the internal purposes of a business. To secure intranet information and resources from outsiders, passwords and data encryption techniques are used.

CLUES TO USE

Understanding the Universal Naming Convention (UNC)

Universal Naming Convention (UNC) is another naming convention (in addition to URL) to locate a file on a network. The structure of a UNC is \\server\sharedfoldername\filename. UNCs are used for local resources, such as a file stored on a local area network. URL addresses are used for Web pages on the Internet or a company intranet.

Unit J

Access 2000

Creating Pages for Interactive Reporting

The **page** object, also called the **data access page (DAP)**, is a special Access object used to create Web pages designed for viewing, editing, and entering data stored in a Microsoft Access database. Data access pages may also include data from other sources such as Microsoft Excel or a Microsoft SQL Server database. You create data access page objects in Access, but the Web pages they create are separate HTML files stored outside the Access database file. DAPs appear when you click Pages on the Objects bar. Table J-3 describes three major purposes for a DAP. David uses the page object to publish interactive reports from the Training-J database that can be viewed using Internet Explorer.

Steps

1. Click **Pages** on the Objects bar, then double-click **Create data access page by using wizard**

   You can create a page object using a wizard or develop it from scratch in Design view.

2. Click the **Tables/Queries list arrow**, click **Query: Attendance Details**, click the **Select All Fields button**, click **Next**, click **Department** as the grouping level, click the **Select Field button**, then click **Next**

   The Page Wizard prompts for sorting fields as well as a page title.

3. Click the **first sort list arrow**, click **Last**, click **Next**, type **Department Training Information**, click the **Open the page option button**, then click **Finish**

   Your screen should look like Figure J-4. The **Expand button** indicates that detail records grouped within the Accounting Department can be viewed by clicking that button. The **navigation buttons** are similar to those for a datasheet or form. The **filter** and **sort buttons** appear on the right side of the navigation buttons of a page object and provide filtering and sorting capabilities to the person who is viewing this information as a Web page when the data access page is posted to an Internet or intranet Web server.

4. Click the **Expand button**, click **1/31/00** in the Attended text box, then click the **Sort Ascending button** on the Attendance Details 1 of 16 navigation bar

   Your screen should look like Figure J-5. The Expand button has become the **Collapse button**. When clicked, the Collapse button collapses the detail records within that group.

5. Click the **Last Record button** on the Attendance Details Department 1 of 11 navigation buttons to display the Video group, click , click **Lee** in the Last field, then click the **Filter by Selection button** on the Attendance Detail 1 of 21 navigation buttons

   Your screen should look like Figure J-6.

6. Click the **Remove Filter button** on the Attendance Details 1 of 11 toolbar to view all 21 detail records within the Video department, click the **Save button** on the Page View toolbar, locate your Project disk, type **Department Training** in the File name text box, then click **Save**

   You do not need to save the HTML file with the same name as the corresponding DAP, but it helps keep them organized if they have similar names. An HTML file named Department Training has been saved to your Project Disk. Internet Explorer opens HTML files as Web pages.

7. Close the Department Training Information page object window

Trouble?

Click the Page View button if you are viewing Page Design view instead of Page view.

Trouble?

If your page doesn't display correctly, click the Page Design View button, then click the Page View button.

Trouble?

When you click a text box on a data access page used for interactive reporting, you may not see the blinking insertion point inside the text box.

FIGURE J-4: Department Training Information data access page

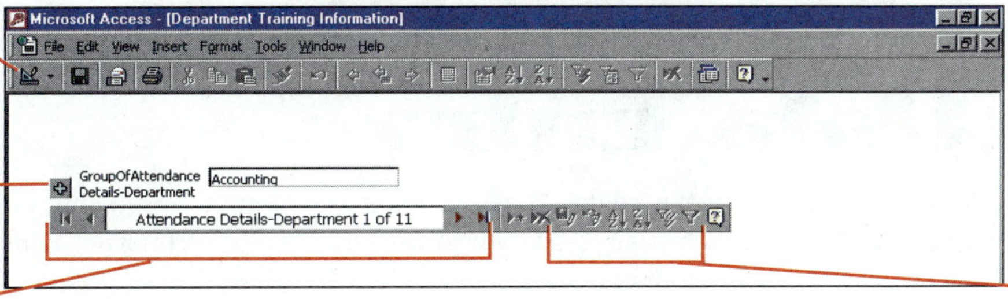

Page Design View button

Expand button

Department Navigation buttons

Filter and Sort buttons

FIGURE J-5: Expanded and sorted data access page

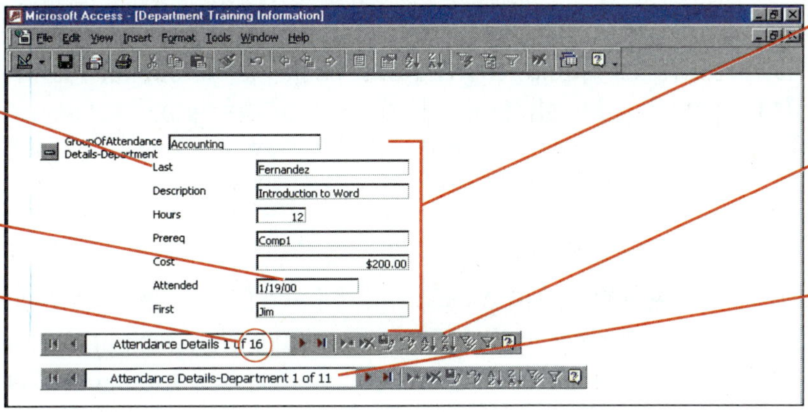

Last field is listed at the top because that's how the detail records are sorted

Attended field

Accounting employees took 16 classes

Detail record for the Accounting Department

Sort Ascending button

11 different departments

FIGURE J-6: Filtered data access page

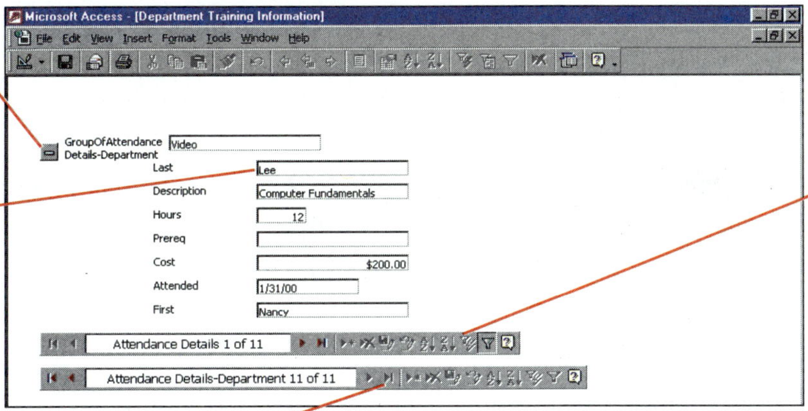

Within the video department, Nancy Lee attended 11 classes

"Lee" entry in Last text box

Filter by Selection button

Department Last Record button

TABLE J-3: Purposes for data access pages

purpose	description
Interactive reporting	To publish summaries of information using sorting, grouping, and filtering techniques.
Data entry	To view, add, and edit records
Data analysis	To analyze the data using pivot tables and charts

Unit J

Access 2000

Creating Pages for Data Entry

Using a data access page for data entry is similar to using an Access form except that the data access page also creates a Web page to be viewed through Microsoft Internet Explorer. Within the data access page you can view, enter, edit, and delete data, just like in a form. The Human Resources department has offered to help David find, enter, and update information on instructors. David creates a data access page based on the Instructors table within the Training-J database to give the HR department the ability to also view and update this data using Internet Explorer.

Steps

1. Double-click the **Create data access page by using wizard**, click the **Tables/Queries list arrow**, click **Table: Instructors**, click the **Select All Fields button** >>, click **Next**, then click **Finish** to accept the rest of the defaults

   The data access page opens in **Page Design view**, as shown in Figure J-7. The Toolbox and the Alignment and Sizing toolbars may be open. The Field list, which organizes fields and objects much like Internet Explorer organizes files and folders, is open. Page objects contain controls just as reports and forms do.

2. Click the **Page View button** on the Page Design toolbar to view the data access page, click the **Save button** on the Page View toolbar, locate your Project Disk, type **Instructor Updates** in the File name text box, then click **Save**

   The Instructors data access page shows the three records that are currently in the Instructors table. You *could* use this page object within Access to enter or edit data, but the purpose of a data access page isn't for data entry (forms are much more powerful data entry tools if you have direct access to the database file). The real power of the data access page object is its ability to create dynamic HTML files (Web pages) that can be used to enter and update data by people who *do not* have direct access to the database, but who *do* have Internet Explorer browser software.

3. Close the **Instructor Updates** data access page

   Use Microsoft Internet Explorer to open the Instructor Updates HTML file to make changes to the Training-J database *even though you are not directly using the Training-J database file.*

4. Click **Start** on the taskbar, point to **Programs**, click **Internet Explorer** (IE), click **File** on the IE menu bar, click **Open**, click **Browse** in the Open dialog box, locate your Project Disk, click **Instructor Updates.htm**, click **Open,** then click **OK**

   The Instructor Updates.htm file opens in Internet Explorer, as shown in Figure J-8.

5. Click the **New Record button** on the navigation bar, type **Sarah**, press **[Tab]**, type **Chalupa**, press **[Tab]**, type **9/1/00**, click the **Previous Record button**, then click the **Next Record button**

   You verify that the record for Sarah Chalupa was entered successfully.

6. Close **Internet Explorer**, click the **Training-J database button** on the taskbar, click **Tables** on the Objects bar, then double-click the **Instructors table** to open it in Datasheet view

   Your screen should look like Figure J-9. The new record appears in the table. You used an HTML Web page opened in Internet Explorer to dynamically update an underlying Access database. If you had been using the Internet or a company intranet, the Instructor Updates.htm file would have to have been stored on a Web server rather than your Project Disk. To open the Instructor Updates.htm file on a Web server, you have to enter the URL or UNC address for the file.

7. Close the **Instructors** datasheet

Trouble?

You do not need to be connected to the Internet to load Web pages stored in your Project Disk.

Trouble?

You cannot press [Page Up] and [Page Down] to move from record to record when viewing records through an HTML file.

FIGURE J-7: Page Design view

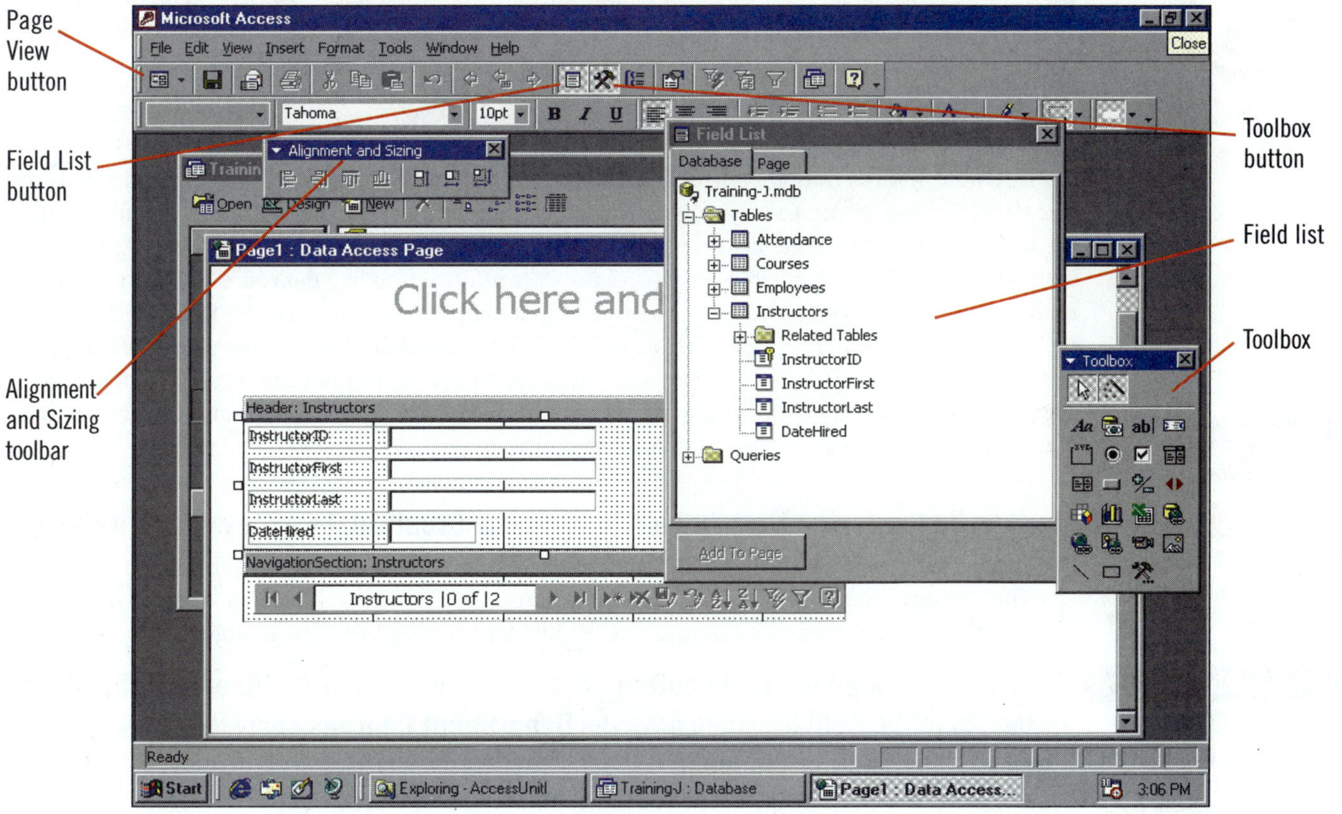

FIGURE J-8: Instructor Updates.htm Web page opened in Internet Explorer

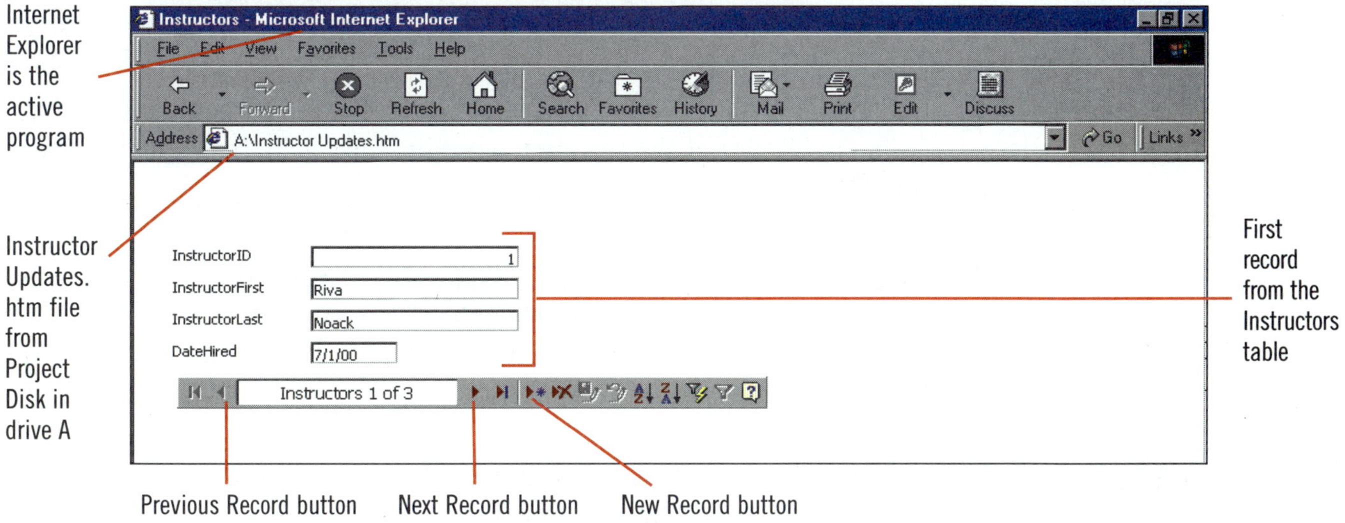

FIGURE J-9: Updated Instructors table

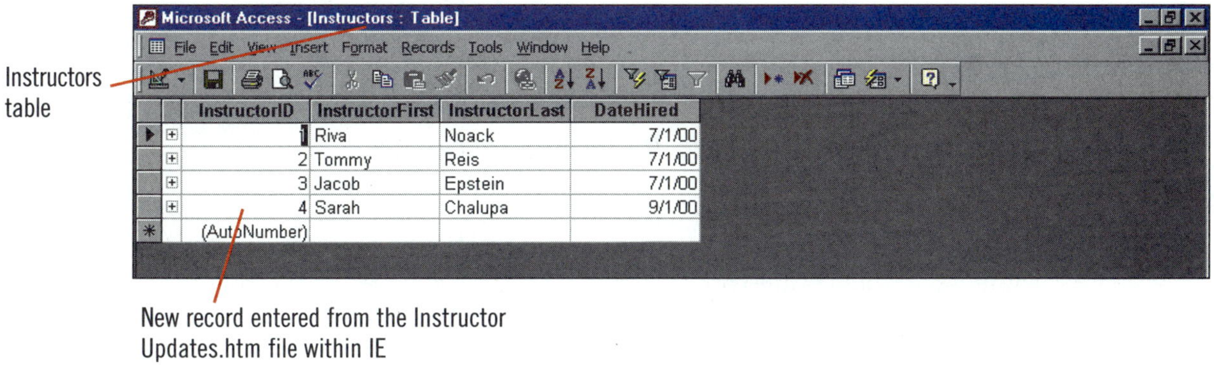

Access 2000

Unit J

Access 2000

Creating Pages for Data Analysis

A **PivotTable list** is a bound control created in Design view of a data access page. It helps you analyze data by allowing you to organize data in many different ways. In a pivot table, one field is used for the column heading, one field is used for the row heading, and one field is summarized for each column and row. The PivotTable list control presents information in a data access page in a way that is similar to how a Crosstab query presents data in a query. You cannot use the PivotTable List control to edit, delete, or add new data. In this respect, DAPs created for data analysis using the PivotTable List control are similar to those created for interactive reporting. Neither can be used to update data. David creates a data access page using the PivotTable list control so that information about course attendance can be viewed in many different ways.

Steps

QuickTip

You can move the Alignment and Spacing toolbar, the Field list, and the Toolbox by dragging their title bars.

Trouble?

Click the Field List button to toggle it on (if necessary), click the Toolbox toolbar button to toggle it on (if necessary).

1. Click **Pages** on the Objects bar, double-click **Create data access page in Design view**, then maximize the Design View window
   The Design view of a page, as shown in Figure J-10, is very similar to that of a form or report. Table J-4 summarizes some of the key terminology used in Design view.
2. Click the **Office PivotTable button** on the Toolbox, click the **Queries Expand button** in the Field list, then drag the **Department Charges** query into the upper-left area of the **Section: Unbound**
   The Layout Wizard helps guide you through the rest of the process.
3. Click the **PivotTable List option button**, click **OK**, then click to toggle the Field list off
   Your screen should look like Figure J-11. The four fields within the Department Charges query are the column headings in the PivotTable List control.
4. Point to the **middle sizing handle** on the right edge of the PivotTable List control, drag ↔ to the right edge of the section to view the Cost field, then click the **Page View button** on the Page Design toolbar
   The data access page appears within Access, and the fields display interactive list arrows.
5. Click the **Department list arrow**, click the **(Show All) check box** to clear all of the check marks, scroll and click the **Video checkbox**, then click **OK**
   Only the records with "Video" in the Department field appear. Choices made within these lists are temporary and are not saved with the page object, so every time you open the page, all of the records are visible.
6. Click the **Design View button** , **click the PivotTable List control**, right-click the **Description field name**, click **Move to Row Area**, then click
   Your screen should look like Figure J-12. The Description field entries are now organized as row headings, and the other fields from the Department Charges query still appear as column headings. The PivotTable List control's major benefit is its ability to quickly rearrange data in many different ways.
7. Click the **Save button** on the Page View toolbar, locate your Project Disk, type **Department Pivot**, click **Save**, then close to access page
   The new Department Pivot data access page object is stored within the Training-J database window and the Department Pivot HTML file is stored on your Project Disk. The PivotTable List control looks and behaves the same way whether you access it as a DAP within Access or view the corresponding HTML file as a Web page within IE.

Trouble?

The PivotTable List control must be selected before you can move the fields within it. The PivotTable List control will have a hashed border when selected.

QuickTip

Saving an HTML file saves both the HTML file and the corresponding DAP with the same name.

FIGURE J-10: Design view of a Page

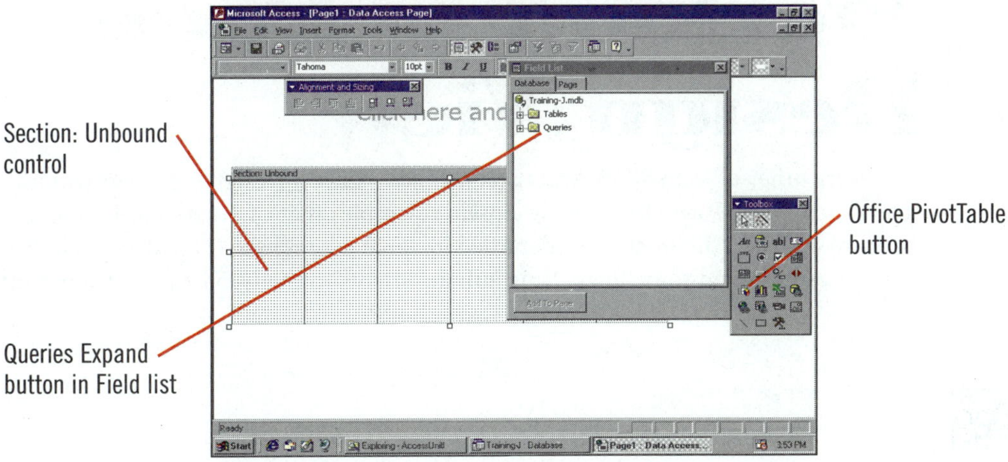

FIGURE J-11: PivotTable List control in Design view

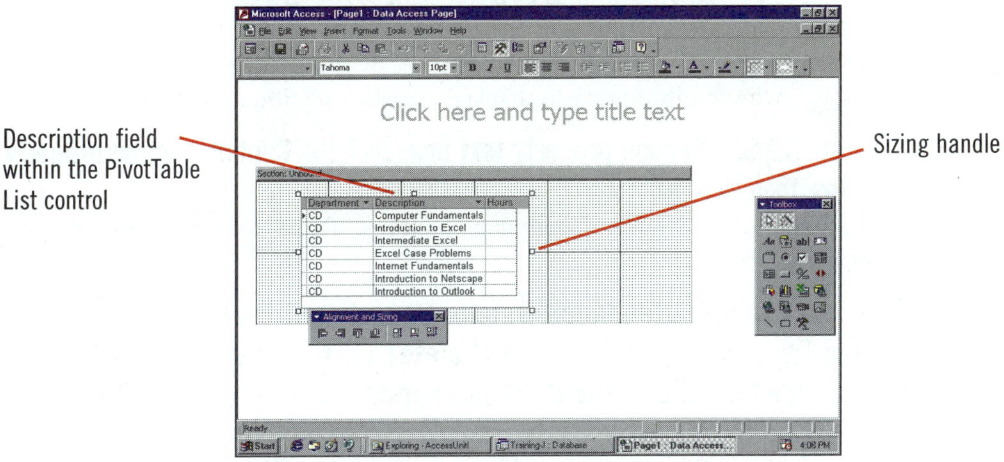

FIGURE J-12: Modified PivotTable List control in Page view

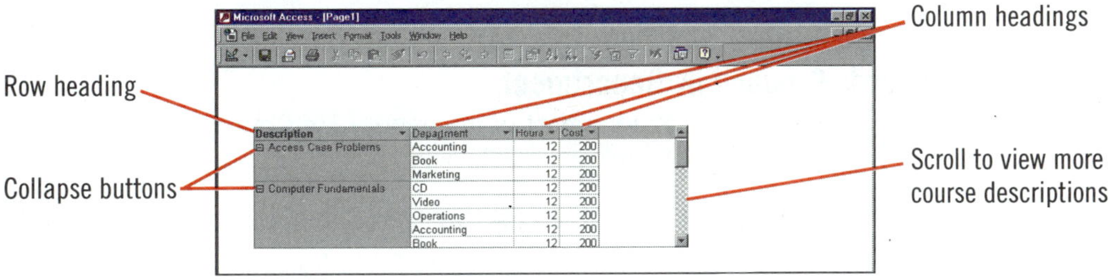

TABLE J-4: Design view terminology

term	definition
Field list	List that contains all of the field names that can be added to an object in Design view
Toolbox toolbar	Toolbar that contains all of the bound and unbound controls that can be added to the object in Design view
Control	Each individual element that can be added, deleted, or modified in an object's Design view
Bound controls	Controls that display data from an underlying recordset. Common bound controls are text boxes, list boxes, and pivot table lists
Unbound controls	Controls that do not display data from an underlying recordset. Common unbound controls for a page are labels, lines, and toolbars
Sections	Areas of the object that contain controls. Sections determine where and how often a control will appear or print
Properties	Characteristics that further describe the selected object, section, or control

Unit J

Access 2000

Working in Page Design View

Like every other object within Access, page objects have a Design view that you use to modify the object's structure. Page Design view closely resembles that of Form and Report Design view, but there are some key differences, as identified in Table J-5. David works in Page Design view to add a caption and some formatting enhancements to the Department Training Page object.

Steps

1. Click the **Department Training page**, click the **Design button** in the Database window, then click the **Sorting and Grouping button** on the Page Design toolbar
   The Sorting and Grouping dialog box opens, as shown in Figure J-13. Several options are available, including the ability to display a caption section and record navigation section.
2. Click the **Caption Section property text box**, click the **Caption section property list arrow**, click **Yes**, then click
   The Sorting and Grouping dialog box closes. The Caption section is often used for descriptive labels.
3. Click the **GroupOfAttendance Details-Department label** in the Header: Attendance Details-Department section, press **[Delete]**, click the **Label button** on the Toolbox, click on the **left side of the Caption section**, then type **DEPARTMENTS**
   Your screen should look similar to Figure J-14. Many of the moving and resizing skills you learned in Form and Report Design view work exactly the same way in Page Design view, so you can move and resize controls if necessary.
4. Click **Click here and type title text** at the top of the page, then type **Attendance Records Grouped by Department**
   The body of the page is not a part of any section, but rather is the title text for the HTML Web page that this DAP creates.
5. Click the **Save button** on the Page Design toolbar, then click the **Page View button**
   The changes you made to the Department Training page are displayed in the Page view.
6. Close the Department Training page object
   The Department Training page looks and behaves the same whether you are viewing it in Page view through Access or as a Web page opened in Internet Explorer.
7. Start **Internet Explorer**, click **File** on the menu bar, click **Open**, click **Browse**, locate your Project Disk, double-click **Department Training**, then click **OK**
   After a few moments, the Department Training HTML file opens within Internet Explorer, as shown in Figure J-15.
8. Close **Internet Explorer**

FIGURE J-13: Sorting and Grouping dialog box for the Data Access page

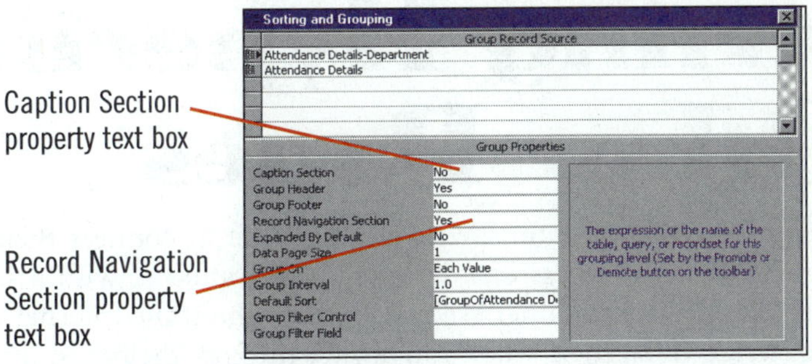

FIGURE J-14: Adding label controls

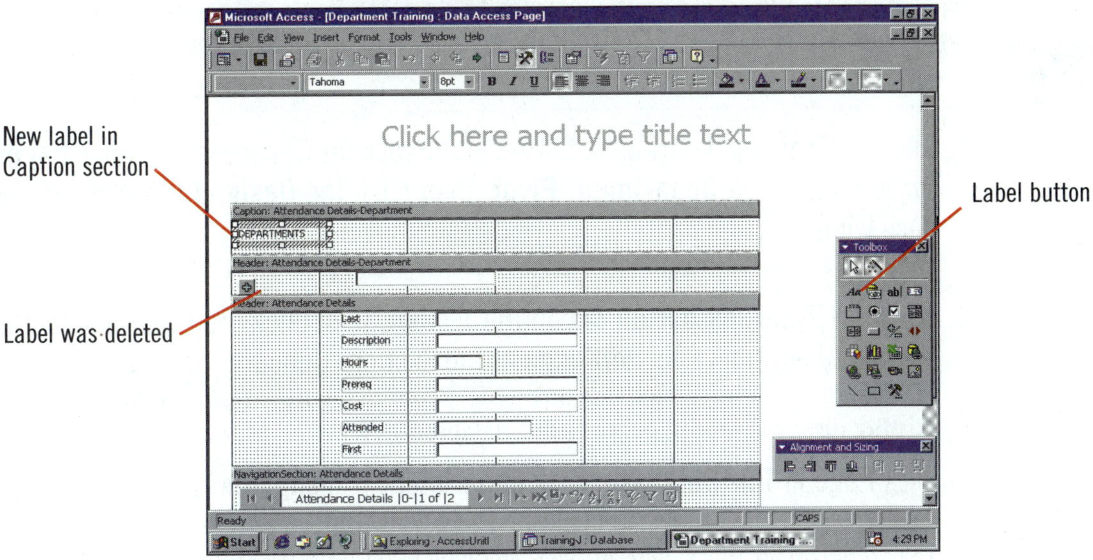

FIGURE J-15: Viewing the updated Web page in Internet Explorer

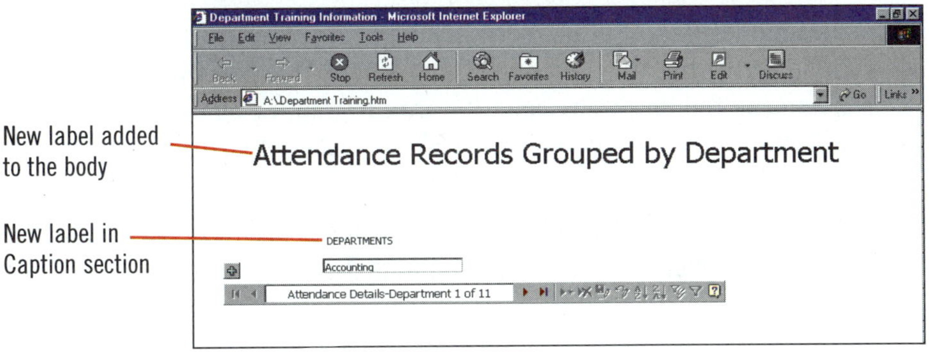

TABLE J-5: New Features within Page Design view

item	description
Body	Basic design surface of the data access page that displays text, controls, and sections. When viewed in Page view or in Internet Explorer, the content in the body automatically adjusts itself to fit the size of the browser
Sections	New sections within a page object include the record navigation section used to display the navigation toolbar and the caption section used to display text. Neither of these two new sections can contain bound controls
Positioning	By default, the position of text, sections, and other elements in the body of a page are relative to one another (determined by the preceding content on the page)
Toolbox	Several new controls are displayed in the Toolbox toolbar that are specific to page objects, including the Office PivotTable, Expand, and Record Navigation controls
Field list	The Field List window displays *all* Tables, Queries, and associated fields within them. The Page tab of the Field list displays the bound controls and grouping choices within the Details section

Unit J

Access 2000

Inserting Hyperlinks to Other Pages

Once the Access page objects are finished, you may wish to connect them using hyperlinks. Hyperlinks allow the user to access one Web page from another with a single click, just like World Wide Web pages reference other Web pages throughout the Internet. You add hyperlinks to pages in Page Design view. Then, when you browse through the pages, you can jump between them by clicking the hyperlinks. David wants to create a hyperlink between the Department Training and Department Pivot data access pages so that one page can be accessed from the other. He uses Page Design view to add the hyperlinks to both pages.

Steps

1. Click the **Training-J** database button in the taskbar (if necessary), click **Pages** on the Objects bar, click **Department Pivot**, then click the **Design button** in the database window
   Hyperlink controls are added to page objects by using the Hyperlink control.
2. Click the **Hyperlink button** on the Toolbox, then click the hyperlink pointer in the page body above the left edge of the Section: Unbound control
   The Insert Hyperlink dialog box opens, as shown in Figure J-16. You may choose links from existing files, Web pages, pages in this database, new pages, or e-mail addresses.
3. Click **Page in This Database**, click **Department Training** from the Select a page in this database list, click **OK**, then click the **Page View button** on the Page Design toolbar
   The Department Pivot page displays the new hyperlink. Pointing to a hyperlink on a page displays information about the hyperlink.
4. Place the pointer over **Department Training** so that the pointer changes to , observe the ScreenTip, then click the **Department Training hyperlink** to test the link
   The Department Training Web page with records grouped by department should be displayed within an IE window. Now add a hyperlink to go from the Department Training Web page back to the Department Pivot Web page.
5. Click the **Department Pivot button** in the taskbar to return to Access, save and close the **Department Pivot** page, click **Department Training** page object in the Training-J database window, then click
6. Click on the Toolbox, then click on the **page body** above the left edge of the Caption: Attendance Details-Department section
7. Click **Page in This Database** in the Insert Hyperlink dialog box, click the **Department Pivot** page, click **OK**, then click
8. Click the **Department Pivot hyperlink**, then click the **Print button** on the IE Standard Buttons toolbar
   The Department Pivot Web page should open in IE, as shown in Figure J-17. Now you can move between the two pages by clicking their hyperlinks.
9. Close IE, then close the Training-J database, saving any changes.

Trouble?

If Netscape opens the Web page, you may want to change file type associations within Explorer so that IE is used to open HTML files.

Trouble?

To make sure that IE is displaying the latest version of a Web page, click the Refresh button on the IE Standard Buttons toolbar.

FIGURE J-16: Insert Hyperlink dialog box

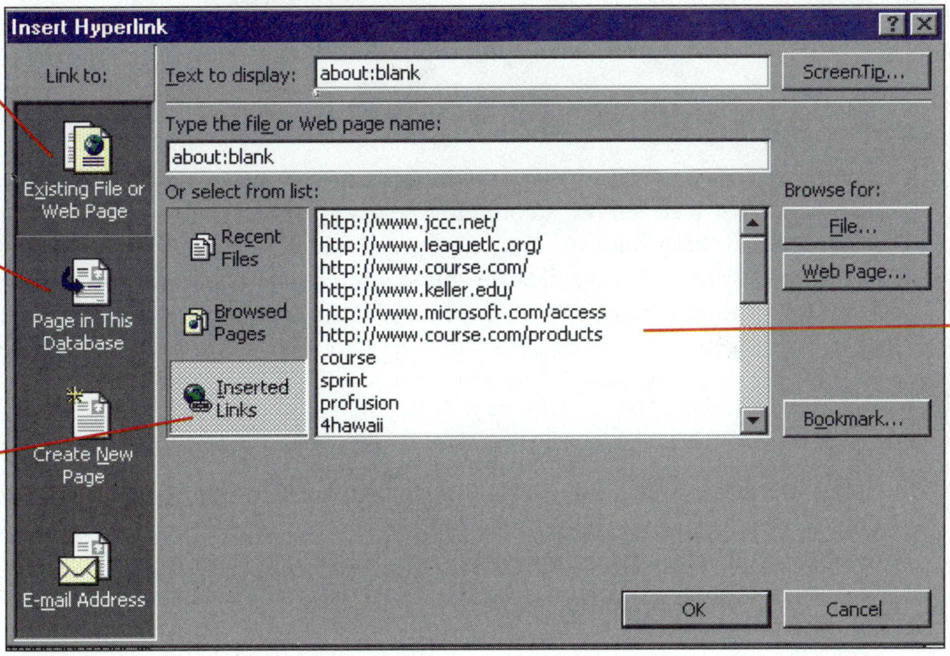

FIGURE J-17: Department Pivot Web page viewed through IE

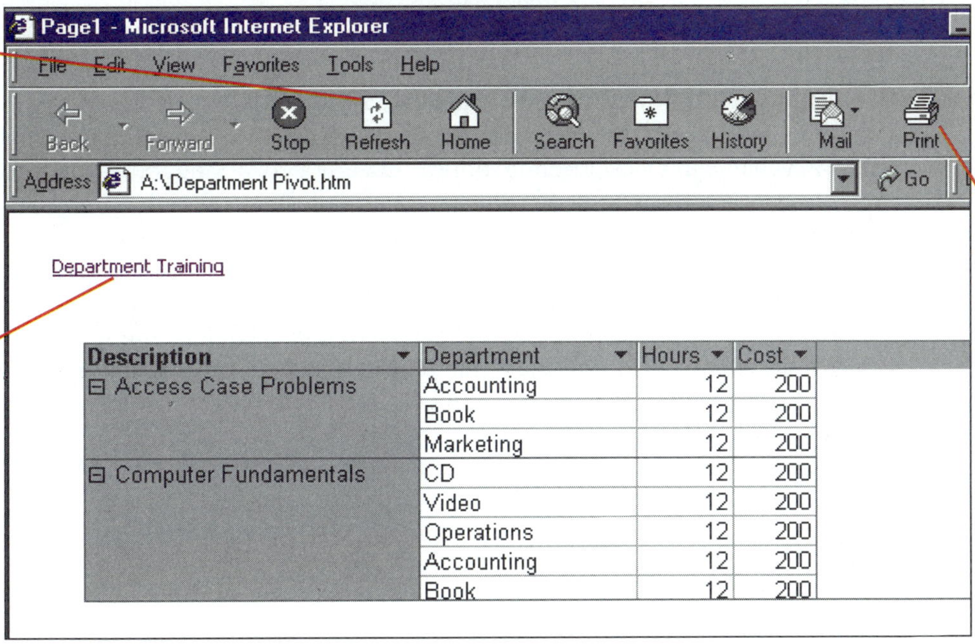

Access 2000

Unit J

Access 2000

Publishing Web Pages to Web Servers

Making Web pages available over the Internet or a company intranet requires publishing your Web pages to a **Web server**, a computer devoted to storing and downloading Web pages. Web servers contain **Web folders**, which are special folders dedicated to storing and organizing Web pages. Once your Web page files are stored appropriately, **clients**, computers with appropriate browser and communication software that have access to the Web folder, may download and use those files. David reviews the steps necessary to publish the Instructor Updates Web page for use over MediaLoft's intranet.

Details

Store the Access database in a shared network folder on the Web server

On a network, most folders are not available to everyone, so you must be sure to put the Access database in a folder that the appropriate people have permission to use (**shared network folder**). Access databases are inherently **multi-user**, so that many people can enter and update information at the same time, provided they are given permission to use the files inside that folder. Two people cannot, however, update the same record at the same time (**record locking**). Also, it doesn't matter whether the individuals are accessing the Access database through the database file itself (for example, two people updating the same database using forms or datasheets) or whether they are using Web pages created by DAPs.

Use the Access database to create DAPs, which in turn create dynamic HTML Web pages

Save the HTML Web page files in the same shared network folder as the Access database

It is not required that the database and HTML files be in the same folder, but this helps keep them organized.

Give the users the URL or UNC address to access the Web pages using IE

URLs are used to access Internet Web pages. UNCs can be used when the file is located on the same local area network as the client computer. As users access the Web pages, the underlying Access database will be updated automatically.

Use professional networking resources as necessary

Publishing a Web page to a Web Folder on a Web Server is very similar to saving an existing file with a new name in a new location, but the existing networking infrastructure (including connectivity between the Web server and your computer), along with appropriate security clearances, needs to be in place before you can save Web pages to any location on a company intranet or on the Internet. This requires the knowledge and skills of professionals dedicated to the field of computer networking. People who build networking infrastructures are often called **network administrators**. Those who work with Web Servers, Web Folders, and supporting Internet technologies are often called **Webmasters**. Table J-6 provides more tips and information about working with Web pages and Access. Figure J-18 illustrates the infrastructure involved with publishing a Web page to a Web server.

FIGURE J-18: Publishing to a Web server

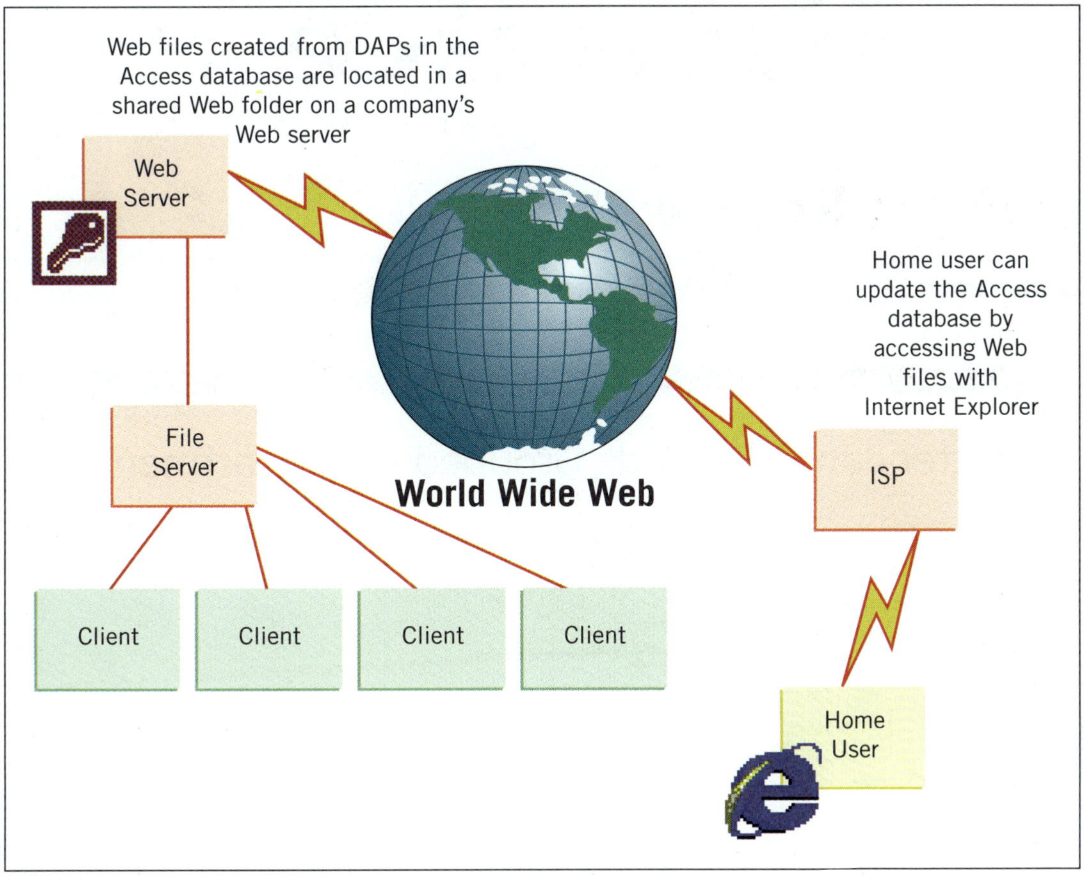

TABLE J-6: Tips for Working with Web pages and Access

to:	do this:
Open dynamic HTML files created by Access in a browser other than IE—dynamic files display live data from the underlying Access database	Use the Export option on the File menu to create server-generated HTML files from tables, queries, and forms (Save as file type ASP for Microsoft Active Server Pages or IDC/HTX Microsoft IIS 1-2 file types.) Server-generated HTML files pages are dynamic, and therefore show current data, but are read-only.
Open static HTML files created by Access in a browser other than IE—static files display data that is current only as of the moment that the Web page was created	Use the Export option on the File menu to create static HTML files from tables, queries, forms, and reports. The files display a snapshot of the data at the time the static HTML file was created.
Open an HTML file created by another program in Access	Right-click the file in the Open dialog box, then click Open in Microsoft Access on the pop-up menu.

Practice

▶ Concepts Review

Identify each element of the form's Design View shown in Figure J-19.

FIGURE J-19

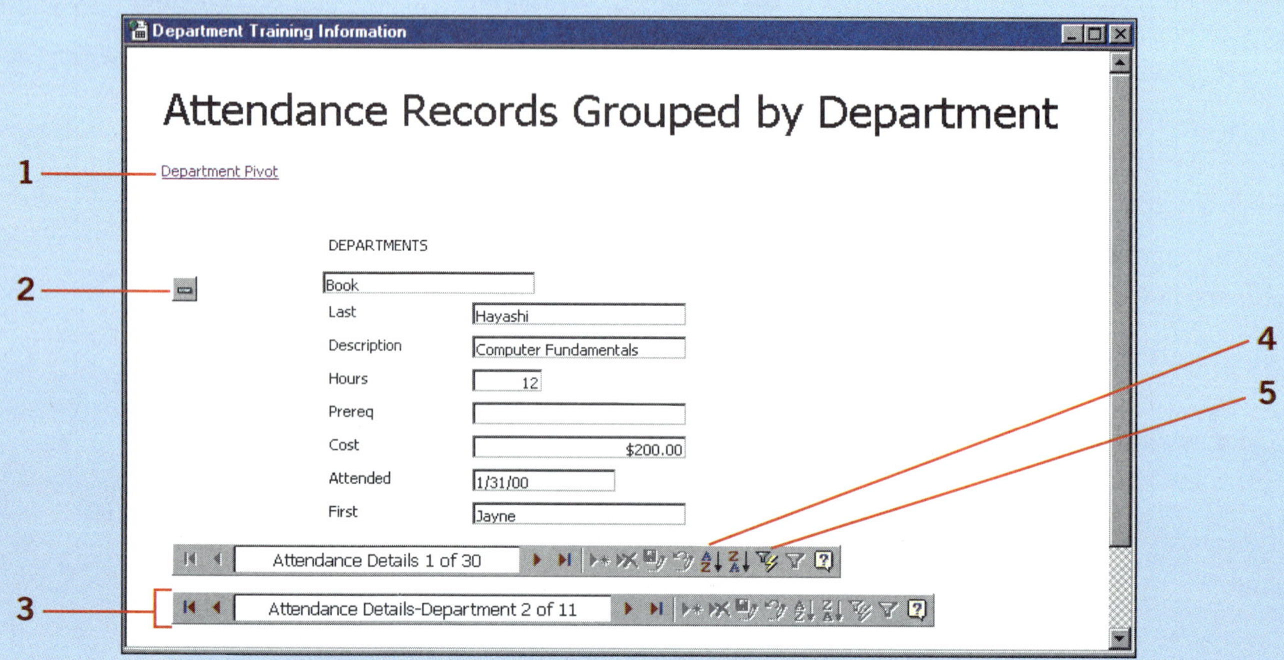

Match each term with the statement that describes its function.

6. data access page
7. URL
8. HTML
9. World Wide Web pages
10. browser
11. World Wide network of computer networks

a. Programming language used to create Web pages
b. Software loaded on a microcomputer and used to find and display Web pages
c. Access 2000 object that provides a connection between Web pages and an Access database
d. Internet
e. Web page address
f. Hyperlinked documents that make the Internet easy to navigate

12. The communications protocol for the Internet is
- **a.** TCP/IP.
- **b.** HTML.
- **c.** URL.
- **d.** ISP.

13. To connect to the Internet through your home computer, you must first call a(n):
- **a.** URL
- **b.** ISP
- **c.** Home page
- **d.** Webmaster

14. Which of the following is NOT a service provided by the Internet?
- **a.** E-mail
- **b.** File transfer
- **c.** World Wide Web
- **d.** Cable TV

15. Which of the following is browser software?
- **a.** Windows NT
- **b.** Internet Explorer
- **c.** Microsoft Access
- **d.** Microsoft Excel

16. Which of the following is a special type of Web page designed for viewing, editing, and entering data stored in a Microsoft Access database?
- **a.** Browser
- **b.** Home page
- **c.** Data access page
- **d.** Pivot table

17. Making Web pages created through Access available to other users is called
- **a.** Publishing.
- **b.** Uploading.
- **c.** Transferring.
- **d.** Rendering.

Skills Review

1. Understanding the World Wide Web.

a. Interview five people and ask them if they have recently used the World Wide Web for the following purposes. If the answer is "Yes," ask them to also identify the URL for the Web page.

- To sell or purchase a product or service
- For entertainment
- To index or reference other Internet resources (search engines)
- To gather information
- To take a class

b. Ask five people who access the Internet from home who they use as their ISP, then write down the names.

2. **Using Hyperlink Fields.**
   a. Open the Machinery-J database, then open the Products table in Design view.
   b. Add a new field named "HomePage" with a Hyperlink Data Type.
   c. Save the Products table, open it in Datasheet view, then enter the following home page URLs into the new field for the first six records:

      1) www.toro.com
      2) www.caseih.com
      3) www.snapper.com
      4) www.deere.com
      5) www.troybilt.com
      6) www.stihl.com

   d. Click the link for www.deere.com and print the first page. If you are not already connected to the Internet, your dialer may appear, prompting you to connect with your chosen ISP. Once connected to your ISP, the John Deere home page should appear.
3. **Creating Pages for Interactive Reporting.**
   a. Click Pages on the Objects bar and double-click Create data access page by using wizard.
   b. Select the ProductName and the ReorderLevel fields from the Products table, then select the TransactionDate and UnitPrice fields from the Inventory Transactions table.
   c. Group the fields by ProductName, and sort in ascending order by TransactionDate.
   d. Type "Product Activity" for the page title, then open the new page in Page view.
   e. Open the Design view, maximize the Design view window, click in the title text area of the body of the Page and type the title "*Your Name's* Garden Shop Orders".
   f. Click the Page View button, click the Product Name text box, sort the ProductName in descending order, expand the ProductName group, then navigate to the 7/1/99 TransactionDate record within the Weed Wacker ProductName and print the page.
   g. Save the HTML file as "Garden Orders" on your Project Disk, then close the page.
4. **Creating Pages for Data Entry.**
   a. Click Pages on the Objects bar, then double-click Create data access page by using the wizard.
   b. Select all of the fields in the Products table.
   c. Do not add any grouping levels, but sort the records in ascending order on ProductName.
   d. Title the page "Product Update Page".
   e. In Design view, click in the title text area of the body of the page and type the title "Your Name's Products".
   f. Save the HTML file as "Products" on your Project Disk, then open Products.htm within Internet Explorer.
   g. Find and change the price of the "Mulcher" from $69.50 to $79.50 by changing the 6 to a 7, then print the Web page within Internet Explorer in which you made this change.
   h. Navigate to the next record within IE, then back to the Mulcher record to make sure that the price change was saved. Close IE.
   i. Open the Products table in the Machinery-J database, and make sure the Mulcher record now displays $79.50 as the Unit Price.
   j. Close the Products table within the Machinery-J database and the Products Web page within IE.
5. **Creating Pages for Data Analysis.**
   a. Click Pages on the Objects bar, then double-click Create data access page in Design view.
   b. Open the Field list window if necessary, then click the Expand button to the left of the Queries folder.
   c. Drag the Products Query to the upper-left corner of the Section: Unbound control, click the PivotTable List option button, then click OK.
   d. Click the PivotTable control to select it, right-click the ProductName field in the PivotTable control, then choose Move to Row Area.

e. Resize the control so that all three columns are clearly visible.
f. Click in the title text area of the body of the page and type the title "*Your Name's* Units Ordered Page", then display the page in Page view.
g. Use the TransactionDate list arrow to select only the 7/1/99 dates, then print the page.
h. Save the HTML file as Units Ordered to your Project Disk.

6. Working in Page Design view.

a. Open the Products page in Design view, then modify all of the labels in the first column so that a space exists between the descriptive words (e.g., change "ProductName" to "Product Name"). (*Hint*: Change these labels by clicking them once to select them, then clicking them again to edit them, just as you would the label control of any form or report.)
b. Click and drag across "*Your Name's* Products" in the body. Format the text to a bright blue, Britannic Bold font. (*Hint*: Use the Formatting (Page) toolbar just as you would when you format a control for any form or report.)
c. Save the changes.

7. Inserting Hyperlinks to other Pages.

a. Open the Products page in Design view, use the Hyperlink button on the toolbox to add a hyperlink control named "Units ordered" above the upper-left corner of the Header: Products section. Create the hyperlink so that it opens the Units Ordered page.
b. Save the Products page and close it.
c. Open the Units Ordered page in Design view, then add a hyperlink control named "Products" that opens the Products page above the upper-left corner of the Section: Unbound control.
d. Save the Units Ordered page and close it.
e. Open the Units Ordered Web page in IE, then click the Products hyperlink to make sure it works.
f. From the opened Products Web page, click the Units Ordered hyperlink to make sure it works.
g. Print the Units Ordered Web page within IE, close IE, and close the Machinery-J database.

8. Publishing Web Pages to Web Servers.

a. Call your ISP and ask for information about the requirements to publish Web pages to their Web server. (If you are not currently connected to the Internet from home, research any ISP of your choice.)
b. If your ISP does not allow members to publish Web pages, continue researching ISPs until you find one that allows members to publish Web pages.
c. Print the documentation on how to publish Web pages to the ISP's Web server.
d. Open IE and type "www.geocities.com" in the Address list box. Follow the links on the Web page to determine how to create your own Web page at the geocities Web site, then print the documentation.

Independent Challenges

1. As the manager of a college women's basketball team, you wish to enhance the Basketball-J database to include hyperlink field entries for opponents. You also wish to develop several Web pages to report information on player statistics.
To complete this independent challenge:

a. Start Access and open the database Basketball-J from your Project Disk.
b. Open the Games table in Design view, then add a field named "Web Site" with a Hyperlink Data Type.
c. Save the Games table, then open it in Datasheet view.
d. For the second record, enter www.creighton.edu in the Web Site field.
e. For the fifth record, enter www.drake.edu in the Web Site field.
f. Click the www.drake.edu link to display the Web page for Drake University, then print the first page.
g. Close the Drake Web page, save and close the Games table, click Pages on the Objects bar, then double-click Create data access page by using wizard.

h. Add all of the fields in the Players Query, group by Last, do not specify any sort fields, and title the page "Player Stats".
i. In Design view, change the label "GroupofPlayersQuery-Last" to "Last".
j. In Design view, click in the title text area of the body of the page and type the title "Iowa State Women's Basketball". Include your initials in the title if you have to identify your name on the printed solution.
k. Save the HTML file as "Player Stats" on your Project Disk, then close the Player Stats DAP in Access.
l. Open the Player Stats HTML file in Internet Explorer, navigate to the player whose last name is Freesen.
m. Click the Expand button to display all of sort the records within the last name of Freesen, sort in descending order on the date, then print that record.
n. Close the Basketball-J database and exit Access.
o. Exit Internet Explorer.

2. As the manager of a college women's basketball team, you wish to enhance the Basketball-J database by developing a Web page to enter new game information.
To complete this independent challenge:

a. Start Access and open the database Basketball-J from your Project Disk.
b. Click Pages on the Objects bar, then double-click Create data access page by using the wizard.
c. Add all of the fields from the Games table, do not add any grouping levels, sort the records in ascending order by Date, and accept Games as the title for the page.
d. In Design view, click in the title text area of the body of the Page and type the title "ISU Games". Include Your Initials in the title if you have to identify your name on the printed solution.
e. Save the HTML file as "Games" to your Project Disk, then open the Games HTML file in IE.
f. Enter the following new record as record 23:

Date:	3/1/01
GameNo:	(No entry required, this is an AutoNumber field. You will not see the AutoNumber entry until you move to a new record, then return to this one.)
Opponent:	State Univ NY-Binghamton
Mascot:	Colonials
Home-Away:	H
Home Score:	100
Opponent Score:	52
Web Site:	www.binghamton.edu

g. Navigate to the first record, then back to the last. (*Note*: The AutoNumber entry for the new record, 23, is automatically entered.)
h. Print this new record, then close IE.
i. Check the Games table to verify the entry in the Basketball-J database.
j. Close the Basketball-J database and exit Access.

3. As the manager of a college women's basketball team, you wish to enhance the Basketball-J database by developing a Web page to display player statistical information as a pivot table.
To complete this independent challenge:

a. Start Access and open the database Basketball-J from your Project Disk.
b. Click Pages on the Objects toolbar, then double-click Create data access page in Design view.
c. Expand the Queries folder in the Field List, then drag the Players Query to the upper-left corner of the Section: Unbound control.
d. Choose the PivotTable List option, then close the Field list.
e. Widen the pivot table control so that all of the seven fields are clearly displayed.

f. Click in the title text area of the body of the Page and type the title "Game Stats". Include your initials in the title if you have to identify your name on the printed solution.
g. Select the pivot table control, right-click the Opponent field, then choose Move to Row Area.
h. Save the HTML file as "Game Stats" to your Project Disk, then close the Game Stats page within Access.
i. Open the Game Stats HTML file within Internet Explorer, click the Last list arrow in the pivot table, click the Show all check box (to clear it), then click the Freesen check box to display only Sydney Freesen's statistics.
j. Print this Web page showing Sydney Freesen's statistics, then close Internet Explorer.
k. Close the Basketball-J database and exit Access.

4. MediaLoft has developed a Web site that provides internal information to their employees. In this independent challenge, you'll find information posted to the Web site from potential new instructors (independent contractors), then enter those records into the Training-J database.

a. Open the Training-J database, click Pages on the Objects bar, then use the Page Wizard to create a new data access page based on all of the fields in the Instructors table.
b. Do not use any grouping levels or sort fields, and title the page "HR Instructors".
c. Save the HTML file as "HR Instructors" to your Project Disk, then open it in Internet Explorer.
d. In a separate IE window, connect to the Internet, then go to the MediaLoft intranet site at http://www.course.com/illustrated/MediaLoft
e. Click the link for Training, then click the link for New HR Instructors.
f. Print this Web page, then close this IE window.
g. Open the IE window that displays the HR Instructors HTML file you created, then enter the four new instructors in the Web page. (*Hint*: The InstructorID field is an AutoNumber field, so you will not type in it.)
h. Add yourself as the ninth new instructor, with a hire date of 11/1/00.
i. Close all IE windows, then return to the Training-J Access database and open the Instructors table.
j. Print the Instructors datasheet, then close the Training-J database and exit Access.

▶ Visual Workshop

As the manager of a college women's basketball team, you wish to enhance the Basketball-J database by developing a Web page to display player scoring information as a pivot table. Figure J-20 shows the data access page, called ISU Scoring, that you need to create. Develop the page in Design view, use the Scoring query as a pivot table control. You will have to move the Home-Away field and the Last field to the Row Area. Include your initials in the title text area. Save the HTML file with the name "Scoring" to your Project Disk. View and print the page in IE. Close all open applications.

FIGURE J-20

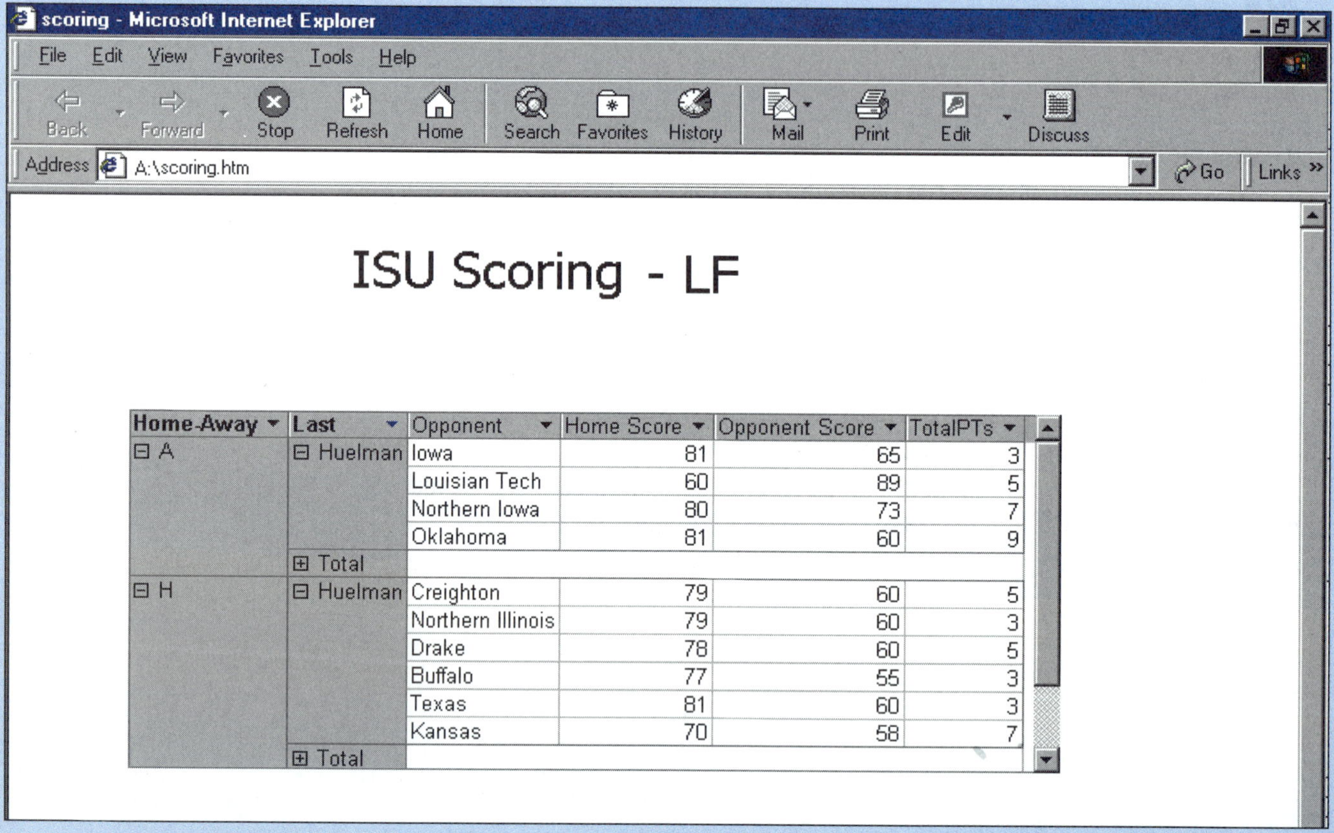

Access 2000

Unit K

Creating
Advanced Queries

Objectives

- MOUS ► Query for Top Values
- MOUS ► Create an Advanced Parameter Query
- MOUS ► Modify Query Properties
- MOUS ► Create an Update Query
- MOUS ► Create a Make-Table Query
- MOUS ► Create an Append Query
- MOUS ► Create a Delete Query
- MOUS ► Specify Join Properties

Queries are database objects that answer questions about the data. The most common query is the **select query**, which displays fields and records that match specific criteria into a single datasheet. Other types of queries, such as top value, parameter, and action queries, are powerful tools for displaying, analyzing, and updating data. An **action query** is one that makes changes to the data. There are four types of action queries: delete, update, append, and make-table. David Dumont, director of training at MediaLoft, has become very familiar with the capabilities of Access. Users come to David with extensive data-analysis and data-update requests, confident that he can provide the information they need. David uses powerful query features and new query types to handle these requirements.

Unit K

Access 2000

Querying for Top Values

Once a large number of records are entered into a table of a database, it is less common to query for all of the records, and more common to list only the most significant records by choosing a subset of the highest or lowest values from a sorted query. The **Top Values** feature within the Query Design view allows you to respond to these types of requests. Employee attendance at MediaLoft classes has grown. To help plan future classes, David wants to print a datasheet listing the names of the top five classes, sorted by number of students per class. David creates a summarized select query to find the total number of attendees for each class, then uses the Top Values feature to find the five most attended classes.

Steps

1. Start Access, open the **Training-K** database, click **Queries** on the Objects bar, click the **New button** in the database window, click **Design View**, then click **OK**
   You need fields from both the Attendance and Courses tables.
2. Double-click **Attendance**, double-click **Courses**, then click **Close** in the Show Table dialog box
   Query Design view now displays two related tables in the upper portion of the screen.
3. Double-click **LogNo** in the Attendance table, then double-click **Description** in the Courses table
   You want to count the LogNo entries for each course Description.
4. Click the **Totals button** on the Query Design toolbar, click **Group By** for the LogNo field, click the **Group By list arrow**, then click **Count**
   You identified the fields and summarized the records by counting the LogNo entries for each Description. Your screen should look like Figure K-1. Sorting determines which records will be on "top."
5. Click the **LogNo field Sort cell**, click the **LogNo field Sort list arrow**, then click **Descending**
   A descending order will put the courses most attended by MediaLoft employees, those with the highest count, at the top.
6. Click the **Top Values list arrow** on the Query Design toolbar
   The Top Values feature is used to display a subset of the records. You can select a number or percentage from the list or enter a specific value or percentage. See Table K-1 for more information on how to use the Top Values feature.
7. Click **5**, then click the **Datasheet View button** on the Query Design toolbar
   Your screen should look like Figure K-2. The Introduction to Access course and the Computer Fundamentals course both had 19 attendees. If more than one course had 14 attendees (a summarized value of 14 in the CountOfLogNo field), then all courses that "tied" for fifth place would have been displayed too.
8. Click the **Save button** on the Query Datasheet toolbar, type **Top 5 Courses**, click **OK**, then close the datasheet
   The Top 5 Courses query appears as a query object in the database window.

QuickTip

Click the Datasheet View button at any time during the query design development process to view the resulting datasheet.

FIGURE K-1: Designing a summary query for top values

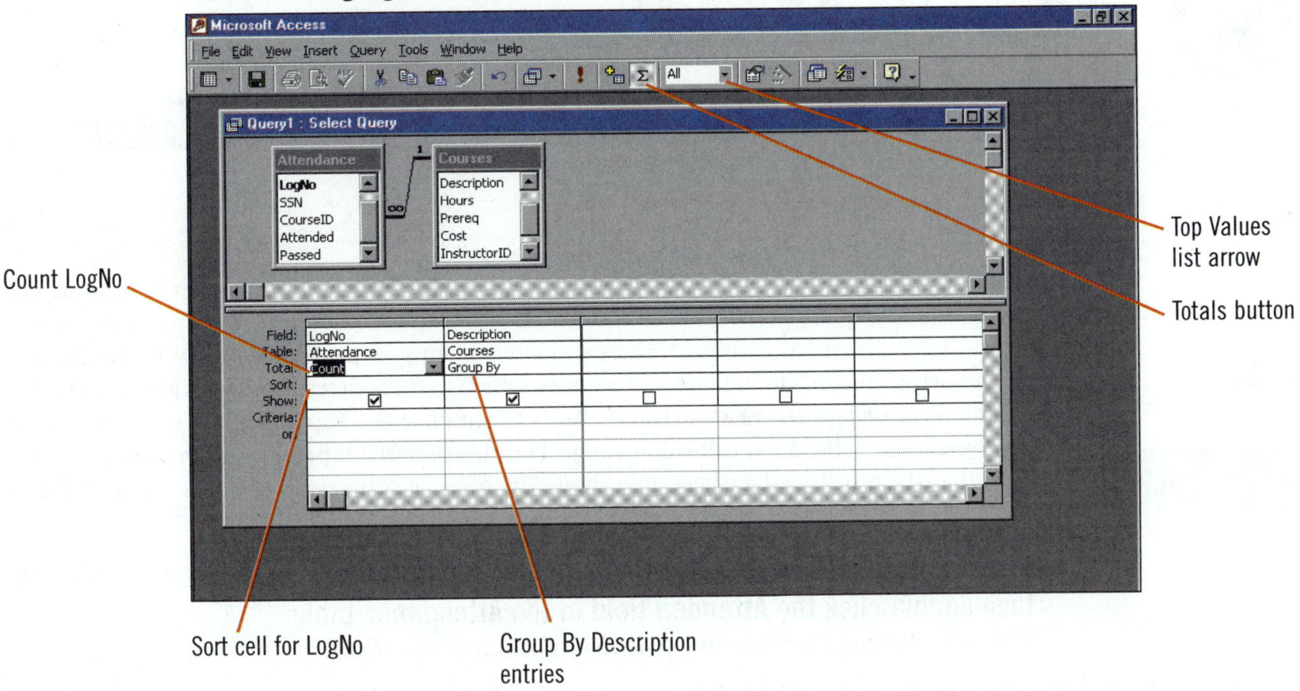

FIGURE K-2: Top Values datasheet

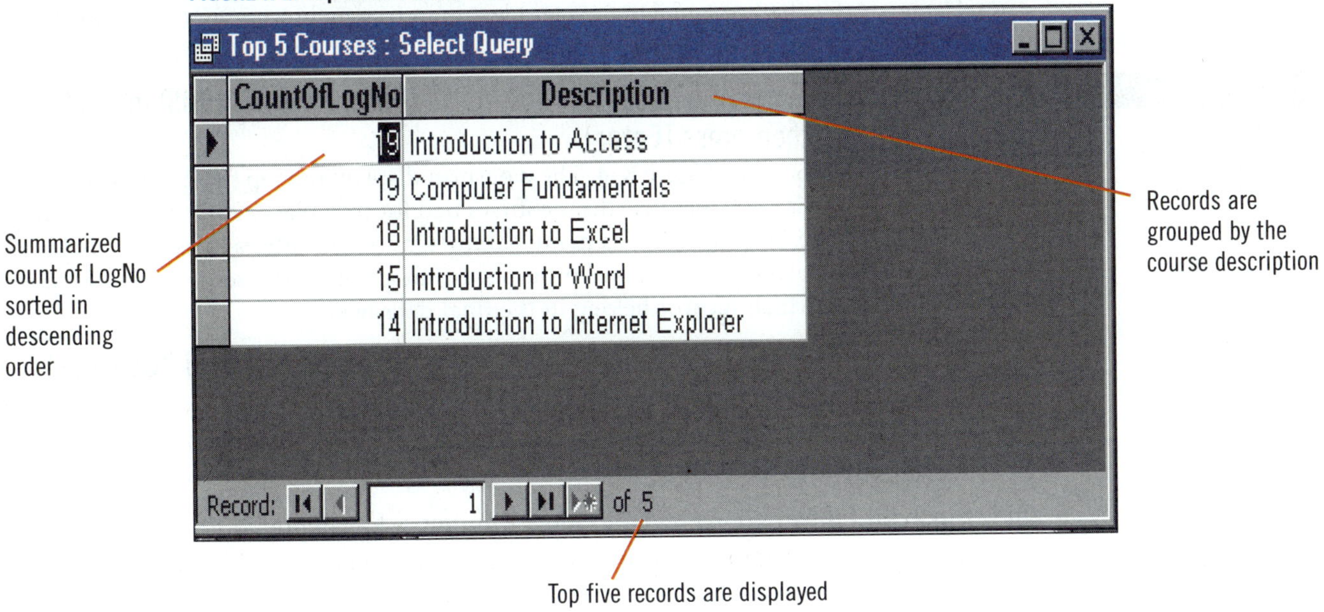

TABLE K-1: Top Values options

action	to display
Click 5, or 25, or 100 from the Top Values list	Top 5, 25, or 100 records
Enter a number such as 10 in the Top Values text box	Top 10 (in this case) records
Click 5% or 25% from the Top Values list	Top 5 or 25 percent of records
Enter a percentage, such as 10%, in the Top Values text box	Top 10 percent (in this case) of records

Unit K

Access 2000

Creating an Advanced Parameter Query

A **parameter query** displays a dialog box prompting you for information to enter as limiting criteria each time the query runs. You can build a form or report based on a parameter query, too. When you open the form or report, the parameter prompt appears. The entry in the prompt determines which records to include in the query, which in turn, determines which records to display in the form or report. David wants to enhance the Top 5 Courses query to display the top five courses within a specific date range. He adds parameter prompts to the Top 5 Courses query so that the resulting datasheet only shows the top five courses for the dates he specifies.

Steps

1. Click the **Top 5 Courses query**, click the **Design button** in the database window, then double-click the **Attended field** in the Attendance table
   The Attended field contains the date that the course was taken.

2. Click the **Attended field Criteria cell**, type **Between [Enter start date:] And [Enter end date:]**, then click the **Datasheet View button**
   Your screen should look like Figure K-3. Parameter criteria must be entered within [square brackets]. The **Between ... And** operator will help you find all records on or between two dates. Using greater than or equal to, >=, and less than or equal to, <=, operators works in the same way.

3. Type **1/1/00** in the Enter start date text box, press **[Enter]**, type **6/30/00** in the Enter end date text box, then press **[Enter]**
   Your screen should look like Figure K-4. The datasheet displays the top five courses attended between 1/1/00 and 6/30/00. Because three courses tied for fifth place, seven records are displayed instead of five. You can enter as many parameter criteria entries in as many fields as you wish. Access displays the parameter prompts one at a time, and uses the entries you've made to determine which records belong in the final datasheet.

4. Click **File** on the menu bar, click **Save As**, click to the left of the word **"Courses"** in the text box, type **– Parameter – Your Initials**, then click **OK**
   Because the object name always appears in the header of a datasheet printout, descriptive query names can help identify the information or creator of the information.

5. Click the **Print button**, then close the Top 5 Courses – Parameter – Your Initials query
   The Top 5 Courses – Parameter – Your Initials query appears as an object in the database window.

QuickTip

Right-click the Criteria cell, then click Zoom or press [Shift][F2] to open the Zoom dialog box, which clearly displays a long entry.

Trouble?

You may have to type 1/1/2000 and 6/30/2000 depending on your computer's settings.

FIGURE K-3: A parameter prompt

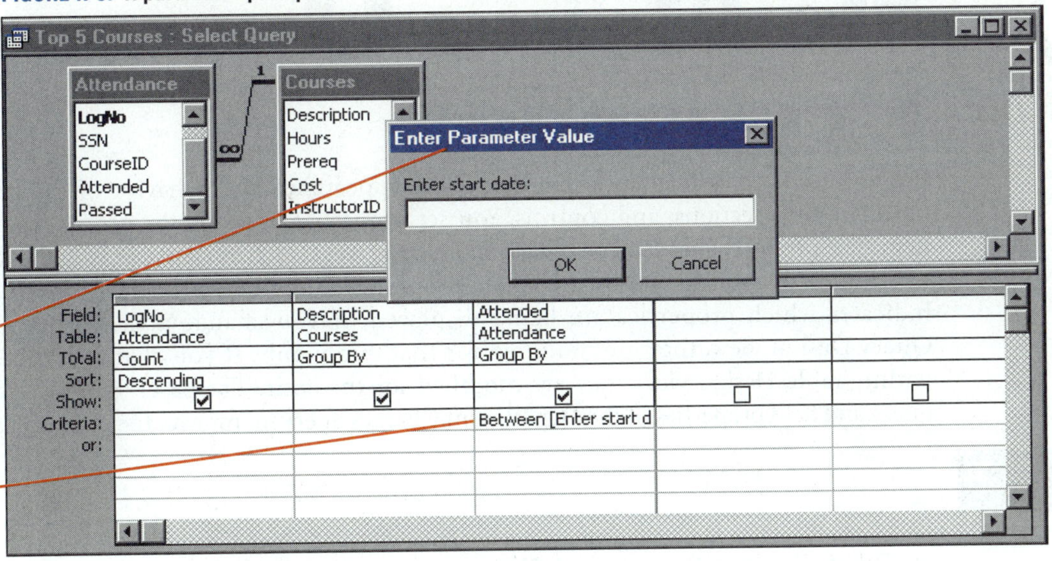

FIGURE K-4: Top 5 Courses – Parameter query

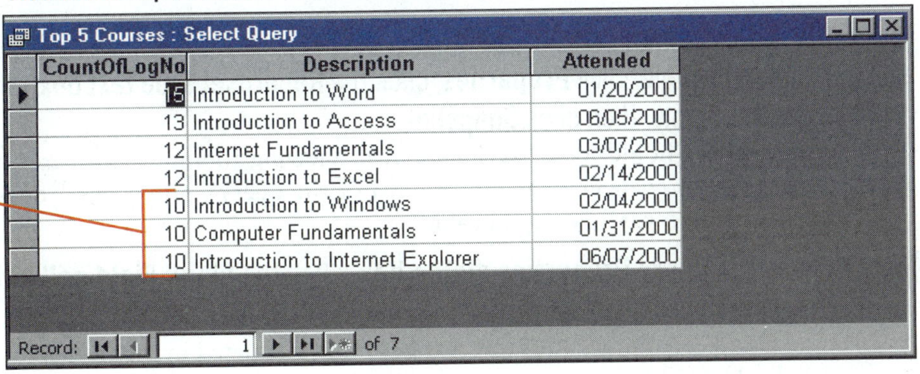

Access 2000

CLUES TO USE

Concatenating a parameter prompt to a wildcard character

You can concatenate parameter prompts with a wildcard character such as the asterisk (*) to create more flexible queries. For example, the entry: **LIKE [Enter the first character of the company name:] & "*"** placed in the Criteria cell of the Company field searches for companies that begin with a specified letter. The entry: **LIKE "*" & [Enter any character(s) to search by:] & "*"** placed in the Criteria cell of the Company field searches for words that contain the specified characters anywhere in the field. The **ampersand (&)** is used to concatenate items in an expression and double quotation marks (" ") are used to surround text criteria.

Unit K

Access 2000

Modifying Query Properties

Properties are characteristics that define the appearance and behavior of the database itself; objects, fields, sections, and controls. You set properties by using the **property sheet** for that item. The property sheet can be displayed in many ways, such as right-clicking the item you wish to examine or modify, and then clicking Properties. The title bar of the property sheet always indicates which properties are being displayed. If you change a field's properties within Query Design view, they are modified for that query only. If you change a field's properties within Table Design view, they are modified for the entire database. David uses the query and field properties of the Department Charges query to improve the datasheet's appearance.

Steps

1. Right-click the **Department Charges** query, then click **Properties**
   The Department Charges Properties dialog box opens, providing information about the query and also allowing you to enter a description for the query.

QuickTip

Click the column headings to sort the objects in ascending or descending order.

2. Type **Lists the department, description, hours, and cost,** click **OK**, click the **Details button** in the Training-K database window, then maximize the database window
   Five columns of information about each query object appear, as shown in Figure K-5. The Description property entry appears in the Description column.

3. Click the **Design button** on the database toolbar, right-click to the right of the Employees table, click **Properties**, click the **Recordset Type text box**, click the **Recordset Type list arrow**, then click **Snapshot**
   Your screen should look like Figure K-6. Viewing the query property sheet from within Query Design view gives a complete list of the query's properties. The Snapshot property makes the Recordset not updateable.

Trouble?

Separate the new field name from the calculated expression with a colon (:) and be sure to surround field names in [square brackets].

4. Close the **Query Properties dialog box**, click the **blank Field cell** in the **fifth** column, type **PerHour:[Cost]/[Hours]**, then click the **Datasheet View button**
   The datasheet appears with the cost per hour calculated in the fifth column, but the calculated values are hard to read because they are unformatted.

Trouble?

The title bar of the property sheet should say "Field Properties." If it doesn't, close the dialog box and try again.

5. Click the **Design View button**, right-click the **PerHour field**, then click **Properties**
   The Field Properties dialog box allows you to change field properties within this query. When you start making an entry in a property, a short description of the property appears in the status bar.

6. Click **Format text box**, click the **Format list arrow**, click **Currency**, click the **Decimal Places text box**, click the **Decimal Places list arrow**, click **2**, click the **Caption property text box**, then type **Cost Per Hour**
   Your screen should look like Figure K-7.

7. Close the property sheet, click the on the Query Design toolbar, type **Video** in the Department field for the first record to view the message in the status bar
   The message "This recordset is not updateable" appears because the query Recordset Type property was set to "Snapshot," which allows you to view the records but not update them. The caption and formatting properties of the calculated field clarify the information.

8. Save and close the Department Charges query

FIGURE K-5: Details

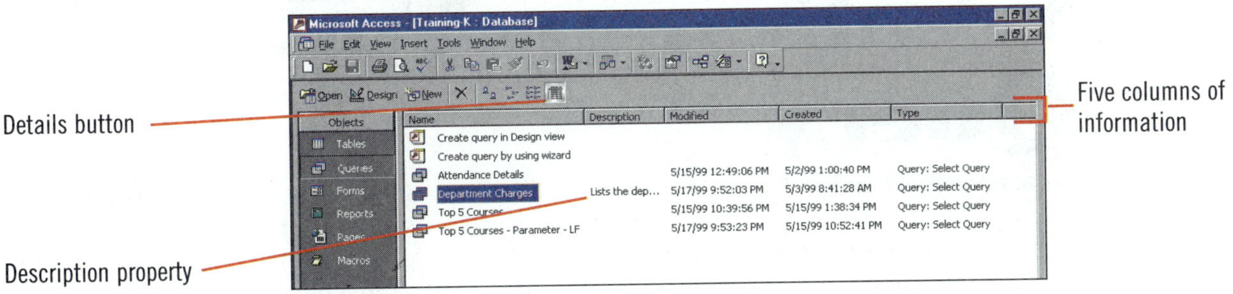

FIGURE K-6: Query property sheet

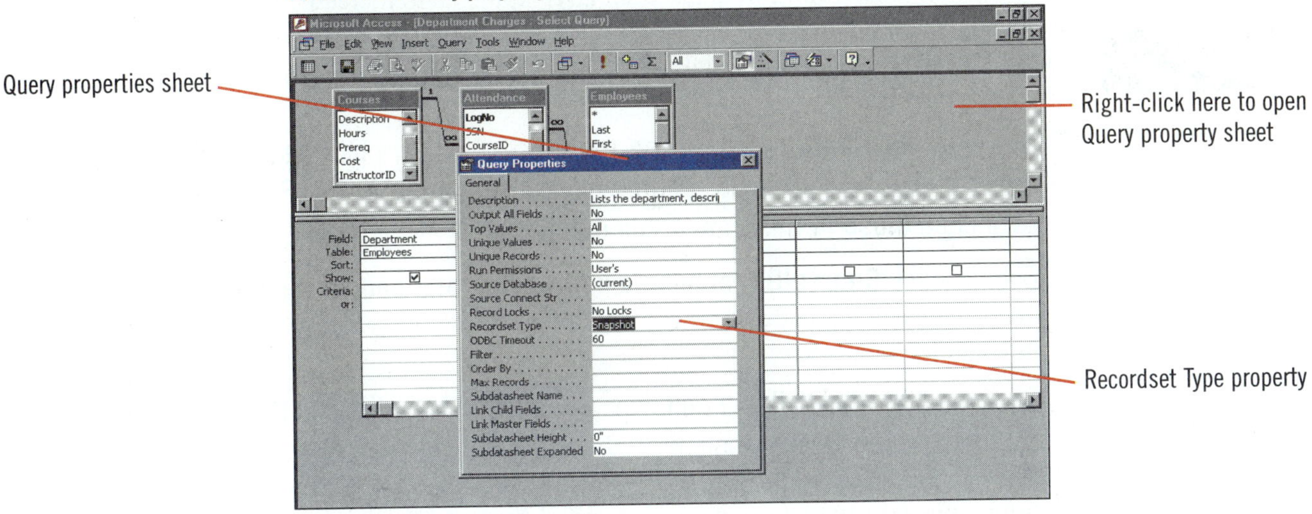

FIGURE K-7: Field property sheet

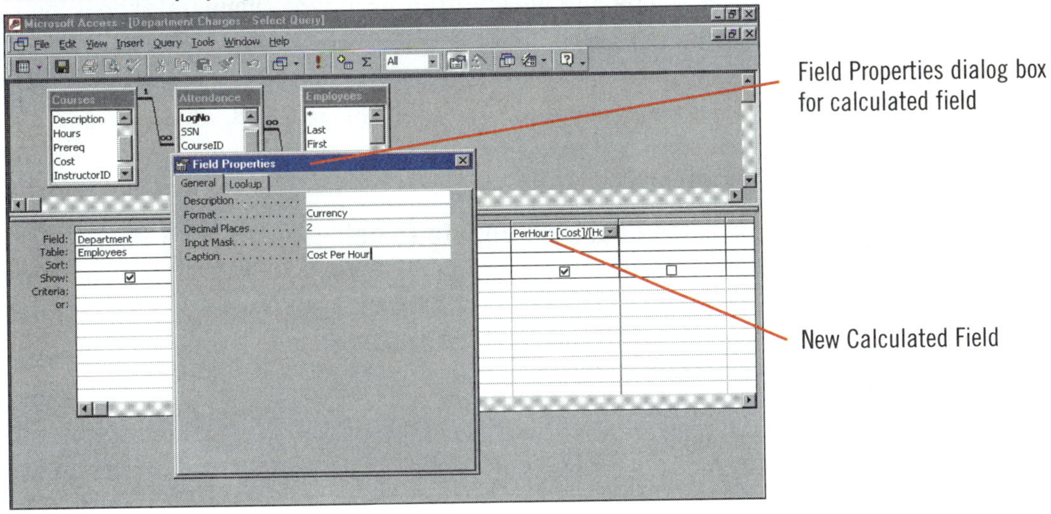

CLUES TO USE

Optimizing queries using indexes and SQL

Indexes are used to speed up queries that are often sorted or grouped. For example, if you commonly sort by a LastName field, setting the **Indexed property** to Yes would improve the performance of any query that also sorted or grouped by the LastName field. You can only set the Indexed property of a field in Table Design view, but if you know **SQL** (Structured Query Language) you can create an index on a field within a query. SQL is a national standard database language for querying a wide range of relational database products. If you want to query an Access database in a manner that is beyond the capabilities of the Query Design view, knowledge of SQL is required. To access the SQL statements for any query, click the Datasheet View list arrow and choose SQL View. To add an index, use the SQL CREATE INDEX statement.

Unit K

Access 2000

Creating an Update Query

An **action query** makes changes to the data of many records. There are four types of action queries: delete, update, append, and make-table. See Table K-2 for more information on action queries. An **update query** is a type of action query that makes a change to the data of the tables. For example, you may wish to increase the price of a product in a particular category by 5% or change an area code with one operation. The Training Department upgraded their equipment on June 1, and David has been given approval to increase by 5% the internal cost of all courses provided after that date to cover the upgrade expense. He creates an update query to change the data in the tables to reflect the cost increase.

Steps

1. Click the **New button** on the database window, click **Design View** in the New Query dialog box, click **OK**, double-click **Attendance** in the Show Table dialog box, then click **Close** in the Show Table dialog box

2. Double-click **CourseID**, double-click **Attended**, and double-click **Cost**
   The three fields are added to the query design grid. You have to change only those courses offered on or after June 1.

3. Click the **Attended Criteria cell**, type **>=6/1/00**, then click the **Datasheet View button** on the Query Design toolbar
   Every action query starts as a select query. Always look at the datasheet of the select query before initiating any action that will change data to make sure which records will be affected.

4. Click the **Design View button** on the Query Datasheet toolbar, click the **Query Type button list arrow** on the Query Design toolbar, then click **Update Query**
   The Query Type button displays the Update Query icon and the Update To: row appears in the query design grid, as shown in Figure K-8. All action query icons include an exclamation point that indicates data will be changed when you click the Run button on the Query Design toolbar.

5. Click the **Cost field Update To cell**, type **[Cost]*1.05**, click the **Run button** on the Query Design toolbar, then click **Yes** to indicate that you want to update 41 rows
   Any time you run an action query, Access prompts you with an "Are you sure?" message before actually updating the data. The Undo button will not undo changes made by action queries.

6. Click on the Query Design toolbar
   Your screen should look like Figure K-9. The datasheet of an update query shows only the updated field.

7. Close the update query without saving the changes
   You rarely need to save an update query, because once the data has been updated, you don't need the query object anymore. Also, if you double-click an action query of any type from the database window, you run the query. Therefore, don't save any queries that you won't need again, especially action queries.

FIGURE K-8: Creating an update query

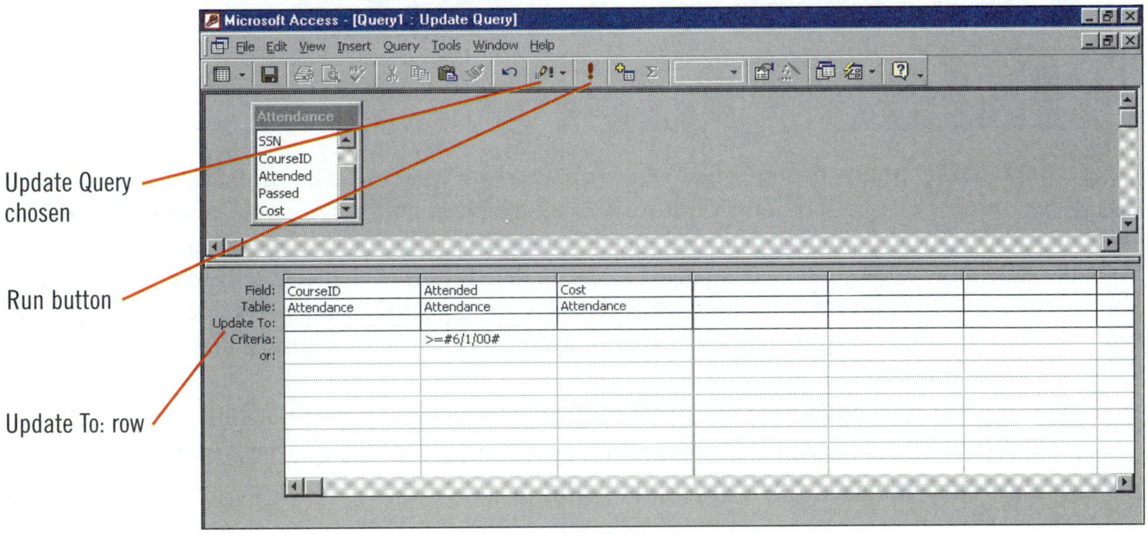

FIGURE K-9: Updated cost fields

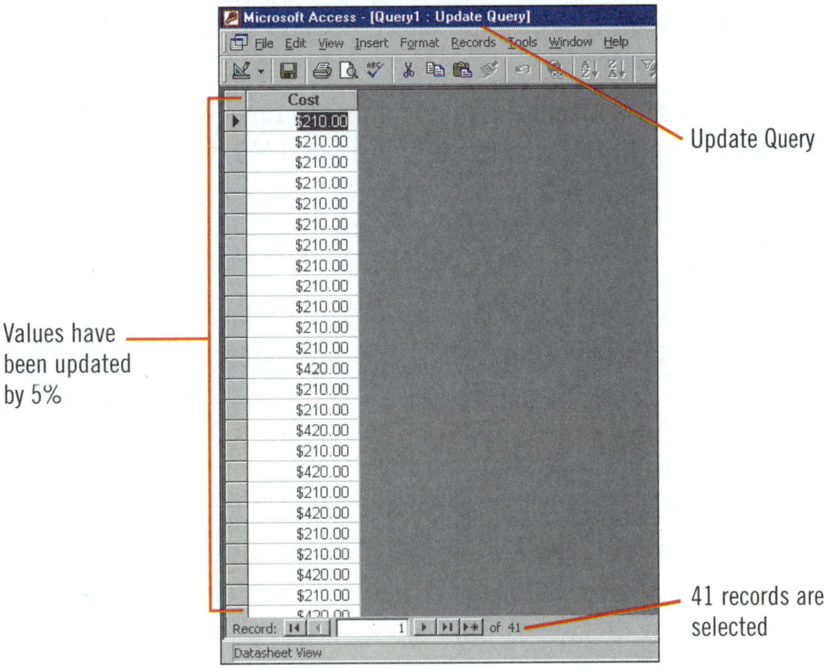

TABLE K-2: Action queries

type of action query	query icon	description	example
Delete		Deletes a group of records from one or more tables	Remove products that are discontinued or for which there are no orders
Update		Makes global changes to a group of records in one or more tables	Raise prices by 10 percent for all products
Append		Adds a group of records from one or more tables to the end of a table	Merge the product table from a business you just acquired to the existing product table for the company
Make-Table		Creates a new table from all or part of the data in one or more tables	Export records to another Access database, make a backup copy of a table, or create reports that display data from a specified point in time

Unit K

Access 2000

Creating a Make-Table Query

Steps 1 2 3 4

A **make-table query** creates a new table in either the current or in another Access database. When using the make-table query feature to make a table in another Access database, it works like an export feature. Sometimes the make-table query is used to create a backup copy of a table or a backup copy of a subset of records for a certain date range. In the latter case, date criteria used in the query design grid determine which records are exported to the new table. David uses a make-table query to archive the records in the Attendance table for the first quarter of 2000.

1. Click the **New button** on the database window, click **OK** to accept Design View in the New Query dialog box, double-click **Attendance** in the Show Table dialog box, then click **Close** in the Show Table dialog box
2. Double-click the *** (asterisk)** at the top of the Attendance table's field list
   Putting the asterisk in the query design grid puts all of the fields in that table in the grid. Later, if fields are added to this table, they also will be automatically added to this query because of the asterisk.
3. Double-click the **Attended field** to add it to the second column of the query grid, click the **Attended field Criteria cell**, type **<4/1/00**, then click the **Attended field Show check box** to uncheck it
   Your screen should look like Figure K-10. Before changing this select query into a make-table query, it is always a good idea to view the datasheet.
4. Click the **Datasheet View button** on the Query Design toolbar, click any entry in the **Attended field**, then click the **Sort Descending button** on the Query Datasheet toolbar
   The descending sort on the Attended field allows you to check that no records on or after 4/1/00 are present in the datasheet. (*Note*: None of the cost values for these records were updated because the previous update query affected courses on or after 6/1/00.)
5. Click the **Design View button**, click the **Query Type list arrow**, click the **Make-Table Query button**, type **First Quarter 2000 Attendance Log** in the Table Name text box, then click **OK**
   Your screen should look like Figure K-11. The Query Type button displays the Make Table icon. The make-table query is ready to be run, but the new table has not yet been created. Action queries do not delete, update, append, or make data until you click the Run button.
6. Click the **Run button** on the Query Design toolbar, click **Yes** when prompted that you are about to paste 102 records, then close but do not save the query
   Make-table queries are rarely saved unless you intend to use them again.
7. Click **Tables** on the Objects bar, then double-click **First Quarter 2000 Attendance Log** to view the new table's datasheet
   All 102 records were pasted into the new table, as shown in Figure K-12. Field properties such as the input mask for the SSN field and the check box display for the Passed field were not duplicated, but you could modify the Design view of this table to change the appearance of the fields just like you could for any other table. (*Note*: -1 is sometimes used to designate "yes" and 0 is used to designate "no" in a Yes/No field).
8. Close the First Quarter 2000 Attendance Log table

QuickTip

The sort and filter buttons work on a query datasheet in exactly the same way that they work in a table datasheet or form.

FIGURE K-10: Using the asterisk in a query grid

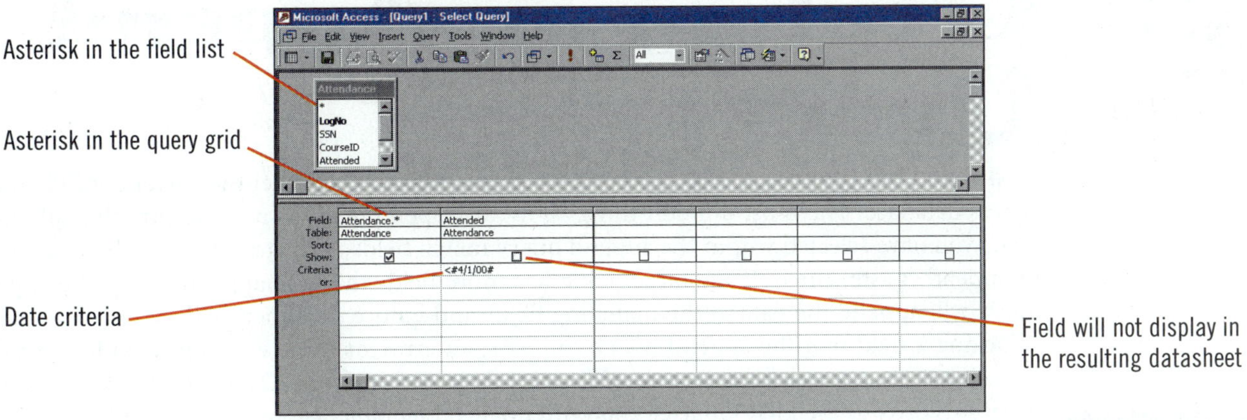

FIGURE K-11: Creating a make-table query

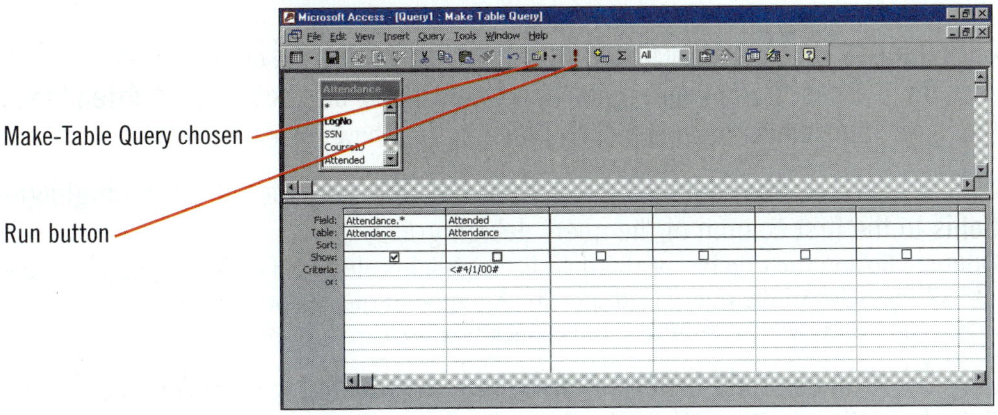

FIGURE K-12: First Half 2000 Attendance Log datasheet

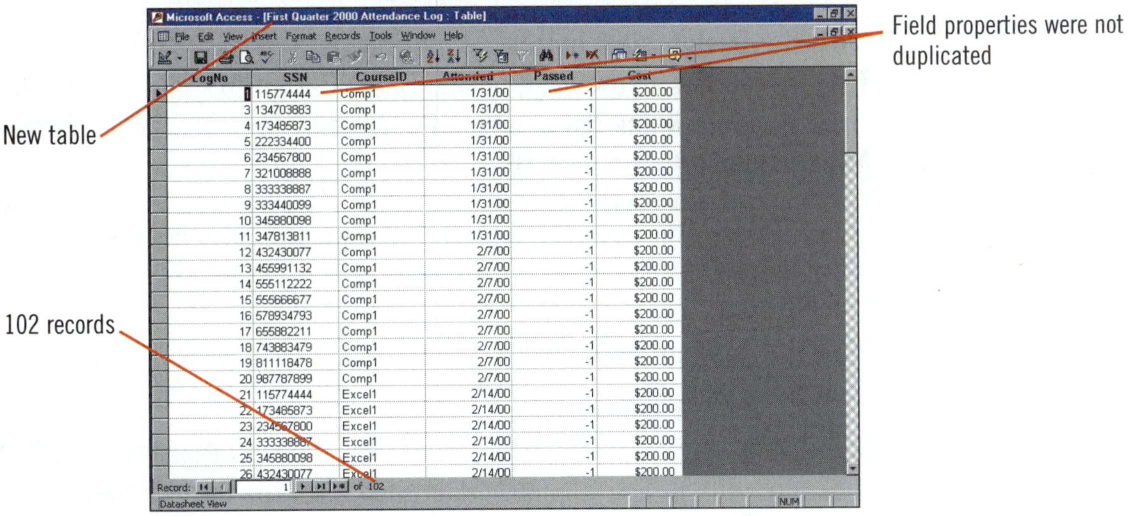

CLUES TO USE

Resolving Year 2000 Issues

If you type only two digits of a date, Access assumes that the digits 00 through 29 are for the years 2000 through 2029. If you type 30 through 99, Access assumes the years refer to 1930 through 1999. If you want years outside these ranges, you must type all four digits of the year or customize the way two-digit date entries are interpreted by using the Microsoft Office 2000 Resource Kit. If you want Access to display all dates with four digits, regardless of how they are entered, click the "Use four-digit year formatting" check box found on the General tab of the Options dialog box. Click the Tools menu item, then click Options to open the Options dialog box.

Unit K

Access 2000

Creating an Append Query

An **append query** adds a group of records to an existing table in either the current or in another Access database. The most difficult thing about an append query is making sure that all of the fields you have selected within the append query match fields in the target table where you wish to append (paste) them. If the target table has more fields than the append query, the append query will append the data in the matching fields and ignore the other fields. If the target table is lacking a field that the append query contains, an error message will appear indicating that there is an unknown field name that will cancel the action. David would like to append April's records to the First Quarter 2000 Attendance Log table. He uses an append query to do this, then he renames the table to accurately reflect its contents.

Steps

1. Click **Queries** on the Objects bar, click the **New button** on the database window, click **OK** to accept Design view in the New Query dialog box, double-click **Attendance** in the Show Table dialog box, then click **Close** in the Show Table dialog box
2. Double-click the **Attendance table's field list title bar**, then drag the **highlighted fields** to the first column of the query design grid

   Double-clicking the title bar of the field list highlights all of the fields, so you were able to add all the fields to the query grid quickly. An append query does not allow the same field to be referenced twice, even if the show check box is cleared for one occurrence of the field.
3. Click the **Attended field Criteria cell**, type **>=4/1/00 and <=4/30/00**, then click the **Datasheet View button** on the Query Design toolbar

   There should be 29 records with an April date in the Attended field.
4. Click the **Design View button** on the Query Datasheet toolbar, click the **Query Type button list arrow** on the Query Design toolbar, click **Append Query**, click the **Table Name list arrow** in the Append dialog box, click **First Quarter 2000 Attendance Log**, then click **OK**

   Your screen should look like Figure K-13. The Query Type button displays the Append Query icon, and the Append To row was added to the query design grid. You would use the Append To row to choose fields in the target table if they were different than the query fields. The append action is ready to be initiated by clicking the Run button.
5. Click the **Run button** on the Query Design toolbar, click **Yes** to indicate that you want to append 29 rows, then close the query without saving the changes
6. Click **Tables** on the Objects bar, double-click the **First Quarter 2000 Attendance Log**, click any entry in the Attended field, then click the **Sort Descending button** on the Table Datasheet toolbar

   The April records were appended to the table for a total of 131 records, as shown in Figure K-14.
7. Close the First Quarter 2000 Attendance Log without saving changes, right-click **First Quarter 2000 Attendance Log** in the database window, click **Rename**, type **Jan-April 2000 Log**, then press **[Enter]**

   The backup table with attendance records from January through April 2000 has been renamed.

FIGURE K-13: Creating an append query

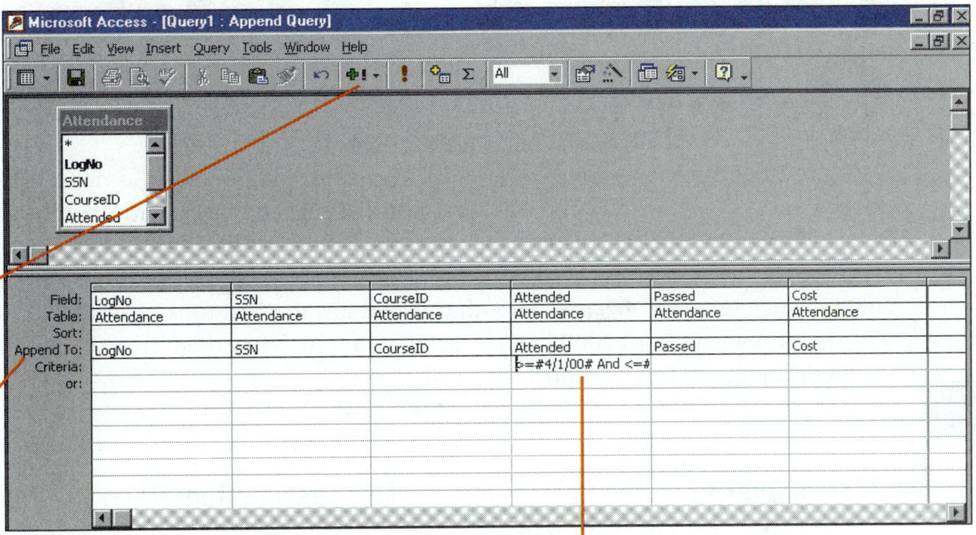

FIGURE K-14: Updated table with appended records

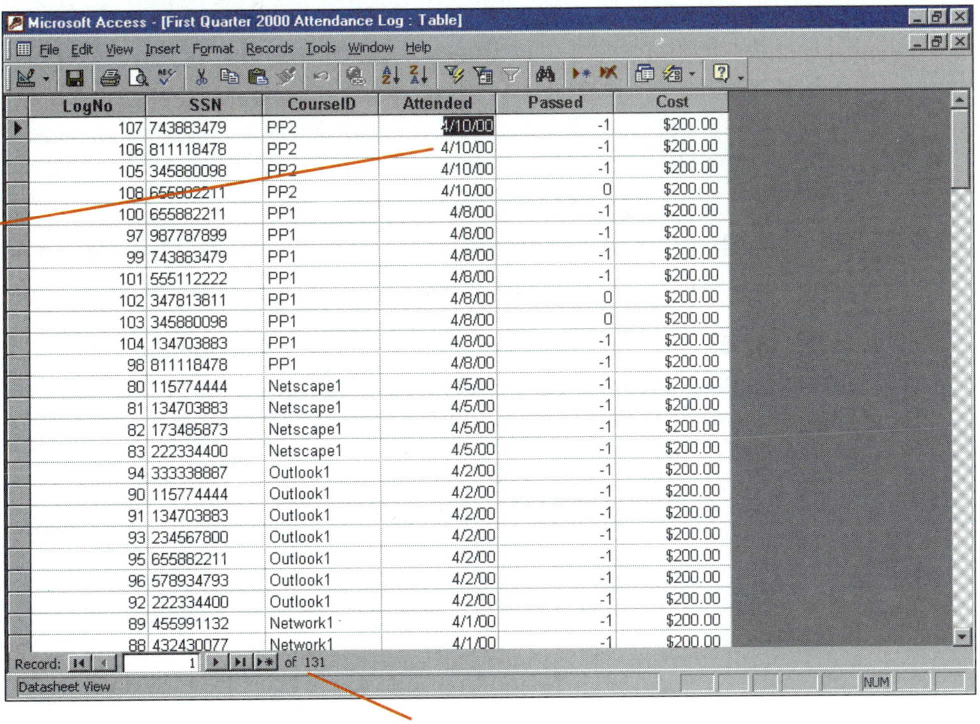

Access 2000

Unit K

Access 2000

Creating a Delete Query

A **delete query** deletes a group of records from one or more tables as defined by a query. Delete queries always delete entire records, and not just selected fields within records, so they should be used carefully. Since the delete query destroys records without the ability to undo the action, it is wise to always have a current backup of the database before running any action query, especially the delete query. Now that David has the first four months of attendance records archived in the Jan-April 2000 Log table, he wishes to delete them from the Attendance table. He uses a delete query to accomplish this task.

Steps

1. Click **Queries** on the Objects bar, click the **New button** on the database window, click **OK** to accept Design view in the New Query dialog box, double-click **Attendance** in the Show Table dialog box, then click **Close** in the Show Table dialog box
2. Double-click the *** (asterisk)** at the top of the Attendance table's field list, then double-click the **Attended** field

   All the fields from the Attendance table are added to the first column of the query design grid, and the Attended field is added to the second column of the query design grid.
3. Click the **Attended field Criteria cell**, type **<=4/30/00**, then press **[Enter]**

   It is important to check the datasheet to make sure that you have selected the same 131 records that are in the Jan-April 2000 Log table.
4. Click the **Datasheet View button** on the Query Design toolbar to confirm that there are 131 records in the datasheet, click the **Design View button** on the Query Datasheet toolbar, click the **Query Type button list arrow**, then click **Delete Query**

   Your screen should look like Figure K-15. The Query Type button displays the Delete Query icon, and the Delete row was added to the query design grid. The delete action is ready to be initiated by clicking the Run button.
5. Click the **Run button** on the Query Design toolbar, click **Yes** to confirm that you want to delete 131 rows, then close the query without saving the changes.
6. Click **Tables** on the Objects bar, double-click **Attendance**, click **any entry in the Attended field**, then click the **Sort Ascending button** on the Table Datasheet toolbar

   The oldest records should start in the month of May, as shown in Figure K-16. All prior records were deleted by the delete query.
7. Save and close the Attendance table datasheet

FIGURE K-15: Creating a delete query

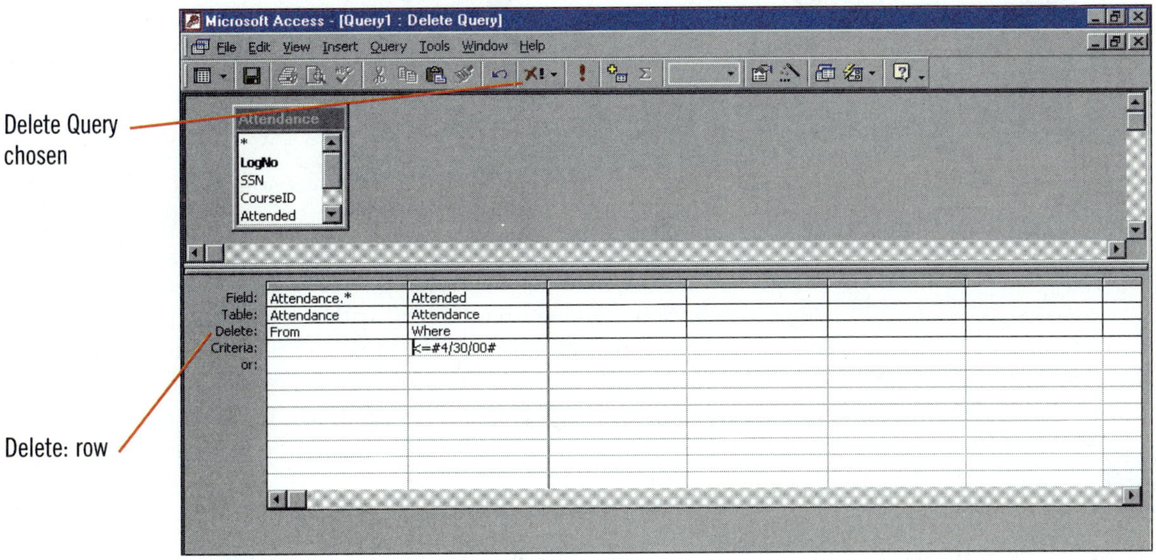

FIGURE K-16: Attendance table without January-April records

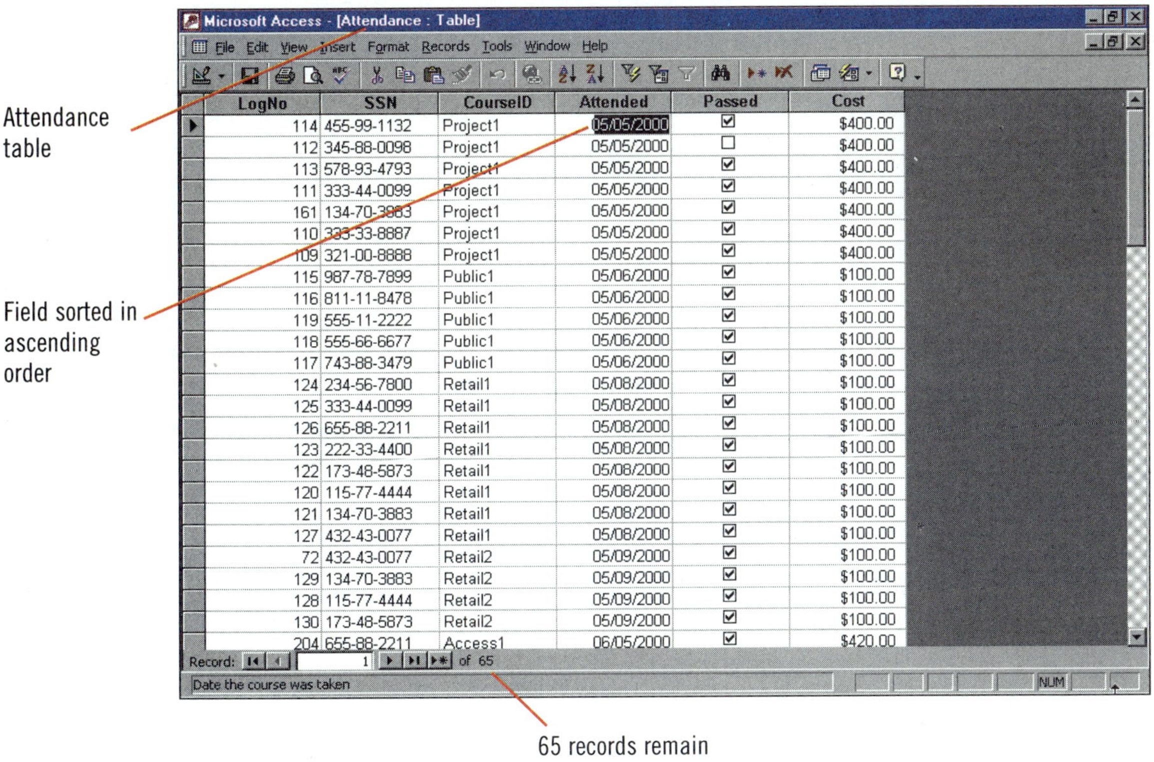

Access 2000

Unit K

Access 2000

Specifying Join Properties

When more than one table's field list is used in a query, the tables are joined as defined in the Relationships window. If referential integrity was enforced, a "1" appears next to the table whose field serves as the "one" side of the one-to-many relationship, and an infinity sign (∞) appears next to the table whose field serves as the "many" side. If no relationships have been established, Access automatically creates join lines if the tables have a field with the same name and comparable data type, and if the field is a primary key in one of the tables. The "one" and "many" symbols do not appear, however, because referential integrity is not enforced. You can edit this relationship by double-clicking the join line. David would like to create a query to find out which courses have never been attended. He modifies the join properties between the Attendance and Courses table to get this answer.

Steps

QuickTip

Right-click a blank spot in the upper portion of the query design grid, then click Relationships to quickly open the Relationships window.

Trouble?

Double-click the middle portion of the join line, not the "one" or "many" symbols.

1. Click **Queries** on the Object bar, click the **New button**, click **OK** to accept Design view, double-click **Courses**, double-click **Attendance**, then click **Close**

   Because the Courses and Attendance tables already have a one-to-many relationship with referential integrity enforced in the Relationships window, the join line appears, linking the two tables using the CourseID field common to both.

2. Double-click the **one-to-many join line** between the field lists

   The Join Properties dialog box opens, as shown in Figure K-17, showing which tables and fields participate in the join. The lower half of the dialog box shows that, by default, option 1 is chosen, which specifies that the query will display only records where joined fields from *both* tables are equal. That means that if any courses exist in which there was no matching attendance record, those courses would not appear in the resulting datasheet.

3. Click the option **2 option button**

   By choosing option 2, you are specifying that you wish to see all of the records in the Courses table, regardless of whether there are any matching records in the Attendance table. Because referential integrity is enforced, option 3 would be the same as option 1, because referential integrity makes it impossible to enter records in the Attendance table that do not have a corresponding record in the Courses table.

4. Click **OK**

   The join line's appearance changes as shown in Figure K-18.

5. Double-click **CourseID** from the Courses field list, double-click **Description** from the Courses field list, double-click **Attended** from the Attendance field list, double-click **Cost** from the Attendance field list, then click the **Datasheet View button**

   All courses are listed in the datasheet. The ones with corresponding attendance records have an entry in the Attended and Cost fields. By using a filter, you can quickly display those with no entry in the Attended field to determine exactly which courses have not been attended.

6. Click the **Access2 Attended field** (it is null), then click the **Filter by Selection button** on the Query Datasheet toolbar

   The 18 filtered records represent those courses as shown in Figure K-19.

7. Click the **Save button** on the Query Datasheet toolbar, type **No Attendance Since 5/1/00 – Your Initials** in the Query Name text box, click **OK**, click the **Access2 Attended field**, click (to refilter for null values), then click the **Print button**

8. Close the datasheet, then exit Access

FIGURE K-17: Join Properties dialog box

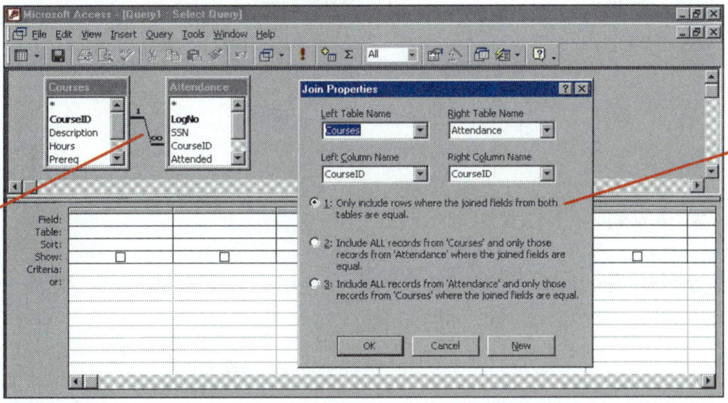

FIGURE K-18: The join line's appearance changes when its properties are changed

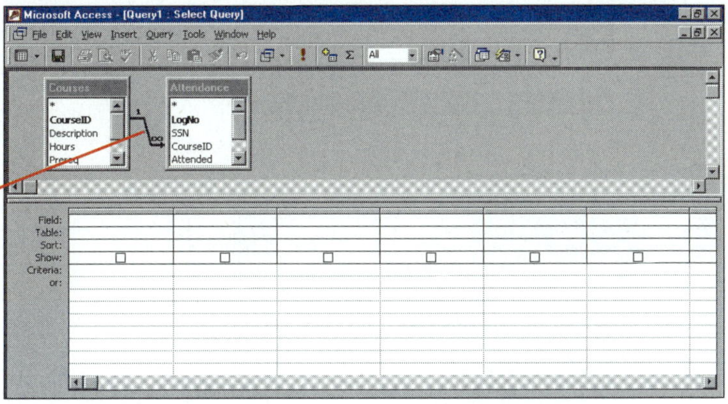

FIGURE K-19: Filtering for courses with no attendance records

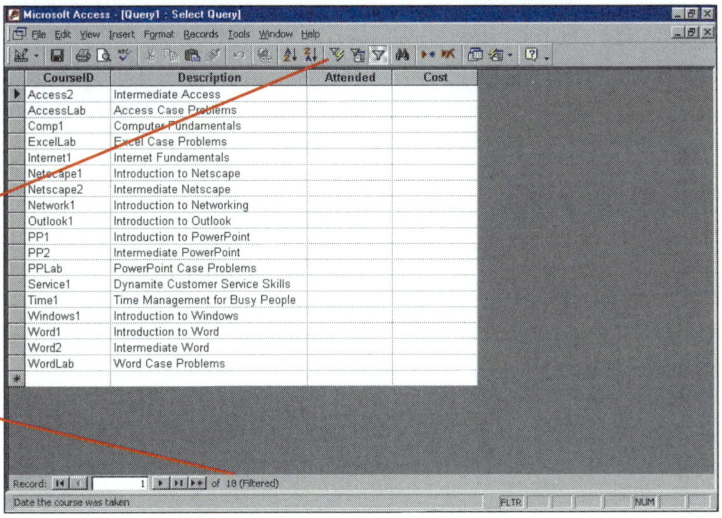

CLUES TO USE

Reviewing referential integrity

Referential integrity between two tables may be established when tables are joined in the Relationships window, and it ensures that no orphaned records are entered or created in the database. An **orphan record** happens when information in the linking field of the "many" table doesn't have a matching entry in the linking field of the "one" table. For the Training-K database, for example, referential integrity ensures that CourseNo entries added to the Attendance table are first recorded in the Courses table. Also, referential integrity prevents the user from deleting a record from the Courses table if matching CourseNo entries are present in the Attendance table.

Practice

► Concepts Review

Identify each element of the form's Design view shown in Figure K-20.

FIGURE K-20

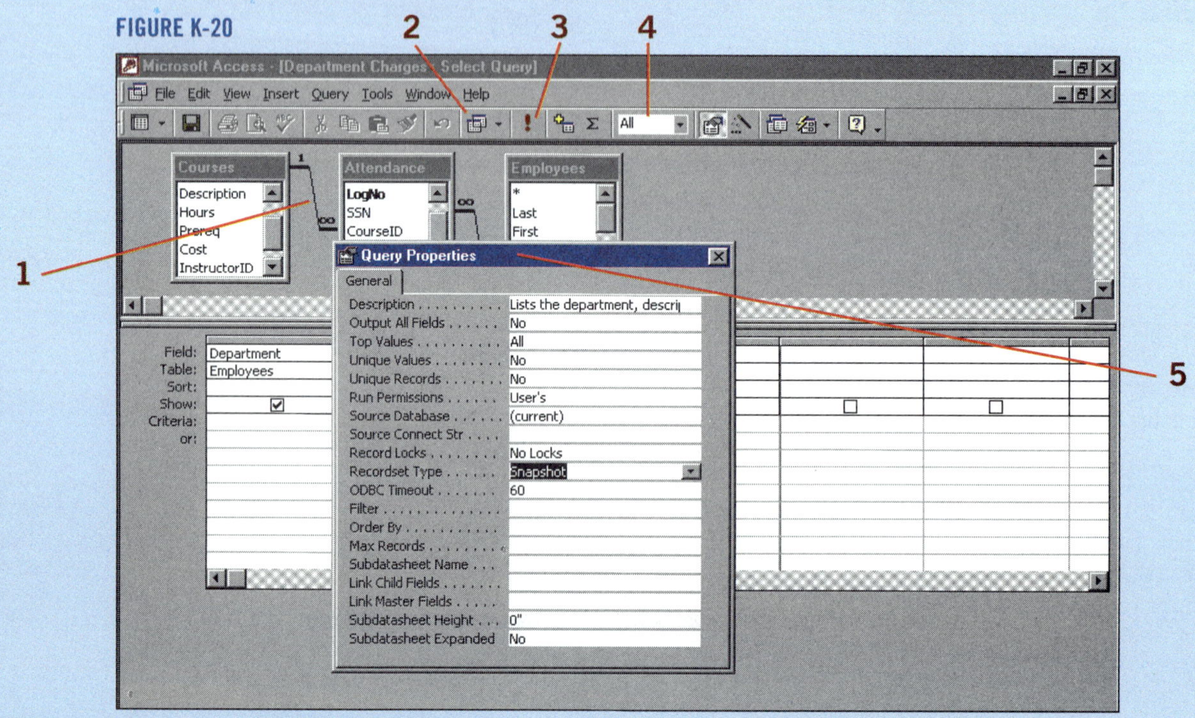

Match each term with the statement that describes its function.

6. **Top values query**
7. **Select query**
8. **Action query**
9. **Properties**
10. **Snapshot**
11. **Parameter query**

a. Displays a dialog box prompting you for information to enter as criteria
b. Makes changes to the data
c. Displays only the highest or lowest values from a sorted query
d. Displays fields and records that match specific criteria into a single datasheet
e. Makes the Recordset not updateable
f. Characteristics that define the appearance and behavior of almost everything within the database

Select the best answer from the list of choices.

12. The entry for the Recordset Type query property that does not allow you to modify any of the data is
- **a.** No Updates.
- **b.** Snapshot.
- **c.** Referential Integrity.
- **d.** Dynaset (No Nulls).

13. Which of the following shows the proper way to enter parameter criteria in the query design grid?
- **a.** >=(Type minimum value here:)
- **b.** >=Type minimum value here: }
- **c.** >=[Type minimum value here:]
- **d.** >=Type minimum value here:

14. You cannot use the Top Values feature to:
- **a.** Display a subset of records.
- **b.** Show the top 30 records.
- **c.** Update the top 10 records.
- **d.** Show the bottom 10 percent of records.

15. Which of the following is not an action query?
- **a.** Union query
- **b.** Delete query
- **c.** Make-table query
- **d.** Append query

16. Which of the following precautions should you take before running a delete query?
- **a.** Check the resulting datasheet to make sure the query selects the right records.
- **b.** Have a current backup of the database.
- **c.** Understand the relationships between the records you are about to delete in the database.
- **d.** All of the above

17. When querying tables in a one-to-many relationship with referential integrity enforced, which records will appear (by default) on the resulting datasheet?
- **a.** Only those with matching values in both tables
- **b.** All records from the "one" table, and only those with matching values from the "many" side
- **c.** All records from the "many" table, and only those with nonmatching values from the "one" side
- **d.** All records from both tables will appear at all times

Skills Review

1. Query for Top Values.
- **a.** Start Access then open the Seminar-K database.
- **b.** Create a select query with the EventName field from the Events table and the RegistrationFee field from the Registration table.
- **c.** Add the RegistrationFee field a second time, then click the Totals button. In the Total row of the query grid, Group By the EventName field, Sum the first RegistrationFee field, and count the second Registration Fee field.
- **d.** Sort in descending order by the Summed RegistrationFee field.
- **e.** Enter 2 in the Top Values list box to display the top two seminars in the datasheet.
- **f.** Save the query as "Top 2 Seminars – Your Initials", view the resulting datasheet, print the datasheet, then close the datasheet.

2. **Create an Advanced Parameter Query.**
   a. Create a select query with the AttendeeLastName field from the Attendees table, and the EventName and Date fields from the Events table. (*Hint*: You'll need to add the Registration table to this query as well as join the Attendees and Events tables.)
   b. Add the parameter criteria "Between [Enter Start Date:] And [Enter End Date:]" in the Date field.
   c. Specify an ascending sort order on the Date field.
   d. Click the Datasheet View button, then enter "5/1/00" as the start date and "6/30/00" as the end date in order to find everyone who has attended a seminar in May or June of the year 2000. You should view 22 records.
   e. Save the query as "May and June Seminar Attendance – Your Initials", then print the datasheet.
3. **Modify Query Properties.**
   a. Open the "May and June Seminar Attendance – Your Initials" query in Design view, open the property sheet for the query, change the Recordset Type property to Snapshot, then close the query property sheet.
   b. Right-click the Date field, and click Properties from the shortcut menu to open the Field Properties dialog box. Enter "Date of Seminar" as the Caption property, change the Format property to Medium Date, then close the property sheet.
   c. Display the records for the months of May and June of 2000, and print the datasheet.
   d. Save and close the query.
4. **Create an Update Query.**
   a. Create a select query and select all the fields from the Registration table.
   b. Add criteria to find those records in which the RegistrationDate is on or after 5/1/00. View the datasheet, and observe and note the values in the RegistrationFee field. There should be six records. Expand the columns to view all of the data.
   c. In Design view, change the query to an update query, then enter "[RegistrationFee]+5" in the RegistrationFee field Update To cell in order to increase each value in that field by $5.
   d. Run the query to update the six records.
   e. Change the query back to a select query, then view the datasheet to make sure that the RegistrationFee fields were updated properly.
   f. Close the query without saving the changes.
5. **Create a Make-Table Query.**
   a. Create a select query and select all the fields from the Registration table.
   b. Add criteria to find those records in which the RegistrationDate is on or before 3/31/00.
   c. View the datasheet. There should be 15 records.
   d. In Design view, change the query into a make-table query that creates a new table in the current database with the Table Name "1Qtr2000 – Your Initials".
   e. Run the query to paste 15 rows into the 1Qtr2000 – Your Initials table.
   f. Close the query without saving it, click Tables on the Objects bar, open the 1Qtr2000 – Your Initials table, view the 15 records, print the datasheet, then close it.
6. **Create an Append Query.**
   a. Create a select query and select all the fields from the Registration table.
   b. Add criteria to find those records in which the RegistrationDate occurred on any day during April 2000. (*Hint*: Use the criteria >=4/1/00 and <=4/30/00.)
   c. View the datasheet. There should be one record.
   d. Change the query to an append query that appends to the 1Qtr2000 – Your Initials table.
   e. Run the query to append the row into the 1Qtr2000 – Your Initials table.
   f. Close the query without saving it.
   g. Rename the 1Qtr2000 – Your Initials table to "Jan-Apr2000 – Your Initials", open the datasheet (there should be 16 records), print it, then close it.

7. **Create a Delete Query.**
   a. Create a select query and select all the fields from the Registration table.
   b. Add criteria to find those records in which the RegistrationDate occurred before May 1, 2000.
   c. View the datasheet. There should be 16 records.
   d. Change the query into a delete query.
   e. Run the query that deletes 16 records from the Registration table.
   f. Close the query without saving it.
   g. Open the Registration table in datasheet view to confirm that there are only six records, then close it.
8. **Specify Join Properties.**
   a. Create a select query with the following fields: AttendeeFirstName and AttendeeLastName from the Attendees table, and RegistrationFee from the Registration table.
   b. Double-click the link between the Attendees and Registration tables to open the Join Properties dialog box. Click the option button to include *all* records from Attendees and only those records from Registration where the joined fields are equal. Click OK to close the dialog box.
   c. View the datasheet, and add your own first and last name as the last record, but do not enter anything in the RegistrationFee field for your record.
   d. Print the datasheet, save the query with the name "Current Attendees", then close the datasheet.
   e. Close the Seminar-K database and exit Access.

Independent Challenges

1. As the manager of a college women's basketball team, you wish to create several queries using the Basketball-K database.

To complete this independent challenge:

a. Start Access and open the database Basketball-K.
b. Open the Players Query in Design view and add parameter criteria to prompt the user to enter a start and end date in the Date field like the following: Between [Enter start date:] and [Enter end date:]
c. Display the datasheet for all of the records in the year 2000. There should be 42 records.
d. Use the Save As option on the File menu to save the query with the name "2000 – Your Initials", then print the datasheet.
e. In Design view of the 2000 - Your Initials query, sort in descending order on the TotalPts field, then choose 5% for Top Values.
f. Display the datasheet for all of the records in the year 2001. There should be two records.
g. Use the Save As option on the File menu to save the query with the name "2001 – Top 5% - Your Initials", then print the datasheet.
h. Close the 2001 – Top 5% - Your Initials query.
i. Open the Scoring query in Design view, then add a new calculated field between the Opponent Score and Last fields with the following expression: Win%:[Home Score]/[Opponent Score]
j. View the datasheet to make sure that the Win% field calculates properly. Because the home score is generally greater than the opponent score, most values will be greater than 1.
k. In Design view, open the property sheet of the Win% field to change the Format property of the Win% field to "Percent" and the Decimal Places property to "0".
l. View the datasheet, use the Save As feature to save the query as "Scoring – Your Initials", then print it.
m. Close the Scoring – Your Initials query and the Basketball-K database, and exit Access.

2. As the manager of a college women's basketball team, you wish to enhance the Basketball-K database and need to create several action queries using the Basketball-K database.
To complete this independent challenge:

a. Start Access and open the database Basketball-K.
b. Create a new select query that includes all of the fields from the Stats table.
c. Add criteria to find all of the statistics for those records with the GameNo field equal to 1, 2, or 3. There should be 18 records.
d. Change the query to a Make-Table query to paste the records into a table in the current database called "Games 1, 2, and 3 – Your Initials".
e. Run the query to paste the 18 rows, then close the query without saving it.
f. Open the Games 1, 2, and 3 – Your Initials table's datasheet and print it.
g. Create another new select query that includes all of the fields from the Stats table.
h. Add criteria to find all of the statistics for those records with the GameNo field equal to 4 or 5. There should be 12 records.
i. Change the query to an append query to append the records to the Games 1, 2, and 3 – Your Initials table.
j. Run the query to append the 12 rows, then close the query without saving it.
k. Rename the Games 1, 2, and 3 – Your Initials table to the "Games 1-5 – Your Initials" table.
l. Open the Games 1-5 – Your Initials table's datasheet, then print it. There should be 30 records.
m. Close the Games 1-5 – Your Initials table, close the Basketball-K database, then exit Access.

3. As the manager of a college women's basketball team, you wish to query the Basketball-K database to find specific information about each player.
To complete this independent challenge:

a. Start Access and open the database Basketball-K.
b. Create a query in Design view with the Players and Stats tables.
c. Double-click the linking line to open the Join Properties dialog box, and change the join properties to include ALL records from "Players" and only those from "Stats" where the joined fields are equal.
d. Add the First and Last fields from the Players table, and the Reb-O, Reb-D, and Assists fields from the Stats table.
e. View the datasheet, then scroll to see if there are any players who do not have rebounding or assist statistics.
f. Click an empty Reb-O field, then click the Filter By Selection button to filter for only those players with null Reb-O statistics.
g. Add your name as the last record, but do not enter anything in the three statistics fields.
h. Print the datasheet, save the query as Redshirts, then close the datasheet.
i. Close Basketball-K and exit Access.

WEB WORK

4. MediaLoft has developed a Web site that provides internal information to their employees. In this independent challenge, you'll find query requests posted to the Web site that you will complete using the Training-K database.

a. Connect to the Internet, go to the MediaLoft intranet site at http://www.course.com/illustrated/MediaLoft

b. Click the link for Training, click the link for Query Requests, then Print the page.

c. Open the Training-K database, click the Queries on the Objects bar, then create the query requested on the printed Web page by including the InstructorFirst and InstructorLast fields from the Instructors table, and the Description field from the Courses table.

d. Double-click the join line to open the Join Properties dialog box, and modify the join properties to include all records from "Instructors" and only those from "Courses" where the joined fields are equal.

e. View the datasheet, add your name in a new record if it doesn't already exist in the datasheet (do not enter a Description in that record), then print the datasheet.

f. Save the query as Instructor Assignments – Your Initials, then close the query and the Training-K database, and exit Access.

▶ Visual Workshop

As the manager of a college women's basketball team, you wish to create a query from the Basketball-K database with the fields shown. The query is a parameter query that prompts the user for a start and end date. Figure K-21 shows the datasheet where the start date of 12/1/00 and end date of 12/31/00 are used. Save and name the query "Offense – Your Initials", then print the datasheet.

FIGURE K-21

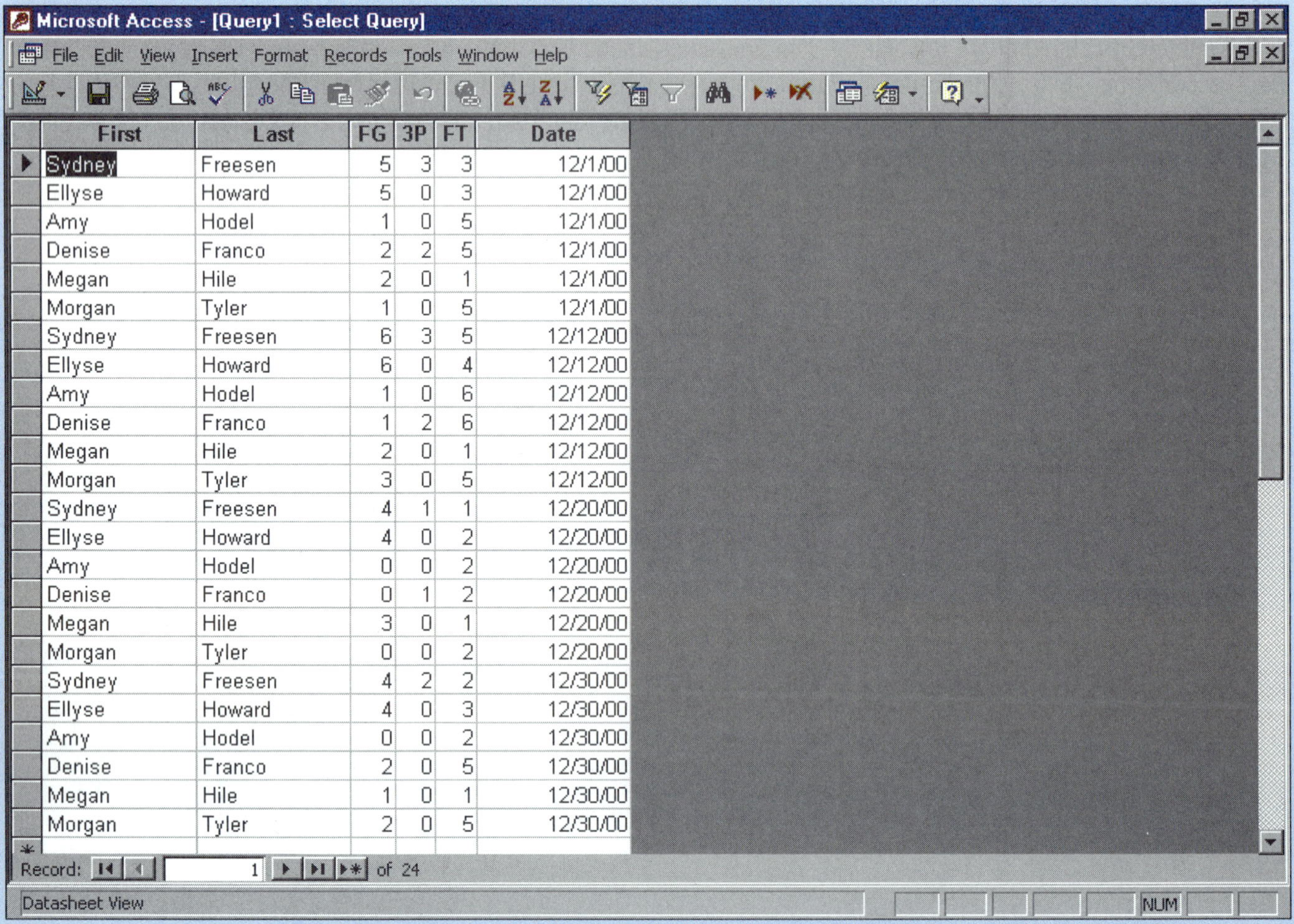

First	Last	FG	3P	FT	Date
Sydney	Freesen	5	3	3	12/1/00
Ellyse	Howard	5	0	3	12/1/00
Amy	Hodel	1	0	5	12/1/00
Denise	Franco	2	2	5	12/1/00
Megan	Hile	2	0	1	12/1/00
Morgan	Tyler	1	0	5	12/1/00
Sydney	Freesen	6	3	5	12/12/00
Ellyse	Howard	6	0	4	12/12/00
Amy	Hodel	1	0	6	12/12/00
Denise	Franco	1	2	6	12/12/00
Megan	Hile	2	0	1	12/12/00
Morgan	Tyler	3	0	5	12/12/00
Sydney	Freesen	4	1	1	12/20/00
Ellyse	Howard	4	0	2	12/20/00
Amy	Hodel	0	0	2	12/20/00
Denise	Franco	0	1	2	12/20/00
Megan	Hile	3	0	1	12/20/00
Morgan	Tyler	0	0	2	12/20/00
Sydney	Freesen	4	2	2	12/30/00
Ellyse	Howard	4	0	3	12/30/00
Amy	Hodel	0	0	2	12/30/00
Denise	Franco	2	0	5	12/30/00
Megan	Hile	1	0	1	12/30/00
Morgan	Tyler	2	0	5	12/30/00

Access 2000

Unit L

Creating
Advanced Forms and Reports

Objectives

- MOUS ► Add Check Boxes and Toggle Buttons
- MOUS ► Use Conditional Formatting
- ► Create Custom Help
- ► Add Tab Controls
- MOUS ► Add Charts
- ► Modify Charts
- MOUS ► Add Subreport Controls
- MOUS ► Modify Section Properties

Advanced controls such as tab controls, charts, and subreports are powerful communication tools. Conditional formatting allows you to highlight exceptional information within a form or report to more clearly present key information. Knowing how to use these advanced features to enhance forms and reports will improve the value of your database to every user. David Dumont wants to enhance existing forms and reports to more professionally and clearly present the information. David will use powerful form and report controls and features such as check boxes, conditional formatting, tab controls, charts, and subreports to improve the training database's forms and reports.

Unit L

Access 2000

Adding Check Boxes and Toggle Buttons

A **check box** is a control that is often used to display Yes/No fields on a form because it can appear in only one of two ways: checked or unchecked. The checked state intuitively means on, yes, or true, and the unchecked state means off, no, or false. It is much easier for a user to answer questions on a form by using the mouse to click a check box control than to type the word "True" or "Yes" in a text box control. By default, Access represents any field with a Yes/No data type as a check box control on a form, regardless of whether the field was added to the form through the Form Wizard, AutoForm options, or in Form Design view. David would like to improve the visual appeal of the Employee Course Attendance form and Attendance Subform. He changes the properties of the Attendance Subform and a Yes/No field.

Steps

1. Open the **Training-L** database, click **Forms** on the Objects bar, then double-click the **Employee Course Attendance form**
   The form opens in Form view and the Attendance Subform appears as a datasheet within it.
2. Click the **Design View button** on the Form View toolbar, then maximize the **Employee Course Attendance form** window
   Your screen should look like Figure L-1. In order to change the appearance of the controls on the subform, the Default View property for the form has to be changed from Datasheet (which allows no special formatting) to Continuous Forms.
3. Double-click the **subform's Select form button**, click the **Format tab** (if necessary) on the property sheet, click the **Default View text box**, click the **Default View list arrow**, click **Continuous Forms**, then click the **Form View button**
   Your screen should look like Figure L-2. The property sheet for the currently selected control, the Last text box, appears because Access allows you to change the properties of some bound controls in Form view. Some modifications can be made only in Design view, however, such as adding, deleting, moving, or resizing a control, or modifying an unbound control such as a label.
4. Close the **property sheet**
   Because of the change to the subform's Default View property, the subform now displays the records in exactly the same way that they appear formatted in Design view, and not as a datasheet.
5. Click on the Form View toolbar, click the **Passed check box** to select it, right-click the **Passed check box**, point to **Change To**, then click **Toggle Button**
   Changing a control into a different control can be accomplished only in Design view. See Table L-1 for more information on which controls are interchangeable by using the "Change To" shortcut menu option.
6. Point to the **middle-right resize handle** on the toggle button, drag ↔ to the right edge of the form, click the **toggle button**, type **Click if Yes**, then click
   Your screen should look similar to Figure L-3. Notice that when the value is "yes," the toggle button appears indented or "pushed in." The text displayed on the button can be changed using the Caption property on the Format tab in the toggle button's property sheet.
7. Click the **Save button** on the Form View toolbar
   The changes are saved to the Employee Course Attendance form and the Attendance Subform.
8. Close the Employee Course Attendance form

Trouble?

If the subform appears as a white rectangle, click the Form View button, then click the Design View button to refresh the screen.

FIGURE L-1: Form and subform in Design view

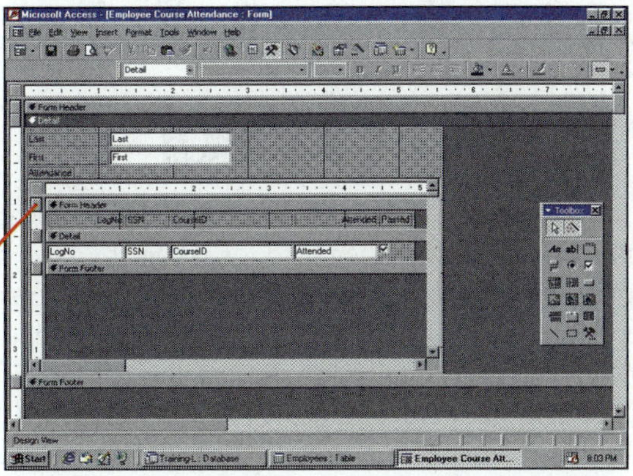

FIGURE L-2: Form view displaying the property sheet

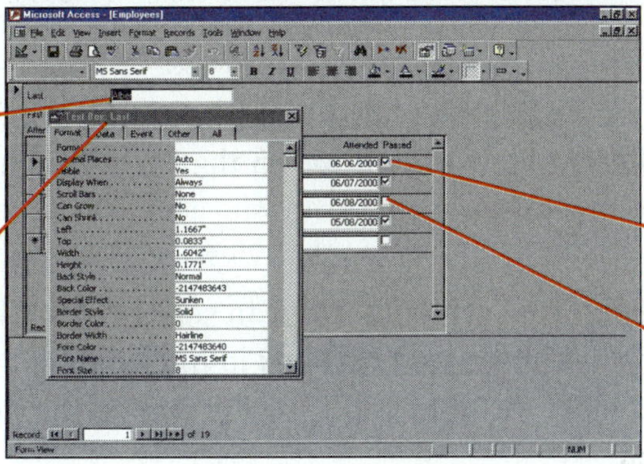

FIGURE L-3: Command buttons displaying "yes" and "no" values

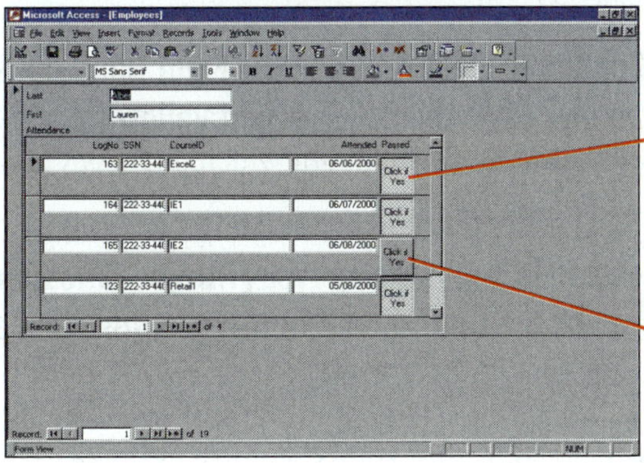

TABLE L-1: Interchangeable bound controls

control	can be interchanged with	used most commonly when the field has:
Text box	List box, combo box	An unlimited number of choices such as a Price, LastName, or Street field
List box	Text box, combo box	A limited number of predefined values such as Manager, Department, or State fields
Combo box	Text box, list box	A limited number of common values, yet you still need the ability to enter a new value from the keyboard, such as the City field
Check box	Toggle button, option button	Only two values, "yes" or "no," such as a Veteran field
Option button	Check box, toggle button	A limited number of values, such as "female" or "male" for a Gender field. The option button is most commonly used in conjunction with an option group that can contain several option buttons, each representing a possible value for the field
Toggle button	Check box, option button	Only two values, "yes" or "no," and you want the appearance of the field to look like a button rather than a check box

Unit L

Access 2000

Using Conditional Formatting

Conditional Formatting can be used to determine the appearance of a field on a form or report based on its value, a value in another field, or when the field has the focus. **Focus** is the ability to receive user input through the keyboard or mouse. Conditional formatting provides a way to alert the user to exceptional situations as data is being entered or reported. Format changes include changing the text color, background color, or style of the control. If you conditionally format a control based on a value in another field, you must use an **expression**, a combination of field names, operators, and values that calculate an answer. The users of the Courses form (which includes the Course-Employee Subform) would like David to modify the form so that they can quickly identify those course attendees with a title of "Salesperson." Additionally, David uses conditional formatting to more clearly show which text box has the focus.

Steps

Trouble?

If the subform appears as a white rectangle, click the Form View button, then click the Design View button to refresh the screen.

1. Double-click the **Courses form**, view the overall layout of the form and subform, then click the **Design View button** on the Form View toolbar

   The subform represents each person who attended the course, and the main form provides four fields of information about the course.

2. Click the **subform horizontal ruler** to select the subform, click the **subform vertical ruler** to the left of the **Last text box** in the subform to select all four text boxes in the Detail section of the subform, click **Format** on the menu bar, then click **Conditional Formatting**

   The Conditional Formatting dialog box opens. The first condition will highlight the field with the focus.

3. Click the **Condition 1 list arrow**, click **Field Has Focus**, click the **Condition 1 Fill/Back Color list arrow**, then click **bright yellow** (fourth row, third box from the left)

   The second condition will highlight which attendees have the title of "Salesperson."

QuickTip

You can include up to three conditions in the Conditional Formatting dialog box.

4. Click **Add** in the Conditional Formatting dialog box, click the **Condition 2 list arrow**, click **Expression is**, press **[Tab]**, type **[Title]="Salesperson"**, click the **Condition 2 Bold button**, click the **Condition 2 Font/Fore Color list arrow**, then click **bright red** (third row, first box from the left)

   Your screen should look like Figure L-4. When an expression is used in the Conditional Formatting dialog box, the expression must evaluate to be either "true," which turns the formatting on, or "false," which turns the formatting off.

5. Click **OK**, click the **Form View button** on the Form Design toolbar, then click **Colletti** (the first field value in the first record) in the subform

   Your screen should look like Figure L-5.

6. Press **[Tab]** three times to move the focus to the Salesperson entry for the first record, press **[Delete]**, then press **[Tab]**

   Your screen should look like Figure L-6, in which the first record in the subform is no longer red and boldface. Conditional formatting reverts to default formatting if the condition is no longer true.

QuickTip

You can also click the Undo button on the Form View toolbar to undo the last action.

7. Click **Edit** on the menu bar, then click the **Undo Saved Record button**

   The Title Salesperson is restored for the first record and it is in red boldface text.

8. Save then close the Courses form

FIGURE L-4: Conditional Formatting dialog box

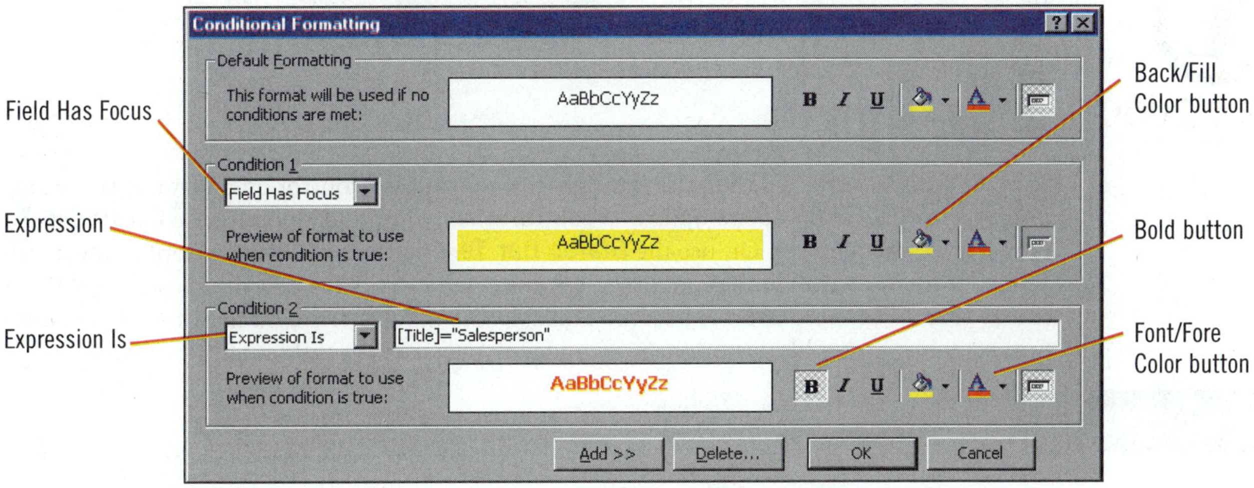

FIGURE L-5: The control with the focus is bright yellow

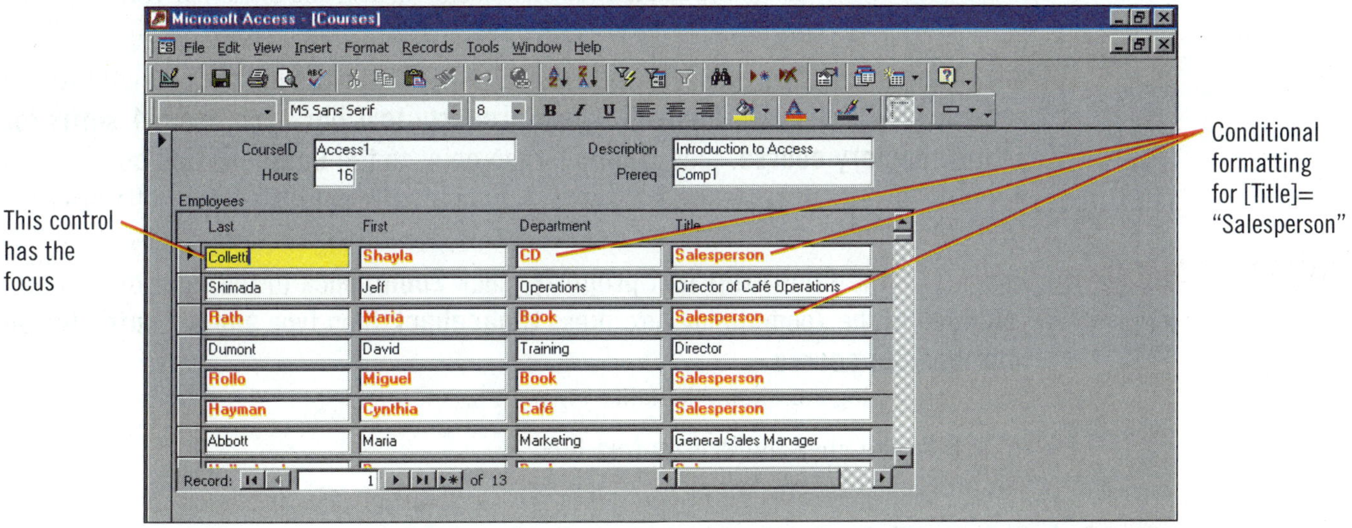

FIGURE L-6: Conditional formats change as data is edited

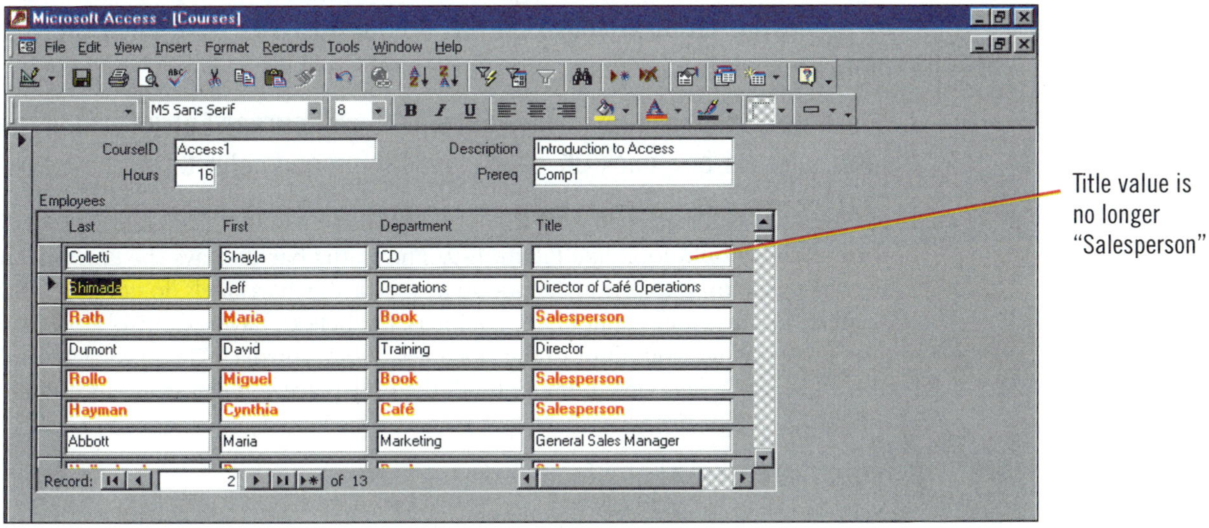

Unit L

Access 2000

Creating Custom Help

You can create several types of custom Help for a form or a control on a form. If you want to display a textual tip that pops up over a control when you point to it, use the **ControlTip Text** property for that control. Or, use the **Status Bar Text** property to display helpful information about a form or control in the status bar. David wants to allow other users to enter new course records as those courses become available. He quickly creates a new form based on the Courses table, then adds custom help to guide the new users as they enter the data.

Steps

1. Click the **New button** in the database window, click **AutoForm: Columnar**, click the **Choose the table or query where the object's data comes from list arrow**, click **Courses**, then click **OK**

   A Courses form is created. You can modify the ControlTip Text and Status Bar Text properties for text boxes and other bound controls from Form view.

2. Click **View** on the menu, click **Properties**, click the **Other tab** in the CourseID text box property sheet, click the **ControlTip Text property text box**, type **Use a 1 suffix for an introductory course**, press **[Enter]**, then point to the **CourseID text box**

   A control tip pops up, as shown in Figure L-7. You can view and enter a long entry using the Zoom dialog box.

3. Right-click the **ControlTip Text property**, click **Zoom**, click to the right of the word "**course**" in the Zoom dialog box, press **[Spacebar]**, then type **and a 2 suffix for an intermediate course**

   The Zoom dialog box should look like Figure L-8.

4. Click **OK**, then click the **Prereq text box**

   The property sheet now shows the properties for the Prereq text box.

5. Click the **Status Bar Text text box** in the Text Box Prereq property sheet

   When the property sheet is open, a short description of the selected property appears in the status bar.

6. Right-click the **Status Bar Text text box**, click **Zoom**, type **Comp1 can be waived by achieving an 80% score on the Computers 101 test**, click **OK**, then close the property sheet

7. Click **File** on the menu bar, click **Save As**, type **Courses Entry Form** in the Save From Form 1 To text box, click **OK**, then close the property sheet and the form

8. Double-click **Courses Entry Form** in the database window, then click the **Prereq text box**

   Your screen should look like Figure L-9. The status bar displays the entry in the Status Bar Text property for this control. Unbound properties such as labels do not have a Status Bar Text property because they cannot have the focus. A label can have a ControlTip Text property that displays text when you point to the label. A label's ControlTip Text property can be modified only in Form Design view, because that's the only place you can select an unbound control in order to access its property sheet.

9. Close the Courses Entry form

QuickTip

Click a property, then press [Shift][F2] to open the Zoom dialog box for that property.

QuickTip

Click a property, then press [F1] to open the Microsoft Access Help window for the specific explanation of that property.

FIGURE L-7: Using the ControlTip Text property

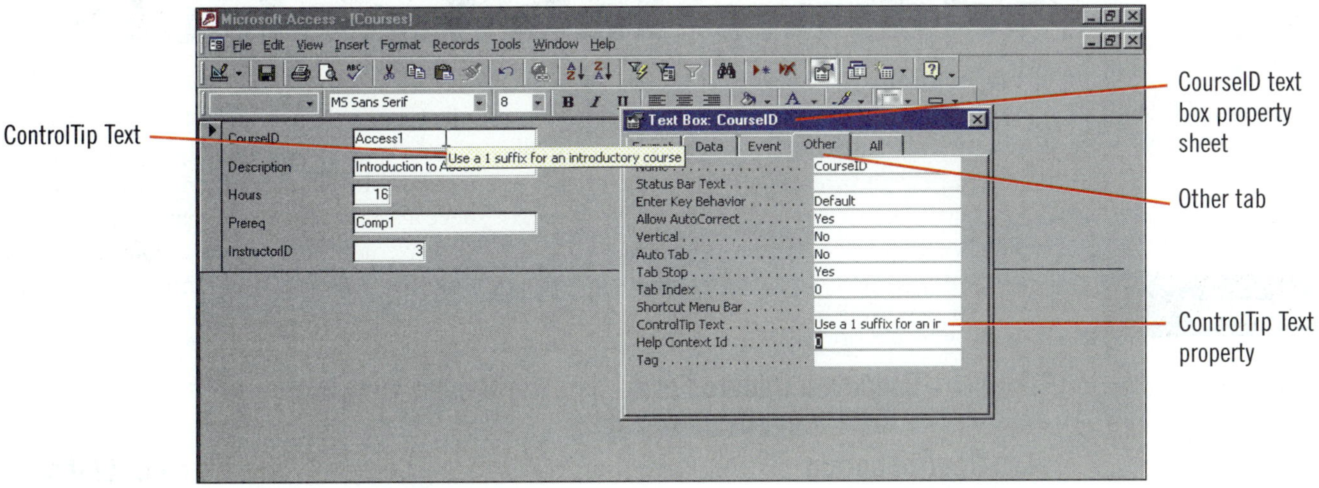

FIGURE L-8: Zoom dialog box

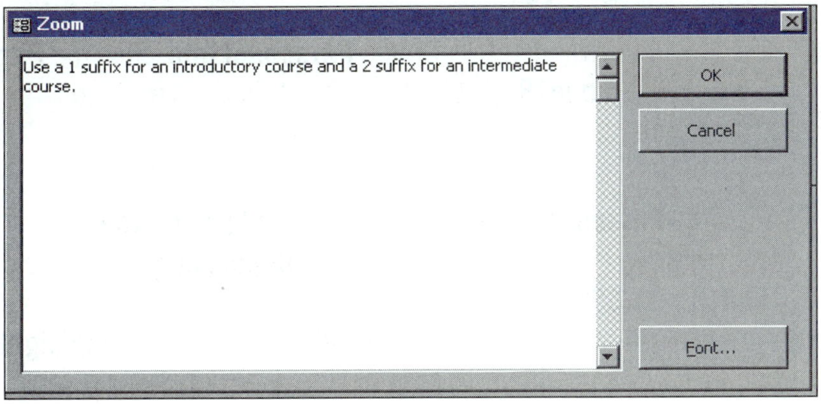

FIGURE L-9: Using the Status Bar Text property

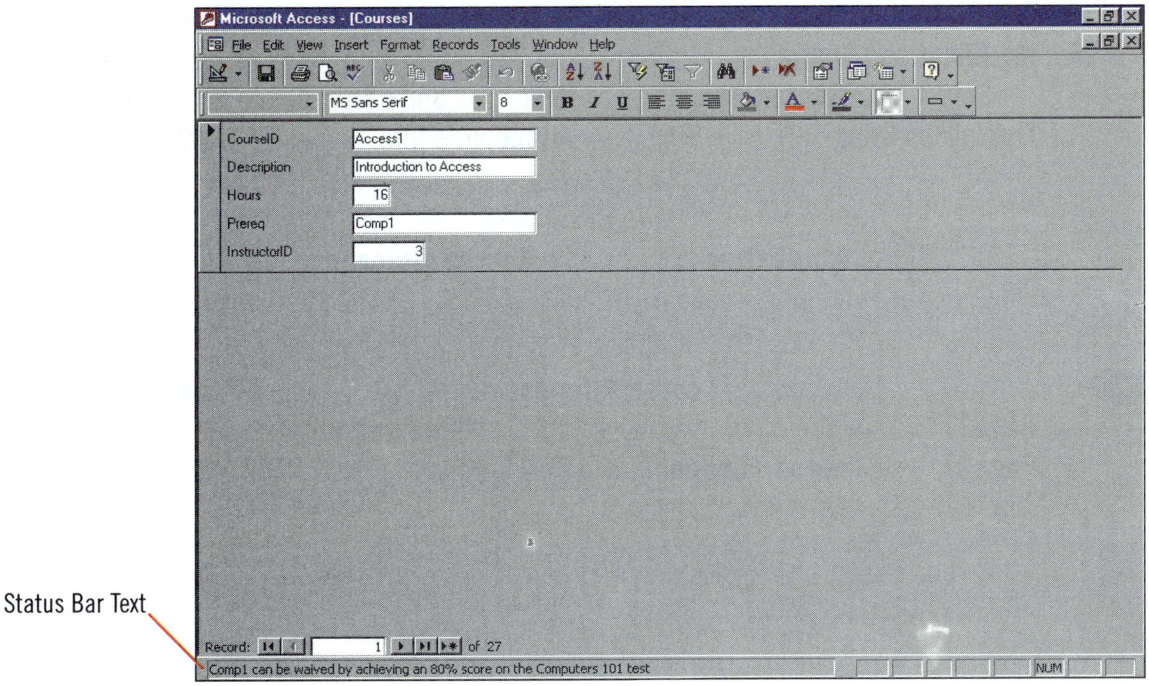

Unit L
Access 2000

Adding Tab Controls

The **tab control** is a powerful unbound control used to organize a form and give it a three-dimensional look by presenting several "pages" on a single form. When you want to show a lot of information on a form at one time, the tab control is an excellent tool to logically organize many fields. You are already familiar with using tab controls because they are used in many Access dialog boxes such as the property sheet. The property sheet also uses tabs to organize properties identified by their category name in the tab (Format, Data, Event, Other, and All). David has started to develop an Employee Update Form, but wants to use the tab control to organize and present employee information in an easy-to-use way.

Steps

1. Click the **Employee Update Form**, click the **Design View button** in the database window, click the **Toolbox button** to toggle the Toolbox on (if necessary), click the **Tab Control button** on the Toolbox toolbar, then click just below the **First label** in the Detail section of the form
   Your screen should look like Figure L-10. The tab control appears with two "pages," with the default names of Page17 and Page18, on the respective tabs.
2. Double-click **Page17** to open its property sheet, click the **Other tab**, verify Page17 is selected in the Name text box, type **Personnel Info**, click the **Page18 tab** on the form, double-click **Page18** in the Name text box of the property sheet, type **Course Attendance**, then close the property sheet
   The tabs now describe the information they will contain.
3. Click the **Personnel Info tab**, click the **Field List button** on the Form Design toolbar to toggle it on (if necessary), click **Department** in the field list, press and hold **[Shift]**, click **SSN** in the field list (you may have to scroll) to select all fields between the Department and SSN, release **[Shift]**, then drag the **highlighted fields** to the middle of the Personnel Info page
   Your screen should look like Figure L-11. The six fields are added to the Personnel Info page on the tab control. You can add any control, even a subform control, to a page.
4. Click the **Course Attendance tab**, click the **Subform/Subreport button** on the Toolbox, click the **upper-left corner of the Course Attendance page**, click the **Use existing Tables and Queries** option button in the SubForm Wizard dialog box, click **Next**, click the **Select All Fields button** , click **Next**, click **Show Attendance for each record in Employees using SSN**, click **Next**, type **Attendance Info**, then click **Finish**
   The tab control as well as the entire form has been automatically widened to better accommodate the wide subform control.
5. Click the **Form View button**, click the **Course Attendance tab**, then maximize the Employee Update Form window
   Your screen should look similar to Figure L-12.
6. Click , right-click the **Course Attendance tab**, click **Insert Page**, double-click **Page27** to open the property sheet, click the **Other tab** (if necessary), double-click **Page27**, type **Course Feedback**, close the property sheet, click , then click all three tabs
   You probably want to move and resize several of the controls on this form before using it, but for now the Course Feedback tab is prepared and ready for you to add controls to it in Design view to hold information for a future time.
7. Save and close the Employee Update Form

QuickTip

The page will become dark gray when you are successfully placing a control on that page.

Trouble?

The Control Wizards button must be selected prior to clicking the Subform/Subreport button on the Toolbox to activate the Subform Wizard.

Trouble?

Your page control number may be different than 27.

FIGURE L-10: Adding a tab control

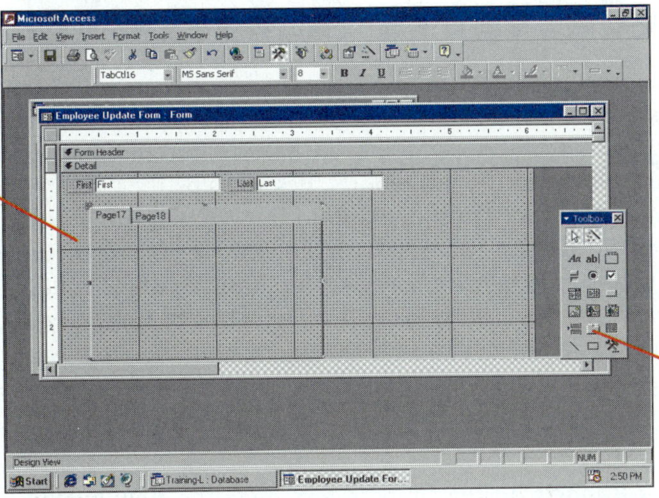

FIGURE L-11: Adding fields to a tab control

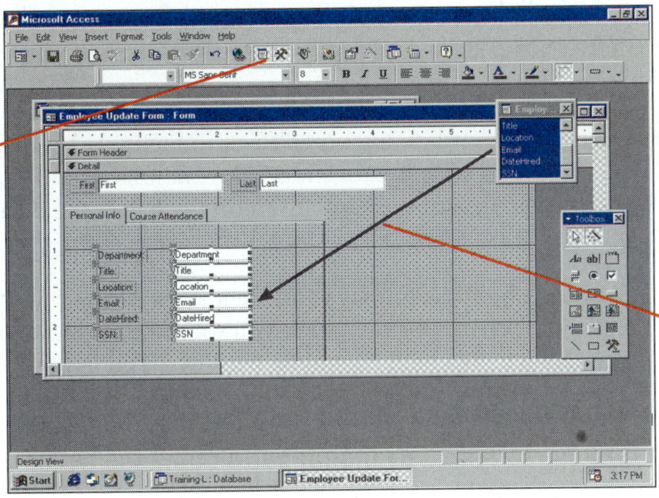

FIGURE L-12: The tab control in Form View

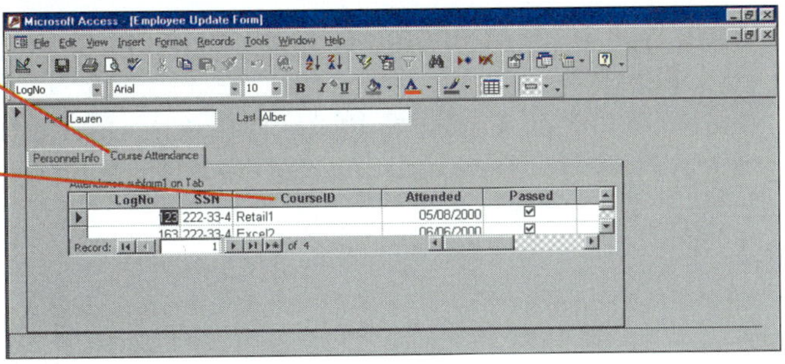

CLUES TO USE

Referencing controls with Text## and Page##

Access sequentially numbers each control on a form and uses that number in the Name property for the control. The label and tab control that display the name property as part of the control, you see the sequential number in the name of the control. For example, when adding a tab control to the form, the word "Page" plus the sequential number of that control are used as the default entry for the Name property and appear on the tab itself. If you add a control and then delete it, that sequential number is not used over. Since users build their forms in different ways, adding and deleting controls as necessary, it is common to reference the new label or tab controls as "Text##" or "Page##" because the exact number represented by ## will be different from user to user.

Unit L

Access 2000

Adding Charts

Charts, sometimes called graphs, are visual representations of numeric data that help users see comparisons, patterns, and trends in data. Charts can be inserted on a form, report, or data access page object. Access provides a **Chart Wizard** that steps you through the process of creating charts within forms and reports. Before using the Chart Wizard, however, you must determine what data you want the graph to show. Often you'll use an intermediate query to gather the specific fields that you wish to graph into one object before using the Chart Wizard to create the graph, especially if the data comes from multiple tables or if you wish to graph a subset of records. David created a Department Summary query with two fields: Attended from the Attendance table and Department from the Employees table. Instead of reporting this information as a datasheet of summarized numbers, he uses the report object's Chart Wizard to visually display a total count of attendance by department.

Steps 1 2 3 4

1. Click **Reports** on the Objects bar, click the **New button** in the database window, click **Chart Wizard**, click the **Choose the table or query where the object's data comes from list arrow**, click **Department Summary**, then click **OK**
   The Chart Wizard starts and presents the fields in the Department Summary query.
2. Click **the Select All Fields button** >>, then click **Next**
   The next Chart Wizard dialog box, shown in Figure L-13, determines the type of chart that will be created. See Table L-2 for more information on common chart types. Column Chart, the button in the first row, first column on the left, is the default chart type.
3. Click **Next**
   The next dialog box determines which fields will be used for the x-axis, bar, and series (legend) areas of the chart. For this chart, you want the bars to represent a count of the Attended field. The Department field should be used as x-axis labels.
4. Drag the **Attended field button** from the field buttons on the right to the **Data** area, then drag the **Attended by month button** from the Series area out of the chart area, as shown in Figure L-14
   Since the Attended field holds date data, bars should count the number of entries.
5. Click **Next**, type **Total Attendance by Department** in the title for your chart text box, then click **Finish**
   Your chart should look similar to Figure L-15. The chart is difficult to read as it currently appears, but Access provides charting tools to improve the appearance of charts.

QuickTip

Click any chart button to read a description of that chart in the lower-right corner of the Chart Wizard dialog box.

QuickTip

If you drag a numeric field into the Data area, you can double-click the button to change the way it is summarized to Sum, Avg, Min, or Max value of the field.

FIGURE L-13: Chart types

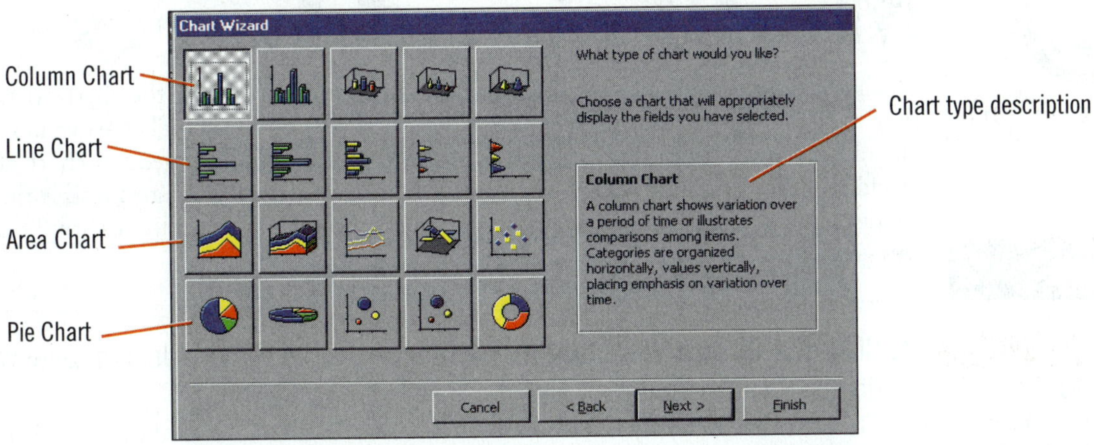

FIGURE L-14: Determining chart layout

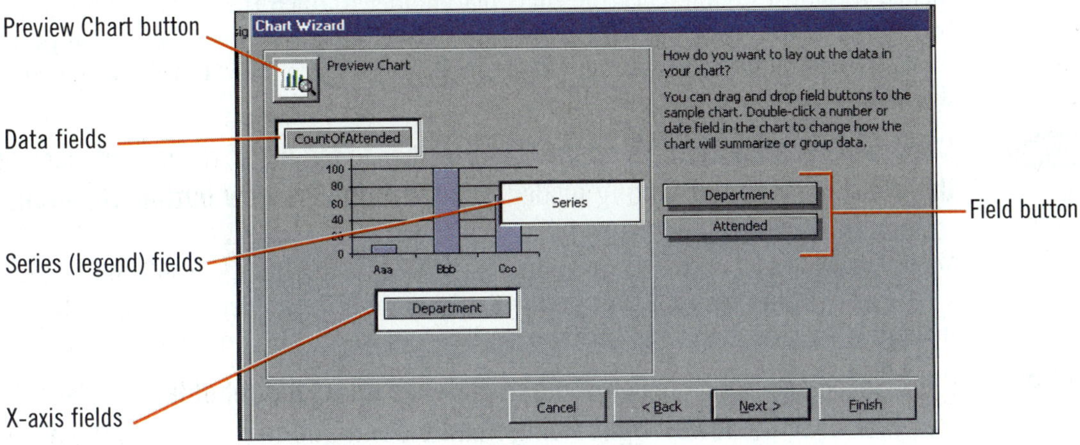

FIGURE L-15: Total Attendance by Department chart

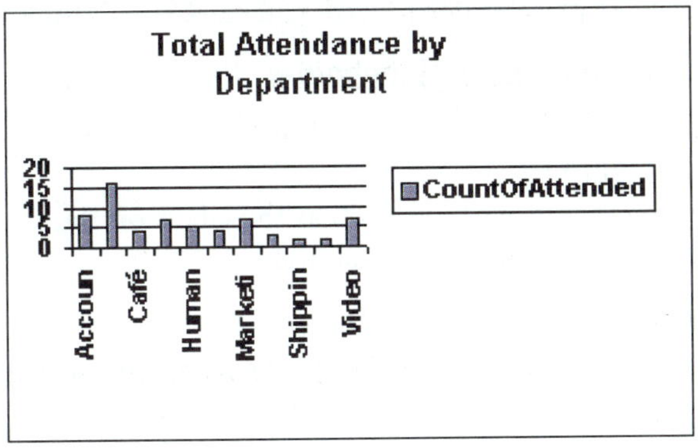

TABLE L-2: Common chart types

chart type	chart icon	most commonly used to show	example
Column		Comparisons of values	Each bar represents the annual sales for a different product for the year 2000
Line		Trends over time	Each point on the line represents monthly sales for one product for the year 2000
Pie		Parts of a whole	Each slice represents total quarterly sales for a company for the year 2000
Area		Cumulative totals	Each section represents monthly sales by representative, stacked to show the cumulative total sales effort for the year 2000

Access 2000

Unit L

Access 2000

Modifying Charts

All charts are modified in Design View of the form or report where the chart exists. Modifying a chart is challenging because Design View doesn't show you the actual chart values and elements, but rather shows you a chart placeholder that represents the embedded chart object. David sees that the chart would be clearer if he removes the legend and resizes the chart to better display the values on the axes. He makes all modifications to the existing chart in Report Design view.

Steps

QuickTip

The hashed border of the chart placeholder control indicates that the Chart is in edit mode.

Trouble?

You may have to click the More Buttons button on the Chart toolbar to locate the Legend button.

Trouble?

Be sure you work within the vertical ruler in the Detail section.

Trouble?

Click the View Datasheet button on the Standard toolbar to close the chart's datasheet if it opens.

QuickTip

The Category Axis is the x-axis, and the Value Axis is the y-axis.

1. Click the **Design View button**, maximize the Report Design View window, then double-click the **chart** to edit it

   The chart is now ready to be edited, as shown in Figure L-16. You can delete, move, or resize the chart object without double-clicking it, but if you want to modify any of the chart elements, you must double-click the chart placeholder to open the chart menu bar and toolbar. If you double-click the edge of the chart placeholder, you will open its property sheet. All chart editing and formatting is done in Report Design view, but the actual chart data displays only in Print Preview.

2. Click the **Legend button** on the Chart toolbar to toggle off the legend, click **outside the chart** to exit chart editing mode, click the **Print Preview button** on the Chart toolbar, then click the chart

   Your chart should look similar to Figure L-17. Because the chart has only one series of bars, a clear title (rather than a legend) can be used to describe the series. Most of the elements, including the y-axis labels and bars, are still too small to clearly display the information.

3. Click on the Print Preview toolbar, click the **chart placeholder** to select the control, then drag the **lower-right sizing handle** down and to the right to the **5"** mark on the horizontal ruler and the **3.5"** mark on the vertical ruler

   With the chart placeholder resized, you can expand the size of the chart within it.

4. Double-click the **chart placeholder**, then drag the lower-right corner sizing handle of the fuzzy border of the chart to just within the border of the chart placeholder, as shown in Figure L-18

   You can modify any element such as the labels on the x-axis or y-axis, but you must select them before you change or format them.

5. Click the **East label** to select the Category Axis, click the **Font Size list arrow** 10, click **8**, click the **Total Attendance by Department Chart Title**, click 12, click **10**, click outside the chart to exit chart edit mode, click on the Report Design toolbar, then click the chart

   The final chart is shown in Figure L-19. It clearly shows that the Book Department has far more attendees at MediaLoft's internal training courses than any other department.

6. Click **File** on the menu bar, click **Save As**, type **Department Graph-Your Initials**, then click **OK**

7. Click the **Print button**, then close the Department Graph-Your Initials report

FIGURE L-16: Editing a chart in Design view

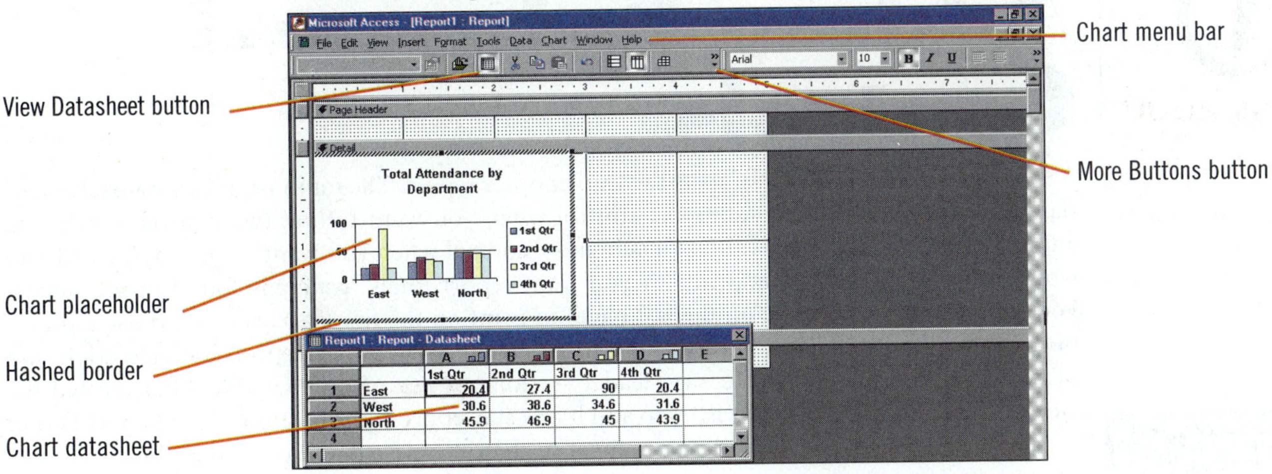

FIGURE L-17: Chart still needs improvement

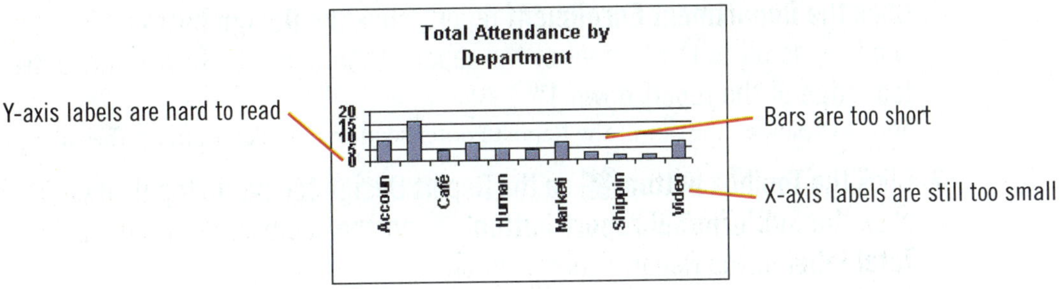

FIGURE L-18: Increasing the chart size

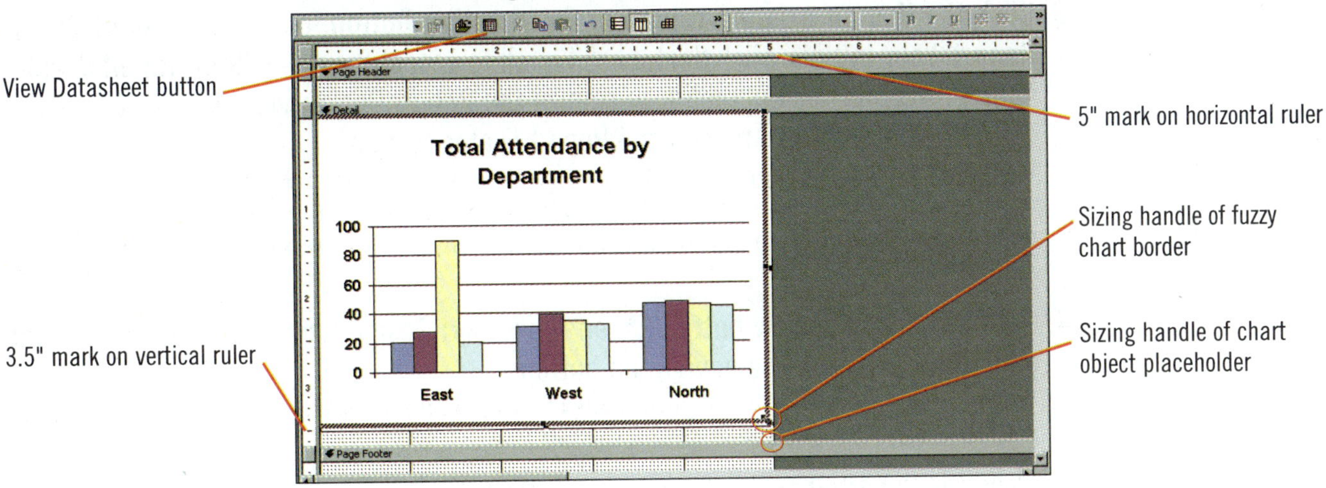

FIGURE L-19: Final chart

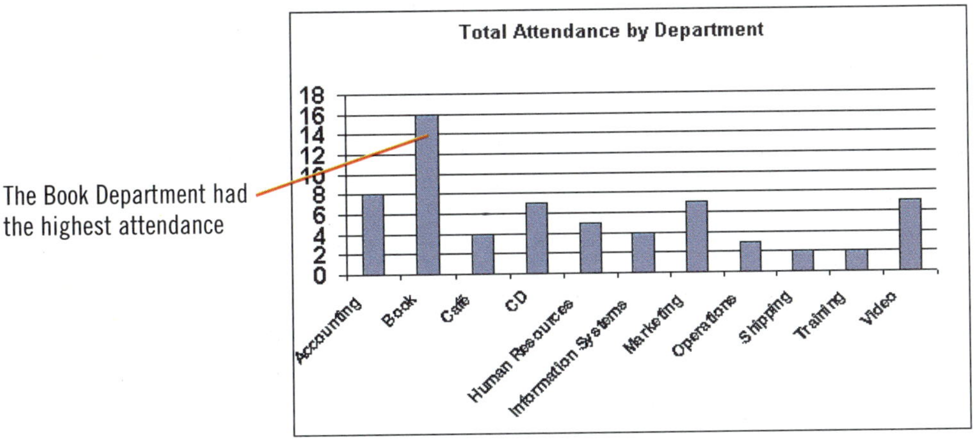

Unit L

Access 2000

Adding Subreport Controls

A **subreport control** displays a report within another report. The **main report** contains the subreport control. You use the subreport control when you want to link two reports together to automate printing. You also can use a subreport control when you want to change the order in which information normally prints. If you want report totals (generally found in the Report Footer section, which prints on the last page) to print on the first page, you could use a subreport control that calculates report grand totals in the subreport's Report Footer section and place it in the main report's Report Header section. Now that David has created the Department Graph report, he wishes to add it as a subreport to the bottom of the Report Footer section of the Department Enrollment report so that it is viewed and printed at the same time.

Steps

1. Click the **Department Enrollment** report, click the **Design button** in the database window, scroll to the bottom of the report, then use the ✛ pointer to drag the bottom edge of the report down **1"**
   You've expanded the size of the Report Footer section to make room for the subreport control.
2. Click the **Toolbox button** on the Report Design toolbar to toggle it on (if necessary), click the **Subform/Subreport button** on the Toolbox, then click below the **Grand Total label** in the Report Footer section
   The SubReport Wizard opens, as shown in Figure L-20.
3. Click the **Use an existing report or form option button**, click **Department Graph Report-Your Initials**, click **Next**, click **Finish** to accept the name **Department Graph-Your Initials** for the subreport, maximize the Report Design view window (if necessary), then scroll down to view the Report Footer section
   The subreport control appears in Report Design view, as shown in Figure L-21, and expands the size of the report to accommodate the large control. You can modify a subreport's controls directly within the main report just as you can modify a subform's controls within a main form.
4. Click the **Print Preview button** on the Report Design toolbar, then click the **Last page button** on the navigation buttons
   Your screen should look like Figure L-22. The Report Footer section contains the subreport and, therefore, displays the graph on the last page.
5. Close the Department Enrollment report, then save the changes when prompted

FIGURE L-20: SubReport Wizard

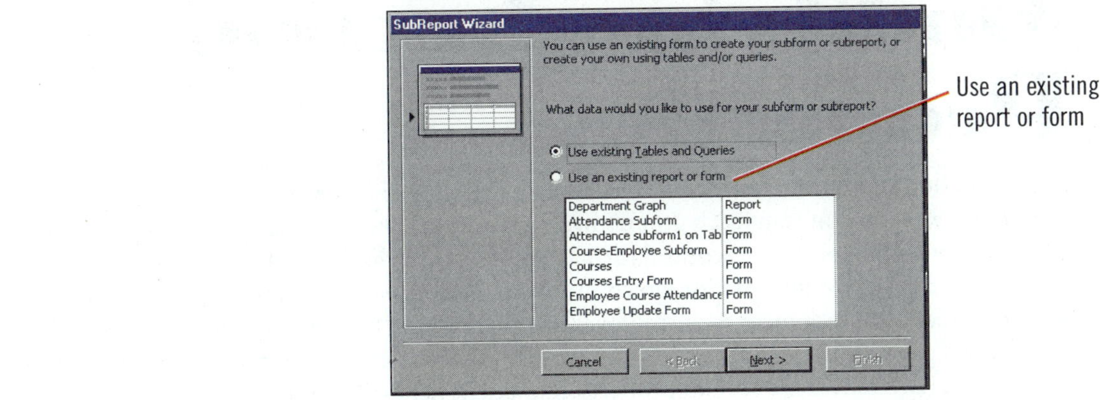

FIGURE L-21: Subreport in Report Design view

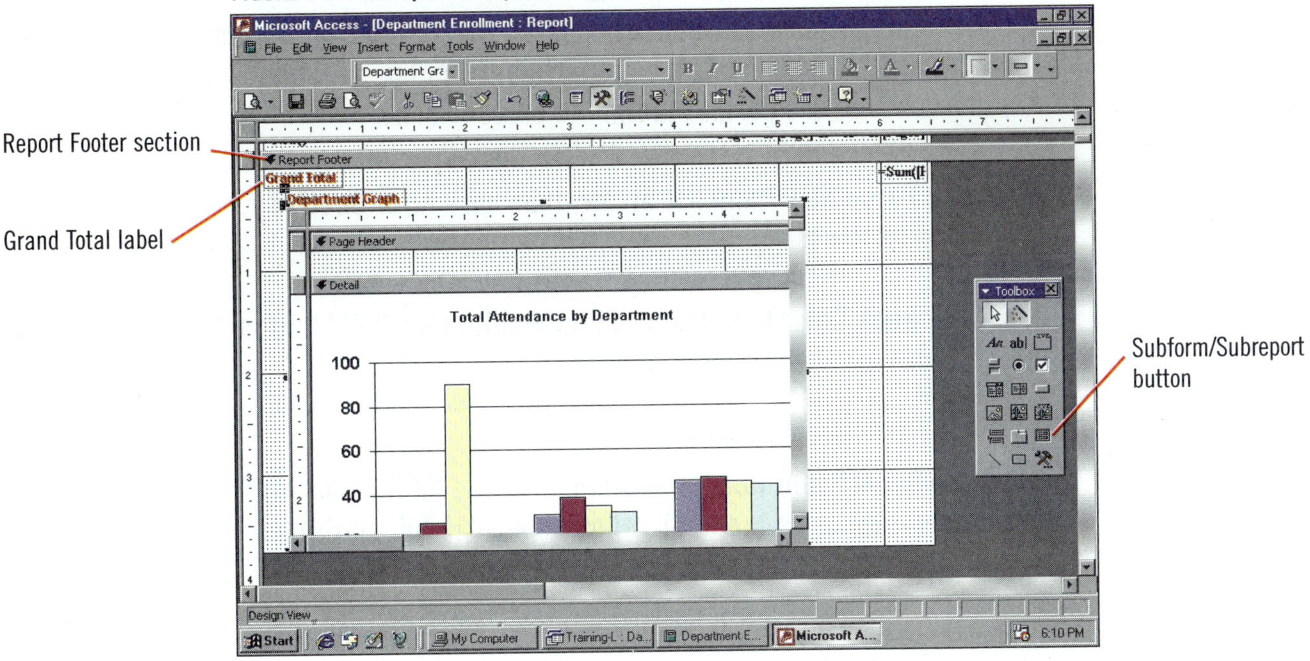

FIGURE L-22: Department graph displayed as a subreport

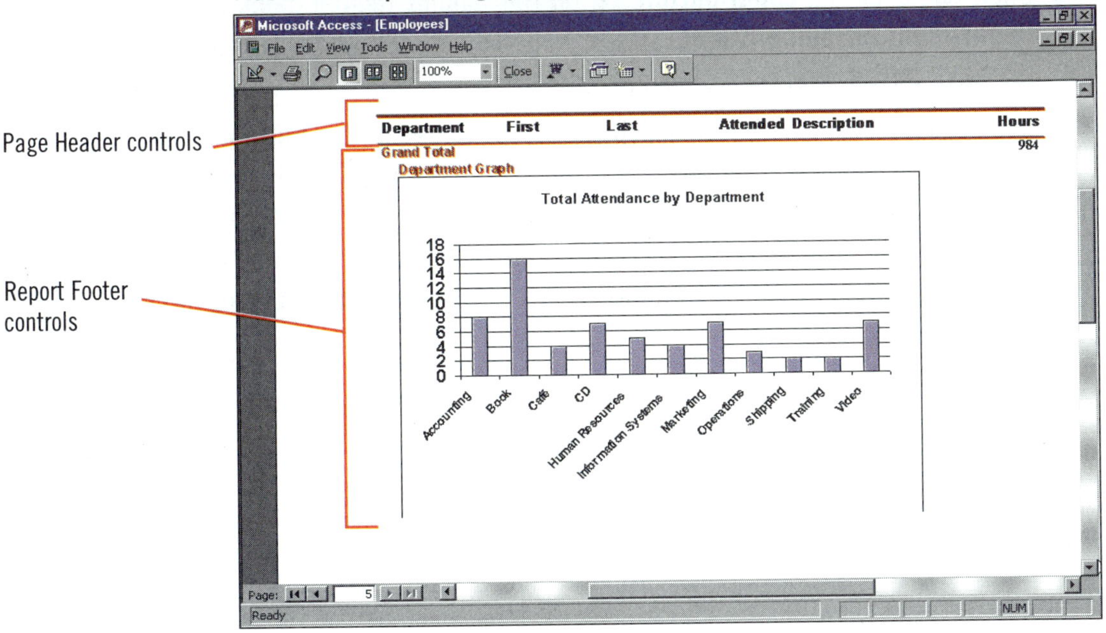

Access 2000

Unit L

Access 2000

Modifying Section Properties

Report **section properties** can be modified to help determine how the sections of the report print. For example, you might want each group's header section to always print at the top of a new page. Other report section properties control formatting issues such as the section's back color property. See Table L-3 for more information on common section properties. David doesn't want the Detail records (the courses each employee has attended) of the Department Enrollment report to span two pages. In addition, he'd like the records for each new department to start at the top of a new page. He makes these section property changes in Report Design view.

Steps

1. Click the **Department Enrollment report**, click the **Design button** in the database window, double-click the **Department Footer section** to open its property sheet, then click the **Format tab** in the property sheet
   The property sheet for the Department Header section opens, as shown in Figure L-23.
2. Click the **Force New Page list arrow**, then click **After Section**
   This property change will force the report to continue at the top of the next page after the Group Footer prints.
3. Click the **Back Color text box**, click the **Back Color Build button**, click the **light yellow box** (second column on the top row), then click **OK**
   Now the entire section will appear with a light yellow background color in print preview, and on the printout if a color printer is used.
4. Click the **Department Header section**, click the **Back Color text box** in the property sheet, click , click the **light yellow box**, click **OK**, close the property sheet, click the **Print Preview button**, then Zoom Out
   Your screen should look like Figure L-24. By modifying section properties, you have clarified where the group starts and stops by shading those sections, and have forced a page break at the end of each Group Footer.
5. Click , click the **Label button** on the Toolbox toolbar, click to the right of the **Department Enrollment label** in the Report Header section, type **Your Name**, click the **Save button**, then click
6. Click **File** on the menu bar, click **Print**, click the **Pages option button** in the Print Range section, type **1** in the From text box, click the **To text box**, type **1**, then click **OK**
   The first page of the Department Enrollment report showing the section shading is sent to the printer.
7. Close the **Department Enrollment** report, close **MediaLoft-L database**, then exit **Access**

FIGURE L-23: Using Section Properties

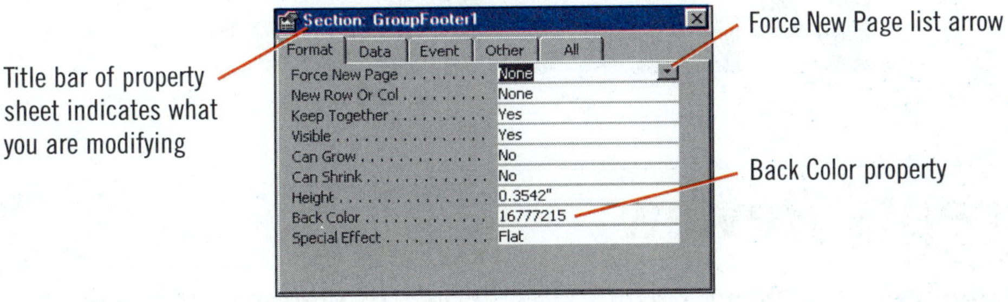

FIGURE L-24: Using Section Colors

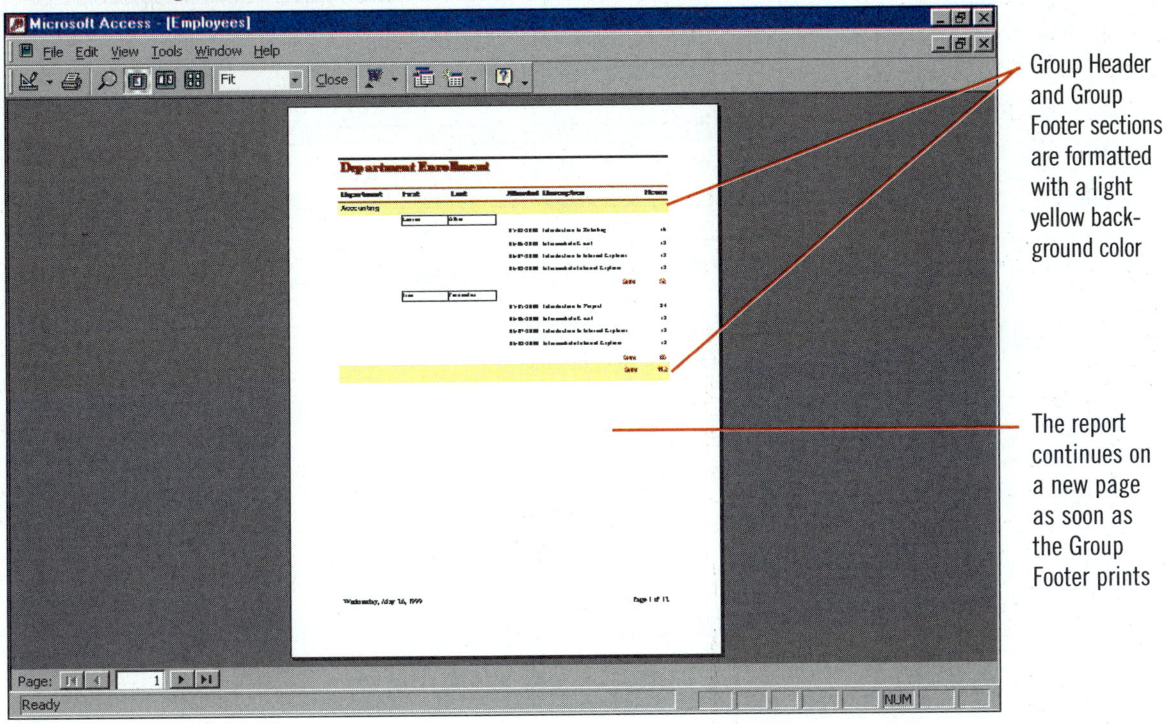

TABLE L-3: Common report section properties

property	options	description
Force New Page	None (default) Before Section After Section Before and After	Determines whether a section starts on the current page or a new page, or whether a new page starts after the section
New Row or Col	None (default) Before Section After Section Before and After	Often used to specify that a Group Header prints at the top of a new column in a multiple-column report
Visible	Yes (default) No	Determines whether the section is visible in Print Preview
Keep Together	Yes (default) No	Determines whether the records in that section must print on the same page or whether they can span multiple pages
Back Color	Number that corresponds to a color	Controls the color of the background of that section

Access 2000

Practice

► Concepts Review

Identify each element of a form's Design view shown in Figure L-25.

FIGURE L-25

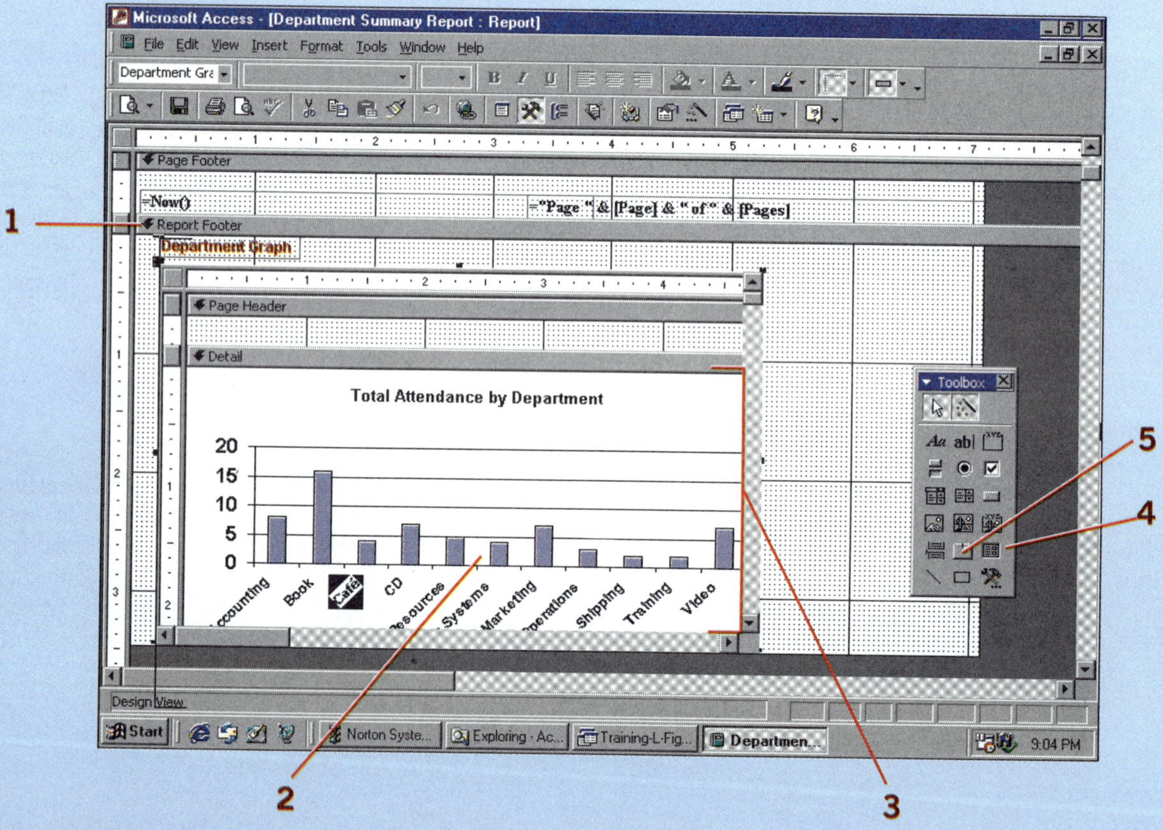

Match each term with the statement that describes its function.

6. Focus
7. Tab control
8. Sections
9. Conditional formatting
10. Charts
11. Check box

a. Allows you to change the appearance of a control on a form or report based on criteria you specify
b. Visual representations of numeric data
c. The ability to receive user input through the keyboard or mouse
d. Determine where and how controls print on a report
e. A control that is often used to display Yes/No fields on a form
f. An unbound control used to organize a form and give it a three-dimensional look

Select the best answer from the list of choices.

12. Which controls are NOT interchangeable?
- **a.** Text box and combo box
- **b.** Combo box and list box
- **c.** Check box and toggle button
- **d.** Check box and option group

13. When would you most likely use a toggle button control?
- **a.** For a field with a limited set of choices
- **b.** For a field with only two choices: Yes or No
- **c.** In place of a command button
- **d.** In place of an unbound label

14. You would most likely use which control for a City field?
- **a.** List box
- **b.** Combo box
- **c.** Check box
- **d.** Command button

15. To display text that pops up over a control when you point to it, you would modify which control property?
- **a.** ControlTip Text
- **b.** Status Bar Text
- **c.** Popup Text
- **d.** Help Text

16. Which type of chart would you most likely use to show an upward sales trend over several months?
- **a.** Pie
- **b.** Column
- **c.** Scatter
- **d.** Line

17. Which type of control would you use to display report totals as the first page of a report?
- **a.** Report Footer
- **b.** Subreport
- **c.** Calculated Properties
- **d.** Main Report

Skills Review

1. Adding Check Boxes and Toggle Buttons.
- **a.** Start Access and open the Seminar-L database from your Project Disk.
- **b.** Open the Attendees form in Form view, and check the EarlyBirdDiscount check box for the first record in the subform of the first person, Phuong Pham.
- **c.** Open Design view of the Attendees form. If the subform doesn't display the controls (but rather a white box), click the Form View button, then click Design view a second time in order to see the controls in the subform.

d. Change the Default View property of the subform to Continuous Forms. (*Hint*: Open the property sheet for the form in the subform control.)
e. Change the EarlyBirdDiscount check box into a toggle button.
f. Expand the subform's height about one inch, then expand the size of the EarlyBirdDiscount toggle button to the width of the subform.
g. Add the text "Click for Early Bird Discount" to the toggle button (either by typing directly on the button or by modifying the toggle button's Caption property).
h. Close the property sheet, then view the form in Form view. Expand the size of the subform control using Design View to clearly display three records in the subform when viewed in Form view.
i. Open the form in Form view, and click the toggle button to enter "Yes" in the EarlyBirdDiscount field for the second record in the subform for Phuong Pham.
j. Enter your own last name in place of "Pham" and print only this record.
k. Save and close the form.

2. Using Conditional Formatting.

a. Open the Attendees form in Design view.
b. Click the RegistrationDate text box, then press and hold [Shift] while clicking the RegistrationFee text box to select both controls in the Detail section of the subform. If you see a white box for the subform control, click the Form View button, then the Design View button to refresh the screen.
c. Click Format on the menu bar, click Conditional Formatting, set Condition 1 to Expression Is, then set the criteria to [RegistrationFee]>10
d. Format the Condition 1 for this expression so any values meeting the criteria display as bold, with a bright blue Font/Fore Color. Close the Conditional Formatting dialog box.
e. Save the changes.
f. Still in Design view, select both the AttendeeFirstName and AttendeeLastName text box controls in the Detail section of the main form.
g. Click Format on the menu bar, click Conditional Formatting, then set Condition 1 to Field Has Focus.
h. The Condition 1 format should be black text against a light blue Fill/Back color.
i. Display the form in Form view, then enter your own first name in place of "Phuong."
j. Change the Registration Fee to $11 for the first record in the subform, then tab through the record to make sure that both the RegistrationDate and RegistrationFee text boxes are conditionally formatted.
k. Save the form, print the first record, then close the form.

3. Creating Custom Help.

a. Open the Attendees form in Design view.
b. Open the property sheet for the EarlyBirdDiscount toggle button, then select the Other tab.
c. Enter the following as the ControlTip Text property: "To qualify, registration must be one month before the event." Use the Zoom dialog box if you wish.
d. Use the Zoom dialog box to enter the following as the Status Bar Text property: "Discounts can also be given for group registrations."
e. Close the property sheet, save the form, then open the form in Form view.
f. Point to the button for the third record in the subform to make sure that the ControlTip Text property works.
g. Point to, then click the command button for the third record in the subform to make sure that the Status Bar Text property works.
h. Close the Attendees form.

4. Adding Tab Controls.
- **a.** Open the Events form in Design view.
- **b.** Add a tab control under the Event Name label.
- **c.** Modify the Page5 Name property of the first tab to be "Event Info".
- **d.** Modify the Page6 Name property of the second tab to be "Participants".
- **e.** Open the Field List, then add the Location, Date, and AvailableSpaces fields from the Field List to the middle of the Event Info page.
- **f.** Add a subform to the Participants page, using the Subform Wizard to guide your actions. Click the Existing tables or queries option button. Select the RegistrationDate field from the Registration table, and the AttendeeFirstName and AttendeeLastName fields from the Attendees table.
- **g.** Link the main form to the subform by using the "Show Registration for each record in Events using EventID" option.
- **h.** Name the subform "Registration".
- **i.** Expand the height of the subform control to fill the page, then view the form in Form view.
- **j.** Click the Participants tab to make sure both tabs work correctly, then print the first record twice, once with the Event Info tab displayed and once with the Participants tab displayed.
- **k.** Save and close the Events form.

5. Adding Charts.
- **a.** Click Reports on the Objects bar, then click the New button in the database window.
- **b.** Click the Chart Wizard, choose Registration as the table or query where the object's data comes from, then click OK.
- **c.** Choose the EventID and RegistrationFee as the fields for the Chart.
- **d.** Choose a Column Chart type.
- **e.** Sum the RegistrationFee field in the Data area, and use the EventID field as the x-axis. (*Hint*: These should be the defaults, but click the Preview Chart button to make sure.)
- **f.** Title the chart "Registration Fee Totals-Your Initials".
- **g.** Print the chart, then save the report as "Registration Fee Totals".

6. Modifying Charts.
- **a.** Open Registration Fee Totals in Design view.
- **b.** Double-click the chart to edit it.
- **c.** Remove the legend, and increase the size of both the control and the chart within it to as large as will comfortably fit on your screen.
- **d.** Click any value in the y-axis to select it, choose Format on the menu bar, then click the Number option.
- **e.** Click the Number tab in the Format Axis dialog box, click the Currency category, change the Decimal places text box to 0, then click OK in the Format Axis dialog box.
- **f.** Click outside the chart object to return to Report Design view, preview the report with the chart, print it, save the changes, then close the Registration Fee Totals report.

7. Adding Subreport Controls.
- **a.** Use the Report Wizard to create a report on all of the fields in the Events table.
- **b.** Do not add any grouping levels, but sort the records in ascending order by EventID.
- **c.** Use a Tabular layout, a Portrait orientation, and a Casual style.
- **d.** Title the report "Event Information".
- **e.** Open Event Information in Design view.
- **f.** Increase the size of the Report Footer section by about one inch.
- **g.** Add a subreport control to the upper-left part of the Report Footer section.

h. Use the SubReport Wizard to guide your actions in creating the subreport. Click the Registration Fee Totals report in the first dialog box, and accept the name "Registration Fee Totals" as the subreport's name in the second.
i. Preview the report, print it, then save and close the Event Information Report.

8. Modifying Section Properties.

a. Use the Report Wizard to create a report on all of the fields in the Registration table, and the EventName field in the Events table.
b. View the data by Events, but do not add any grouping levels or sorting fields.
c. Use an Outline 2 layout, a Landscape orientation, and a Compact style.
d. Title the report "Event Details".
e. Open Event Details in Design view, then open the property sheet for the Events_EventID Header section.
f. Change the Force New Page property on the Format tab to Before Section. Change the Back Color property to light blue. (*Hint*: Use the Build button to locate the color on the palette.)
g. Close the property sheet, add your name as a label in the Report Header section, preview the report, then print the first two pages.
h. Save and close the Event Details report.
i. Close Seminar-L and exit Access.

Independent Challenges

1. As the manager of a college women's basketball team, you wish to enhance the forms within the Basketball-L database. To complete this independent challenge:

a. Start Access and open the database Basketball-L from your Project Disk.
b. Click the Forms button on the Object bar, then double-click the Create form by using wizard option.
c. Choose all of the fields in the Players table.
d. Use a Columnar layout, a Standard style, and title the form "Player Information."
e. Maximize the Player Information form, open it in Design view, then change the Lettered? check box into a toggle button with the text "Click if earned a varsity letter".
f. Resize the toggle button so that it is as wide as the form and clearly displays the text.
g. Open the toggle button's property sheet and add the following ControlTip Text property: "Must have 200 minutes of playing time to letter".
h. In the toggle button's property sheet, add the following Status Bar Text property: "For the year 2000".
i. Close the property sheet, display the form in Form view, enter your own last name in the first record, then click the toggle button to indicate you've earned a varsity letter.
j. Print the first record, save the form, then close the Player Information form and the Basketball-L database.
k. Exit Access.

2. As the manager of a college women's basketball team, you wish to enhance the forms within the Basketball-L database. To complete this independent challenge:

a. Start Access and open the database Basketball-L from your Project Disk.
b. Open the Player Statistics form in Design view.
c. Add a tab control just below the Last label.
d. Modify the Page5 Name property of the first tab to be "Player Background".
e. Modify the Page6 Name property of the second tab to be "Statistics".

f. Add the Height, PlayerNo, Year, Position, HomeTown, and HomeState fields from the Field List to the middle of the Player Background page.
g. Add a subform to the Statistics page based on all the fields from the Stats table.
h. Link the main form to the subform by using the "Show Stats for each record in Players using PlayerNo" option.
i. Name the subform "Stats subform".
j. Expand the height of the subform control to fill the page, then view the form in Form view.
k. Click the Participants tab to make sure both tabs work correctly, then print the first record.
l. Save and close the Player Statistics form.
m. Close the Basketball-L database, then exit Access.

3. As the manager of a college women's basketball team, you wish to create a chart from the Basketball-L database to summarize three-point goals.

To complete this independent challenge:

a. Start Access and open the Basketball-L database from your Project Disk.
b. Click the Reports button on the Objects bar, click the New button in the database window, click Chart Wizard, then choose the Stats table.
c. Choose the PlayerNo, 3P (three pointers), and 3PA (three pointers attempted) fields for the chart.
d. Choose a Column Chart.
e. Drag the 3PA field to the Data area of the chart so that both the SumOf3P and SumOf3PA fields are in the Data area, and the PlayerNo field is in the Axis area of the chart.
f. Title the chart "3 Pointers – Your Initials".
g. Print the chart, then close and save the report as "3 Pointers".
h. Close the Basketball-L database, then exit Access.

WEB WORK

4. MediaLoft has developed a Web site that provides internal information to its employees. In this independent challenge, you'll surf the Internet to find Web pages that present information organized similarly to how tab controls are used on Access forms.

a. Connect to the Internet, go to the MediaLoft intranet site at http://www.course.com/illustrated/MediaLoft
b. Click the link for Research, click the link for Competition: Other Bookstores, and browse for a Web page that organizes information on "pages" accessed by clicking "tabs" in a manner similar to how tab controls are used within Access forms.
c. If you are not familiar with Web browsing techniques, click the Back button until you return to the MediaLoft Research page, where you can start a new search.
d. When you find a Web page that contains "tab-like" controls to organize information, print the Web page and circle the tab controls.
e. Close your browser window, then disconnect from the Internet.

▶ Visual Workshop

As the manager of a college women's basketball team, you wish to create a form that highlights outstanding statistics if either their scoring or their rebounding totals are equal to or greater than 10 for an individual game effort. Start Access and open the Basketball-L database. Open the Players form in Design view, and use the conditional formatting feature to format the FG (field goals), 3P (three-point shots), and FT (free throws) text boxes in the Stats Subform1 to have a bright yellow background if the following expression that totals their scoring for that game is true: 2*[FG]+3*[3P]+[FT]>=10. Conditionally format the Reb-O (offensive rebounds) and Reb-D (defensive rebounds) text boxes to be have a light blue background if the following expression that totals rebounds is true: [Reb-O]+[Reb-D]>=10. Display the second record for Ellyse Howard, which should look like Figure L-26. Print the form.

FIGURE L-26

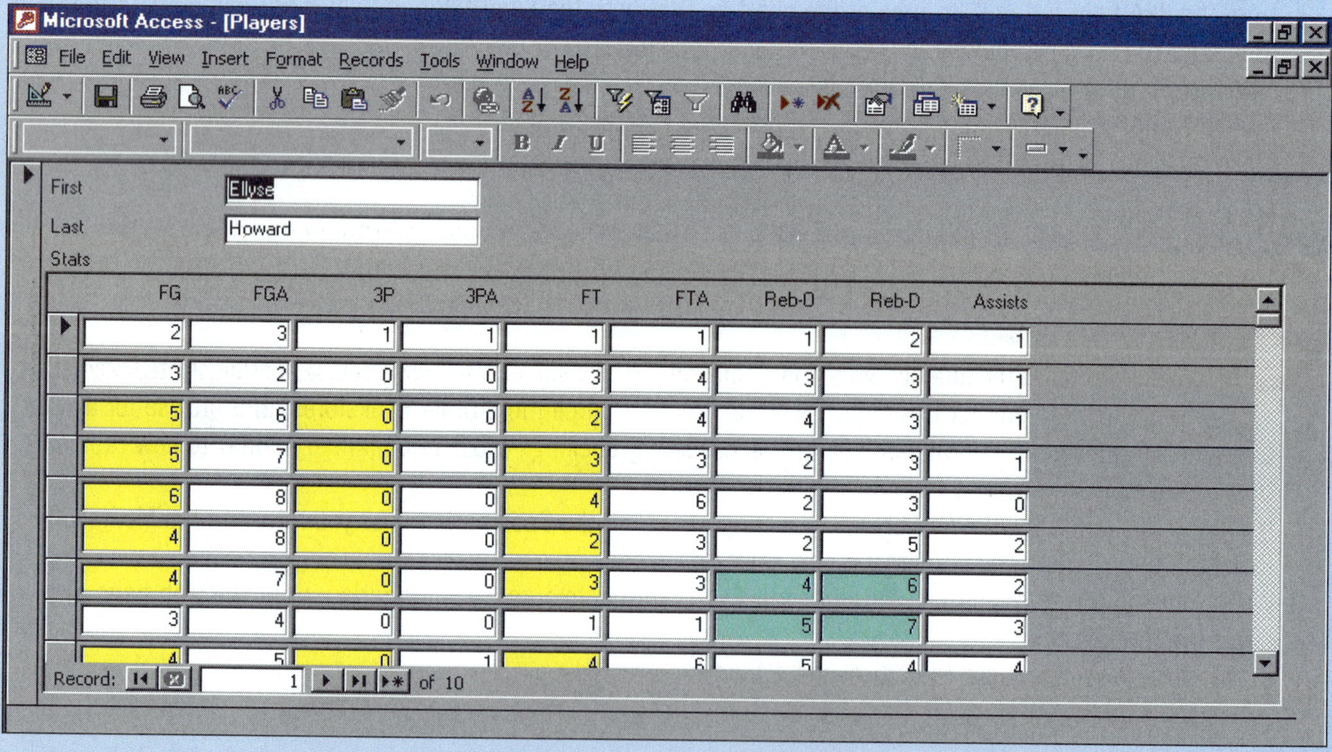

Access 2000

Unit M

Managing
Database Objects

Objectives

- Work with Objects
- MOUS Use the Documenter
- Group Objects
- Modify Groups
- Create a Dialog Box
- Create a Pop-up Form
- MOUS Create a Switchboard
- Modify a Switchboard

As your database grows in size and functionality, the number of objects (especially queries and reports) will grow as well. Your ability to find, rename, delete, and document objects as well as your proficiency to present objects in an organized way to other database users through groups and switchboards will become important skills. Kristen Fontanelle is the network administrator at MediaLoft headquarters. She has developed a working database to document MediaLoft computer equipment in use throughout the company. The large quantity of objects within the database makes it increasingly difficult to find and organize information. Kristen will use powerful Access documentation, object grouping, and switchboard features to manage the growing database.

Unit M
Access 2000

Working with Objects

Working with Access objects is very similar to working with files in Windows Explorer. For example, the **View buttons** (Large Icons, Small Icons, List, and Details) on the database window toolbar can be used to arrange the objects in four different ways just as files can be arranged within Explorer. Similarly, you right-click an object within Access to open, copy, delete, or rename it just as you would right-click a file within Explorer. Kristen wants to work with several objects to improve the database window interface. She deletes, renames, sorts, and adds descriptions to several objects.

Steps

1. Start Access, open the **Technology-M database** on your Project Disk, maximize the database window, click **Queries** on the Objects bar, then click the **Details button** on the database window toolbar

   Your screen should look like Figure M-1, with five columns of information for each object: Name, Description, Modified (date the object was last changed), Created (date the object was originally created), and Type. By default, objects are sorted in ascending order by name, and the Description column is blank.

2. Click the **Modified column heading** to sort the objects in ascending order on the date they were last modified, click **Modified column heading** again to sort the objects in descending order on the date they were last modified, then click the **Name column heading**

   The query objects are now sorted in ascending order by name. The Description column is a special object property that is used to further describe the object.

QuickTip

Point to the line between column headings, then drag ↔ left or right to resize that column.

3. Right-click the **Equipment Specs query**, then click **Properties**

   The Equipment Specs Properties dialog box opens, as shown in Figure M-2.

4. Type **Includes RAM, hard drive, and processor information for PCs**, then click **OK**

   Part of the description appears in the database window and helps describe the object. If an object is no longer needed, you should delete it to free up disk space and keep the database window organized.

5. Right-click the **Employees Query**, click **Delete**, then click **Yes** when prompted

   Even though object names can be 64 characters long and can include any combination of letters, numbers, spaces, and special characters except a period (.), exclamation point (!), accent (`), or brackets ([]), they should be kept short yet descriptive. Short names make them easier to reference in other places in the database such as in the Record Source property for a report.

6. Right-click the **Human Resources query**, click **Rename**, type **HR**, press **[Enter]**, right-click the **Information Systems query**, click **Rename**, type **IS**, then press **[Enter]**

   Your final screen should look like Figure M-3. With shorter query names, all of the object names are visible in the database window without resizing the columns.

FIGURE M-1: Viewing object details

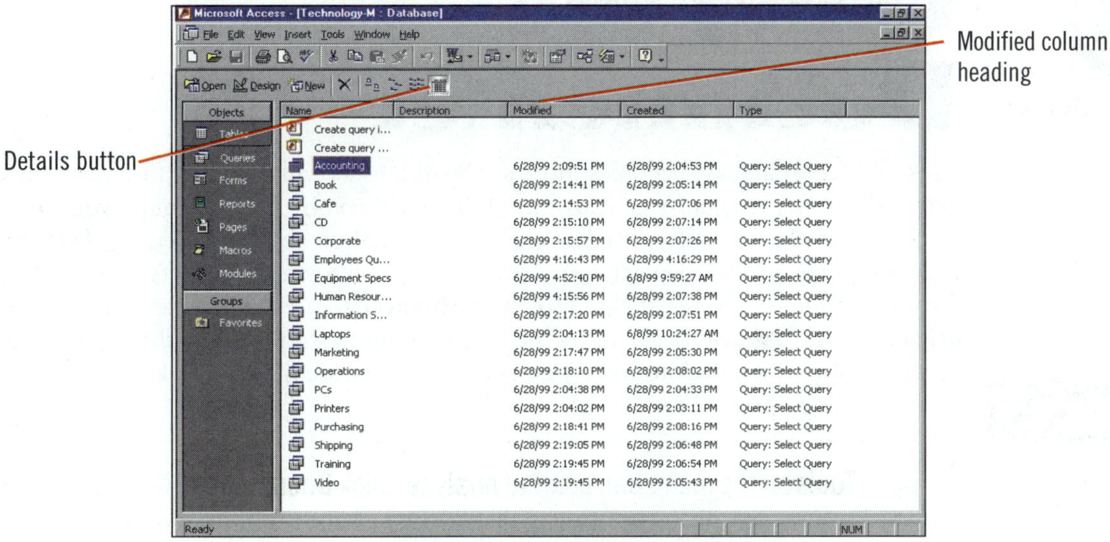

FIGURE M-2: Equipment Specs Properties dialog box

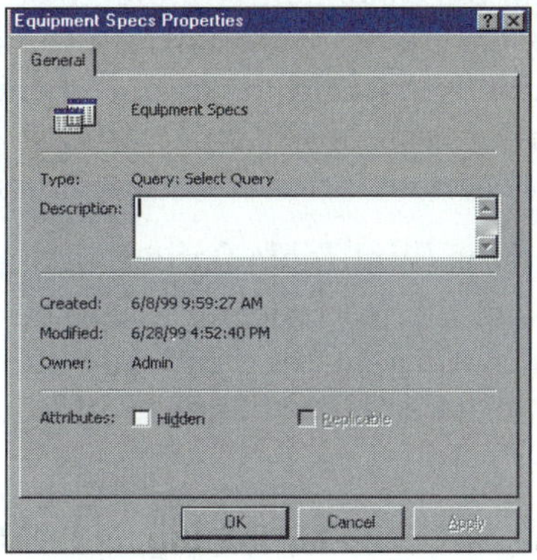

FIGURE M-3: Final Query object window

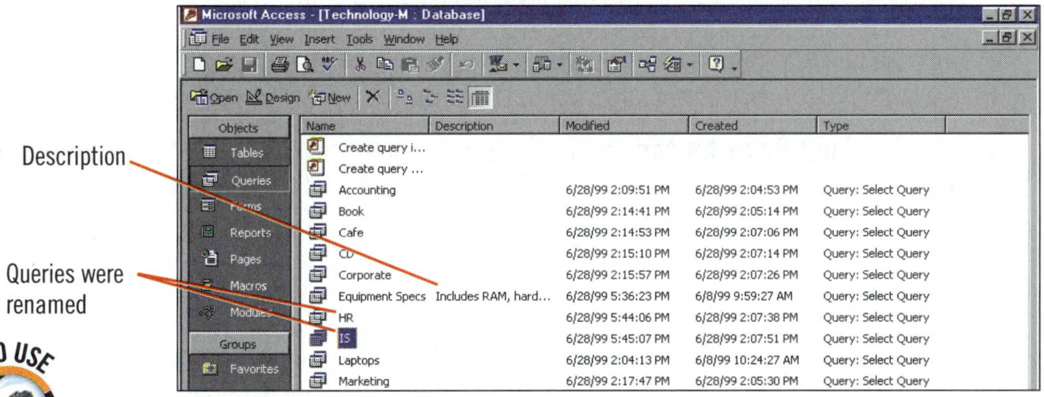

Clues to Use

Updating names with Name AutoCorrect

Name AutoCorrect fixes discrepancies between references to field names, controls, and objects when you rename them. For example, if a report is based on a query named "Department Income," and the query name is changed to "Dept Inc," the Name AutoCorrect feature will automatically update the Record Source property for the report to "Dept Inc." Similarly, if a query includes a field name of "LastName" that changes to "LName" in the Design view of the original table, the Name AutoCorrect feature will update the field name reference within the query as well. Name AutoCorrect will not repair references in Visual Basic code, replicated databases, linked tables, or a number of other database situations. Click Tools on the menu bar in the database window, click Options, and then click the General tab to view the Name AutoCorrect options. By default, the first two of the three Name AutoCorrect options should be checked.

Unit M

Access 2000

Using the Documenter

As your Access database becomes more successful, users will naturally find new ways to use the data. Your ability to modify an existing database will revolve largely around your understanding of existing database objects. Access provides an analysis feature called the **Documenter** that creates reports on the properties and relationships between the objects in your database. This documentation is especially helpful to those who need to use the database but did not design the original tables. Kristen uses the Documenter to start creating the paper documentation that will support the Technology-M database for other MediaLoft employees.

Steps

1. Click **Tools** on the menu bar, point to **Analyze**, click **Documenter**, then click the **Tables tab**
   The Documenter dialog box opens, displaying tabs for the object types.
2. Click **Options** in the Documenter dialog box
   The Print Table Definition dialog box, shown in Figure M-4, opens. This dialog box gives you some control over what type of documentation you wish to print for the table. The documentation for each object type varies slightly. For example, the documentation on forms and reports would include information on controls and sections.
3. Click **Cancel** in the Print Table Definition dialog box
   You work through the Documenter dialog box, deciding which objects and options you want to document. Clicking the Select All button is a fast way to select all of the objects on that tab. You can also select or deselect individual objects by clicking the check box beside their name.
4. Click **Select All**, click the **Forms tab**, click **Select All**, then click **OK**
   Documenter is now creating a report about all of the table and form objects in the Technology-M database, and will display it as an Access report. This can be a lengthy process (several minutes) depending on the speed of your computer and the number of objects that Documenter is examining. When completed, your screen will look like Figure M-5, which shows a report that displays information about the first table, Assignments, on the first page.
5. Click the **Last Page button** in the navigation buttons, click the **Previous Page button**, then scroll down so that your screen looks like Figure M-6
   The report contains about three pages of documentation for each table, and about six pages per form. The properties for each control on the form are listed in two columns. Because most form controls have approximately 50 properties, you can quickly see why the documentation that lists each control and section property can become so large. You can print or send the report to a Word document using the OfficeLinks buttons, but you cannot work in the report's Design view or save the report as an object within the database window.
6. Click the **Close button** on the Print Preview toolbar

QuickTip

Information about the progress of Documenter will appear in the status bar.

FIGURE M-4: Print Table Definition dialog box

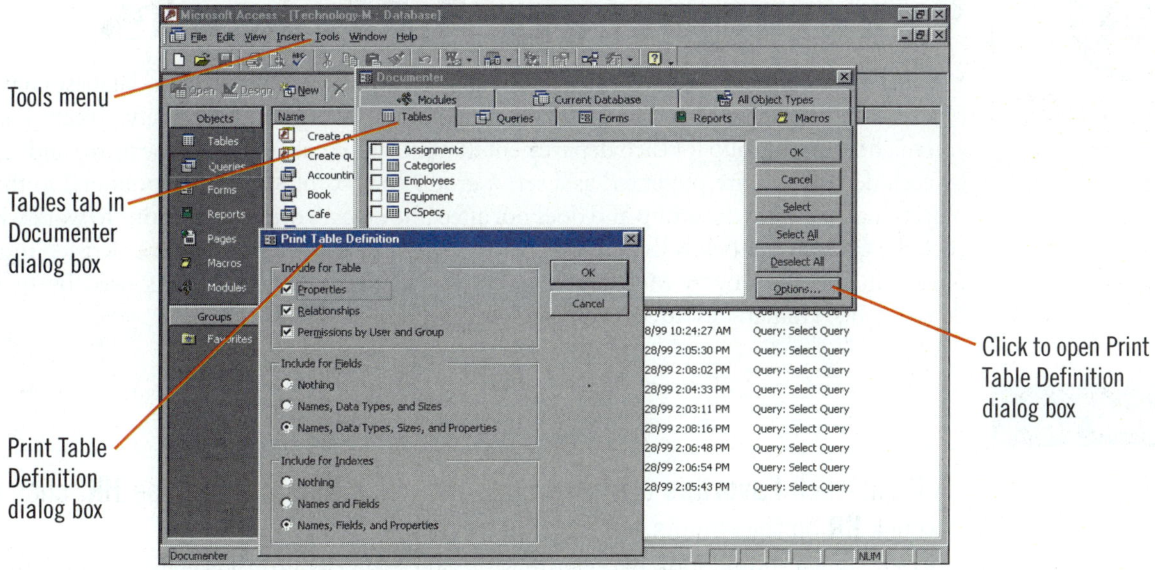

FIGURE M-5: First page of documentation

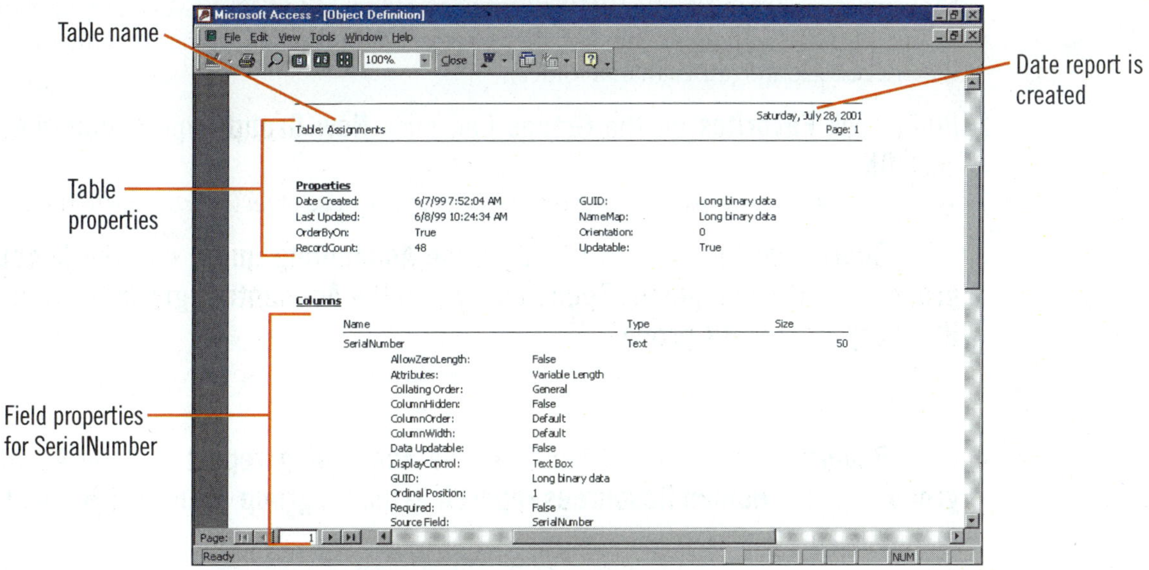

FIGURE M-6: Second to last page of documentation

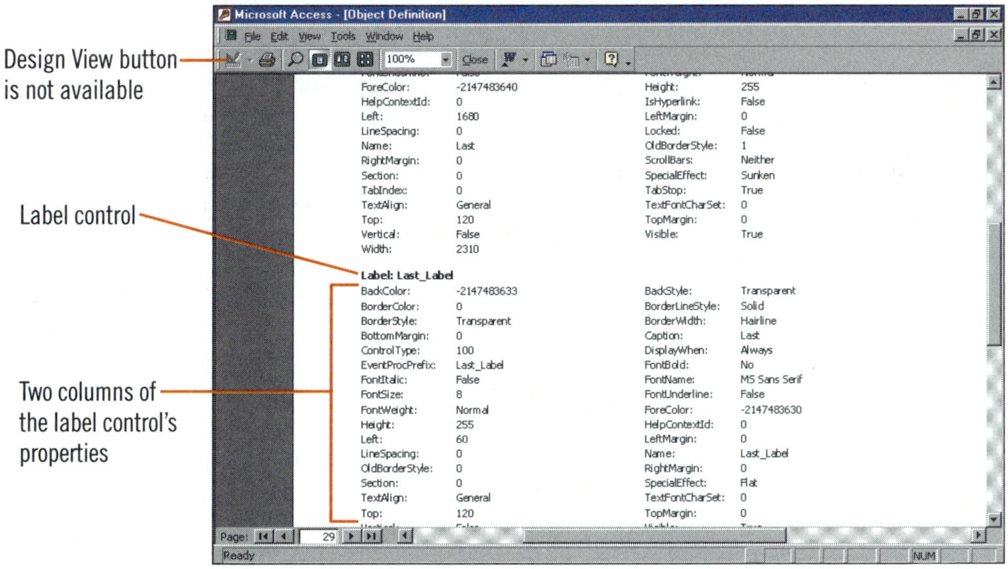

Unit M

Access 2000

Grouping Objects

Viewing every object in the database window can be cumbersome when your database contains many objects. Objects can be placed in **groups** to help you easily organize or classify objects. For example, you might create a group for each department that uses the database so that the forms and reports used by each department are presented as a set. A group consists of **shortcuts** (pointers) to the database objects that belong to the group and does not affect the object's original location. To work with groups, click the **Groups bar** below the Objects bar in the Database window. Kristen organizes the objects in the Technology-M database by creating groups for the objects used by two different departments: Human Resources (HR) and Accounting.

Steps

1. Right-click **Favorites** on the Groups bar, click **New Group**, type **HR**, click **OK**, then click **HR** on the Groups bar

   Your screen should look like Figure M-7. Since the HR group was just created, there are no objects referenced in that group. The Favorites group is provided for every new Access database and is similar in function to the Favorites folder used in other Microsoft applications. Within an Access database, the Favorites group organizes *objects* rather than files because it is an Access group (rather than a folder).

2. Right-click **Favorites** on the Groups bar, click **New Group**, type **Accounting**, then click **OK**

   With the two new groups in place, you are ready to organize objects according to these groups.

3. Click **Queries** on the Objects bar, drag the **Accounting query** into the **Accounting group**, drag the **Equipment Specs query** into the **Accounting group**, then drag the **HR query** into the **HR group**

   Shortcuts to these three queries have been placed in their respective groups; the original objects do not move.

4. Click **Reports** on the Objects bar, drag the **Accounting report** into the **Accounting group**, drag the **Human Resources report** into the **HR group**, then click **Accounting** on the Groups bar

   Your screen should look like Figure M-8, with three shortcut icons representing two queries and one report in the Accounting group. Because both an original query and a report object were named "Accounting," Access added a "1" to the second "Accounting" shortcut icon. These shortcuts are just pointers to the original objects and, therefore, do not change the name of the original object. You can open or design an object by clicking its shortcut icon. You also can drag an object to more than one group, thereby creating more than one shortcut to it.

5. Click **Groups** on the Groups bar

   Clicking Groups expands the Groups bar and collapses the Objects bar, as shown in Figure M-9.

6. Click **Groups** on the Groups bar

   Clicking Groups when it is expanded collapses the Groups bar. The Objects bar works in the same way.

7. Place the pointer on the top edge of **Groups**, and drag up with the ÷ mouse pointer to just below **Modules** on the Objects bar

   Displaying all of the Objects and all of the Groups is a good way to arrange the Objects and Groups bars when you start a new Access database.

FIGURE M-7: Creating groups

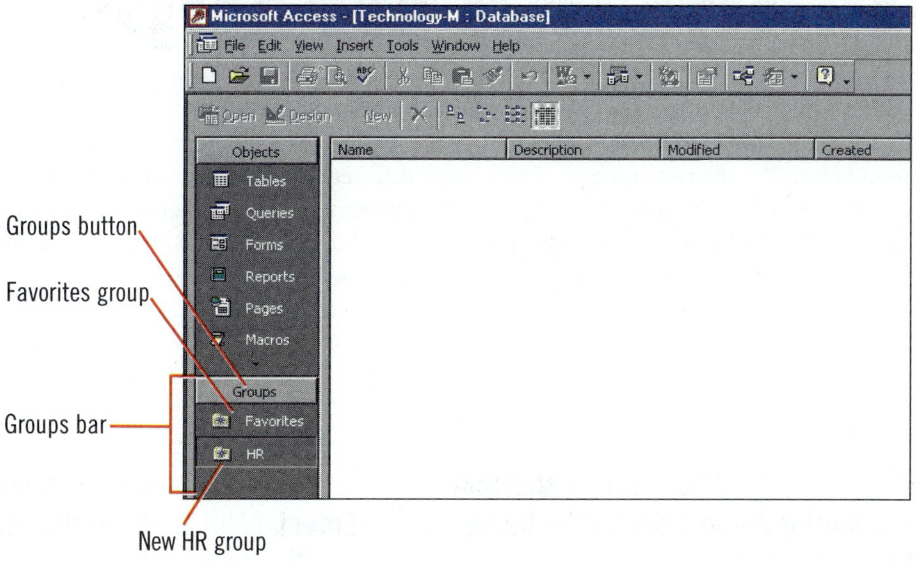

FIGURE M-8: Dragging objects to groups

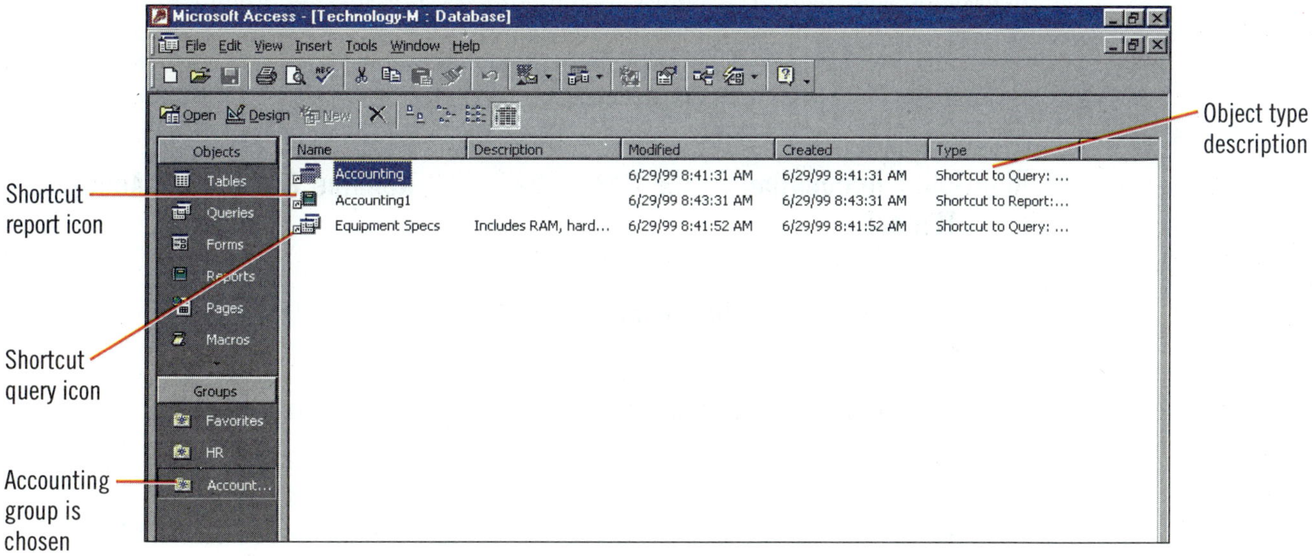

FIGURE M-9: Expanding groups

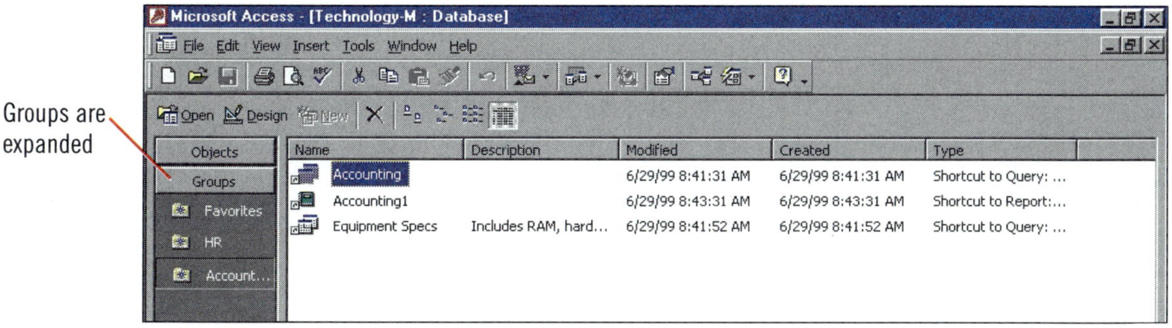

Unit M

Access 2000

Modifying Groups

Once groups are created and object shortcuts are added to them, you modify the shortcuts in each group similarly to how you work with the actual objects themselves. For example, you can delete, rename, copy, or print a shortcut by right-clicking it and choosing the appropriate command from the short-cut menu. The biggest difference between working with shortcuts and actual objects is that if you delete a shortcut, you do not permanently delete the object. Groups also can be renamed and deleted. Kristen modifies both the groups and the shortcuts within them to clarify the Technology-M database.

Steps

1. Right-click the **Accounting1 shortcut** in the Accounting group, click **Rename**, type **Accounting Report Sorted by Name**, press **[Enter]**, point to the **right edge of the Name column** so that the pointer changes to ✛, then double-click the column separator

   The Name column resizes to display the full shortcut name. A shortcut name does not have to have the same name as the object that it points to, but, it is important that the shortcuts be clearly named. The shortcut icon to the left of the shortcut indicates the type of object it represents. See Tables M-1 and M-2 for information about a popular object and field type naming convention developed by the Kwery Corporation, called the Leszynski Naming Convention.

2. Right-click **Accounting** on the Groups bar, click **Rename Group**, type **Acctg**, then press **[Enter]**

   The Groups bar should look like Figure M-10.

3. Right-click **Acctg**, click **New Group**, type **IS** in the New Group dialog box, then press **[Enter]**

4. Drag the **Equipment Specs shortcut** from the Acctg group to the IS group

   Shortcuts to the same object can be found in multiple groups. They can have the same or different names within each group.

5. Click **IS** on the Groups bar, double-click the **Equipment Specs shortcut** in the IS group to open the query's datasheet, double-click **32** in the Memory field for the second record (SerialNo RT55XLQ5), type **64**, then close the datasheet

   Edits and entries made to data in this query's datasheet (whether you opened the datasheet from the original query object or from a shortcut) are stored in the original table object.

6. Click **Tables** on the Objects bar, double-click the **PCSpecs table** to open its datasheet, then click the **Sort Descending button** on the Table Datasheet toolbar

   The records are sorted in descending order on SerialNo, as shown in Figure M-11. Note that the entry for the Memory field for SerialNo RT55XLQ5 is 64.

7. Close the PCSpecs datasheet without saving changes

FIGURE M-10: Modifying groups

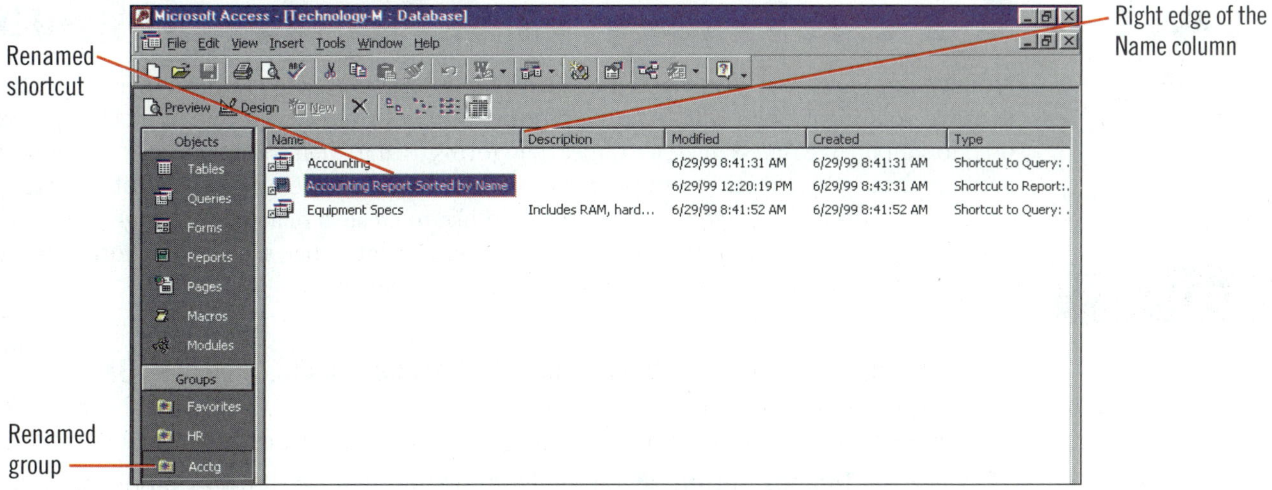

FIGURE M-11: A change made through a shortcut

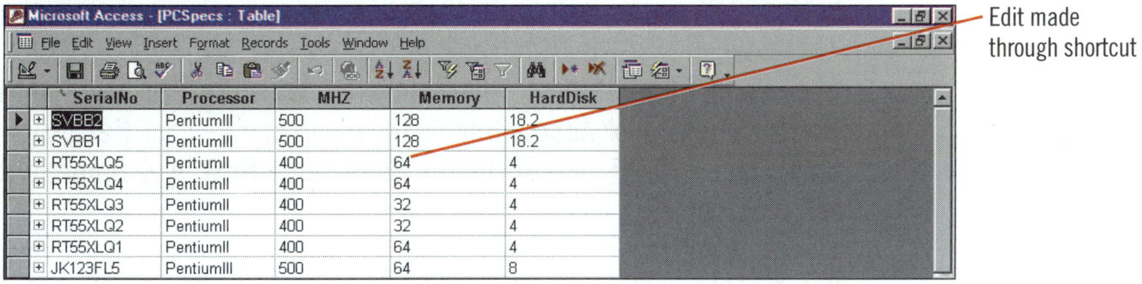

TABLE M-1: Leszynski Naming Convention for objects

object	tag	example
Table	tbl	TblEmployees
Form	frm	FrmEmployeeEntry
Query	qry	qryIncome2000
Report	rpt	rptAccount1Qtr
Macro	mcr	McrHRToolbar

TABLE M-2: Leszynski Naming Convention for data types

field data type	tag	example
Currency	cur	CurRetail
Date/Time	dtm	DtmSaleDate
Number (Integer)	int	IntDistrictNo
Number (Double)	dbl	DblMicrons
Number (Single)	sng	SngMillimeters
Memo	mem	MemComments
OLE Object	ole	OlePicture
Text	str	StrFName
Yes/No	ysn	YsnGoldClub

Unit M

Access 2000

Creating a Dialog Box

A **dialog box** is a special form that is used to display information or to prompt a user for a choice. For example, you might create a dialog box to prompt the user to select a report to print. Dialog boxes are used to simplify the Access interface rather than forms used in their traditional role (to support easy, accurate data entry). Special form properties such as **Border Style** and **Auto Center** make a form appear like a dialog box. Kristen would like to create a dialog box that gives access to the three reports that the Accounting Department regularly prints. Then she'll add a shortcut to the dialog box in the Accounting group to simplify the printing process.

Steps

1. Click **Forms** on the Objects bar, click the **New button**, then click **OK**
   A dialog box is not bound to an underlying table or query and doesn't use the form's Record Source property. A dialog box often contains command buttons to automate tasks.
2. Click the **Toolbox button** on the Form Design toolbar (if necessary), verify that the **Control Wizards button** is selected on the Toolbox, click the **Command Button button** on the Toolbox, then click in the upper-left corner of the form
   The **Command Button Wizard** dialog box opens.
3. Click **Report Operations** in the Categories list, click **Preview Report** in the Actions list, click **Next**, click **Accounting** as the report choice, click **Next**, click the **Text option button**, press **[Tab]**, type **Sorted by Name**, click **Next**, type **Name** in the button name text box, then click **Finish**
   The command button appears in Form Design view, as shown in Figure M-12. The dialog box will contain two more buttons to preview the other two Accounting reports.
4. Click, click below the first command button, click **Report Operations** in the Categories list, click **Preview Report** in the Actions list, click **Next**, click **Accounting Manufacturer**, click **Next**, click the **Text option button**, press **[Tab]**, type **Sorted by Manufacturer**, click **Next**, type **Mfg**, then click **Finish**
5. Click, click below the second command button, click **Report Operations** in the Categories list, click **Preview Report** in the Actions list, click **Next**, click **Accounting MHz**, click **Next**, click the **Text option button**, press **[Tab]**, type **Sorted by Speed**, click **Next**, type **Speed**, then click **Finish**
   The Design view of the form should look like Figure M-13.
6. Double-click the **Form Selector button** to open the form's property sheet, click the **Format tab**, click the **Border Style text box**, click the **Border Style list arrow**, then click **Dialog**
   The **Dialog** option for the Border Style property indicates that the form will have a thick border and can include only a title bar, a close button, and a control menu button. The form cannot be maximized, minimized, or resized.
7. Click the **Navigation Buttons text box**, click the **Navigation Buttons list arrow**, click **No**, click the **Record Selectors text box**, click the **Record Selectors list arrow**, then click **No**
8. Close the property sheet, restore the form, resize the form to 3" wide by 3" tall, save the form as **Accounting Reports**, then click the **Form View button**
   Restoring and resizing the form best displays the property changes you made to the Border Style, Navigation Buttons, and Record Selectors properties as shown in Figure M-14.
9. Click the **Sorted by Speed command button**
   The report sorts the PCs in the Accounting Department in descending order by MHz (megahertz).
10. Close the **Accounting MHz report**, then close the **Accounting Reports form**

Trouble?

Every command button must be given a unique name that is referenced in underlying Visual Basic code. Deleting a command button from Design view does not delete the underlying code, so each new button name must be different, even if the button has been deleted.

FIGURE M-12: Adding a command button

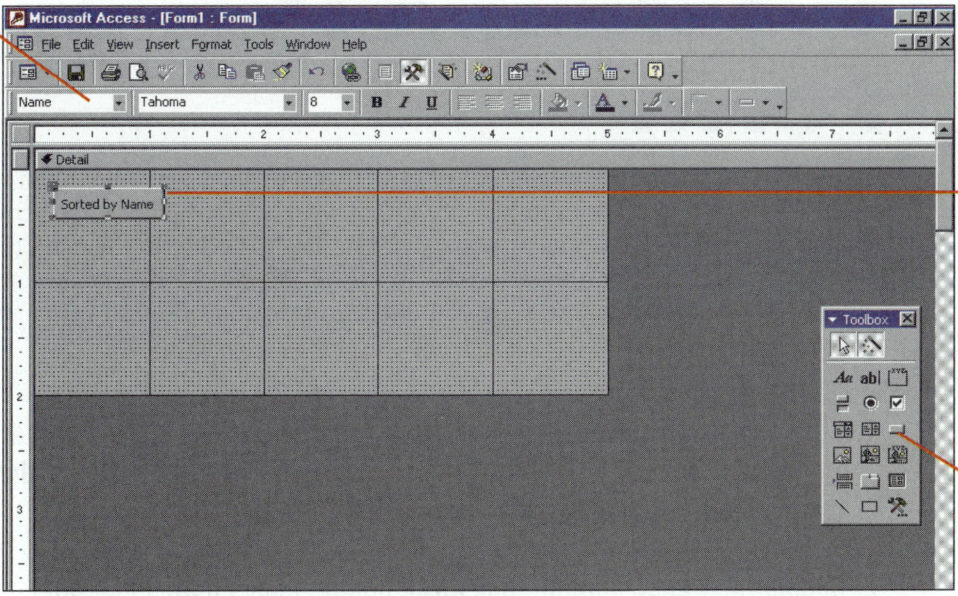

FIGURE M-13: The final dialog box in Form Design view

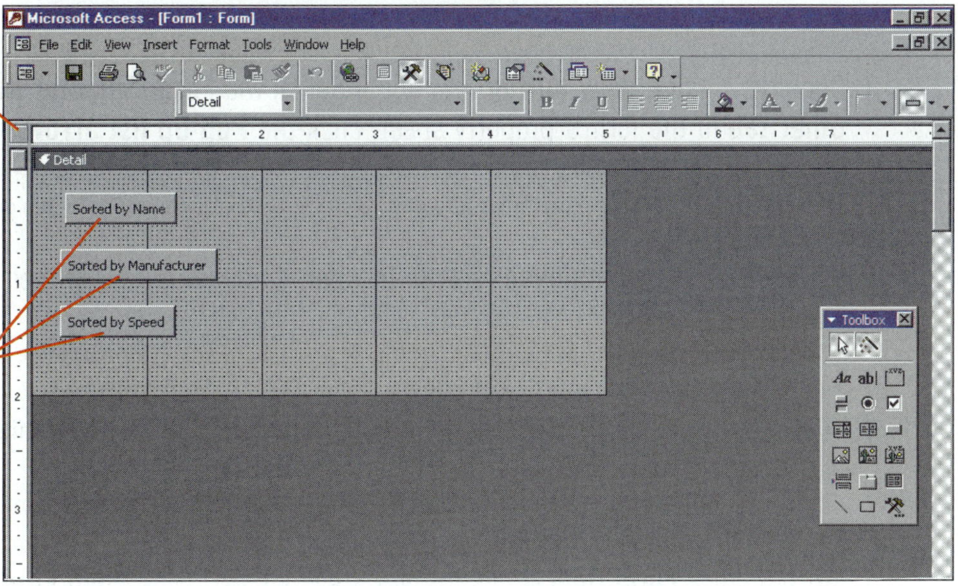

FIGURE M-14: The final dialog box in Form view

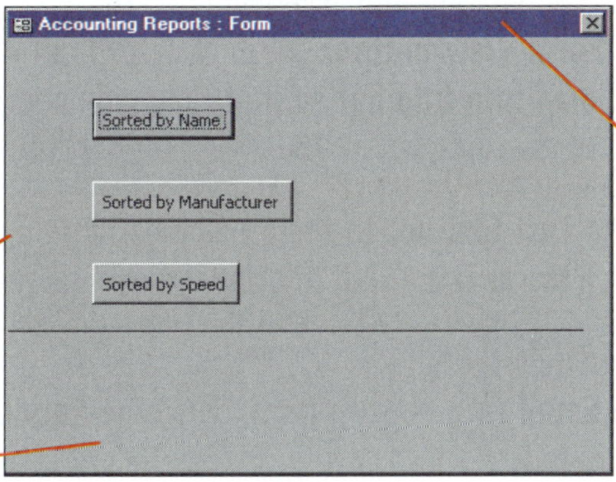

Access 2000

Unit M

Access 2000

Creating a Pop-up Form

A **pop-up form** is another special type of form that stays on top of other open forms, even when another form is active. For example, you might want to create a pop-up form to give the user detailed information about an employee that isn't always visible on the main form. A command button is usually used to open the pop-up form. Kristen creates a pop-up form to access employee e-mail information, and adds a command button on the Employees form to open the pop-up form.

Steps

1. Click **Forms** on the Objects bar, click the **New button** in the database window, click **Form Wizard**, click the **Choose the table or query where the object's data comes from list arrow**, click **Employees**, then click **OK**
   You need only three fields of information in the pop-up form.
2. Double-click **Last**, double-click **First**, double-click **Email**, click **Next**, click **Tabular** for the layout, click **Next**, click **Standard** for the style, click **Next**, type **Email Info** for the title of the form, then click **Finish**
   The Email Info form opens in Form view, as shown in Figure M-15. You can modify the form so that it behaves as a pop-up form in Form Design view.
3. Click the **Design View button**, double-click the **Form Selector button**, click the **Other tab** in the form's property sheet, click the **Pop Up list arrow**, click **Yes**, close the property sheet, save the form, then close the form
   With the Email Info pop-up form created, you are ready to connect it via a command button to the Employees form.
4. Double-click the **Employees form** to open it in Form view, then maximize the Employees form
   The Employees form contains four bound fields: Last, First, Department, and Title, as well as a subform that displays the equipment assigned to that employee.
5. Click on the Form view toolbar, place the pointer on the **right edge of the form**, then drag to the **6.5"** mark on the horizontal ruler
   The command button will be placed in the upper-right corner of the form.
6. Click the **Command Button button** on the Toolbox, click to the right of the Title text box, click **Form Operations** in the Categories list, click **Open Form** in the Actions list, click **Next**, click the **Email Info** form, click **Next**, click the **Open the form and show all the records option button**, click **Next**, click the **Text option button**, press **[Tab]**, type **Email Addresses**, click **Next**, type **Email** as the name of the button, then click **Finish**
   Your screen should look similar to Figure M-16.
7. Click the **Form View button**, click the **Email Addresses command button**, then drag the **Email Info title bar** so that your screen looks like Figure M-17
   The power of pop-up forms is that they stay on top of all other forms and can be turned on and off as needed by the user.
8. Click in the **Last text box** in the Employees form, click the **Sort Ascending button**, double-click **Maria** in the First text box of the Employees form, type **Mary**, then press **[Tab]**
   "Maria" also changed to "Mary" in the pop-up form because both forms are tied to the underlying Employee table.
9. Close the **Email Info** pop-up form, close the **Employees** form and save the changes when prompted

FIGURE M-15: Creating the Email Info pop-up form

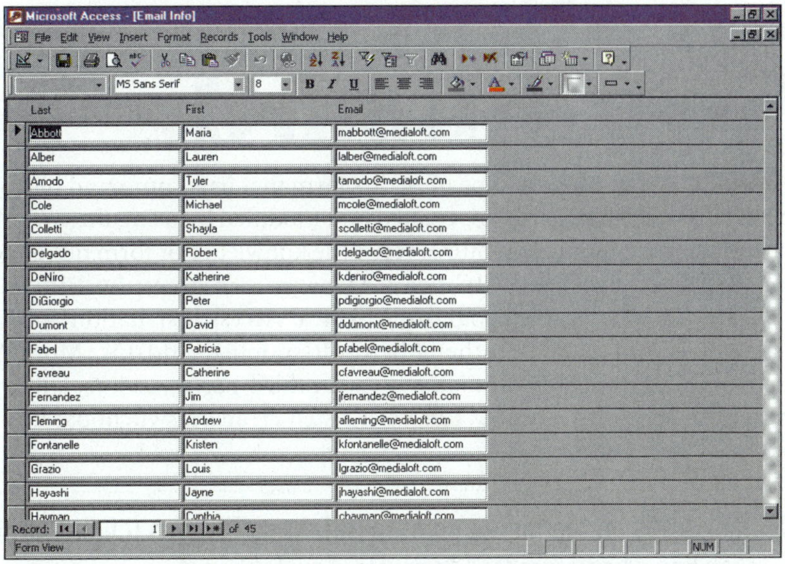

FIGURE M-16: Adding a command button to the Employees form

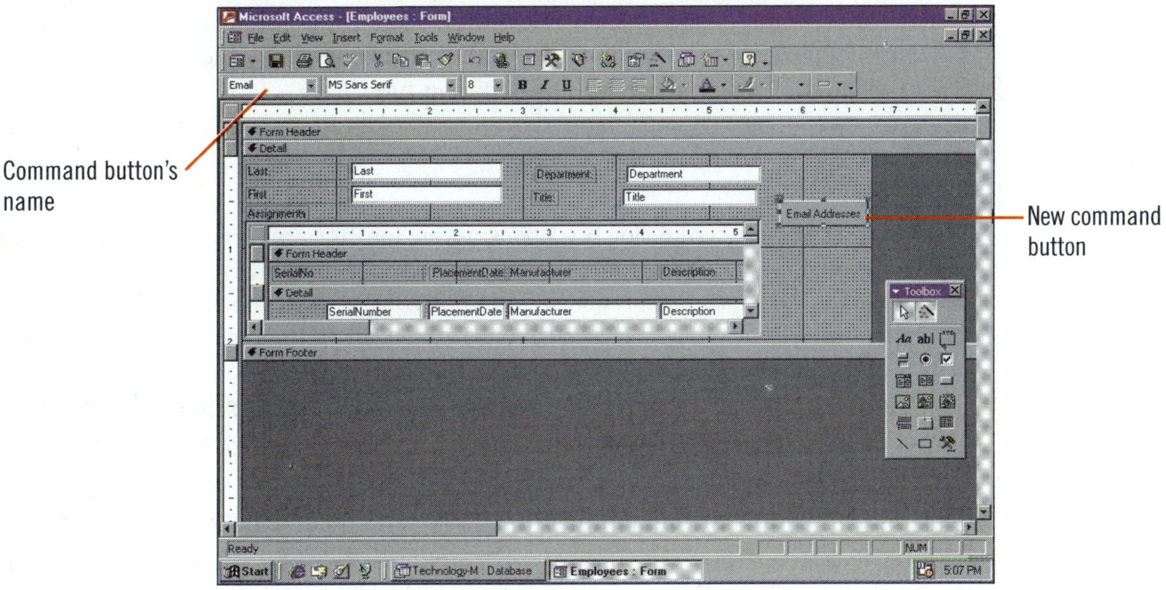

FIGURE M-17: The final form and pop-up form

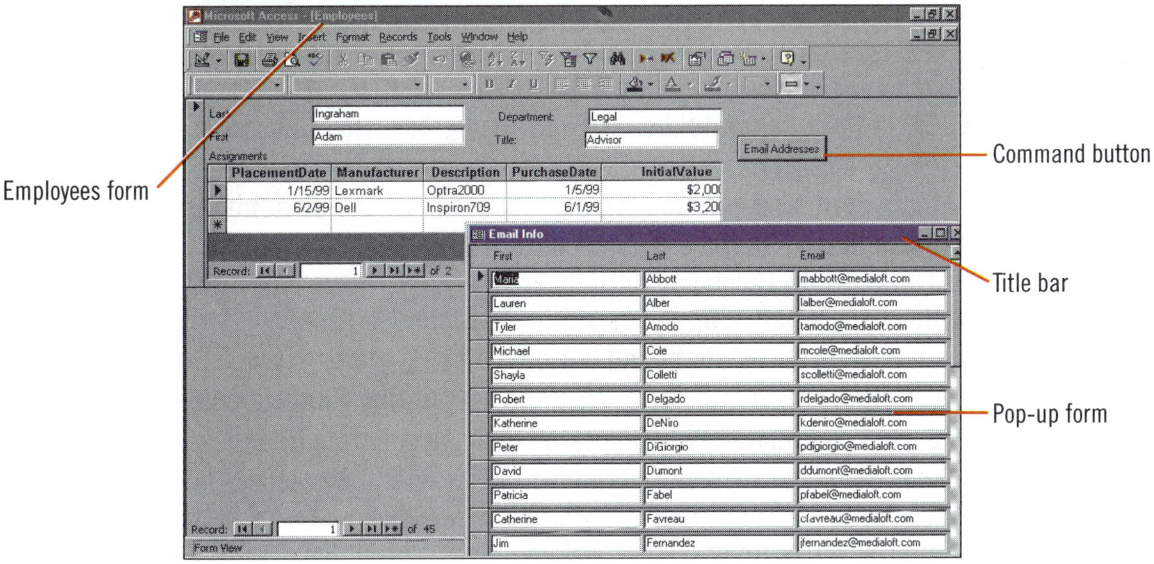

Access 2000

Unit M

Access 2000

Creating a Switchboard

A **switchboard** is a special type of Access form that uses command buttons to simplify and secure the database. Switchboards are created and modified by using the **Switchboard Manager**. Using the Switchboard Manager requires very little knowledge of form design techniques, control types, or property settings. The Switchboard Manager is an Access **Add-In**, an extra feature that is not a part of the core Access program. A typical Access installation will include the Switchboard Manager as well as a few other Microsoft-supplied Add-Ins. More Add-Ins that extend the capabilities of Access are available through third-party vendors, and many can be downloaded from the Microsoft Web site. Kristen creates a switchboard form to make the database extremely easy to navigate.

Steps

1. Click **Tools** on the menu, point to **Database Utilities**, click **Switchboard Manager**, then click **Yes** when prompted to create a switchboard
   The Switchboard Manager dialog box opens, displaying one switchboard with the name of "Main Switchboard (Default)." One switchboard is always identified as the default switchboard, a designation that can be used to automatically open the switchboard form when the database opens.
2. Click **Edit** in the Switchboard Manager dialog box
   The Edit Switchboard Page dialog box opens. There are no items currently on the switchboard form.
3. Click **New**
   The Edit Switchboard Item dialog box opens, asking for three important items: Text (a label on the switchboard form that identifies the corresponding command button), Command (which corresponds to a database action that will be chosen), and Switchboard (which further defines the command button action). The Switchboard option changes depending on the action chosen in the Command list.
4. Type **Open Employees Form** in the Text text box, click the **Command list arrow**, click **Open Form in Edit Mode**, click the **Form list arrow**, then click **Employees**
   The Edit Switchboard Item dialog box should look like Figure M-18.
5. Click **OK** to add the first command button to the switchboard, click **New**, type **Accounting Reports** in the Text text box, click the **Command list arrow**, click **Open Form in Edit Mode**, click the **Form list arrow**, click **Accounting Reports**, then click **OK**
   The Edit Switchboard Page dialog box should look like Figure M-19. Each entry in this dialog box represents a command button that will appear on the final switchboard. Recall that the object "Accounting Reports" is a form with three command buttons that allow the user to preview three different reports.
6. Close the Edit Switchboard Page dialog box, then close the Switchboard Manager dialog box
7. Click **Forms** on the Objects bar, double-click the **Switchboard form**, then click the **Switchboard Restore Window button** (if it is maximized)
   The finished switchboard opens in Form view, as shown in Figure M-20.
8. Click the **Open Employees Form command button** on the Switchboard, click the **Email Addresses command button** on the Employees form, close the **Email info form**, close the **Employees form**, click the **Accounting Reports command button**, click the **Sorted by Name command button** in the Accounting Reports dialog box, maximize the report window, then close the report window and the Accounting Reports dialog box
   You have successfully tested the Switchboard, which should be on the screen. Most users consider Switchboard forms to be the easiest way to navigate through the objects of a large database.

FIGURE M-18: Edit Switchboard Item dialog box

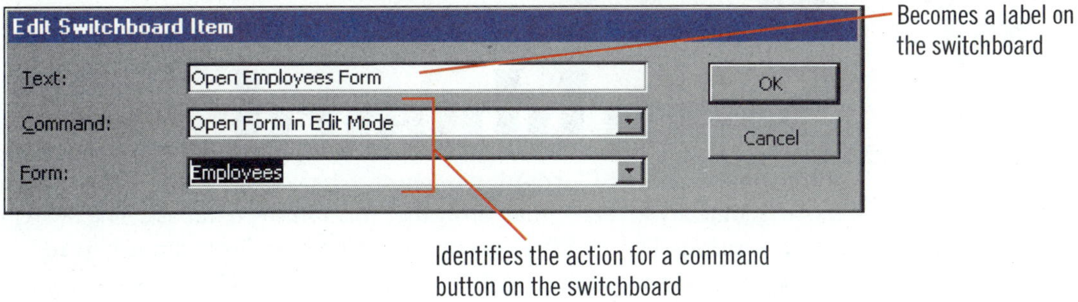

FIGURE M-19: Edit Switchboard Page dialog box

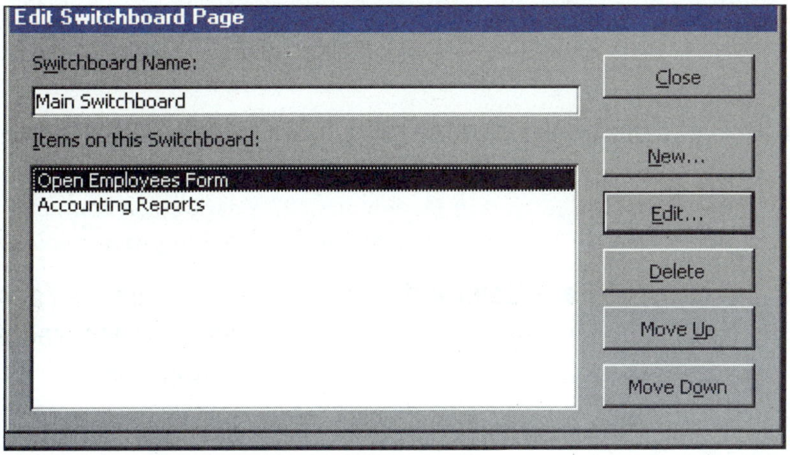

FIGURE M-20: Finished Switchboard

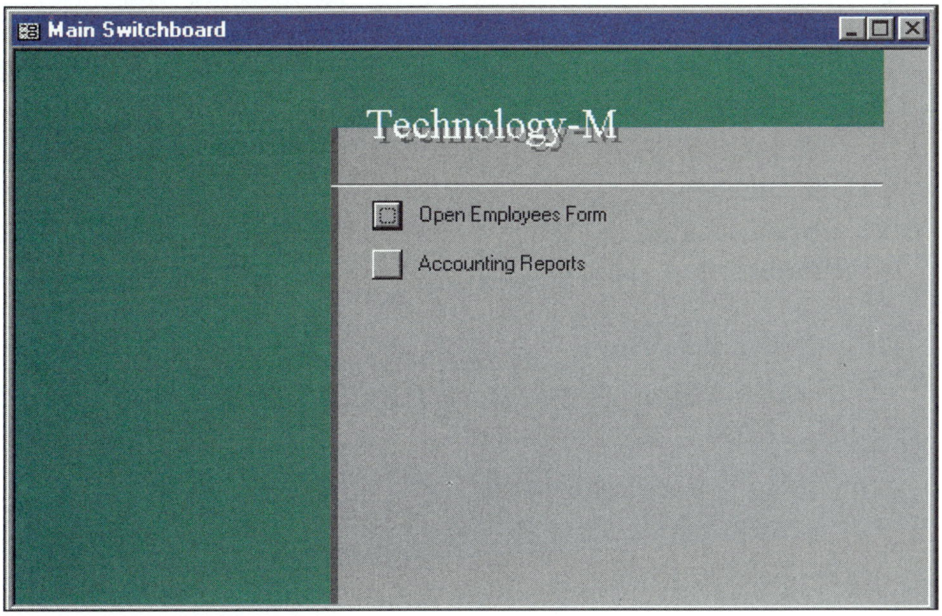

Access 2000

Unit M
Access 2000

Modifying a Switchboard

Although switchboard forms don't *appear* to be very complex, in reality they are probably much more technically involved than any other form in the database. The Switchboard Manager hides that complexity by providing a series of dialog boxes you can use to add, delete, move, and edit the command buttons displayed on the switchboard. Cosmetic changes to a switchboard form, such as changing the label that serves as the title of the form, or changing form colors, can be accomplished in the form's Design view, but *always* use the Switchboard Manager to make changes to the command buttons and associated labels. Kristen is happy with the initial switchboard form she created, but she would like to improve it by changing the title, colors, and order of the command buttons. She uses Form Design view to make the formatting changes and the Switchboard Manager to change the order of the buttons.

Steps

QuickTip

If you need to uniquely identify your switchboard, add a label to the upper-right corner with your name.

Trouble?

The Switchboard Manager creates a table called Switchboard Items that stores a record of information for each item in each switchboard. Deleting this table deletes all switchboards created within the database.

1. Click the **Design View button** on the Form View toolbar, then click the **dark green rectangle** on the left of the Detail section
   The Switchboard form is in Design view. The dark green colors on the left and top portion of the switchboard are actually just clip art, added to provide color to the form.
2. Click the **Fill/Back Color button list arrow** on the Formatting (Form/Report) toolbar, click **bright yellow**, click the **dark green rectangle** on the top of the Detail section, click , then click **bright red**
3. Click the **white Technology-M label**, drag the **white Technology-M label** using up into the red rectangle, click the **gray Technology-M** label, then press **[Delete]**
   Your screen should look like Figure M-21. Other than changing colors, the title label, and adding or deleting clip art, there isn't much more you should modify in Form Design view when you are working with a switchboard. The Switchboard Manager gives you all the power you need to make changes to the command buttons.
4. Save and close the switchboard, click **Tools** on the menu, point to **Database Utilities**, click **Switchboard Manager**, then click **Edit**
   You can create more than one switchboard form, and chain them together through command buttons. In this case, you have only one switchboard.
5. Click **Accounting Reports**, click **Edit**, click to the left of the **A** in the Text text box, type **Preview**, press **[Spacebar]**, then click **OK**
   In addition to changing the labels connected to each command button on a switchboard, you can add, delete, move, or edit them from the Edit Switchboard Page dialog box.
6. Click **Move Up** to make Preview Accounting Reports the first item in the switchboard, click **Close**, then click **Close**
7. Double-click the **Switchboard** form to open it in Form view
   The modified switchboard should look like Figure M-22.
8. Print and close the switchboard, then exit Access

FIGURE M-21: Switchboard in Design view

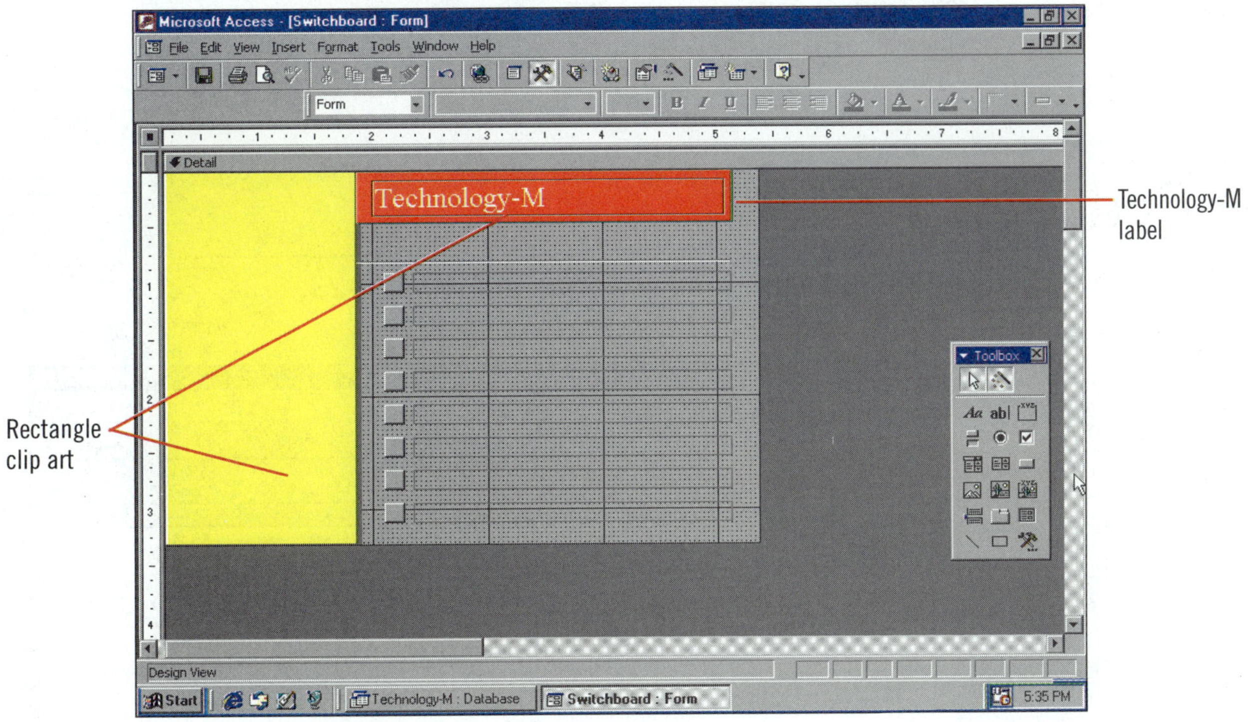

FIGURE M-22: Modified Switchboard

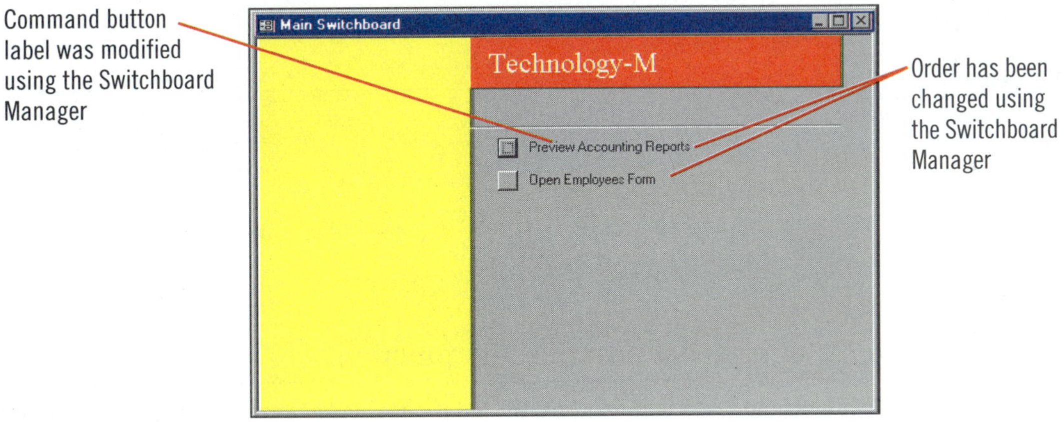

CLUES TO USE

Illustrating Access features with Sample Databases

Microsoft provides four sample databases with Access 2000 that illustrate many different ways to use Access objects and features. All four databases are installed on first use in a default installation (or can be installed to your hard drive directly from the Microsoft Office 2000 CD from the Microsoft Access for Windows; Sample Databases installation category). The Northwind database, in particular, provides several examples of exciting switchboards and dialog boxes.

Practice

► Concepts Review

Identify each element of the database window shown in Figure M-23.

FIGURE M-23

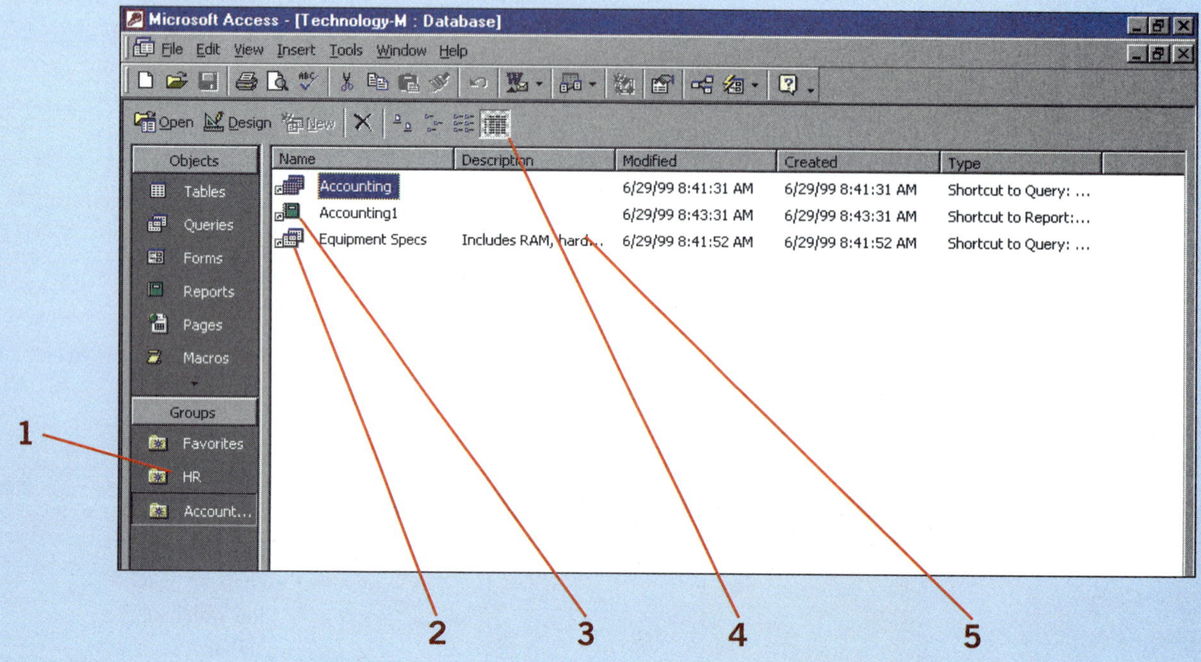

Match each term with the statement that describes its function.

6. **Group**
7. **Pop-up form**
8. **Shortcut**
9. **Add-In**
10. **Documenter**
11. **Switchboard**

a. Creates reports on the properties and relationships between the objects in your database
b. Pointer to database objects
c. Special type of form that stays on top of other open forms, even when another form is active
d. Special type of Access form that uses command buttons to simplify and secure access to database objects
e. Extra feature that is not a part of the core Access program
f. Helps you easily organize and classify objects

Select the best answer from the list of choices.

12. Which View button do you use to see the date that the object was created?
- **a.** List
- **b.** Small Icons
- **c.** Date
- **d.** Details

13. Which feature fixes discrepancies between references to field names, controls, and objects when you rename them?
- **a.** Documenter
- **b.** Renamer
- **c.** Name AutoCorrect
- **d.** Switchboard Manager

14. If you wanted to add another command button to a switchboard, which technique would you use?
- **a.** Modify the switchboard in Form Design view.
- **b.** Modify the switchboard in Report Design view.
- **c.** Use the Switchboard Manager.
- **d.** Use the Switchboard Analyzer.

15. Which technique would NOT provide much help to organize the Access objects that the Human Resources (HR) Department most often uses?
- **a.** Create a report that lists all HR employees.
- **b.** Create a switchboard that provides command buttons to the appropriate HR objects.
- **c.** Create a dialog box with command buttons that reference the most commonly used HR reports.
- **d.** Create an HR group and add shortcuts to the objects the HR Department most commonly uses.

16. Northwind is the name of a sample
- **a.** Switchboard form.
- **b.** Database.
- **c.** Pop-up form.
- **d.** Dialog box.

17. A dialog box is really a ____________ with special property settings.
- **a.** Table
- **b.** Form
- **c.** Macro
- **d.** Report

Skills Review

1. Working with Objects.
- **a.** Open the Basketball-M database.
- **b.** Click the Details button to view the details, click Reports on the Objects bar, then resize the Name column so that the entire report name is visible in the database window.

c. Right-click the Player Field Goal Stats report, click Properties, type "Forwards and Guards" as the Description, then click OK.
d. Click Queries on the Objects bar, right-click the Games query, click Rename, then type "Score Delta" as the new query name.
e. Open the Games Summary Report in Design view, open the report property sheet, then check the Record Source property on the Data tab. Because the Games Summary Report was based on the former Games Query object, the new query name should appear in the Record Source property. (*Hint*: If the query name, Score Delta, doesn't appear in the Record Source property, click the Record Source property list arrow, then click Score Delta. Check the AutoCorrect options. From the database window, click Tools on the menu bar, click Options, click the General tab, then check the Name AutoCorrect options. By default, the first two of the three Name AutoCorrect options should be checked. Close the Options dialog box by clicking OK.)
f. Close the property sheet, then save and close the report.

2. Using the Documenter.

a. Click Tools on the menu bar, point to Analyze, then click Documenter.
b. Click the Tables tab, click Select All, click the Reports tab, click the Games Summary Report check box, then click OK
c. Watch the status bar to track the Documenter's progress.
d. The final report is 20 pages long. Click File on the menu bar, click Print, click the Pages option button, type "1" in the From text box, type "1" in the To text box, then click OK to print the first page.
e. Click File on the menu bar, click Print, click the Pages option button, type "20" in the From and To text boxes, then click OK to print page 20.
f. Close the report created by Documenter.

3. Grouping Objects.

a. Right-click Favorites on the Groups bar, click New Group, then type Forwards to create a new group named "Forwards".
b. Drag the Forward Field Goals query to the Forwards group, then drag the Forward Field Goal Stats report to the Forwards group. Verify that the shortcuts are on the Forwards group.
c. Create a new group named "Guards", then add shortcuts for the Guard Field Goals query and Guard Field Goal Stats report objects to it. Verify that the shortcuts are on the Guards group.

4. Modifying Groups.

a. Click Forwards on the Groups bar, right-click the Forward Field Goals query shortcut, then rename the shortcut as "Forward FG Query".
b. Rename the Forward Field Goal Stats report as "Forward FG Report".
c. Click Guards on the Groups bar. Rename the Guard Field Goals query shortcut as "Guard FG Query".
d. Rename the Guard Field Goal Stats report shortcut to "Guard FG Report".
e. Click Forwards on the Groups bar, double-click the Forward FG Query shortcut, then enter your own name to replace Amy Hodel on any record her name currently occupies. As soon as you move off the record you are editing, the change will be made to the underlying Players table, which will update every record in this datasheet.
f. Print the datasheet, then close it.

5. Creating a Dialog Box.

a. Start a new form in Design view. Do not select any underlying tables or queries.
b. Using the Toolbox, add a command button to the upper-left corner of the form using the Command Button Wizard. Select Report operations from the Categories list, then select Preview Report from the actions list since this is a form to preview the Games Summary Report.
c. The Text for the button should be "Preview Games Summary Report" and the name of the button should be "Games".
d. Using the Toolbox and the Command Button Wizard, create a second command button below the first to preview the Player Field Goal Stats report.

e. The Text for the button should be "Preview Player FG Stats" and the name of the button should be "Players".
f. Below the two buttons, add a label to the form with your name in it.
g. Open the Form's property sheet, click the Format tab, change the form's Border Style property to Dialog, change the form's Record Selectors property to No, then change the form's Navigation Buttons property to No.
h. Close the property sheet, restore the form (if it is maximized), resize it to approximately 3" wide by 3" tall, save the form as "Team Reports", click the Form View button, test the buttons, then print the form.

6. **Creating a Pop-up Form.**
   a. Using the Form Wizard, create a form with the following fields from the Players table: First, Last, and PlayerNo.
   b. Use a Tabular layout, a Standard style, and title the form "Player Pop-up".
   c. In Design view of the Player Pop-up form, resize the First and Last labels and text boxes to about half of their current width.
   d. Move the Last and PlayerNo labels and text boxes close to the First label and text box so that the entire form can be narrowed to no larger than 3" wide. Resize the form to 3" wide.
   e. Open the Forms property sheet, change the Pop Up property on the form's Other tab to Yes. Close the property sheet.
   f. Save and close the Player Pop-up form.
   g. In the Design view of the Team Reports form, use the Toolbox and Command Button Wizard to create a command button on the right side of the form that opens the Player Pop-up form and shows all of the records.
   h. The Text for the new button should be "Open Player Pop-up" and the name of the button should be "Player Pop-up".
   i. Save and view the Team Reports form in Form view, then click the Open Player Pop-up command button to test it. Test the other buttons as well. The Player Pop-up form should stay on top of all other forms and reports unless you close it.
   j. Save and close all open forms and reports.

7. **Creating a Switchboard.**
   a. Click Tools, point to Database Utilities, click Switchboard Manager, then click Yes to create a new switchboard.
   b. Click Edit to edit the Main Switchboard, then click New to add the first item to it.
   c. The Text for the first item should be "Choose a Team Report", the Command should be Open Form in Add Mode, and the Form should be Team Reports.
   d. Click New to add a second item to the switchboard. The Text for the second item should be "Open Player Entry Form", the Command should be Open Form in Add Mode, and the form should be Player Entry Form.
   e. Close the Edit Switchboard manager dialog box, close the Switchboard Manager dialog box. Open the Switchboard form and click both command buttons to make sure they work. Notice that when you open a form in "Add Mode" (rather than using the Open Form in Edit Mode action within the Switchboard Manager), the navigation buttons indicate that you can only add a new record, and not edit an existing one.
   f. Close all open forms including the Switchboard form.

8. **Modifying a Switchboard.**
   a. Click Tools, point to Database Utilities, click Switchboard Manager, then click Edit to edit the Main Switchboard.
   b. Click Open Player Entry Form, then click Edit.
   c. Change the Command to Open Form in Edit Mode, choose the Player Entry Form in the Form list, then click OK.
   d. Move the Open Player Entry Form item above the Choose a Team Report item, then close the Switchboard Manager.
   e. In Design view of the Switchboard Manager, delete both the white and gray Basketball-M labels, add a label with your team's name, then add a label with your own name. Place the two new labels at the top of the Switchboard form, and be sure to format them with a color that is visible in Form view.
   f. Save, print, and close the Switchboard form.
   g. Close the Basketball-M database.
   h. Exit Access.

Independent Challenges

1. As the manager of a doctor's clinic, you have created an Access database called Patients-M to track insurance claim reimbursements that are fixed (paid at a predetermined fixed rate), or denied (not paid by the insurance company). You wish to create two groups to organize database objects.

To complete this independent challenge:

a. Start Access and open the database Patients-M from your Project Disk.
b. Create two new groups: Fixed and Denied.
c. Add shortcuts for the Monthly Query – Fixed query, the Date of Service Report – Fixed report, and the Monthly Claims Report – Fixed report to the Fixed group.
d. Add shortcuts for the Monthly Query – Denied query, the Date of Service Report – Denied report, and the Monthly Claims Report – Denied report to the Denied group.
e. Click Queries on the Objects bar, click the Details button in the database window, then sort the queries by date they were modified.
f. For the two queries that were last modified in May, add the Description "For Board Meeting" by accessing their properties.
g. Click the Tools menu, point to Analyze, then click Documenter. On the Current Database tab, click Relationships, then click OK.
h. Print the Documenter's report, then close it.
i. Close the Patients-M database.
j. Exit Access.

2. As the manager of a doctor's clinic, you have created an Access database called Patients-M to track insurance claim reimbursements that are fixed (paid at a predetermined fixed rate) or denied (not paid by the insurance company). You wish to create a new dialog box for your database.

To complete this independent challenge:

a. Start Access and open the database Patients-M from your Project Disk.
b. Start a new form in Design view.
c. Using the Toolbox and the Command Button Wizard, add a command button to the form to preview the Date of Service Report – Denied.
d. The Text for the button should be "Preview Date of Service – Denied" and the name of the button should be "PDOSD".
e. Using the Toolbox and the Command Button Wizard, create a second button below the first to preview the Date of Service Report – Fixed.
f. The Text for the button should be "Preview Date of Service – Fixed" and the name of the button should be "PDOSF".
g. Create a third command button below the second to preview the Monthly Claims Report – Denied.
h. The Text for the button should be "Preview Monthly Claims – Denied" and the name of the button should be "PMCD".
i. Create a fourth and final command button below the third to preview the Monthly Claims Report – Fixed.
j. The text for the button should be "Preview Monthly Claims – Fixed" and the name of the button should be "PMCF".
k. Below the buttons, add a label to the form with your name in it.
l. Change the form's Border Style property to Dialog.

m. Change the form's Record Selectors property to No.
n. Change the form's Navigation Buttons property to No.
o. Close the property sheet, restore the form (if it is maximized), resize it to approximately 3" wide by 3" tall, save the form as "Report Dialog Box", click the Form View button, test the buttons, then print the form.
p. Close the Patients-M database.
q. Exit Access

3. As the manager of a doctor's clinic, you have created an Access database called Patients-M to track insurance claim reimbursements that are fixed (paid at a predetermined fixed rate), or denied (not paid by the insurance company). You wish to create a pop-up form to provide physician information. You'll access the pop-up form from the Claim Entry Form via a command button.

To complete this independent challenge:

a. Start Access and open the database Patients-M database from your Project Disk.
b. Use the Form Wizard to create a form with all three fields in the Doctors table.
c. Use a Tabular layout, a Standard style, and title the form "Doctor Pop-up".
d. In Design view of the Doctor Pop-up form, resize all three labels and text boxes to about half their current width.
e. Move the PodLastName and PodCode labels and text boxes close to the PodFirstName label and text box so that the entire form can be narrowed to no larger than 3" wide.
f. Change the Pop-Up property on the form's Other tab to Yes.
g. Save and close the Doctor Pop-up form.
h. In Design view of the Claim Entry Form, use the Toolbox and Command Button Wizard to create a command button to the right of the Form Header section that opens the Doctor Pop-up form and shows all of the records.
i. The Text for the new button should be "Open Doctor Pop-up" and the name of the button should be "Doctor Pop-up".
j. Save and view the Claim Entry Form in Form view, then click the Open Doctor Pop-up command button.
k. Move through the records of the Claim Entry form. The Doctor Pop-up form should stay on top of all other forms unless you close it.
l. Save and close all open forms.
m. Close the Patients-M database.
n. Exit Access.

WEB WORK

4. MediaLoft has developed a Web site that provides internal information to their employees. In this independent challenge, you'll surf the Internet to find Web pages that present information organized similarly to how a switchboard is used to organize an Access database.

a. Connect to the Internet, go to the MediaLoft intranet site at http://www.course.com/illustrated/MediaLoft
b. Print the home page. Identify which hyperlinks on the home page are analogous to command buttons on a switchboard.
c. Click the center link Research, click the link for Competition: Other Bookstores, and browse for a Web page that organizes information like switchboards.
d. If you are not familiar with Web browsing techniques, click the Back button until you return to the MediaLoft Research page, where you can start a new search.
e. When you find a Web page that contains "switchboard-like" hyperlinks to organize information, print the Web page and identify the hyperlinks. Print at least two other non-MediaLoft Web pages that act like switchboards, providing an organized method to access the rest of the information on that Web site.
h. Close your browser window.
i. Disconnect from the Internet.

Visual Workshop

As the manager of a doctor's clinic, you have created an Access database called Patients-M to track insurance claim reimbursements that are fixed (paid at a predetermined fixed rate), or denied (not paid by the insurance company). Create a switchboard form to give the users an easy interface, as shown in Figure M-24. Both command buttons on the switchboard open forms in edit mode. Add and modify the two labels in the switchboard's Design view, and be sure to add your own name as the manager.

FIGURE M-24

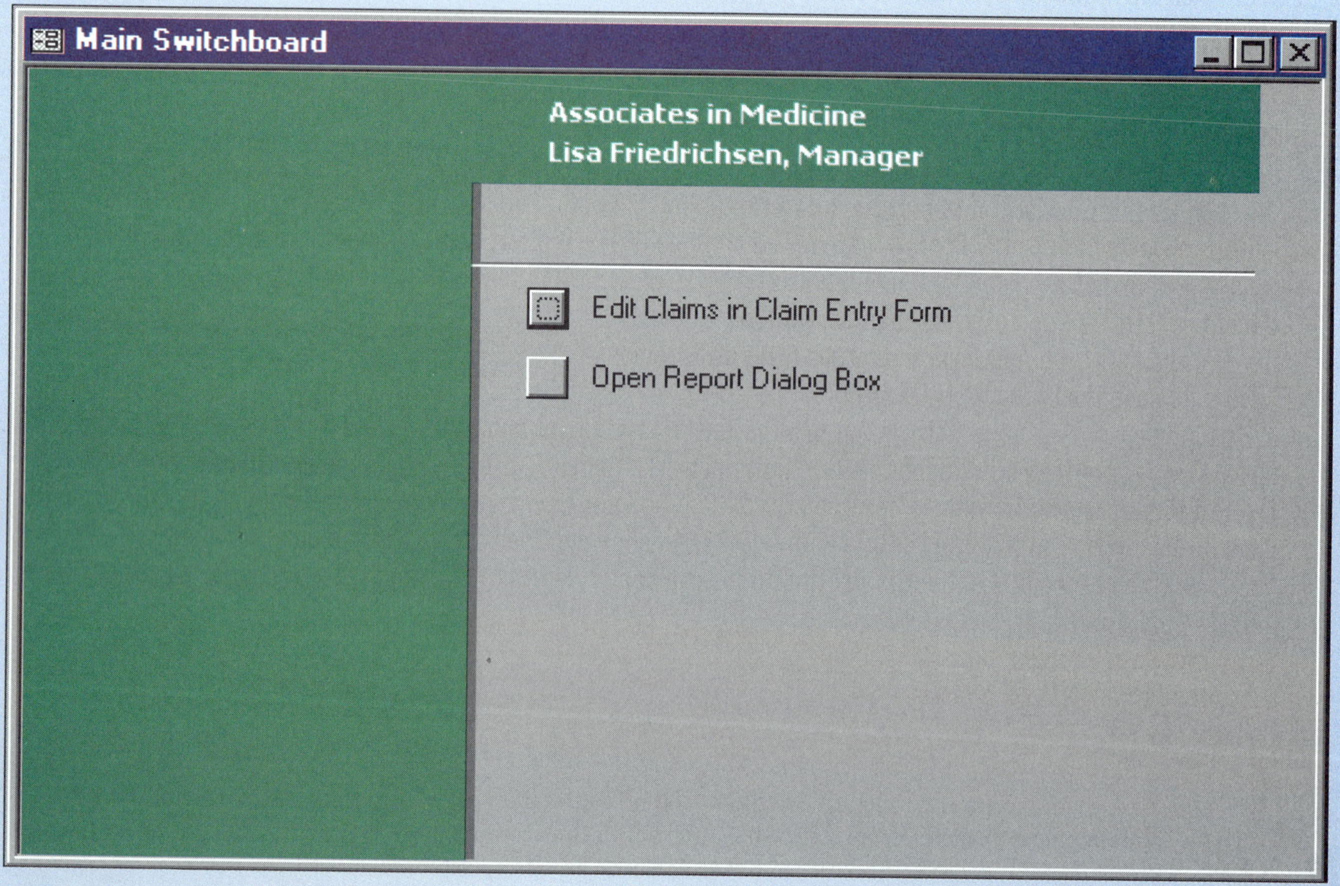

Creating Macros

Objectives

- Understand Macros
- MOUS Create a Macro
- Modify Actions and Arguments
- Create a Macro Group
- Set Conditional Expressions
- MOUS Assign a Macro to an Event
- Customize Toolbars with Macros
- Troubleshoot Macros

A **macro** is a database object that stores Access actions. When you run a macro, you execute the stored set of actions. Almost any repetitive Access task such as printing a report, opening a form, or exporting data is a good candidate for a macro. Automating routine and complex tasks as stored actions in a macro builds efficiency, accuracy, and flexibility into your database. Kristen noticed that several tasks are repeated on a regular basis and could be automated with macros. Although she hasn't worked with macros before, Kristen recognizes the benefits and is excited to get started.

Unit N

Access 2000

Understanding Macros

A macro may contain one or more **actions**, the tasks that you want Access to perform. When you **run** a macro, the actions execute in the order in which they are listed in the **Macro window**. Each action has a specified set of **arguments** that provide additional information on how to carry out the action. For example, if the action were OpenForm, the arguments would include specifying the Form Name, the view (Form or Design) that the form should open to, and whether you want to apply any filters when you open the form. Kristen studies the major benefits of using macros, the key terminology she needs to know when developing macros, and the components of the Access Macro window before she builds her first macro.

Details

The major benefits of using macros:

- Save time by automating routine tasks.
- Increase accuracy by ensuring that tasks are executed consistently.
- Make forms and reports work together by providing command buttons bound to macros that enable users to quickly and easily move between the objects.
- Make the database easier to use by providing command buttons bound to macros to filter and find records automatically.
- Ensure data accuracy in forms by responding to errors in data entry with different messages developed in macros.
- Automate data transfers such as exporting data to an Excel workbook.
- Create your own customized environment by customizing toolbars and the menu system.

Key macro terminology:

- **macro**: An Access object that stores a series of actions to perform one or more tasks.
- **action**: Each task that you want the macro to perform. Each macro action occupies a single row in the macro window.
- **macro window**: The window in which you create a macro, as shown in Figure N-1. See Table N-1 for a description of the macro window components.
- **arguments**: Properties of an action that provide additional information on how the action should execute.
- **macro group**: An Access macro object that stores more than one macro. The macros in a macro group run independently of one another, but are grouped together to organize multiple macros that have similar characteristics. For example, you may wish to put all of the macros that print reports in one macro group.
- **expression**: A combination of values, identifiers (such as the value in a field), and operators that result in a value.
- **conditional expression**: An expression that results in either a "true" or "false" answer that determines if a macro action will execute or not. For example, if the field Country contained a null value, you may wish for the macro to execute an action that sends the user a message.
- **event**: Something that happens on a form, window, toolbar, or datasheet—such as the click of a command button or an entry in a field—that can be used to initiate the execution of a macro.

FIGURE N-1: Macro window of a macro group

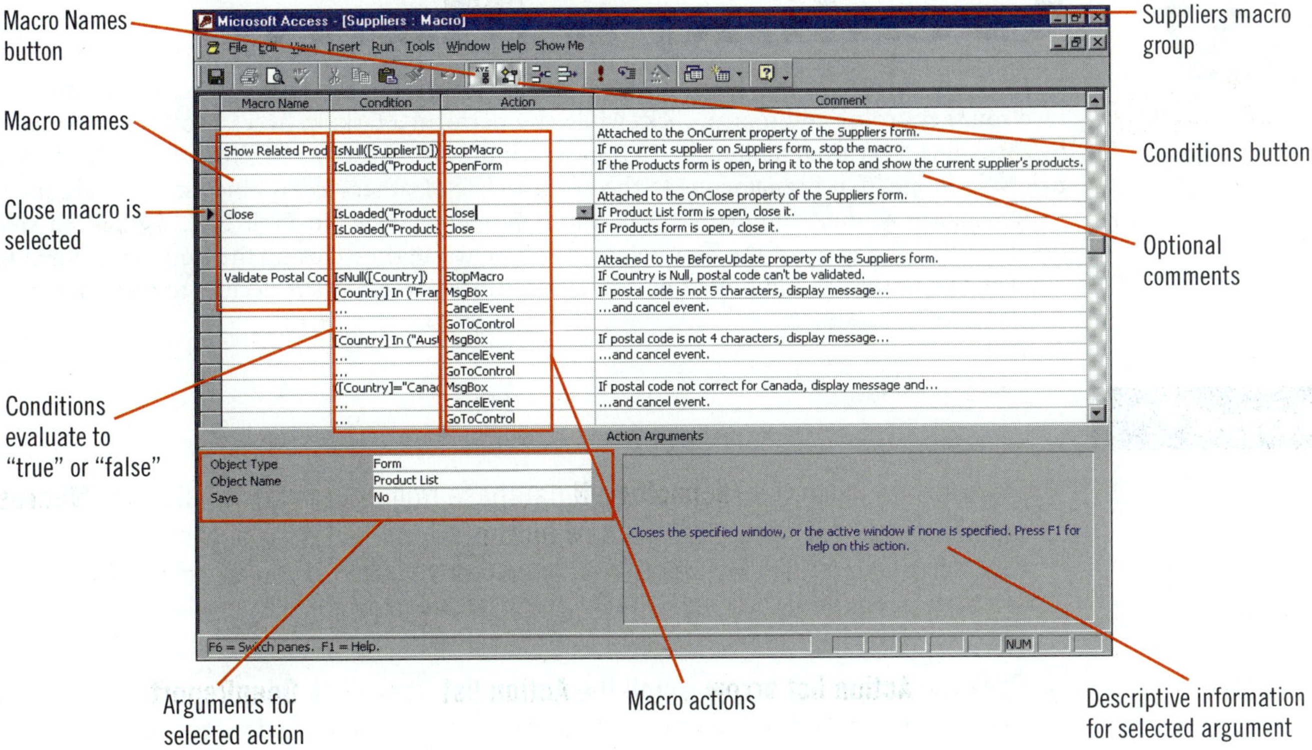

TABLE N-1: Macro window components

component	description
Macro Name column	Contains the names of individual macros within a macro group. If the macro object contains only one macro, it isn't necessary to use this column because you can run the macro by referring to the macro object's name. View this column by clicking the Macro Names button.
Condition column	Contains conditional expressions that are evaluated either "true" or "false." If "true," the macro action on that row is executed. If "false," the macro action on that row is skipped. View this column by clicking the Conditions button.
Action column	Contains the actions (steps, instructions, or commands) that the macro executes when it runs.
Comment column	Contains optional explanatory text for each macro action.
Close macro	Is only two actions long. Both actions are "close" actions and will be executed only if the conditional expression in the corresponding row is "true."
Action arguments	Displays action characteristics and values that further define the selected macro action. In Figure N-1, the Close action has three arguments. Action Arguments change based on the action.

Unit N

Access 2000

Creating a Macro

In some software programs, you can create a macro by having a "macro recorder" monitor and save your keystrokes and mouse clicks while you perform a task. In Access, you create a macro by specifying a series of actions in the Macro window. Because the Macro window is where a macro is designed, it is analogous to the Design view of other Access objects. There are more than 50 macro actions, and many of the common ones are listed in Table N-2. Kristen observed that the users of the Technology database waste time closing the Employees form to open and print the All Equipment report several times a week, so she decides to create a macro to automate this task.

Steps

1. Start Access, open the **Technology-N** database from your Project Disk, click **Macros** on the Objects bar, then click the **New button** in the database window
   The Macro1 Macro window opens, ready to accept your first action statement. The Macro Name and Condition columns are not visible by default, but could be toggled on by clicking their respective buttons on the Macro Design toolbar.
2. Click the **Action list arrow**, scroll the **Action list**, then click **OpenReport**
   The OpenReport action is added as the first line of the Macro window, and the arguments that further define the action appear in the Action Arguments panel. The Open Report action has two required arguments: the name of the report that you want to open and the view in which you want to open the report. The Filter Name and Where Condition arguments are optional.
3. Click the **Report Name text box** in the Action Arguments panel, click the **Report Name List arrow**, then click **All Equipment**
   All of the report objects in the Technology-N database display in the Report Name list when you choose the OpenReport action.
4. Click the **View text box** in the Action Arguments panel, click the **View list arrow**, then click **Print**
   Your screen should look like Figure N-2. Macro actions can contain conditional expressions that execute only if the result of the conditional expression is true. Macros can be one or many actions long. In this case, the macro is only one action long and there are no conditional expressions.
5. Click the **Save button** on the Macro Design toolbar, type **Print All Equipment Report** in the Macro Name text box, click **OK**, then close the Macro window
   The Technology-N database window shows the Print All Equipment Report object as a Macro object.
6. Click the **Run button** in the Technology-N Database window
   The All Equipment report prints.

QuickTip

Add a label with your name to the All Equipment report if you need to uniquely identify your printout.

FIGURE N-2: Macro window with OpenReport action

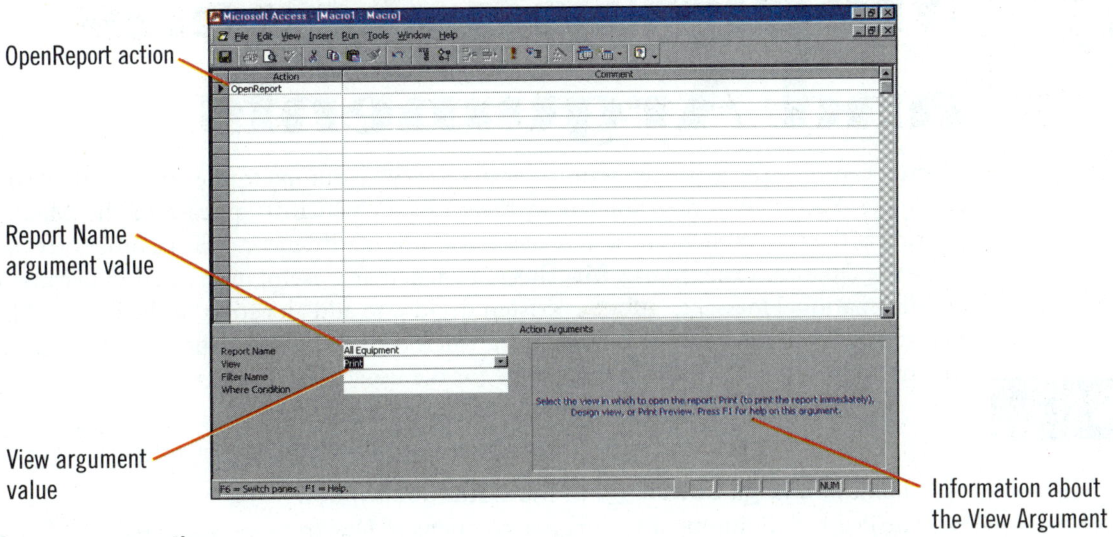

TABLE N-2: Common macro actions

subject area	macro action	description
Handling data in forms	ApplyFilter	Restricts the number of records that appear in the resulting form or report by applying limiting criteria
	FindRecord	Finds the first record that meets the criteria
	GoToControl	Moves the focus (where you are currently typing or clicking) to a specific field or control
	GoToRecord	Makes a specified record the current record
Executing menu options	RunCode	Calls a Visual Basic function (a series of programming statements that do a calculation or comparison and return a value)
	RunCommand	Carries out a specified menu command
	RunMacro	Runs a macro or attaches a macro to a custom menu command
	StopMacro	Stops the currently running macro
Importing/Exporting data	TransferDatabase TransferSpreadsheet TransferText	Imports, links, or exports data between the current Microsoft Access database and another database, spreadsheet, or text file
Manipulating objects	Close	Closes a window
	Maximize	Enlarges the active window to fill the Access window
	OpenForm	Opens a form in Form view, Design view, Print Preview, or Datasheet view
	OpenQuery	Opens a select or crosstab query in Datasheet view, Design view, or Print Preview; runs an action query
	OpenReport	Opens a report in Design view or Print Preview, or prints the report
	OpenTable	Opens a table in Datasheet view, Design view, or Print Preview
	PrintOut	Prints the active object, such as a datasheet, report, form, or module, in the open database
	SetValue	Sets the value of a field, control, or property
Miscellaneous	Beep	Sounds a beep tone through the computer's speaker
	MsgBox	Displays a message box containing a warning or an informational message
	SendKeys	Sends keystrokes directly to Microsoft Access or to an active Windows-based application

Unit N

Access 2000

Modifying Actions and Arguments

Macros can contain as many actions as necessary to complete the process that you want to automate. Each action is evaluated in the order in which it appears in the Macro window, starting at the top. While some macro actions manipulate data or objects, others are used only to make the database easier to use. **MsgBox** is a particularly useful macro action because it displays an informational message. Kristen decides to add an action to the Print All Equipment Report macro to clarify what is happening when the macro runs. She adds a MsgBox action to the macro to display a descriptive message for the user.

Steps

1. Click the **Design button** in the database window
   The Print All Equipment Report macro opens in Design view.
2. Click the **Action cell** just below the OpenReport action, click the **Action list arrow**, scroll the **Action list**, then click **MsgBox**
   Each action has its own arguments that further clarify what the action will accomplish.
3. Click the **Message text box** in the Action Arguments panel, then type **The All Equipment Report has just been sent to the printer**
   The Message argument determines what text appears in the message box. By default, the Beep argument is set to "Yes" and the Type argument is set to "None."
4. Click the **Type text box** in the Action Arguments panel, read the description in the lower-right corner of the Macro window, click the **Type list arrow**, then click **Information**
   The Type argument determines which icon will appear in the dialog box that is created by the MsgBox action.
5. Click the **Title text box** in the Action Arguments panel, then type **Important Information!**
   Your screen should look like Figure N-3. The Title argument specifies what text will display in the title bar of the resulting dialog box. If you leave the Title argument empty, the title bar of the resulting dialog box will display "Microsoft Access."
6. Click the **Save button** on the Macro Design toolbar, then click the **Run button** on the Macro Design toolbar
   If your speakers are turned on, you should hear a beep, then the message box should appear, as shown in Figure N-4. The report prints a second time.
7. Click **OK** in the dialog box, then close the Print All Equipment Report Macro window
   The modified Print All Equipment Report macro is saved.

QuickTip

Press [F1] to display Help text for the action and argument currently selected.

FIGURE N-3: Print All Equipment Report macro with additional MsgBox action

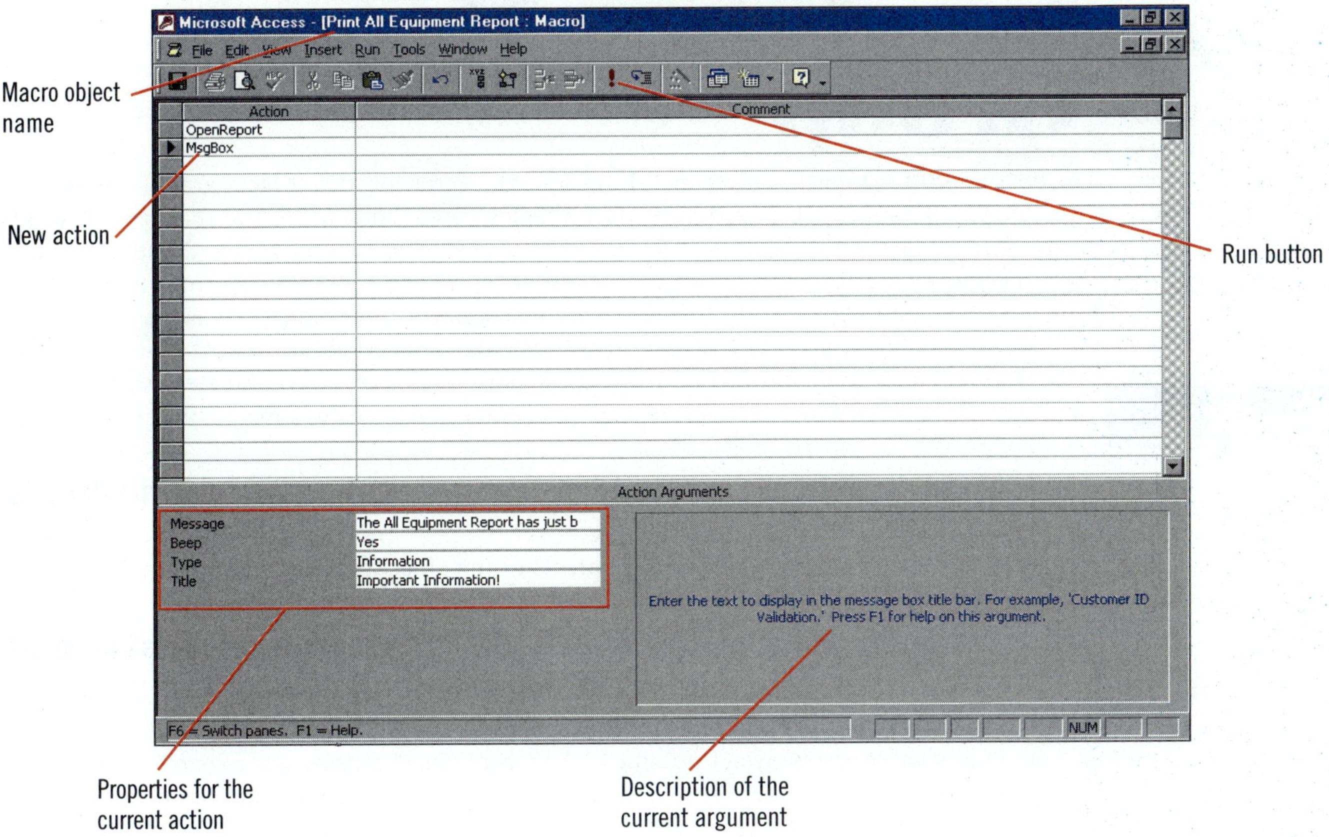

FIGURE N-4: Dialog box created by MsgBox action

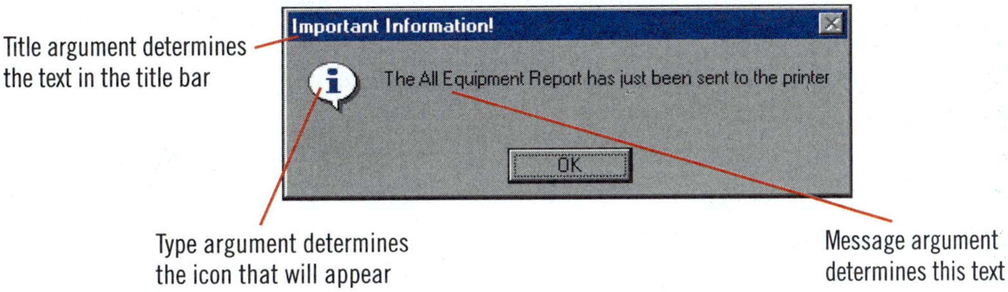

Creating a Macro Group

A **macro group** is a macro object that stores several macros together. Macro groups are used to organize multiple macros that have similar characteristics, such as all the macros that print reports or all the macros that are attached to the same form through command buttons. When you put several macros in the same macro object to create a macro group, you must enter a unique name for each macro in the Macro Name column (in the same row as the first macro action) to identify where each macro starts. Kristen adds a macro that prints the Accounting Report to the Print All Equipment Report macro object. By adding this new macro and any additional macros that print reports in one object, she creates a macro object.

Steps

1. Right-click the **Print All Equipment Report macro**, click **Rename**, type **Print Reports Macro Group**, then press **[Enter]**
   The object name should explain the contents of the object as clearly as possible. The name should reflect the fact that the macro object contains more than one macro.
2. Click the **Design button** in the database window, click the **Macro Names button** on the Macro Design toolbar, type **Print All Equipment** in the Macro Name column, then press **[Enter]**
   An individual macro is given the name of the macro object *unless* a macro name is entered in the Macro Name column. If several macros are stored as a macro group in one object, it is imperative that each be given a unique name so that each can be clearly referenced later.
3. Click in the **Macro Name cell** in the third row, type **Print Accounting Report**, then press **[Enter]**
   A new macro starts when a new name is entered in the Macro Name column.
4. Click the **Action list arrow**, scroll and click **OpenReport**, click in the **Report Name text box** in the Action Arguments panel, click the **Report Name list arrow**, then click **Accounting Report**
   Your screen should look like Figure N-5. The other two arguments associated with the OpenReport action are already correctly specified.
5. Click the **row selector of the MsgBox action of the Print All Equipment macro**, click the **Copy button** on the Macro Design toolbar, click the **fourth row selector**, then click the **Paste button** on the Macro Design toolbar
   Being able to copy and paste actions in a Macro window is another benefit of using macro groups. Action argument values are copied and pasted along with the action, so they don't need to be reentered. Sometimes, however, the arguments need to be edited.
6. Delete **All Equipment** in the Message text box in the Action Arguments panel, type **Accounting**, then click the **Save button** on the Macro Design toolbar
   To run a specific macro from within a macro group's window, you must use the menu.
7. Click **Tools** on the menu bar, point to **Macro**, click **Run Macro**, click the **Macro Name list arrow** in the Run Macro dialog box, click **Print Reports Macro Group.Print Accounting Report**, then click **OK**
   Your screen should look like Figure N-6. Referring to a specific macro within a macro group by separating them with a period is called **dot notation**. Dot notation syntax is also used when developing modules with Visual Basic programming code.
8. Click **OK**, then close the Macro window
   The Print Reports Macro Group object containing two macros is shown in the database window.

QuickTip

Some macro developers leave a blank row between macros to further clarify where a new macro starts.

QuickTip

Add a label with your name to the Accounting Report if you need to uniquely identify your printout.

FIGURE N-5: Creating a macro group

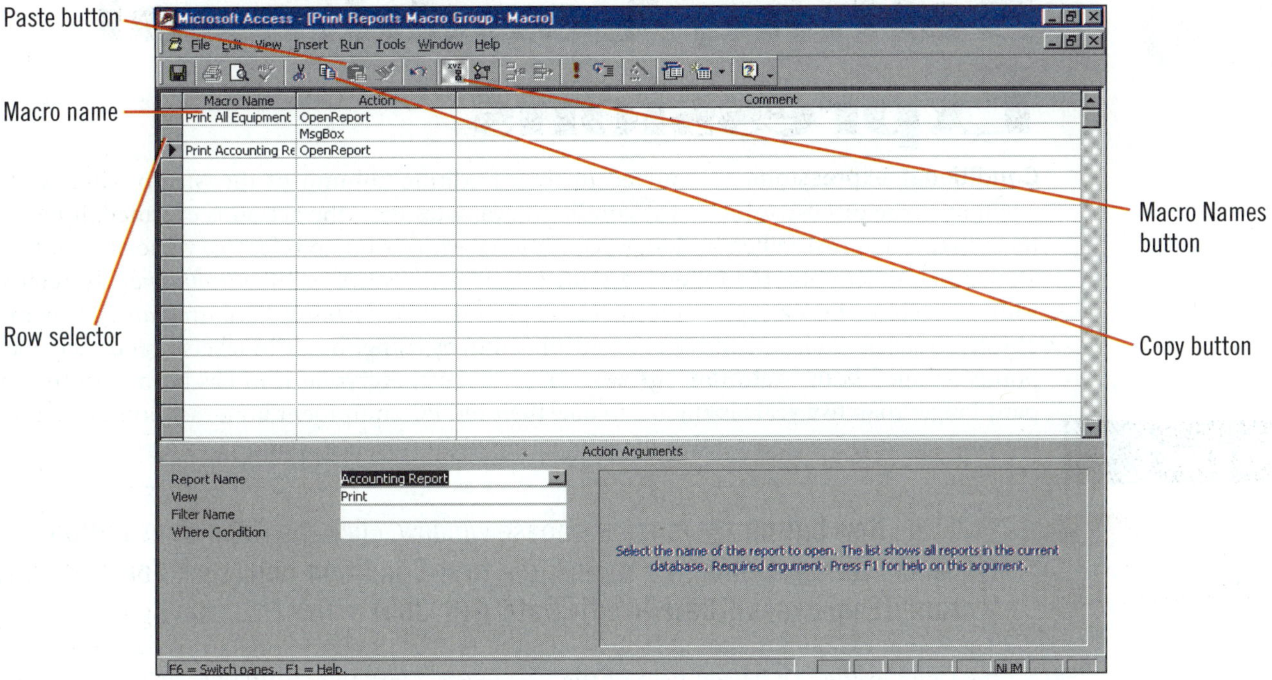

FIGURE N-6: Running the Print Accounting Report macro

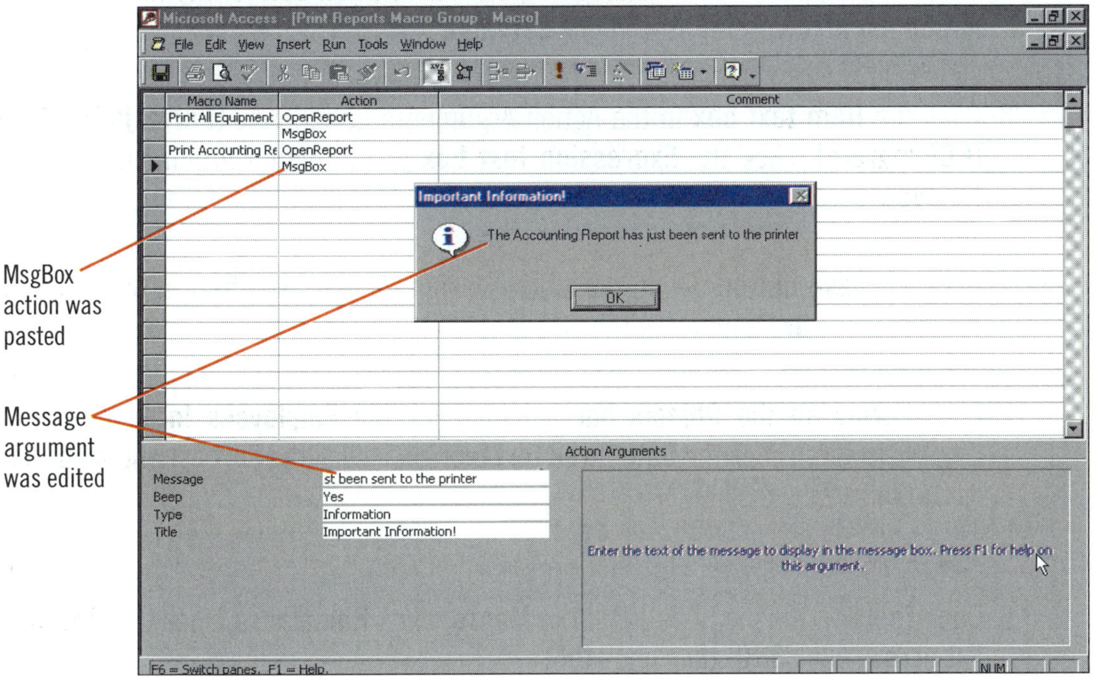

CLUES TO USE

Assigning a macro to a key combination

You can assign macros to a key combination (such as Ctrl+L) by creating a macro group object called **AutoKeys**. In the Macro Names column of the AutoKeys Macro window, enter the key combination to press when you want to run the macro. Any key combination assignments you make in the AutoKeys macro override those that Access has already specified (for example, Ctrl+C is the key combination for copy).

Unit N

Access 2000

Setting Conditional Expressions

Conditional expressions are entered in the Condition column of the Macro window. They result in a true or false value. If the condition evaluates true, the action is executed: if false, the macro skips that row. When building a conditional expression, to refer to a value of a control on a form in a macro, use the following syntax: [Forms]![*formname*]![*controlname*]. To refer to a value of a control on a report, the syntax is [Reports]![*reportname*]![*controlname*]. Separating object types from object names from control names by using square brackets [] and exclamation points is called **bang notation**. At MediaLoft, everyone who has been with the company longer than five years is eligible to take their old PC equipment home as soon as it has been replaced. Kristen uses a conditional macro to highlight this information in a form.

Steps

QuickTip

The columns of the Macro window can be resized using the ✥ mouse pointer.

1. Click the **New button** in the database window, click the **Conditions button** on the Macro Design toolbar, right-click the **first Condition cell**, click **Zoom**, then type **[Forms]![Employees]![DateHired]<Date()-(5*365)** in the Zoom dialog box

   The Zoom dialog box should look like Figure N-7. This conditional expression says "Check the value in the DateHired field of the Employees form to see if it is earlier than five years before today's date."

2. Click **OK** to close the Zoom dialog box, click the **Action cell** for the first row, click the **Action list arrow**, scroll, then click **SetValue**

   The SetValue macro action has two arguments.

3. Click the **Item text box** in the Action Arguments panel, type **[Forms]![Employees]![PCProgram]**, click the **Expression text box** in the Action Arguments panel, then type **yes**

   Your screen should look like Figure N-8.

4. Click the **Save button** on the Macro Design toolbar, type **5PC** in the Macro Name text box, click **OK**, then close the 5PC macro

   Test the macro using the Employees form.

5. Click **Forms on the Objects bar**, double-click the **Employees form**, maximize the Employees form, click the **Date Hired text box**, then click the **Sort Ascending button** on the Form View toolbar

   The record for Evelyn Storey, hired 1/1/92, appears. Because she has five years of service with MediaLoft, she is eligible for the PC program.

6. Click **Tools** on the menu bar, point to **Macro**, click **Run Macro**, click the **Macro Name list arrow**, click **5PC**, then click **OK**

   After evaluating the date of this record and determining that this employee has been working at MediaLoft longer than five years, the PC Program check box was automatically checked (set to "Yes"), as shown in Figure N-9.

7. Click the **Last Record button** on the Main Form Navigation buttons, click **Tools** on the menu bar, point to **Macro**, click **Run Macro**, verify that **5PC** is in the **Macro Name text box**, then click **OK**

   Because Kristen Fontanelle was hired recently, the PC Program check box was not checked (set to "yes") by running the macro.

8. Close the Employees form

FIGURE N-7: Zoom dialog box

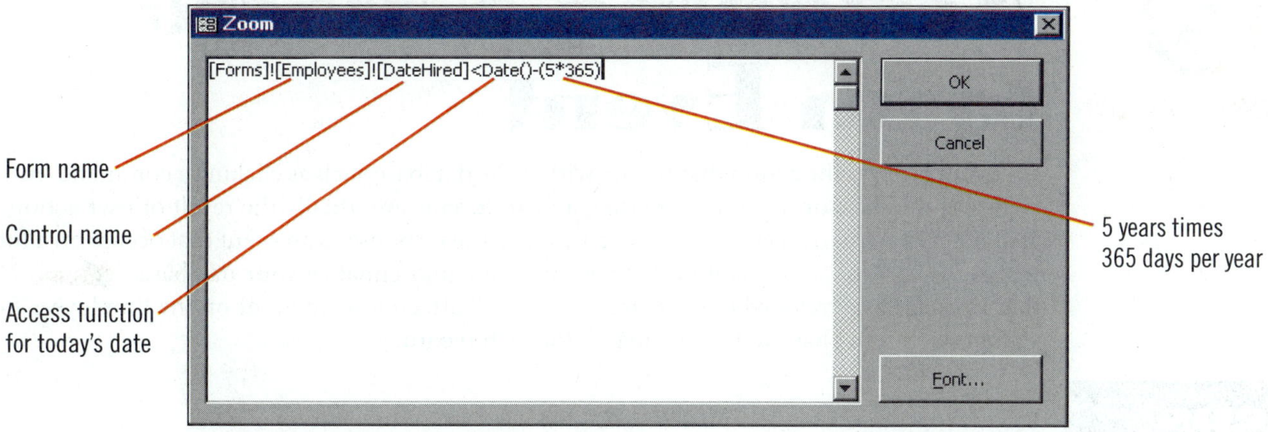

FIGURE N-08: Creating a conditional expression

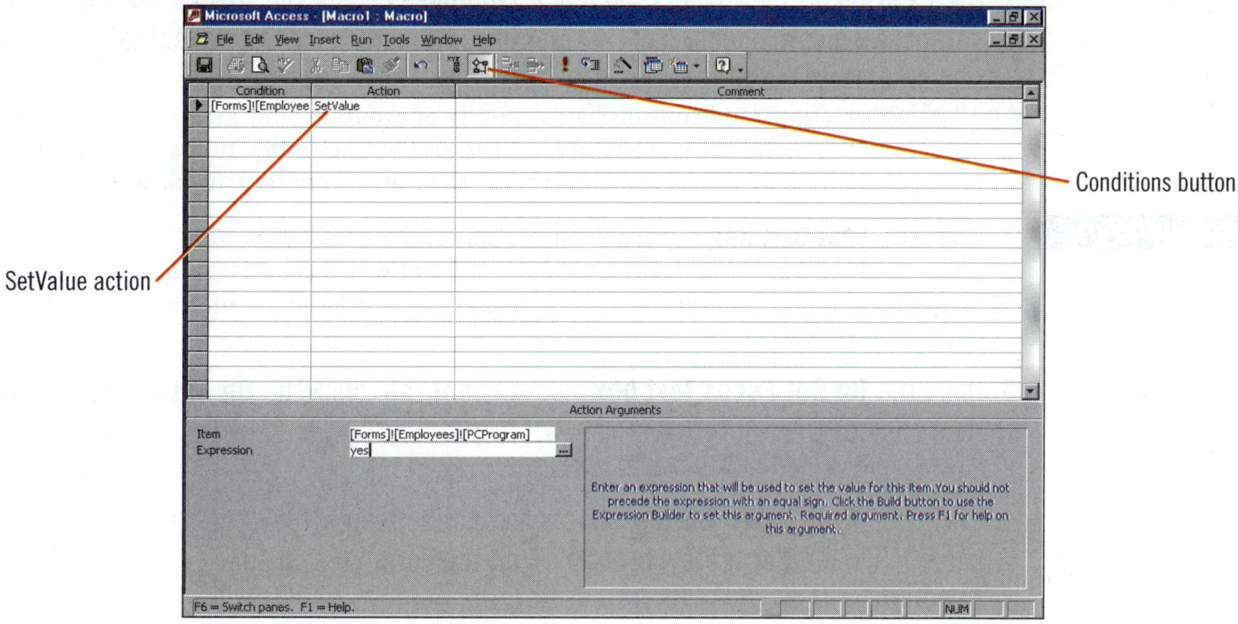

FIGURE N-9: Running the 5PC macro

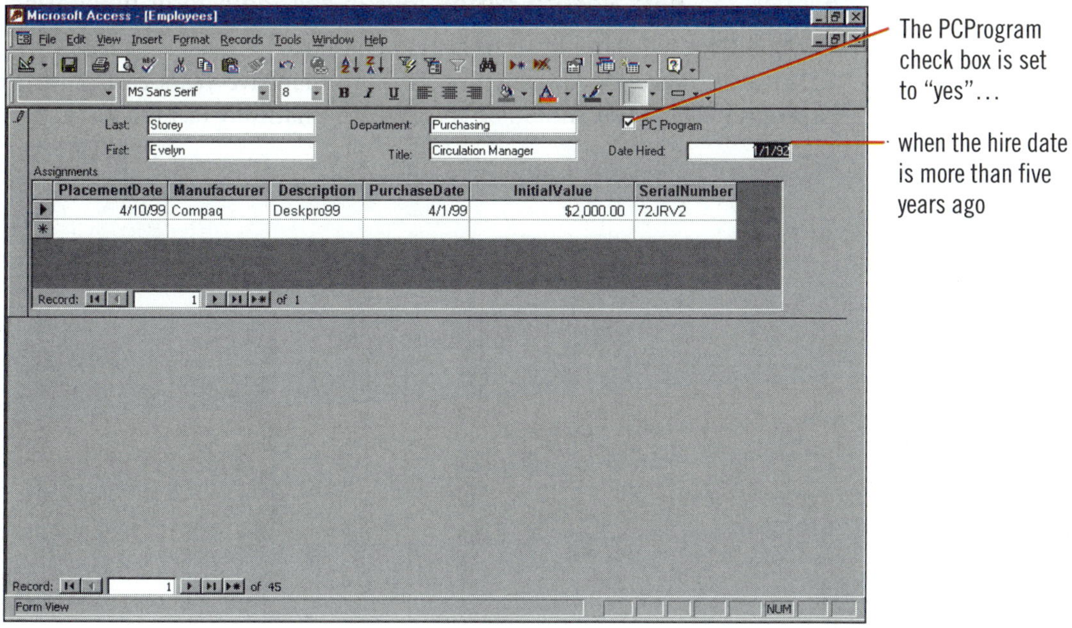

Access 2000

Unit N

Access 2000

Assigning a Macro to an Event

An **event** is a specific action that occurs within the database such as clicking a command button, changing the data, or opening or closing a form. Events are usually the result of user action. By assigning a macro to an event, you can customize the response to an event that occurs on a form, report, or control, and therefore further automate and enhance your database. Now that Kristen has developed the 5PC macro, she will attach it to an event on the Employees form so that she doesn't have to run the macro for each record.

Steps

QuickTip

Click any event property text box, then press [F1] for more help on that property.

Trouble?

Close the Toolbox and Field list and move the property sheet to better view the form.

1. Click **Forms** on the Objects bar, click **Employees**, click the **Design button** in the database window, double-click the **Detail section**, then click the **Event tab** in the Detail section property sheet

   All objects, sections, and controls have a variety of events to which macros can be attached. Most event names are self-explanatory, such as the On Click event for the Detail section. Any macro attached to this event would run when the Detail section of the form is clicked.

2. Click the **Last text box** in the Detail section of the Employees form

   There are 15 different events for a text box, many of which are very similar. Knowing which to use is a matter of experience. The Help manual provides more information on the subtle differences between the events.

3. Click the **On Got Focus text box** on the Event tab, click the **On Got Focus list arrow**, then click **5PC**

   Your screen should look like Figure N-10.

4. Click the **Properties button** on the Form Design toolbar to close the property sheet, click the **Form View button** on the Form View toolbar

   As you move through the records of the form, the Last text box will automatically have the focus because it is listed first in the form's tab order, and the 5PC macro will automatically run.

5. Click the **Next Record button** in the main form navigation buttons ten times while observing the PC Program check box

   For every Date Hired value that is more than five years earlier than today's date, the PC Program check box should be checked automatically (set to "yes").

6. Save and close the Employees form

FIGURE N-10: Assigning a macro to a text box event

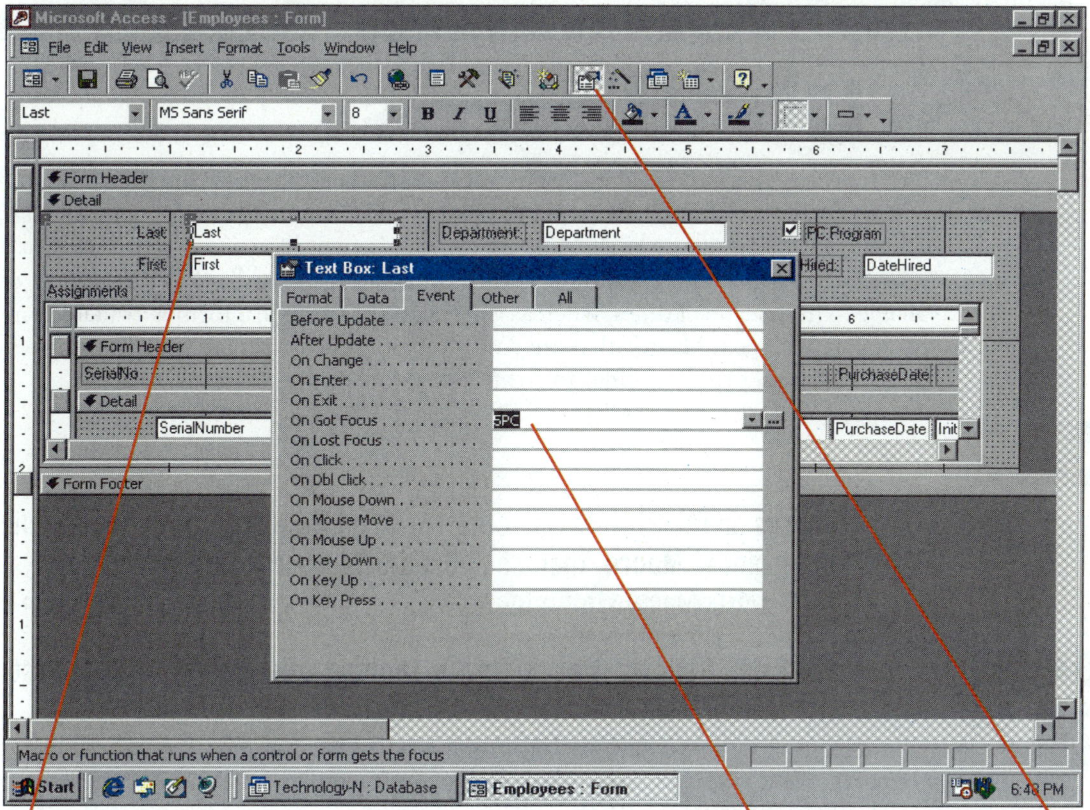

CLUES TO USE

Assigning a macro to a command button

You can add a command button on a form to run a macro. One way to accomplish this is to build the command button using the Command Button Wizard. Use the wizard to specify the Run Macro action found in the Miscellaneous category. Another way to assign a macro to a command button is to open the command button's property sheet and enter the macro name in the appropriate event property. The most common event property for a command button is the **On Click** event, which triggers as soon as you click the command button in Form view.

Unit N

Access 2000

Customizing Toolbars with Macros

There are many ways to run a macro: by clicking the Run button in the Macro window, by going through the Tools menu, by assigning the macro to an event on a control, or by assigning it to a button on a toolbar, menu, or shortcut menu. The benefit of assigning a macro to a toolbar button over assigning it to a command button on a specific form is that the toolbar can be made available to the user at all times, whereas a command button on a form is available only when that specific form is open. Macros that are run from multiple forms are great candidates for custom toolbars. Kristen decides to create a new toolbar for the print macros.

Steps

1. Click **Macros** on the Objects bar, click the **Print Reports Macro Group**, click **Tools** on the menu, point to **Macro**, then click **Create Toolbar from Macro**
   The Print Reports Macro Group toolbar appears on your screen. All of the macros in that group are automatically added to the toolbar.
2. Drag the **Print Reports Macro Group toolbar title bar** to dock it just below the Database toolbar, as shown in Figure N-11
   Because this toolbar contains buttons for only two macros (the two found in the Print Reports Macro Group), the entire name of the macro fits comfortably on the toolbar. If you add several more macros to the toolbar, however, you will quickly run out of room.
3. Right-click the **Print Reports Macro Group toolbar**, click **Customize** to open the Customize dialog box, right-click the **Print All Equipment macro button** on the Print Reports Macro Group toolbar, then point to **Change Button Image**
   Your screen should look like Figure N-12. The shortcut menu that allows you to modify toolbar button images and text is available only when the Customize dialog box is open.
4. Click the **Shoes icon** on the icon palette, right-click the **Print All Equipment macro button** again, then click **Default Style**
   The Default Style for a button displays only the button image, not the text.
5. Right-click the **Print Accounting Report macro button** on the Print Reports Macro Group toolbar, point to **Change Button Image**, click the **Scales icon** on the icon palette, right-click the **Print Accounting Report macro button**, then click **Default Style**
   The image on a toolbar button can be edited.
6. Right-click , then click **Edit Button Image**
   The Button Editor dialog box opens, which allows you change the appearance of the picture pixel by pixel.
7. Click the **bright green color box** on the Colors palette, then click all 11 squares in the **left scale**, as shown in Figure N-13
   With enough time and patience, you could create any number of unique button images. Once created, the images can be copied and pasted from one button to another.
8. Click **OK**, then click **Close** to close the Customize dialog box
   The Print Reports Macro Group toolbar can be turned on or off from anywhere within the database. As with buttons on other toolbars, these buttons can be deleted and modified, and new ones can be added later.
9. Point to the , then point to the on the Print Reports Macro Group toolbar
   Each button on the new Print Reports Macro Group toolbar has a ScreenTip and functions like the buttons on other toolbars.

Trouble?

If the new toolbar docks in an undesirable location, point to the left edge of the toolbar so that your mouse pointer changes to ✥, then drag it to the desired location.

FIGURE N-11: Print Reports Macro Group toolbar

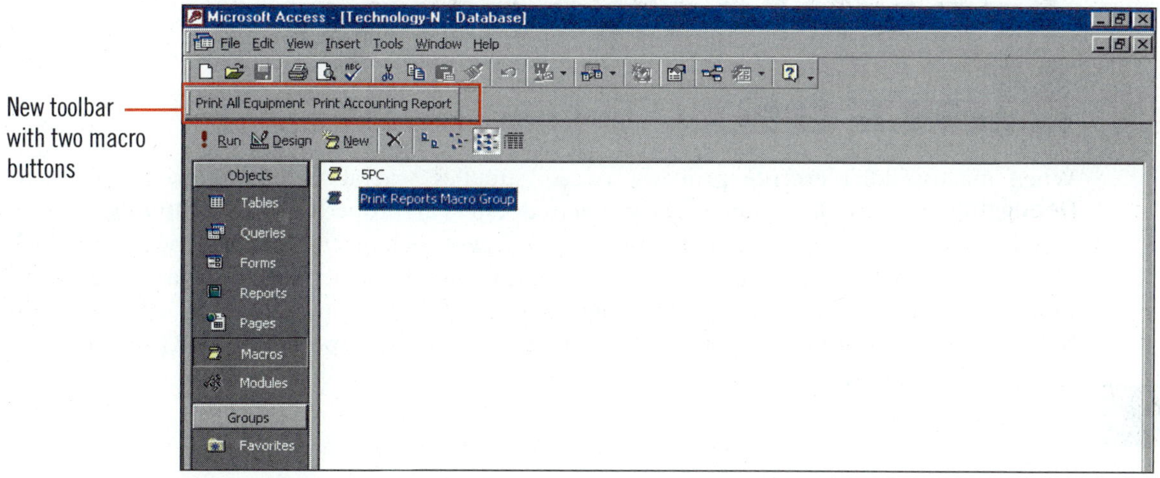

FIGURE N-12: Customizing a button image

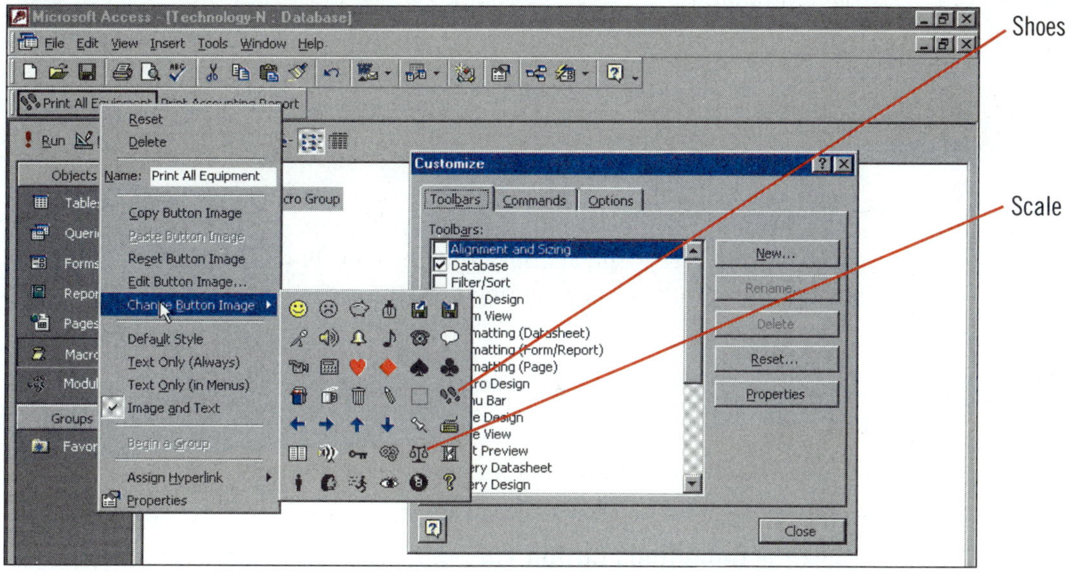

FIGURE N-13: Button Editor dialog box

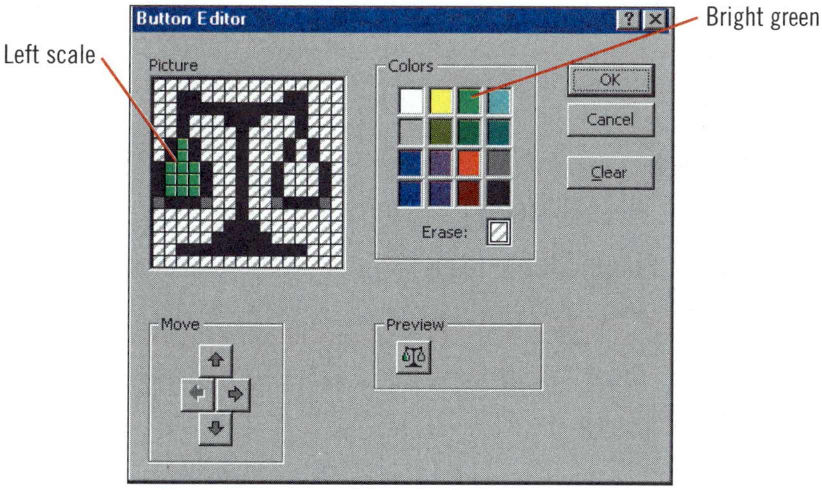

Troubleshooting Macros

When macros don't execute properly, Access supplies several techniques to debug them. **Debugging** means to determine why the macro doesn't run properly. **Single stepping** runs the macro one line at a time, so you can observe the effect of each macro action in the Macro Single Step dialog box while it executes. Another option is to disable a macro action by entering "False" in the Condition cell in the row of the action that you wish to temporarily skip. Before building more sophisticated macros, Kristen uses the Print Reports Macro Group to learn debugging techniques.

Steps

1. Click **Print Reports Macro Group**, click the **Design button**, click the **Single Step button** on the Macro Design toolbar, then click the **Run button** on the Macro Design toolbar
   The screen should look like Figure N-14, with the Macro Single Step dialog box open. This dialog box displays information including the macro's name, whether the current action's condition is true, the action's name, and the action arguments. From the Macro Single Step dialog box you can step into the next macro action, halt execution of the macro, or continue running the macro without single stepping.
2. Click **Step** in the Macro Single Step dialog box
   Stepping into the second action allows the first action to execute. The Macro Single Step dialog box now displays information about the second action.
3. Click **Step**
   The second action, the MsgBox action, executes, displaying the message box.
4. Click **OK**
   You can use the Condition column to temporarily ignore an action while you are debugging a macro.
5. Click the **Conditions button** on the Macro Design toolbar, click the **Condition cell** for the first row, then type **False**
   Your screen should look like Figure N-15.
6. Click the **Save button** on the Macro Design toolbar, then click
   The Macro Single Step dialog box still displays description information about the action, but because the Condition value is False, the OpenReport action will not execute, so the All Equipment report will not be sent to the printer.
7. Click **Halt** in the Macro Single Step dialog box, double-click **False** in the Condition cell, then press **[Delete]**
8. Click the **Single Step button** on the Macro Design toolbar to turn it off
   You could leave the Single Step feature on for future work, but you should turn it off now so that the next time you open a database and run a macro it will not be on.
9. Save and close the Print Reports Macro Group, close the Technology–N database, then exit Access

FIGURE N-14: Single stepping through a macro

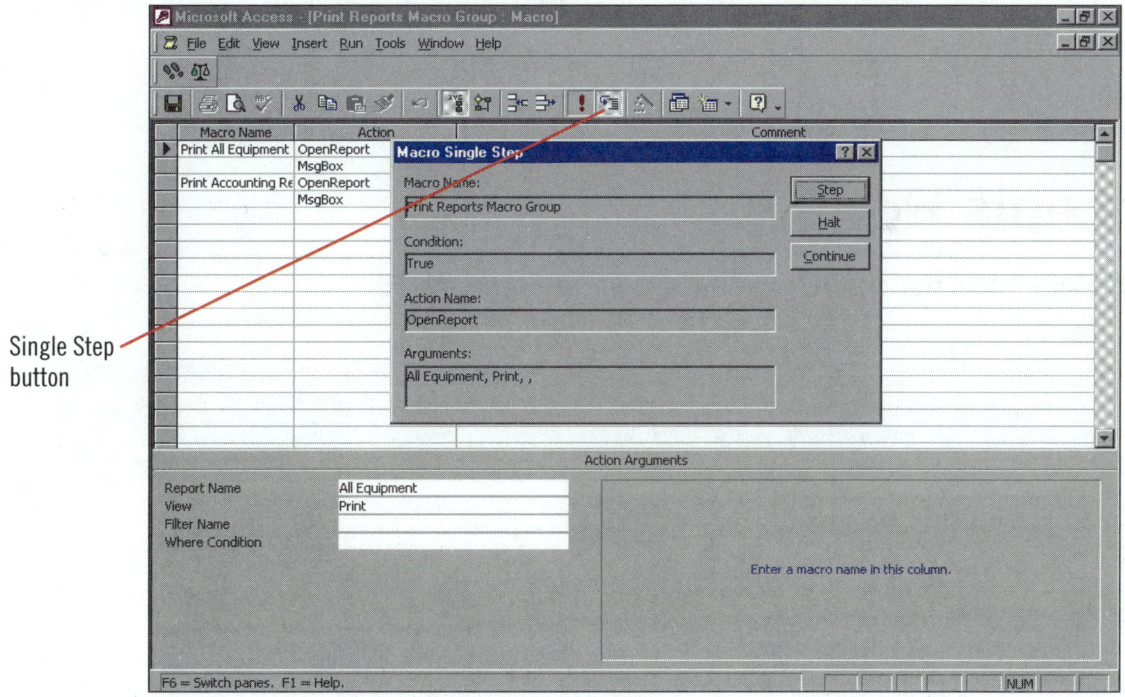

FIGURE N-15: Using a False condition

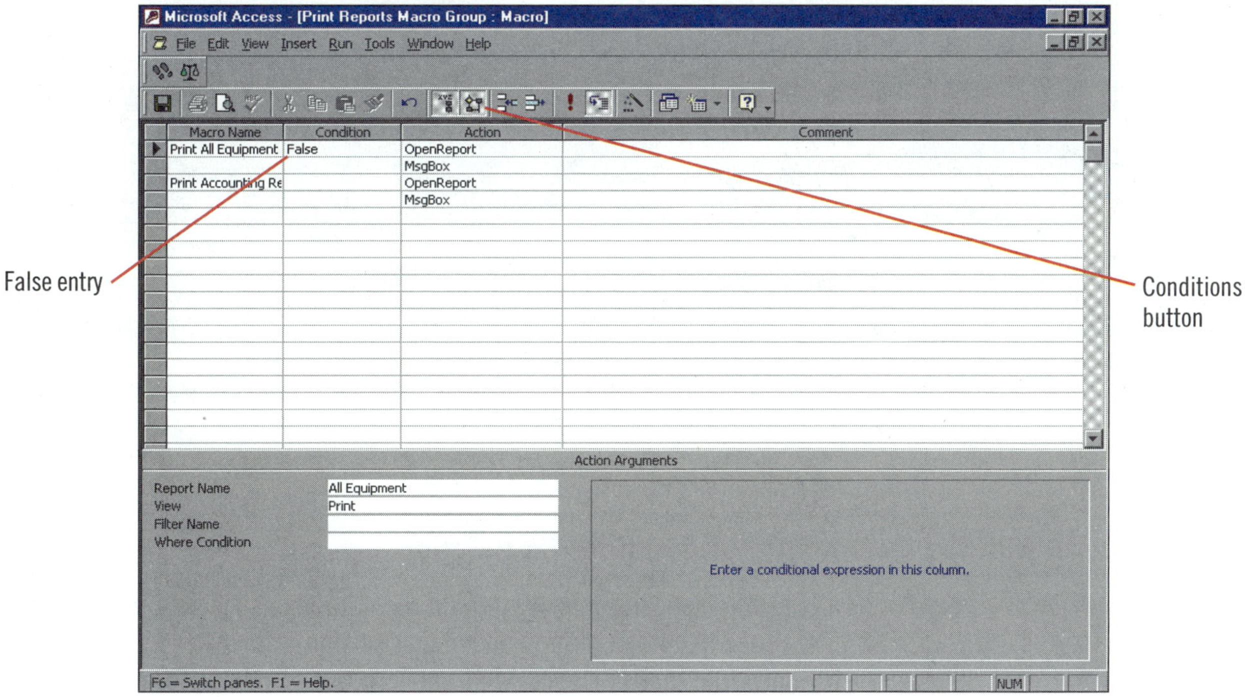

Practice

▶ Concepts Review

Identify each element of the macro window shown in Figure N-16.

FIGURE N-16

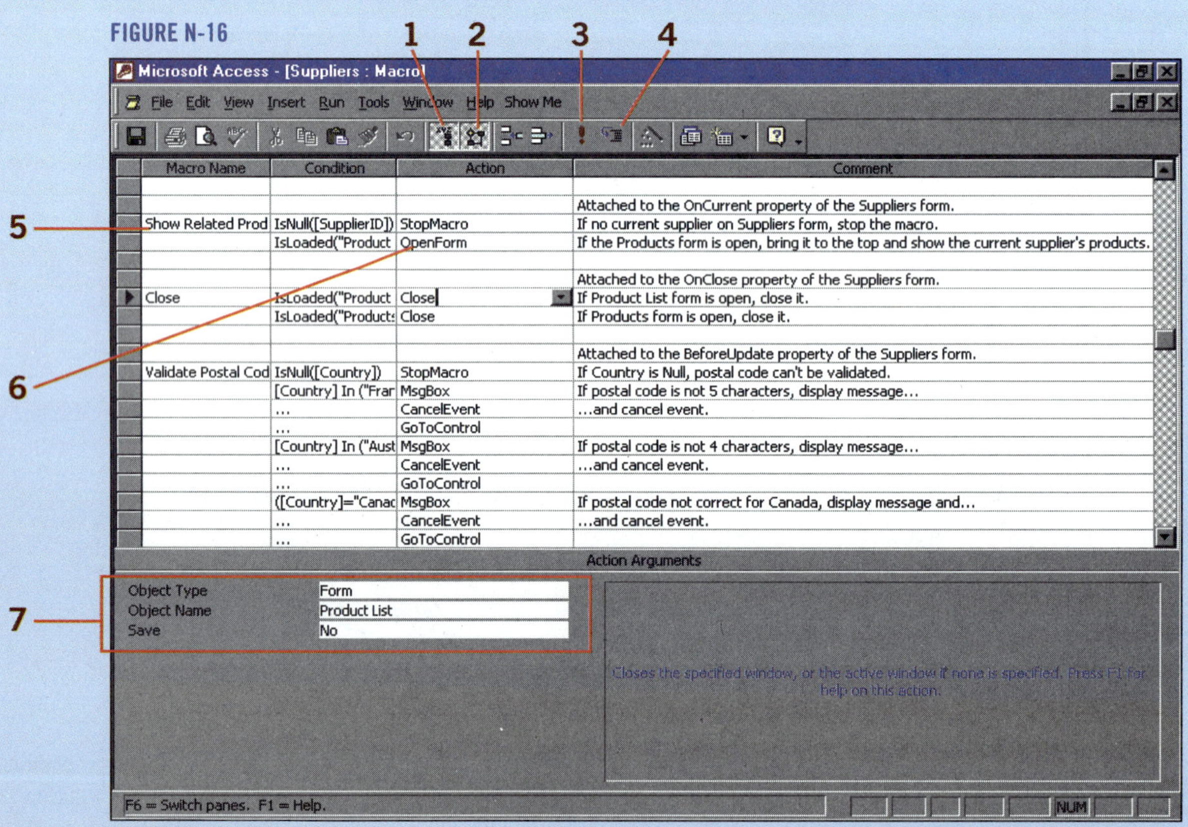

Match each term with the statement that describes its function.

8. **Macro**
9. **Conditional expression**
10. **Arguments**
11. **Debugging**
12. **Actions**
13. **Event**

a. Specific action that occurs within the database such as a mouse click, a change in data, or a form opening or closing

b. Individual tasks that you want the Access macro to perform

c. Access object that stores a series of actions that perform a series of tasks

d. Determining why a macro doesn't run properly

e. Provide additional information to define how an Access action will perform

f. Evaluates as either true or false, which determines whether Access will execute a macro action or not

Select the best answer from the list of choices.

14. Which of the following is *not* a major benefit of using a macro?
- **a.** To save time by automating routine tasks
- **b.** To ensure consistency in executing routine or complex tasks
- **c.** To make the database more flexible by adding macro command buttons to forms
- **d.** To redesign the relationships among the tables of the database

15. Which of the following *best* describes the process of creating an Access macro?
- **a.** Use the macro recorder to record clicks and keystrokes as you complete a task
- **b.** Use the single-step recorder feature to record clicks and keystrokes as you complete a task
- **c.** Use the Macro Wizard to determine which tasks are done most frequently
- **d.** Open the Macro window and add actions, arguments, and conditions to accomplish the desired task

16. Which of the following does *not* run a macro?
- **a.** Click the macro name in the Database window, then click Run
- **b.** Assign the macro to an event of a control on a form
- **c.** Add the macro to a toolbar
- **d.** Add the macro as an entry on the title bar

17. Which is *not* a reason to run a macro in single-step mode?
- **a.** You want to change the arguments of a macro while it runs
- **b.** You want to observe the effect of each macro action individually
- **c.** You want to debug a macro that isn't working properly
- **d.** You want to run only a few of the actions of a macro

18. Which is *not* a reason to use conditional expressions in a macro?
- **a.** More macro actions are available when you are also using conditional expressions
- **b.** Conditional expressions allow you to skip over actions when the expression evaluates to false
- **c.** You can enter "False" in the Conditions column of the Macro window to skip that action
- **d.** Conditional expressions give the macro more power and flexibility

19. Which example illustrates the proper syntax to refer to a specific control on a form?
- **a.** {Forms}!{*formname*}!{*controlname*}
- **b.** (Forms)!(*formname*)!(*controlname*)
- **c.** Forms!*formname.controlname*
- **d.** [Forms]![*formname*]![*controlname*]

Skills Review

1. Understanding Macros.
- **a.** Start Access and open the Basketball-N database from your Project Disk.
- **b.** Open the Macro Design window of the Print Macro Group and record your answers to the following questions on a sheet of paper:
  - How many macros are in this macro group?
  - What are the names of the macros in this macro group?

Access 2000

- What actions does the first macro in this macro group contain?
- What arguments does the first action contain? What values were chosen for those arguments?

c. Close the Macro window for the Print Macro Group object.

2. Creating a Macro.

a. Open a new Macro window.
b. Add the OpenQuery action to the first row of the Macro window.
c. Select Score Delta as the value for the Query Name argument of the OpenQuery action.
d. Select Datasheet for the View argument of the OpenQuery action.
e. Select Edit for the Data Mode argument for the OpenQuery action.
f. Save the macro object with the name "Score Delta".
g. Run the macro to make sure it works, then close Score Delta query and the Score Delta Macro window.

3. Modifying Actions and Arguments.

f. Open the Score Delta macro in Macro Design view.
b. Add a MsgBox action in the second row of the Macro window.
c. Type "We had a great season!" for the Message argument in the Action Arguments panes of the MsgBox action.
d. Select Yes for the Beep argument of the MsgBox action.
e. Select Warning! for the Type argument of the MsgBox action.
f. Type "Iowa State Cyclones" for the Title argument of the MsgBox action.
g. Save the macro, then run it to make sure the MsgBox action works as intended.
h. Click OK in the dialog box created by the MsgBox action, then close the Score Delta query and close the Macro window.

4. Creating a Macro Group.

a. Rename the Score Delta macro with the name "Query Macro Group".
b. Open the Query Macro Group's Macro Design window.
c. Open the Macro Name column and type the name "Score Delta Macro" on the first line for the first macro.
d. Create another macro and name it "Forward FG Macro".
e. Add an OpenQuery action for the first action of the Forward FG Macro.
f. Select Forward Field Goals for the Query Name argument of the OpenQuery action and use the default entries for the other two arguments.
g. Add a MsgBox action for the second action of the Forward FG Macro.
h. Type "Forward Field Goals" as the Message argument for the MsgBox action.
i. Select Yes for the Beep argument of the MsgBox action.
j. Select Critical for the Type argument of the MsgBox action.
k. Type "2000-2001 Season" for the Title argument of the MsgBox action.
l. Save the macro.
m. Click Tools on the menu bar, point to Macro, click Run macro, then run the Forward FG Macro.
n. Click OK in the 2000-2001 Season dialog box created by the MsgBox action, then close the query datasheet and close the Macro window.

5. **Setting Conditional Expressions.**
   a. Open a new Macro window.
   b. Click the Conditions button to open the Condition column.
   c. Type the following condition in the condition cell of the first row: [Forms]![Game Summary Form]![Home Score]>[Opponent Score] (*Hint*: Use the Zoom dialog box or widen the column to more clearly view the entry.)
   d. Add the SetValue action to the first row.
   e. Type the following entry in the Item argument value for the SetValue action: [Forms]![Game Summary Form]![Victory]
   f. Type "Yes" for the Expression argument for the SetValue action.
   g. Save the macro as "Victory Calculator" and close the Macro window.

6. **Assigning a Macro to an Event.**
   a. Open the Game Summary Form in Design view.
   b. Open the Property sheet for the Detail section.
   c. Assign the Victory Calculator macro to the On Click event of the Detail section.
   d. Close the property sheet, save the form, then open it in Form view.
   e. Navigate through the first four records, while single clicking each record in the Detail section (click to the right of the text box controls). The Victory checkbox should be marked for the first three records, but not the fourth.
   f. Close the Game Summary form.

7. **Customizing Toolbars with Macros.**
   a. Click Macros on the Objects bar, click the Print Macro Group, click Tools on the menu bar, point to Macro, then click Create Toolbar from Macro.
   b. Dock the toolbar with the three text buttons just below the Database toolbar in the database window.
   c. Right-click the new toolbar, then click Customize to open the Customize dialog box.
   d. Change the button image for each of the three macros to the question mark icon and a default style (image only).
   e. Edit the button images so that the second macro question mark button is bright red (instead of yellow) and the third is bright blue (instead of yellow).
   f. Close the Customize dialog box and point to each icon to make sure that the ScreenTip relates to the three macro names in the Print Macro Group.

8. **Troubleshooting Macros.**
   a. Open the Print Macro Group's Macro window.
   b. Click the Single Step button on the Macro Design toolbar, then click the Run button.
   c. Click Step twice to step through the two actions of this macro, then click OK on the resulting message box.
   d. Open the Condition column by clicking the Conditions button on the Macro Design toolbar (if it's not already opened).
   e. Add the value "False" as a condition to the first row, the OpenReport action of the Games Summary macro.
   f. Save the macro, then click the Run button.
   g. Click the Step button twice to move through the actions of the macro. This time the Games Summary report should *not* be printed. Click OK when prompted.
   h. Delete the False condition in the first row, save the macro, then close the Macro window.
   i. Turn off the Single Step button.
   j. Close the Basketball-N database.
   k. Exit Access.

Independent Challenges

1. As the manager of a doctor's clinic, you have created an Access database called Patients-N to track insurance claim reimbursements. You wish to use macros to help automate the database.

To complete this independent challenge:

a. Start Access and open the database Patients-N from your Project Disk.
b. Open the Macro window of the CPT Form Open macro (CPT stands for Current Procedural Terminology, which is a code that describes a medical procedure.)
c. On a separate sheet of paper, identify the macro actions, arguments for each action, and values for each argument.
d. In two or three sentences, explain in your own words what tasks this macro automates.
e. Close the CPT Form Open Macro window.
f. Open the Claim Entry Form in Design view. Maximize the window.
g. In the footer of the Claim Entry Form are several command buttons. (*Hint*: Scroll the main form to see these buttons.) Open the property sheet of the Add CPT Code button and click the Event tab.
h. On your paper, write the event to which the CPT Form Open macro is assigned.
i. Open the Claim Entry Form in Form view and click the Add CPT Code button in the form footer.
j. On your paper, write the current record number that is displayed for you.
k. Scroll up the CPT form and find the record for CPT Code 99243. Write the RBRVS value for this record, then close the CPT form and Claim Entry form. (RBRVS stands for Resource Based Relative Value System, a measurement of relative value between medical procedures.)
l. Close the Patients-N database.
m. Exit Access.

2. As the manager of a doctor's clinic, you have created an Access database called Patients-N to track insurance claim reimbursements. You wish to use macros to help automate the database.

To complete this independent challenge:

a. Start Access and open the database Patients-N from your Project Disk.
b. Open a new Macro Window and click the Macro Names button to open the Macro Name column.
c. Enter "Preview DOS-Denied" as the first macro name, and use the OpenReport macro action in the first row.
d. Select Date of Service Report – Denied for the ReportName argument, and Print Preview for the View argument of the OpenReport action. Leave the other two arguments blank.
e. Enter "Preview DOS-Fixed" as the second macro name, and use the OpenReport macro action in the second row.
f. Select Date of Service Report – Fixed for the ReportName argument, and Print Preview for the View argument of the OpenReport action. Leave the other two arguments blank.
g. Save the object with the name "Preview Group", then close the Macro window.
h. Run the Preview DOS-Fixed macro.
i. Close the Patients-N database.
j. Exit Access.

3. As the manager of a doctor's clinic, you have created an Access database called Patients-N to track insurance claim reimbursements. You wish to use macros to help automate the database.

To complete this independent challenge:

a. Start Access and open the Patients-N database from your Project Disk.
b. Open a blank Macro window and click the Conditions button to open the Condition column.
c. Enter the following in the Condition cell of the first row:
[Forms]![CPT Form]![RBRVS]=0
d. Select the SetValue action for the first row.
e. Type the following as the Item argument value for the SetValue action:
[Forms]![CPT Form]![Research]
f. Enter "Yes" as the Expression argument value for the SetValue action.
g. Save the macro with the name "Value Research" and close the Macro window.
h. Open the CPT Form in Design view, and open the property sheet for the CPTCode text box.
i. Assign the Value Research macro to the On Got Focus event of the CPTCode text box.
j. Close the property sheet, save the form, and open it in Form view.
k. Use the Next Record button to move quickly through all 64 records in the form. Notice that the macro automatically places a check mark in the Research check box when the RBRVS value is equal to zero.
l. Save and close the CPT form, and close the Patients-N database.

WEB WORK

4. MediaLoft has developed a Web site that provides internal information to their employees. In this independent challenge, you will complete research on macros for upcoming MediaLoft projects.

a. Connect to the Internet, go to the MediaLoft intranet site at http://www.course.com/illustrated/MediaLoft
b. Click the link for the Research center, then click the link for Microsoft Access Information.
c. Find the Search This Site text box and enter "Access macro" to request information on this subject. (*Hint*: Web sites change often, and you may need to find and click a "Search" button before you are able to enter your search criteria.)
d. Refine your search as necessary, then find and print two articles with both the words "Access" and "macro" in the summary line.
e. Close your browser window.

Visual Workshop

As the manager of a doctor's clinic, you have created an Access database called Patients-N to track insurance claim reimbursements. Develop the macro group called Query Group with the actions and argument values shown in Figure N-17 and Table N-3. Run both macros to test them. Debug them if necessary.

TABLE N-3: Macro actions and arguments for the Query Group

macro name	action	argument	argument value
Denied	OpenQuery	Query Name	Monthly Query – Denied
		View	Datasheet
		Data Mode	Edit
	Maximize		
	MsgBox	Message	These claims were denied
		Beep	Yes
		Type	Information
		Title	Denied
Fixed	OpenQuery	Query Name	Monthly Query – Fixed
		View	Datasheet
		Data Mode	Edit
	Maximize		
	MsgBox	Message	These claims were fixed
		Beep	Yes
		Type	Information
		Title	Fixed

FIGURE N-17

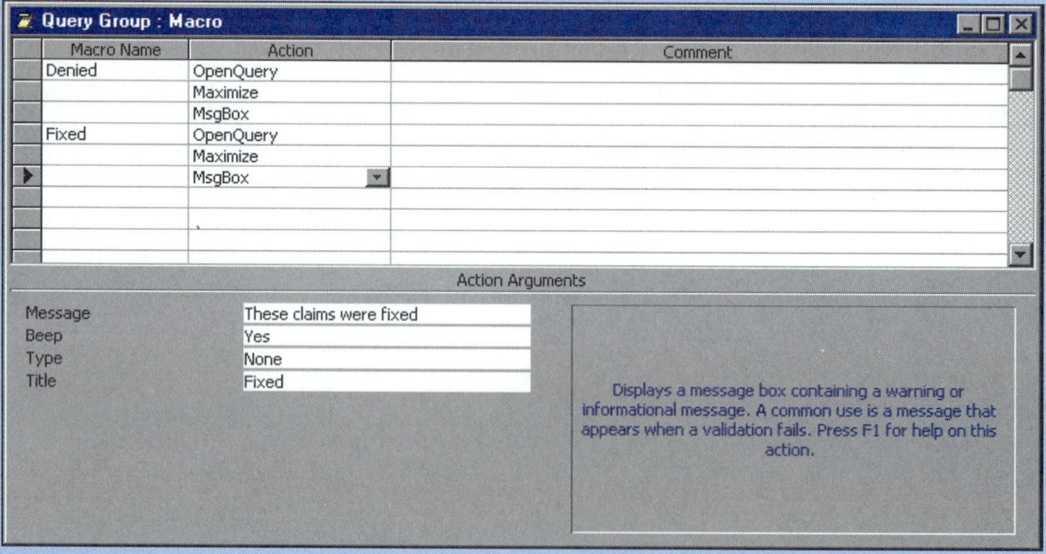

Access 2000

Unit O

Creating Modules

Objectives

- Understand Modules
- Compare Macros and Modules
- Create a Function Procedure
- Use If Statements
- Document a Procedure
- Examine Class Modules
- Create a Sub Procedure
- Troubleshoot Modules

Access is an extremely robust and easy-to-use relational database program. Reports and screens that took hours to create using complex programming code are now created using wizards, graphical tools, and property sheets. Macros that formerly took hours to debug can now be written, tested, and attached to a command button or control event in minutes. Because Access provides so many user-friendly tools to accomplish tasks, many Access database administrators don't need to work with the Access programming language, **Visual Basic for Applications** (**VBA**), to meet the needs of the users. When programming is required, however, the Visual Basic code is stored in a database object called a **module**. Kristen learns about and creates some small Access modules to enhance the capabilities of the Technology database.

Unit O

Access 2000

Understanding Modules

A **module** is an Access object that contains Visual Basic for Applications programming code, and it is written in the **Visual Basic Editor Code window** (**Code window**), shown in Figure O-1. The components and text colors of the Code window are described in Table O-1. Programming code contained within the module can be executed by clicking a command button or in response to an event. A database has two kinds of modules: **class modules**, which are used only with a particular form or report and are, therefore, stored as a part of the form or report object; and **standard modules**, which can be executed from anywhere in the database and are displayed as module objects in the database window. Kristen wants to learn more about VBA modules, so she studies several key questions that explain the purpose and terminology of modules.

Details

What does a module contain?

A module contains VBA programming code organized in units called **procedures**. A procedure may be a few or several lines (**statements**) long. Modules also contain **comment lines** to help document and explain the code. Comment lines in Visual Basic are preceded by an apostrophe.

What is a procedure?

A **procedure** is a series of VBA programming statements that perform an operation or calculate an answer. There are two types of procedures: Functions and Subs. **Declaration statements** precede procedure statements and help set rules for how the statements in the module are processed.

What is a function?

A **function** is a procedure that returns a value. Access supplies many built-in statistical, financial, and date functions, such as Sum, Pmt, and Now, that can be used in an expression in a query, form, or report to calculate a value. Using VBA, you could create a new function called StockOptions, for example, which calculates the date an employee is eligible for the corporate stock options, and use the unique method of calculating that date specified by your company.

What is a sub?

A **sub** (or **sub procedure**) performs a series of VBA statements, but does not return a value and cannot be used in an expression. You use subs to manipulate controls and objects. For example, you might create a sub called SetSchoolNameFocus that moves the focus on a form to a text box bound to a SchoolName field when the user marks a check box that indicates he or she is a college graduate.

What are arguments?

Arguments are constants, variables, or expressions passed to a procedure (function or sub) that are required for it to execute. For example, the full syntax for the Sum function is Sum(*expr*), where *expr* represents the argument for the Sum function. Arguments are specified immediately after a procedure's name and are enclosed in parentheses. When there are multiple arguments, they are separated by commas.

What is a method?

A **method** is an action that an object can perform. For example, the GoToPage method moves the focus to the first control on a specified page in the active form. Procedures are often written to invoke methods (database actions) in response to user actions. For example, you may wish to invoke the GoToPage method when the user clicks a command button.

FIGURE O-1: Visual Basic Editor Code window for a standard module

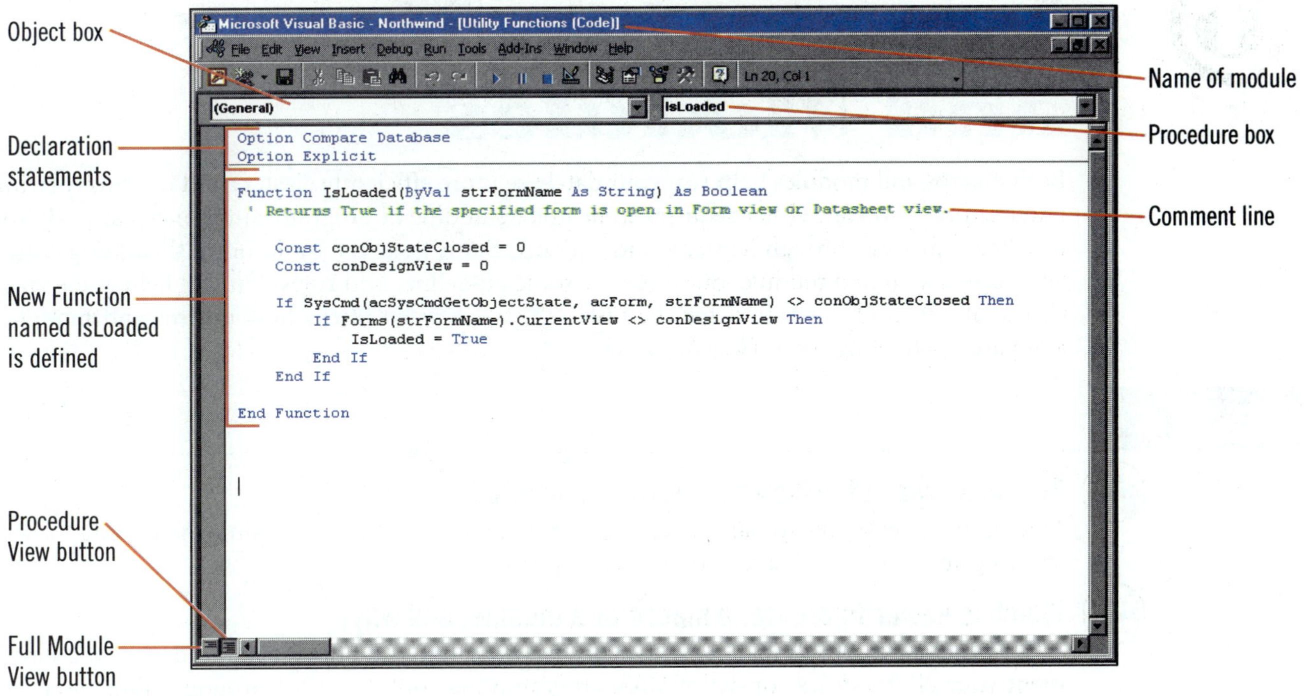

TABLE O-1: Components and Text Colors of the Code window

component or color	description
Procedure View button	Shows the statements that belong only to the current procedure
Full Module View button	Shows all the lines of VBA (all of the procedures) in the module
Declaration statements	Contains statements that apply to every procedure in the module such as declarations for variables, constants, user-defined data types, and external procedures in a dynamic link library
Object box	In a class module, lists the objects associated with the form or report (in VBA, "**objects**" are the form or report's controls, sections, the form or report itself, and subs already defined)
Procedure box	In a standard module, lists the procedures in that module. In a class module, lists the events (such as Click or Dblclick) that the item selected in the Object box can use
Comment line	Descriptive text that serves as explanatory documentation; comment lines start with an apostrophe
Blue	Keyword text—blue words are reserved by VBA and are already assigned specific meanings
Black	Normal text—black words are the unique VBA code developed by the user
Red	Syntax error text—a line of code in red indicates that it will not execute correctly because there is a syntax error (perhaps a missing parenthesis or a spelling error)
Green	Comment text—any text after an apostrophe is considered documentation, and is therefore ignored in the execution of the procedure

Unit O

Access 2000

Comparing Macros and Modules

Both macros and modules help run your database more efficiently (faster) and effectively (with fewer errors). To create either requires some understanding of programming concepts, an ability to follow a process through its steps, and patience. Some tasks can be accomplished using either an Access macro or a module, but there are some guidelines and rules that will help guide your choice of which object is best for the task. Kristen learns how macros and modules compare by studying several key questions.

Details

For what types of tasks are macros best suited?

Macros are an easy way to handle repetitive, simple details such as opening and closing forms, showing and hiding toolbars, and printing reports.

Which is easier to create, a macro or a module, and why?

To create a module, you must know the correct syntax for each line of code, and write the statement yourself. Modules consist of VBA programming code, a robust programming language with endless possibilities. Macros are generally easier to create because you don't have to know about programming syntax. With a macro, you choose actions (a limited list of about 50) from a list. Once the action is chosen, the arguments associated with that action are displayed automatically in the Action Arguments panel.

Is there ever a situation when I must use a macro?

You must use macros to make global shortcut key assignments. You can also use an automatic macro that carries out a series of actions that are beyond the capabilities of the startup options when the database first opens.

When should I use a module?

There are at least five reasons to use a module rather than a macro:

- Class modules, like the one shown in Figure O-2, are stored as part of the form or report object in which they are created. Therefore, if you develop forms and reports in one database and copy them to another, class modules are copied with the object.
- You must use modules to create unique function procedures. For instance, you might want to create a function called COMMISSION that calculates the appropriate commission on a sale using your company's unique commission formula.
- Modules can contain procedures used to mask error messages. Access error messages can be confusing to the user. But using VBA procedures, you can detect the error when it occurs and display your own message or take some action.
- You can't use a macro to accomplish many tasks outside Access, but VBA code stored in modules works with other products in the Microsoft Office suite to pass information back and forth between the programs.
- VBA code can contain nested If statements, Case statements, and other programming code, which makes it more powerful and flexible than macros. Some of the most common VBA keywords are shown in Table O-2. Because each is a reserved VBA keyword, each appears in blue in the Code window.

FIGURE O-2: Code window for a class module

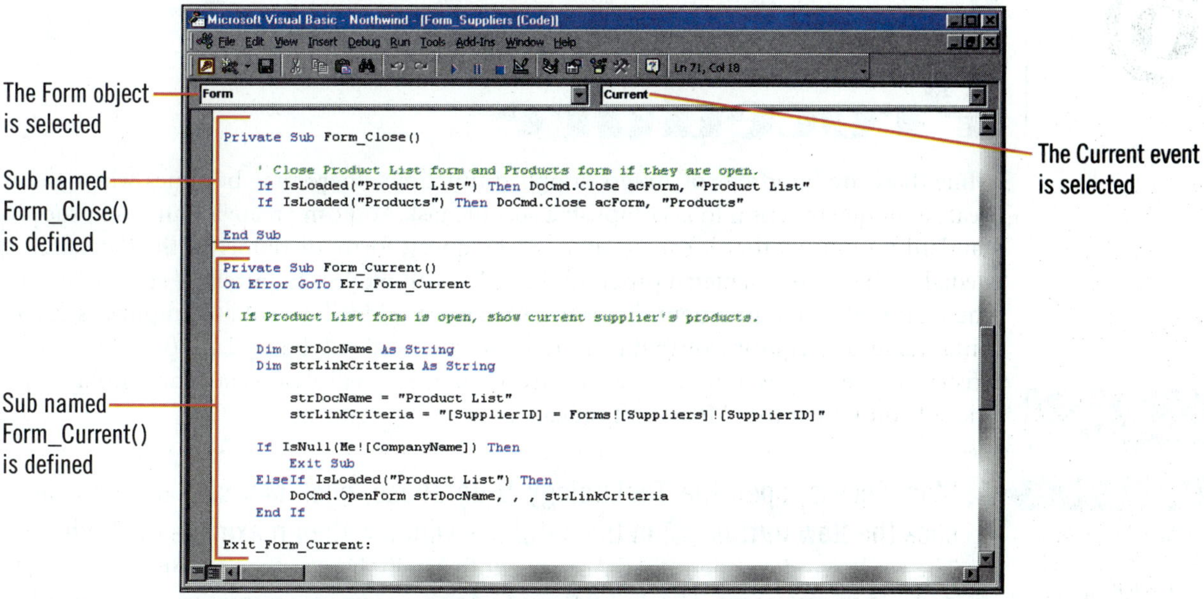

TABLE O-2: Common VBA keywords

statement	explanation
Function	Declares the name and arguments that create a new function procedure
End Function	When defining a new function, the End Function statement is required as the last statement to mark the end of the VBA code that defines the function.
Sub	Declares the name, arguments, and code that create a new sub procedure. **Private Sub** indicates that the sub procedure is accessible only to other procedures in the module where it is declared
End Sub	When defining a new sub, the End Sub statement is required as the last statement to mark the end of the VBA code that defines the sub.
If **Then**	Used to execute code (code that follows the Then statement) if the value of the expression is true (the expression follows the If statement). The If...Then statement has additional optional parts including Then, and ElseIf statements.
End If	When creating an If...Then statement, the End If statement is required as the last statement.
Const	Declares the name and value of a **constant**, an item that retains a constant value throughout the execution of the code
Option Compare Database	A declaration statement that determines the way string values (text) will be sorted
Option Explicit	A declaration statement that specifies that you must explicitly declare all variables used in all procedures. If you attempt to use an undeclared variable name, an error occurs at **compile time**, the period during which source code is translated to executable code.
Dim	Declares a **variable**, a named storage location that contains data that can be modified during program execution
On Error GoTo	Upon error in the execution of a procedure, the On Error GoTo statement specifies the location (the statement) where the procedure should continue. If you don't use an On Error statement, any run-time error that occurs is fatal; that is, an error message is displayed and execution stops.
Select Case	Executes one of several groups of statements, depending on the value of an expression. Each group of statements is a new **Case**. Use the Select Case statement as an alternative to using **ElseIf** in **If...Then...Else** statements when comparing one expression to several different values.
End Select	When defining a new Select Case group of statements, the End Select statement is required as the last statement to mark the end of the VBA code.

Unit O

Access 2000

Creating a Function Procedure

While there are hundreds of Access-supplied functions, there may be times when you want to create a unique function to accomplish a specific task. You can create a Function procedure in a standard module so that it can be used in any query, form, or report in the database. MediaLoft has implemented a program that allows employees to purchase corporate equipment when it is replaced. Equipment that is less than a year old will be sold to employees at 75% of its initial value, and equipment that is more than a year old will be sold at 50% of its initial value. Kristen defines a new function called StreetValue that will determine the employee purchase price of equipment that MediaLoft replaces.

Steps

Trouble?

If the Projects or Properties windows are open as small windows on the left side of the screen, click their Close buttons to close them.

1. Start Access, open the **Technology-O** database, click **Modules** on the Objects bar, click the **New button** in the database window, then maximize the Code window
   The Code window opens, and Access automatically inserts the Option Compare Database declaration statement. The Technology-O database window minimizes on the taskbar.
2. Type **Function StreetValue(corpvalue)**, then press **[Enter]**
   This statement declares a new function name, StreetValue, which contains one argument, corpvalue. VBA automatically adds the End Function statement because it is required to mark the end of the code that defines the new function. Because both Function and End Function are VBA keywords, they are colored blue. The insertion point is positioned between the statements so that you can further define how the new StreetValue function will calculate.
3. Press **[Tab]**, type **StreetValue = corpvalue * 0.5**, then press **[Enter]**
   Your screen should look like Figure O-3. This statement explains how StreetValue will calculate. StreetValue will be equal to the corpvalue argument times 0.5. It is not necessary to indent statements, but many programmers indent code between matching Function/End Function, Sub/End Sub, or If/End If statements to enhance the program's readability.
4. Click the **Save button** on the Standard toolbar, type **Functions** in the Save As dialog box, then click **OK**
   Now that the function is created, it can be used in a query, form, or report. You need to close the Visual Basic window and return to Access.
5. Click **File** on the menu bar, then click **Close and Return to Microsoft Access**
   The Visual Basic window closes, and the Microsoft Access window and the Technology-O database window are open on your screen.
6. Click **Queries** on the Objects bar, click **Employee Pricing**, then click the **Design button** in the database window
   The Employee Pricing query opens in Design view. You can create calculated expressions in a query using either Access functions or the ones you define in modules.
7. Maximize the Query Design window, click the **blank Field cell** to the right of the InitialValue field, type **EmployeePrice:StreetValue([InitialValue])**, then click the **Datasheet View button** on the Query Design toolbar
   Your screen should look like Figure O-4. In this query you created a new field called EmployeePrice that used the StreetValue function that contains one argument (called corpvalue in the module). The value in the InitialValue field (stored in the Equipment table) was entered as the corpvalue argument. The StreetValue function multiplied the InitialValue field by 0.5 to determine the EmployeePrice field. By creating the StreetValue function in a module, you can add powerful logic to it that calculates different StreetValues depending on the age of the equipment and use it over and over again.
8. Save the Employee Pricing query, then close the datasheet

QuickTip

Right-click the blank Field cell, then click Zoom to enter the calculated expression in a Zoom dialog box.

FIGURE O-3: Creating the StreetValue function

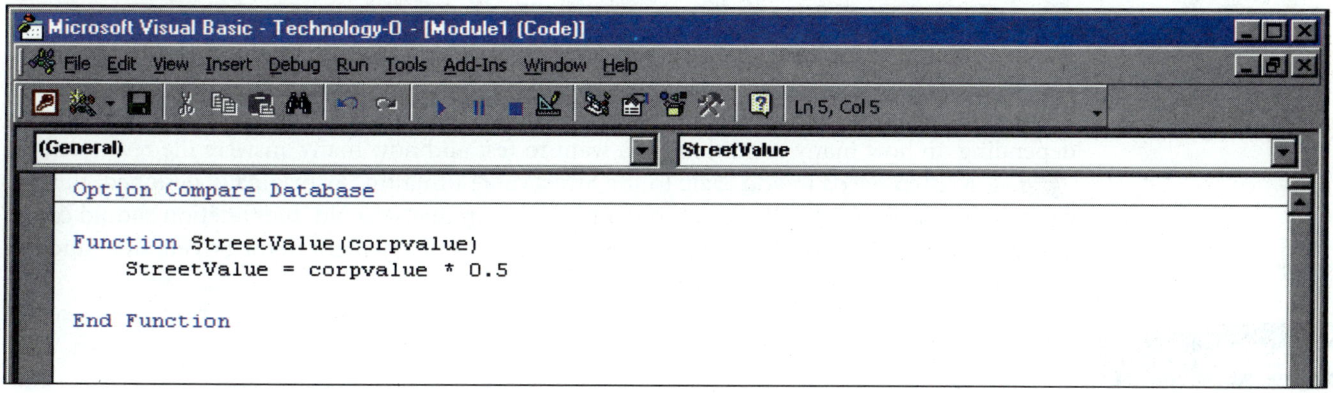

FIGURE O-4: Creating the EmployeePrice field using the StreetValue function

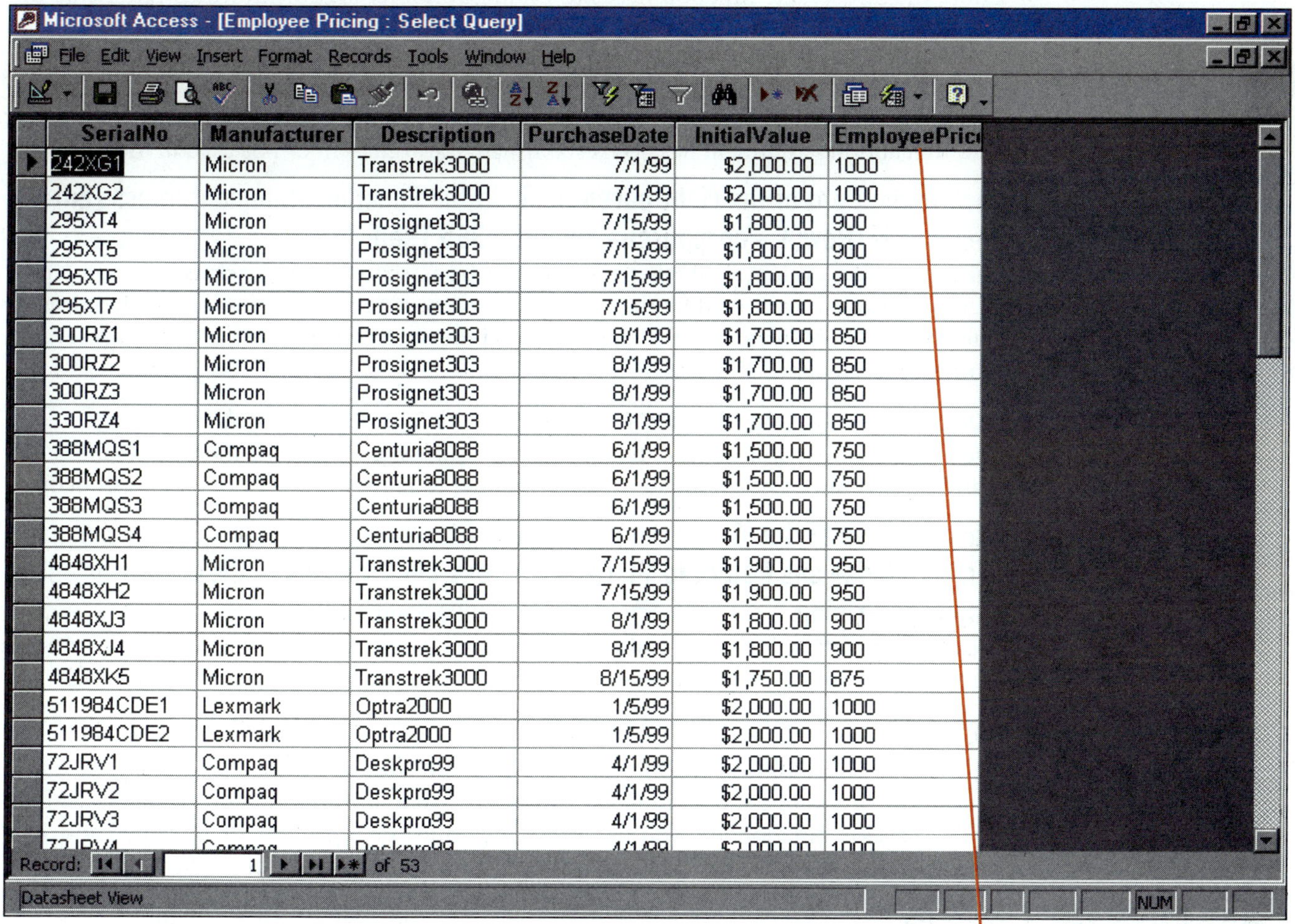

SerialNo	Manufacturer	Description	PurchaseDate	InitialValue	EmployeePric
242XG1	Micron	Transtrek3000	7/1/99	$2,000.00	1000
242XG2	Micron	Transtrek3000	7/1/99	$2,000.00	1000
295XT4	Micron	Prosignet303	7/15/99	$1,800.00	900
295XT5	Micron	Prosignet303	7/15/99	$1,800.00	900
295XT6	Micron	Prosignet303	7/15/99	$1,800.00	900
295XT7	Micron	Prosignet303	7/15/99	$1,800.00	900
300RZ1	Micron	Prosignet303	8/1/99	$1,700.00	850
300RZ2	Micron	Prosignet303	8/1/99	$1,700.00	850
300RZ3	Micron	Prosignet303	8/1/99	$1,700.00	850
330RZ4	Micron	Prosignet303	8/1/99	$1,700.00	850
388MQS1	Compaq	Centuria8088	6/1/99	$1,500.00	750
388MQS2	Compaq	Centuria8088	6/1/99	$1,500.00	750
388MQS3	Compaq	Centuria8088	6/1/99	$1,500.00	750
388MQS4	Compaq	Centuria8088	6/1/99	$1,500.00	750
4848XH1	Micron	Transtrek3000	7/15/99	$1,900.00	950
4848XH2	Micron	Transtrek3000	7/15/99	$1,900.00	950
4848XJ3	Micron	Transtrek3000	8/1/99	$1,800.00	900
4848XJ4	Micron	Transtrek3000	8/1/99	$1,800.00	900
4848XK5	Micron	Transtrek3000	8/15/99	$1,750.00	875
511984CDE1	Lexmark	Optra2000	1/5/99	$2,000.00	1000
511984CDE2	Lexmark	Optra2000	1/5/99	$2,000.00	1000
72JRV1	Compaq	Deskpro99	4/1/99	$2,000.00	1000
72JRV2	Compaq	Deskpro99	4/1/99	$2,000.00	1000
72JRV3	Compaq	Deskpro99	4/1/99	$2,000.00	1000

Access 2000

Unit O

Access 2000

Using If Statements

The **If...Then...Else** statement allows you to test a logical condition and execute commands only if the condition is true. The If...Then...Else statement can be one or several lines of code, depending on how many conditions you want to test and how many answers the result can be. Kristen needs to add logic to the StreetValue function. As originally designed, the calculation is *always* at 50%. If the equipment is less than one year old, the function should calculate the answer at 75% of the original value. She uses an If statement in the StreetValue function to determine the correct value based on age.

Steps

1. Click **Modules** on the Objects bar, click **Functions**, then click the **Design button**
   The Functions Code window with the StreetValue function opens. To determine the age of the equipment, which in turn determines whether 50% or 75% should be used in the calculation, the StreetValue function needs to evaluate another argument, which represents the purchase date.

Trouble?

Be sure to type the arguments exactly as specified to avoid getting errors later.

2. Click between the **e** in **corpvalue** and the **right parenthesis** in the Function statement, type , (a comma), press **[Spacebar]**, then type **corppurchasedate**
   Now that another argument has been established, the argument can be used in the function.
3. Click to the right of the **right parenthesis** in the Function statement, press **[Enter]**, then type **If (Now( ) – corppurchasedate) >365 Then**
   This expression evaluates whether today's date (represented by the Access function Now) minus the value represented by the corppurchasedate argument is greater than 365 days. If true, this would indicate that the equipment is older than one year old and the StreetValue should be recalculated at 50%.
4. Type the Else and End If statements precisely as shown in Figure O-5
   The Else statement will be executed only if the expression is false (if the equipment is less than 365 days old). The End If statement is needed to mark the end of the If block of code.
5. Click the **Save button** on the Visual Basic Standard toolbar, click **File** on the menu bar, click **Close and Return to Microsoft Access**, click **Queries** on the Objects bar, click **Employee Pricing**, then click in the database window
   Because you modified the StreetValue function to include two arguments, you have to change the expression in the query to include two arguments for the StreetValue function as well.
6. Right-click the **EmployeePrice field** in the query design grid, click **Zoom**, click to the right of the **right square bracket**, then type **,[PurchaseDate]**
   Your Zoom dialog box should look like Figure O-6. Both of the arguments used to calculate the StreetValue function are field names, so they must be typed exactly as shown and surrounded by square brackets. Commas separate multiple arguments in the function.

Trouble?

If you get a compile or syntax error, open the query design grid, check your function against Figure O-6, and correct any errors.

7. Click **OK** in the Zoom dialog box, then click the **Datasheet View button** on the Query Design toolbar
8. Click any entry in the **PurchaseDate field**, then click the **Sort Ascending button**
   The StreetValue function now calculates two ways, depending on the age of the equipment determined by the date in the PurchaseDate field, as shown in Figure O-7. The EmployeePrice will calculate based on the current date on your computer, so your results may vary. Check to make sure that all records with PurchaseDate values more recently than one year ago calculate the EmployeePrice field at 75% of the InitialValue field.
9. Save and close the Employee Pricing query

FIGURE O-5: If...Then...Else statements

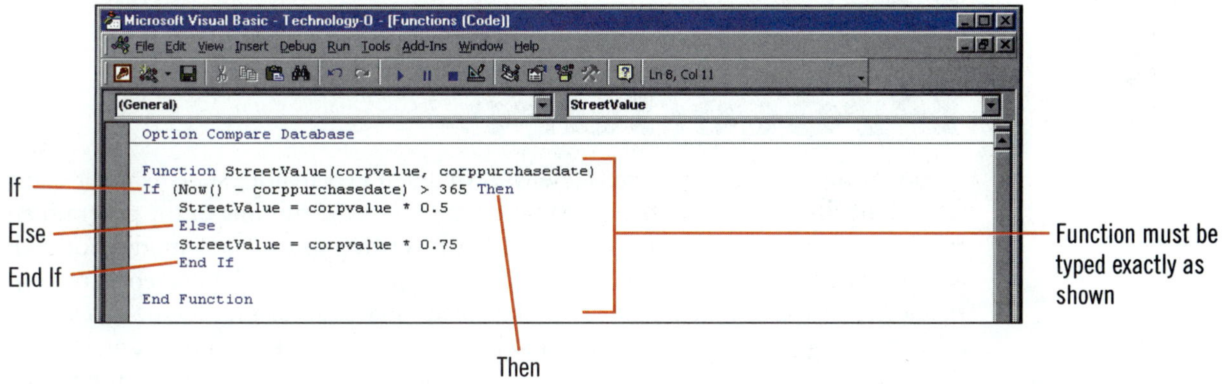

FIGURE O-6: Modifying the expression

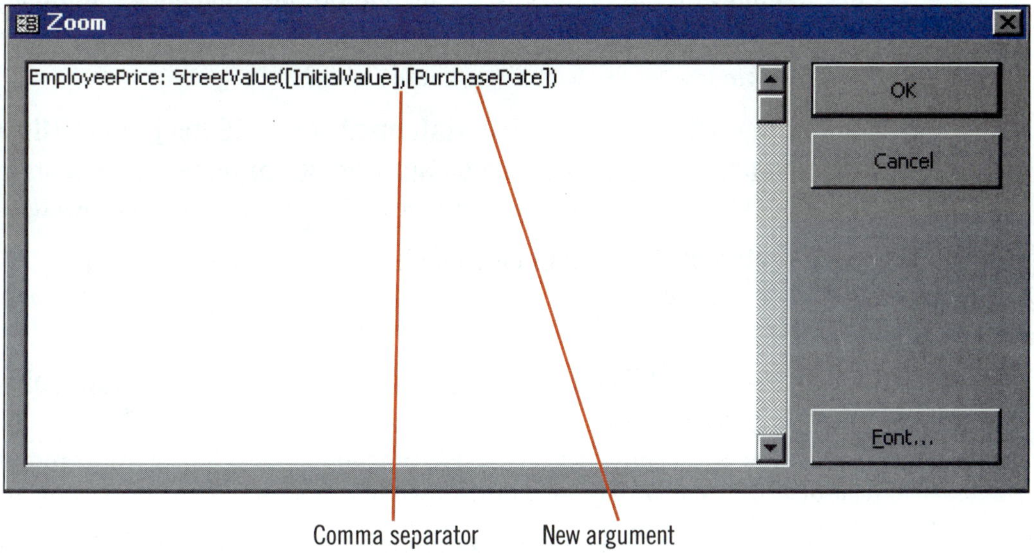

FIGURE O-7: Final EmployeePrice field is calculated using the StreetValue function

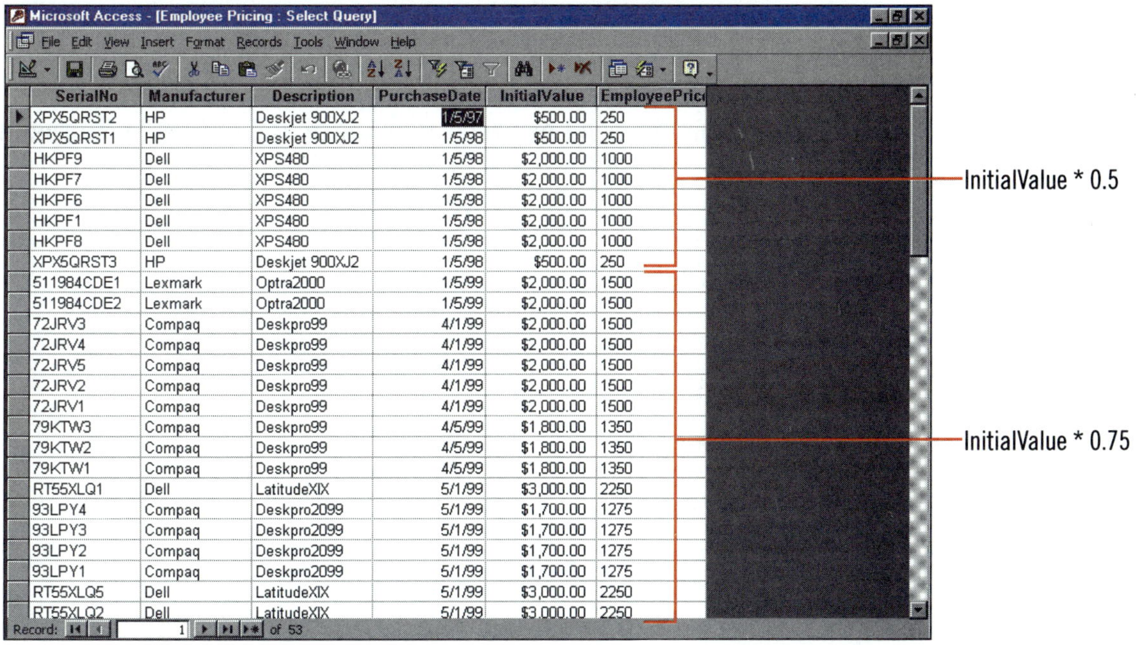

SerialNo	Manufacturer	Description	PurchaseDate	InitialValue	EmployeePric
XPX5QRST2	HP	Deskjet 900XJ2	1/5/97	$500.00	250
XPX5QRST1	HP	Deskjet 900XJ2	1/5/98	$500.00	250
HKPF9	Dell	XPS480	1/5/98	$2,000.00	1000
HKPF7	Dell	XPS480	1/5/98	$2,000.00	1000
HKPF6	Dell	XPS480	1/5/98	$2,000.00	1000
HKPF1	Dell	XPS480	1/5/98	$2,000.00	1000
HKPF8	Dell	XPS480	1/5/98	$2,000.00	1000
XPX5QRST3	HP	Deskjet 900XJ2	1/5/98	$500.00	250
511984CDE1	Lexmark	Optra2000	1/5/99	$2,000.00	1500
511984CDE2	Lexmark	Optra2000	1/5/99	$2,000.00	1500
72JRV3	Compaq	Deskpro99	4/1/99	$2,000.00	1500
72JRV4	Compaq	Deskpro99	4/1/99	$2,000.00	1500
72JRV5	Compaq	Deskpro99	4/1/99	$2,000.00	1500
72JRV2	Compaq	Deskpro99	4/1/99	$2,000.00	1500
72JRV1	Compaq	Deskpro99	4/1/99	$2,000.00	1500
79KTW3	Compaq	Deskpro99	4/5/99	$1,800.00	1350
79KTW2	Compaq	Deskpro99	4/5/99	$1,800.00	1350
79KTW1	Compaq	Deskpro99	4/5/99	$1,800.00	1350
RT55XLQ1	Dell	LatitudeXIX	5/1/99	$3,000.00	2250
93LPY4	Compaq	Deskpro2099	5/1/99	$1,700.00	1275
93LPY3	Compaq	Deskpro2099	5/1/99	$1,700.00	1275
93LPY2	Compaq	Deskpro2099	5/1/99	$1,700.00	1275
93LPY1	Compaq	Deskpro2099	5/1/99	$1,700.00	1275
RT55XLQ5	Dell	LatitudeXIX	5/1/99	$3,000.00	2250
RT55XLQ2	Dell	LatitudeXIX	5/1/99	$3,000.00	2250

Access 2000

Documenting a Procedure

A good programmer documents code with frequent explanatory statements or comment lines. **Comment lines** are text in the code that do not affect the running of the program and are used simply to document the code. At any future time, when you want to modify the code, you'll be able to write the modifications much more quickly if the existing statements are properly documented. If you expect someone else to be able to maintain or modify the code, comment lines are a must. Kristen documents the StreetValue function in the Functions module with descriptive comments so she can easily follow the purpose and logic of the function.

Steps

1. Click **Modules** on the Objects bar, click **Functions**, then click the **Design button** in the database window
   The Code window for the Functions module opens.
2. Click to the left of the **Function statement**, press **[Enter]**, press **[Up arrow]**, type **'This function is called StreetValue and has two arguments**, then press **[Enter]**
   Comments always start with an apostrophe and are green in the Code window.
3. Type **'Created by Your Name on Today's Date**, then press **[Enter]**
   Your screen should look like Figure O-8. Comments also can be placed at the end of an existing line. Either way, however, they always start with an apostrophe.
4. Click to the right of **Then** at the end of the If statement, press **[Spacebar]**, then type **'Now( ) is today's date**
   This comment explains that the Now() function is today's date. All comments are green, regardless of whether they are on their own line or at the end of an existing line.
5. Click to the right of **0.5**, press **[Spacebar]**, then type **'If > 365 days, value is 50%**
6. Click to the right of **0.75**, press **[Spacebar]**, then type **'If < 365 days, value is 75%**
   Your screen should look like Figure O-9. Table O-3 provides more information about the Standard toolbar buttons in the Code window.
7. Click the **Save button** on the Standard toolbar, click **File** on the menu bar, click **Print**, then click **OK**
8. Click **File** on the menu bar, then click **Close and Return to Microsoft Access**

Trouble?

Be sure to use an ' (apostrophe) and not a " (quotation mark) to begin the comment line.

FIGURE O-8: Adding comments to the Code window

Comment lines

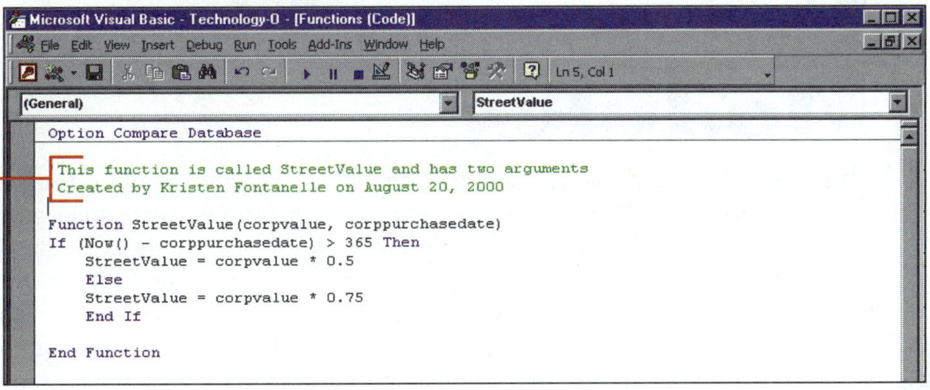

FIGURE O-9: Adding comments at the end of a statement

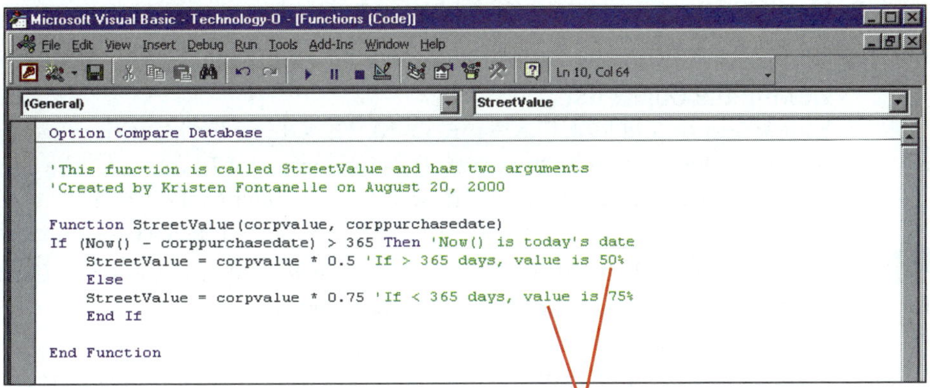

Comment lines at the end of an existing line

Access 2000

TABLE O-3: Standard toolbar buttons in the Code window

button name	button	description
View Microsoft Access		Toggles between the host application and the active Visual Basic document
Insert		Opens a new module or class module code window, or inserts a new procedure in the current code window
Run Sub/UserForm		Runs the current procedure if the insertion point is in a procedure or runs the UserForm if it is active
Break		Stops execution of a program while it's running and switches to **break mode**, the temporary suspension of program execution in which you can examine, debug, reset, step through, or continue program execution
Reset		Resets the procedure
Project Explorer		Displays the **Project Explorer**, which displays a hierarchical list of the currently open **projects**, (set of modules) and their contents
Object Browser		Displays the **Object Browser**, which lists the defined modules and procedures as well as available methods, properties, events, constants, and other items that you can use in the code

Unit O

Access 2000

Examining Class Modules

Class modules are contained and executed within specific forms and reports. Class modules most commonly contain sub procedures and execute in response to an event such as the click of a command button. You do not always have to know VBA code to create class modules. The Command Button Wizard, for example, creates sub procedures. You can examine them to see how sub procedures work and how they are associated to specific events. Kristen used the Command Button Wizard to create four command buttons on the Equipment Entry Form. She examines the sub procedures in this form in order to understand class modules.

Steps

1. Click **Forms** on the Objects bar, click the **Equipment Entry Form**, then click the **Design button** in the database window
   The Equipment Entry Form opens in Design view. The form has four command buttons: three to manipulate records and one to close the form.
2. Maximize the form, click the **Add New Record command button**, view the **Object list** on the Formatting (Form/Report) toolbar, then click each command button while viewing the Object list
   Your screen should look like Figure O-10. The Object list identifies the name of the selected control as determined by the control's Name property. In this case, the word "object" is used as a VBA programmer would use it, and does not refer to the seven basic object types (tables, queries, forms, pages, reports, macros, and modules) of an Access database.
3. Click the **Code button** on the Form Design toolbar, then maximize the Form_Equipment Entry Form (Code) window
   The Code window for the VBA code stored in the Equipment Entry Form class module appears, as shown in Figure O-11. This code was created by using the Command Button Wizard. The names of the two subs displayed at the top of the code window correspond with the first two command buttons on the form, the AddNewRecordButton and the DeleteThisRecordButton. The _Click() suffix on the sub names identifies the event that will cause this sub to execute.
4. Click **File** on the menu bar, click **Close and Return to Microsoft Access**, double-click the **AddNewRecord command button** to open its property sheet, click the **Event tab**, click the **On Click text box**, then click the **Build button**
   The class module is opened in the specific location where the AddNewRecordButton_Click() sub is stored. If you wanted to create another sub that was executed from another event associated with that command button (for example, to display a message box when the command button gets the focus) you could use the property sheet to help you with the syntax of correctly defining the sub's name.
5. Click **File** on the menu bar, click **Close and Return to Microsoft Access**, click the **On Got Focus text box** on the Command Button AddNewRecordButton property sheet, click , click **Code Builder** in the Choose Builder dialog box, then click **OK**
   The class module Code window opens, as shown in Figure O-12. Because you entered the Code window through a specific event (On Got Focus) of a specific control (AddNewRecordButton), VBA knew what to name the sub and to automatically supply the last line of the procedure, the End Sub statement. The rest of the sub's statements, however, require individual programming, because you are not using a wizard to create the code.
6. Select all of the statements from **Private Sub AddNewRecordButton_GotFocus()** through the **End Sub** statement, press **[Delete]**, click the **Save button** on the Microsoft Visual Basic Standard toolbar, click **File** on the menu bar, click **Close and Return to Microsoft Access**, close the property sheet, then close the Equipment Entry Form

QuickTip

The Command Button Wizard prompts you for the command button's name as its last question.

Trouble?

If the Immediate Window is open below the code window, close it.

FIGURE O-10: Four command buttons in Form Design view

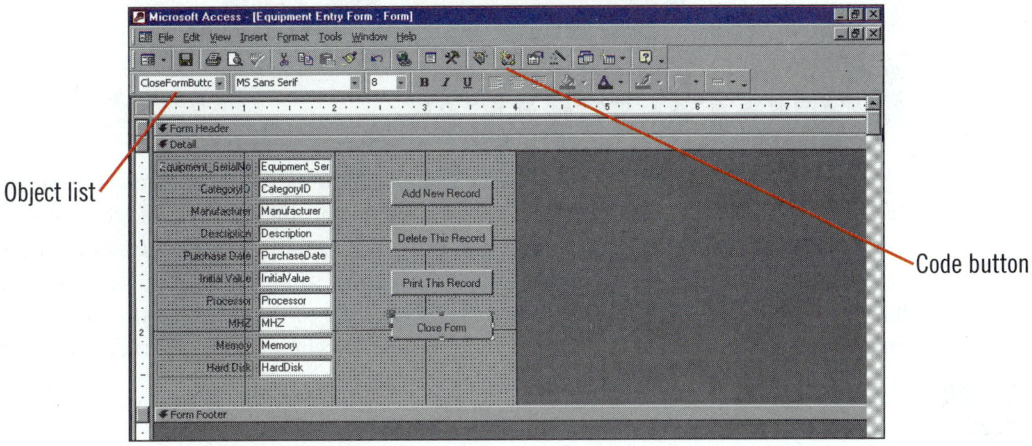

FIGURE O-11: Class module containing four subs that correspond with the four command buttons

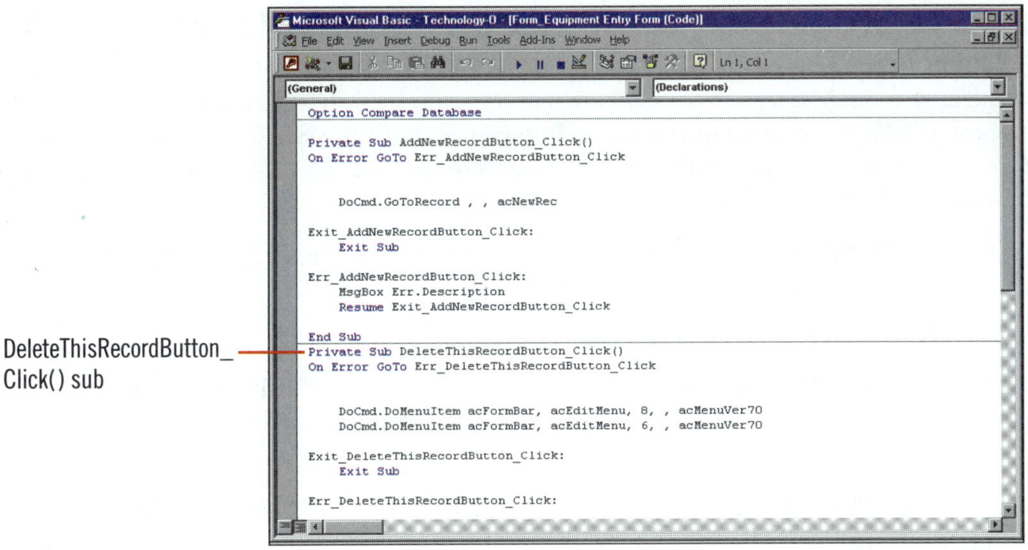

FIGURE O-12: Examining a new sub for a command button

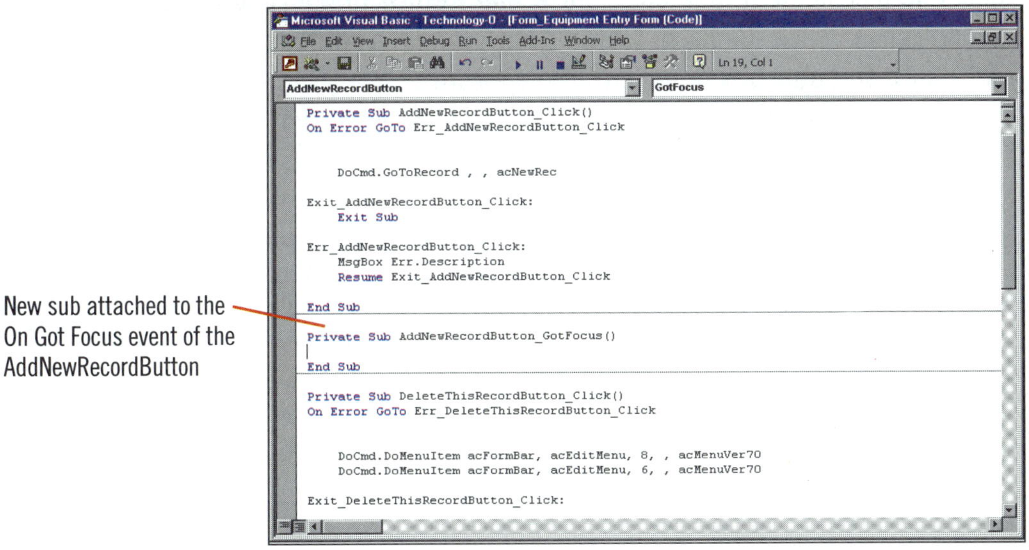

Unit O

Access 2000

Creating a Sub Procedure

While it is easiest to create class module sub procedures using wizards, not all subs can be created this way. The Command Button Wizard, for example, always attaches its code to the Click event of a command button. You might want to create a sub that executes based on another action, such as double-click, or one that is assigned to a control (called objects in VBA) other than a command button. Kristen would like to create all of the Technology forms with built-in documentation that the user can access by clicking the form. To accomplish this, she writes a sub procedure in the form's class module.

Steps

1. Click the **Equipment Entry Form**, click the **Design button** in the database window, then click the **Properties button** to open the form's property sheet

2. Click the **Event tab**, click the **On Click text box**, click the **Build button**, click **Code Builder** in the Choose Builder dialog box, then click **OK**

   The class module opens with two new statements to identify the new sub, which is called Form_Click( ). The name of the new sub references both the specific object and event you were examining through the property sheet. You can use the Object and Procedure lists within the Code window to find specific statements.

3. Click the **Object list arrow** below the Standard toolbar, click **FormFooter**, then scroll up so that your screen is similar to Figure O-13

   A new sub, named FormFooter_Click( ), was created.

4. Click the **Procedure list arrow** below the Standard toolbar, then click **DblClick**

   A new sub, named FormFooter_DblClick( ), was created. You do not wish to keep the FormFooter subs.

5. Click the **Undo button** twice, type **MsgBox ("Created by Your Name on Today's Date")** as the single statement of the Form_Click() sub, then click the **Save button** on the Standard toolbar

   Your screen should look like Figure O-14.

6. Click **File** on the menu bar, click **Close and Return to Microsoft Access**, close the property sheet, click the **Form View button** on the Form Design toolbar, then click the **record selector box** to the left of the record

   The MsgBox statement in the Form_Click( ) sub created the dialog box, as shown in Figure O-15.

7. Click **OK** in the message box, then close the form

   Visual Basic for Applications programming code is as robust and powerful as the Access application itself. It takes years of experience to appreciate the vast number of objects, events, methods, and properties that are available. With only modest programming skills, however, you can create basic modules as well as edit those that do not work as intended.

FIGURE O-13: Using the Object and Procedure lists

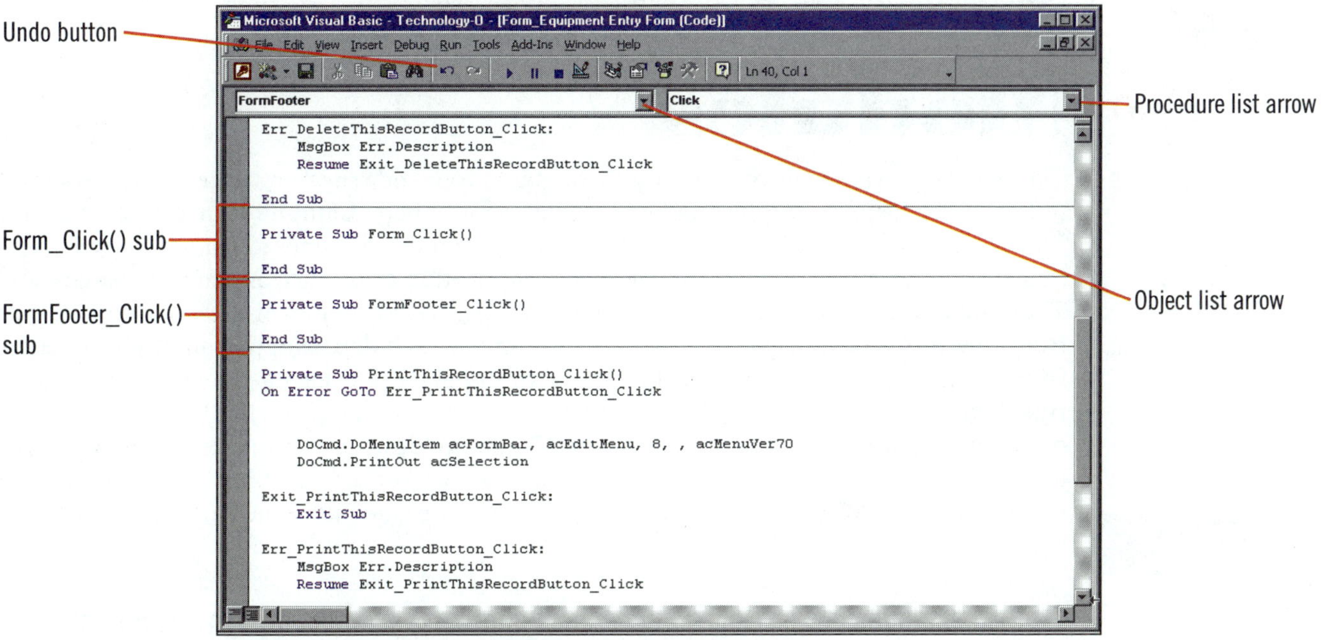

FIGURE O-14: Creating a sub procedure

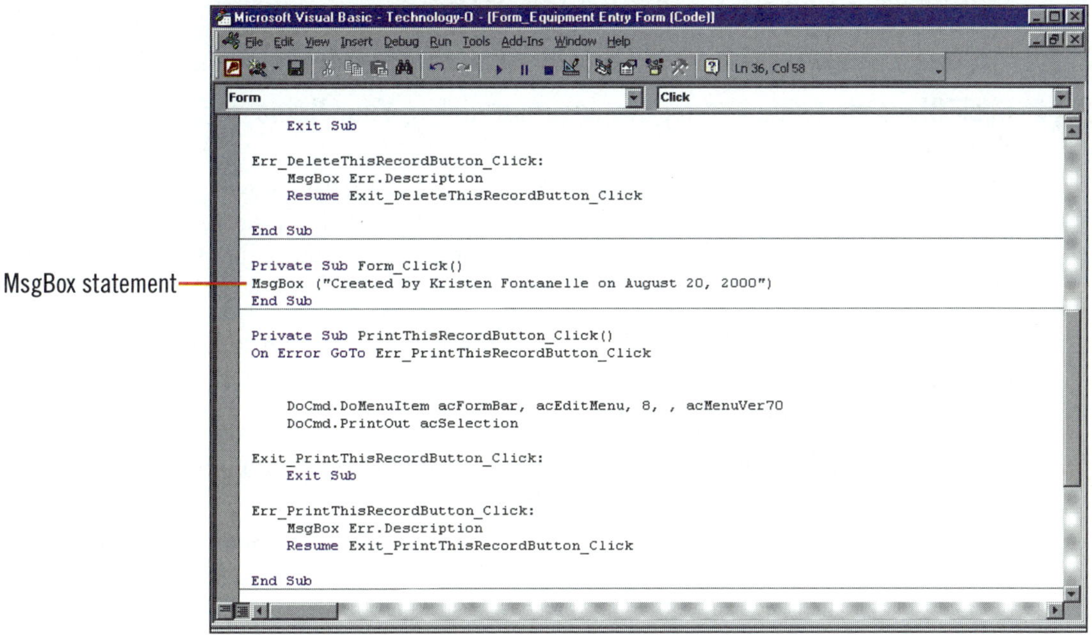

FIGURE O-15: The MsgBox action

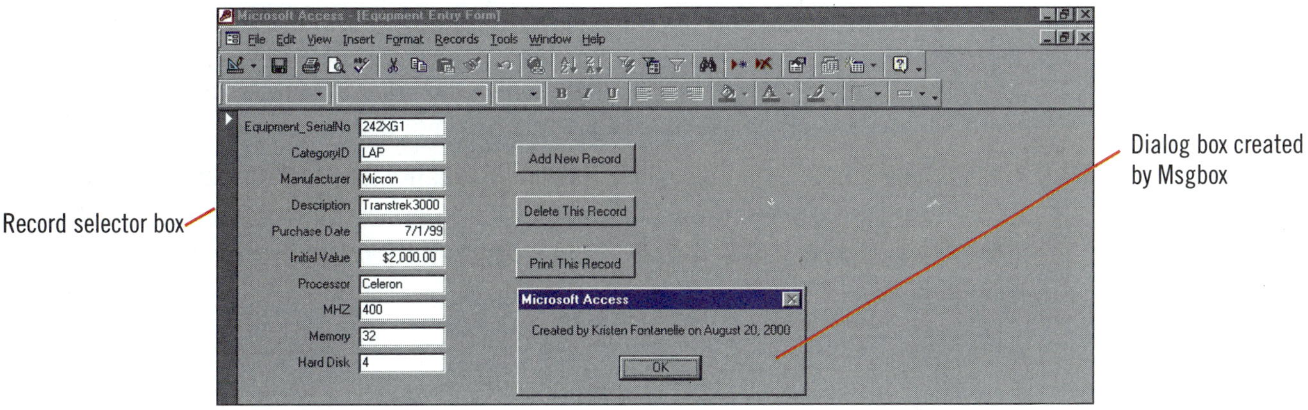

Access 2000

Unit O

Access 2000

Troubleshooting Modules

There are three types of errors you may encounter as your code runs, and Access provides several techniques to help you **debug** (find and resolve errors) them. **Compile-time errors** occur as a result of incorrectly constructed code. For example, you may have forgotten to write an End If statement following an If clause, or you may have a **syntax error**, such as a missing parenthesis. These are easiest to find because your code will turn red as soon as it detects a syntax error. **Run-time errors** occur after the code starts to run and include attempting an illegal operation such as dividing by zero or moving focus to a control that doesn't exist. When you encounter a run-time error, VBA will stop the execution of your procedure at the line in which the error occurred so you can examine it. **Logic errors** are more difficult to troubleshoot because they occur when the code runs without problems, but the procedure still doesn't produce the expected results. Kristen studies debugging techniques using the Functions module.

Steps

1. Click **Modules** on the Objects bar, click **Functions**, click the **Design button** in the database window, click to the left of the **Option Compare Database** statement, type **Your Name**, then press the **[Down arrow key]**

   The Functions module opens in the Code window, and when you attempt to move out of that line of code, VBA notices the syntax error and displays the statement in bright red.

2. Click **OK** in the Compile error message box, delete **Your Name**, then click in another statement

   The Option Compare Database statement changes to blue (because it uses reserved VBA keywords) as soon as you successfully delete your name and click elsewhere in the code window. One debugging technique is to set a **breakpoint**, a bookmark that suspends execution of the procedure at that point in time to allow the user to examine what is happening.

3. Click anywhere in the **If** statement, click **Debug** on the menu bar, then click **Toggle Breakpoint**

   Your screen should look like Figure O-16.

4. Click the **View Microsoft Access button** on the Standard toolbar, click **Queries** on the Objects bar, then double-click **Employee Pricing**

   When the Employee Pricing query opens, it immediately runs the StreetValue function. Because you set a breakpoint at the If statement, that statement is highlighted, as shown in Figure O-17, indicating that the code has been suspended at that point.

5. Click **View** on the menu bar, click **Immediate Window**, type **? corppurchasedate**, then press **[Enter]**

   Your screen should look like Figure O-18. The **Immediate Window** is a scratch pad window in which statements are evaluated immediately, so you can determine the value of any argument at any point in the procedure. There are many other debugging tools available in the Code window when you are working with more complex code.

6. Click **Debug** on the menu bar, click **Clear All Breakpoints**, click the **Continue button** on the Standard toolbar to execute the rest of the function, close the **Immediate Window**, click **File** on the menu bar, then click **Close and return to Microsoft Access**

   The Employee Pricing query's datasheet should be visible.

7. Close the Employee Pricing datasheet, close the Technology-O database, save the changes to Functions, then exit Access

QuickTip

Click the gray bar to the left of the VBA statement to toggle breakpoints on and off.

QuickTip

If you suspend the execution of a procedure by using a breakpoint, pointing to an argument in the Code window will display a pop-up with the argument's current value.

FIGURE O-16: Setting a breakpoint

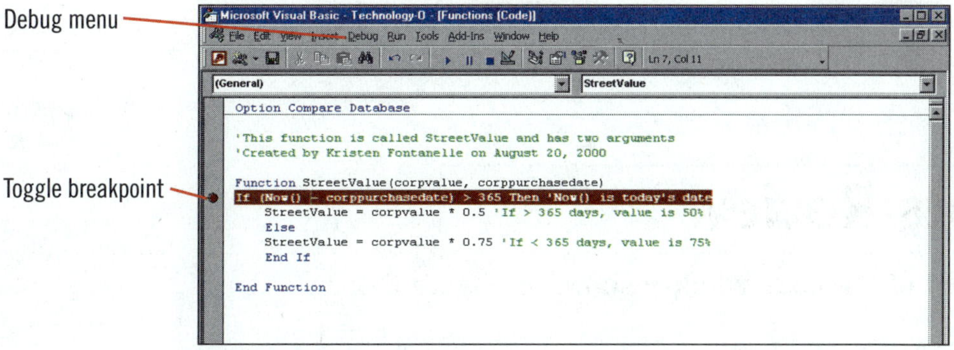

FIGURE O-17: Stopping execution at a breakpoint

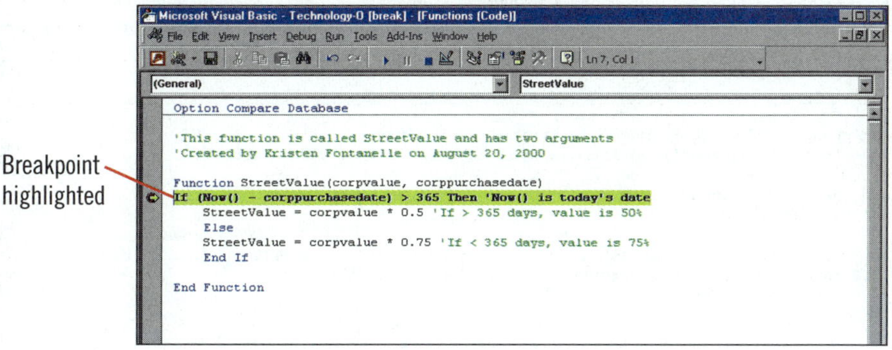

FIGURE O-18: Using the Immediate window

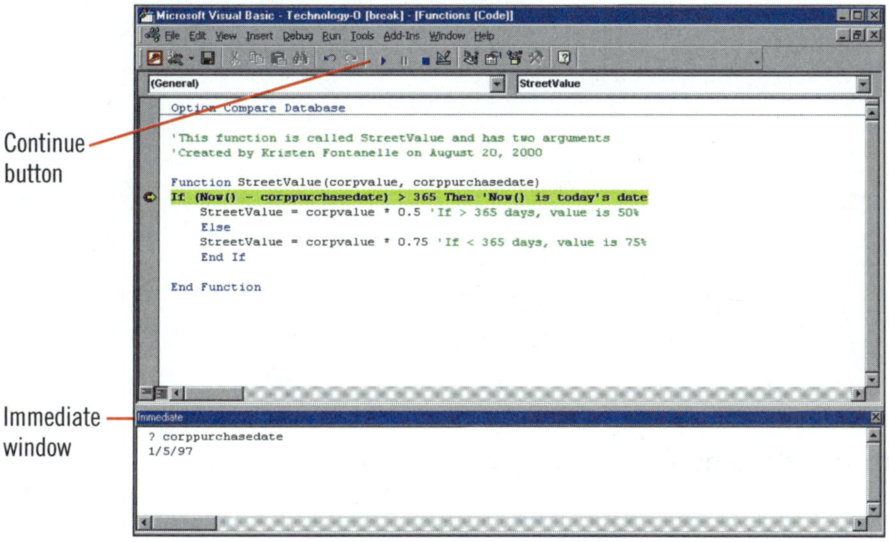

CLUES TO USE

Interpreting Visual Basic syntax

When you enter a Visual Basic keyword such as MsgBox, shown in Figure O-19, Visual Basic prompts appear to help you complete the statement. In the MsgBox function syntax, the bold italic words are **named arguments** of the function. **Arguments** enclosed in brackets are optional. (Do not type the brackets in your Visual Basic code.) For the MsgBox function, the only argument you must provide is the text for the prompt.

FIGURE O-19: MsgBox function

```
MsgBox |
MsgBox(Prompt, [Buttons As VbMsgBoxStyle = vbOKOnly], [Title], [HelpFile], [Context])
As VbMsgBoxResult
```

Access 2000

Practice

▶ Concepts Review

Identify each element of the code window shown in Figure O-20.

FIGURE O-20

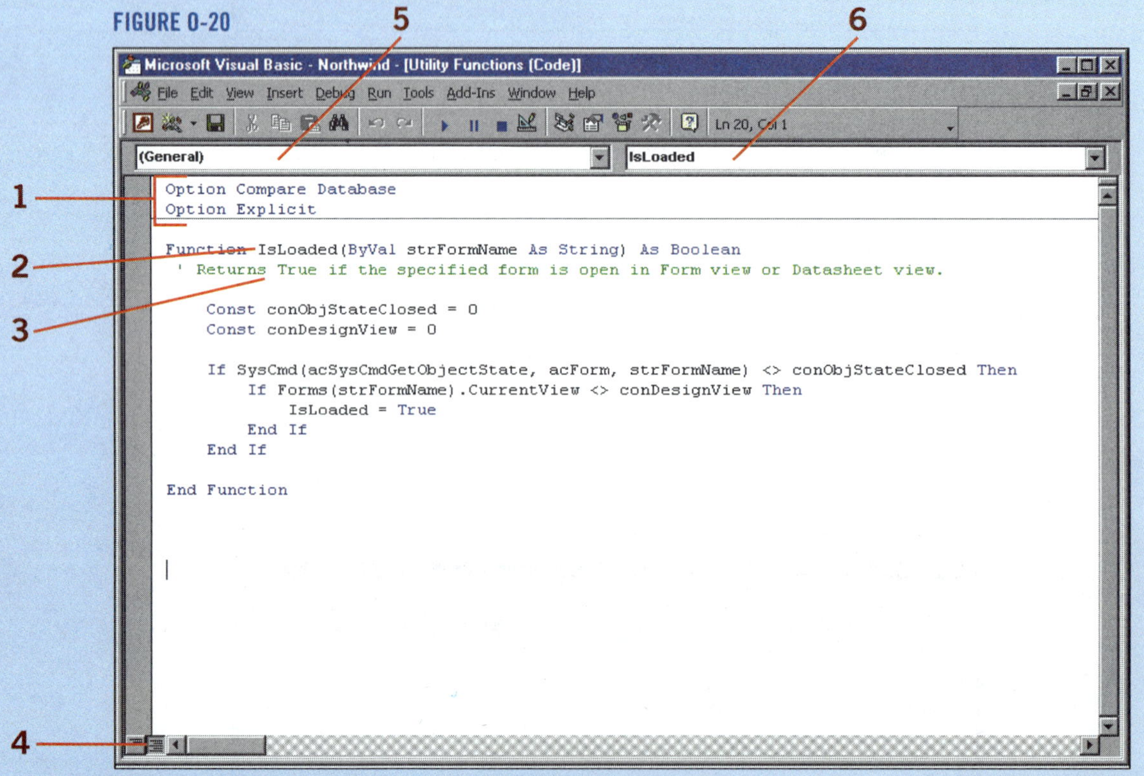

Match each term with the statement that describes its function.

7. **Procedure**
8. **If...Then...Else statement**
9. **Debugging**
10. **Class modules**
11. **Visual Basic for Applications**
12. **Function**
13. **Arguments**
14. **Breakpoint**
15. **Module**

a. Allows you to test a logical condition and execute commands only if the condition is true
b. The programming language used in Access modules
c. A line of code that automatically suspends execution of the procedure
d. A procedure that returns a value
e. Constants, variables, or expressions passed to a procedure to further define how it should execute
f. Stored as part of the form or report object in which they are created
g. The Access object where VBA code is stored
h. A series of VBA statements that perform an operation or calculate a value
i. A process to find and resolve programming errors

Select the best answer from the list of choices.

16. A module contains VBA programming code organized in units called:
- **a.** Macros.
- **b.** Arguments.
- **c.** Breakpoints.
- **d.** Procedures.

17. Which type of procedure does NOT return a value?
- **a.** Sub
- **b.** Function
- **c.** Module
- **d.** Macro

18. Which of the following is NOT a reason to use modules rather than macros?
- **a.** Modules are used to create unique functions.
- **b.** Modules contain code that can work with other Microsoft Office software programs.
- **c.** Modules can contain procedures that mask error messages.
- **d.** Modules are usually easier to write than macros.

19. Which of the following is NOT a type of VBA error?
- **a.** Compile time
- **b.** Run time
- **c.** Logic
- **d.** Class action

Skills Review

1. Understanding Modules.
- **a.** Start Access and open the Basketball-O database.
- **b.** Click Modules on the Objects bar, click the Shot Statistics module, then click the Design button.
- **c.** Record your answers to the following questions on a sheet of paper.
  - What is the name of the function defined in this module?
  - What are the names of the arguments defined in this module?
  - In your own words, what is the purpose of the If statement?
  - What is the purpose of the End Function statement?
  - Why is the End Function statement in blue?
  - Why are some of the lines indented?

2. Comparing Macros and Modules.
- **a.** If not already opened, open the Code window for the Shot Statistics module.
- **b.** Record your answers to the following questions on a sheet of paper.
  - Why was a module rather than a macro used to create this function?
  - Why is code written in the Shot Statistics code window generally more difficult to create than a macro?
  - Identify each of the keywords or keyword phrases, and explain the purpose for each.

3. Creating a Function Procedure.
- **a.** If not already opened, open the Code window for the Shot Statistics module.
- **b.** Create a function called "Contribution" below the End Function statement of the TotalShotPercentage function by typing the following VBA statements: (*Hint*: Type the function exactly as written below.)

```
Function Contribution(fg, threept, ft, offreb, defreb, assists)
    Contribution = (fg * 2 + threept * 3 + ft + offreb * 2 + defreb + assists * 2)
End Function
```

c. Click the Save button to save the Shot Statistics code
d. Close the Visual Basic Code window and return to Access.
e. Use Query Design view to create a new query using the First and Last fields from the Players table and all of the fields from the Stats table.
f. Create a calculated field called Rank in the first available column by carefully typing the Contribution function as follows:
   Rank: Contribution([FG],[3P], [FT], [Reb-O], [Reb-D], [Assists])
g. View the query datasheet
h. Change PlayerNo 21 to your first and last name, then print the first page of the datasheet in landscape orientation.
i. Save the query as "Rankings" and close the datasheet.

4. Using If Statements.

a. Click Modules on the Objects bar, open the Shot Statistics Code Design window, click to the right of the Function Contribution statement, press [Enter], then type the following If statements:
   (*Hint:* You can use copy and paste to copy repeating statements, then edit for the differences.)

```
    If fg+threept+ft = 0 Then
    Contribution = (fg * 2 + threept * 3 + ft + offreb * 2 + defreb + assists * 2)/2
    ElseIf offreb+defreb = 0 Then
    Contribution = (fg * 2 + threept * 3 + ft + offreb * 2 + defreb + assists * 2)/3
    Else
    Contribution = (fg * 2 + threept * 3 + ft + offreb * 2 + defreb + assists * 2)
    End If
End Function
```

b. Save and close the Shot Statistics Code window and return to Access.
c. Open the Rankings query, then print the first pages of the datasheet in landscape orientation. You should see the calculated Ranking field change for PlayerNo 21 for Games 1, 2, and 3 in which the player had either zero offense or zero rebounds.
d. Close the datasheet.

5. Documenting a Procedure.

a. Click Modules on the Objects bar, open the Shot Statistics Code design window, and edit the Contribution function to include the following five comment statements:

```
Function Contribution(fg, threept, ft, offreb, defreb, assists)
'If no field goals, 3 pointers, or free throws were made
        If fg + threept + ft = 0 Then
'Then the Contribution statistic should be divided by 2
        Contribution = (fg * 2 + threept * 3 + ft + offreb * 2 + defreb + assists * 2) / 2
'If no offensive or defensive rebounds were grabbed
        ElseIf offreb + defreb = 0 Then
'Then the Contribution statistic should be divided by 3
        Contribution = (fg * 2 + threept * 3 + ft + offreb * 2 + defreb + assists * 2) / 3
        Else
        Contribution = (fg * 2 + threept * 3 + ft + offreb * 2 + defreb + assists * 2)
        End If
End Function
'This function was created by Your Name on Today's Date
```

b. Save the changes to the Contribution function and Shot Statistics module, print and close the Code window, then return to Access.

6. **Examining a Class Module.**
   a. Open the Player Entry Form in Design view.
   b. Select the Command Button on the right side of the form that does the Print Record Action. It has the picture of a printer on the button and is named PrintCurrentRecord.
   c. Open the property sheet for the button, click the Event tab, click the On Click property, then click the Build button to open the class module.
   d. Edit the comment on the last line to document your name and the current date; save, print, then close the Code window.

7. **Creating a Sub Procedure.**
   a. Open the Player Entry Form in Design view, if not already opened.
   b. Open the property sheet for the form, click the Event tab, click the On Mouse Move text box, click the Build button, click Code Builder, then click OK.
   c. Enter the following statement between the Private Sub and End Sub statements:
      [First].ForeColor = 255
   d. Enter a comment below this statement as follows:
      'When the mouse moves, the First control will become bright red
   e. Save and close the Code window. Return to Access.
   f. Close the property sheet, then open the Player Entry Form in Form view.
   g. Move the mouse beyond the edge of the Detail section of the form. The color of the First text box should turn bright red.
   h. Save and close the Player Entry Form.

8. **Troubleshooting a Module.**
   a. Open the Code window for the Shot Statistics module.
   b. Click anywhere in the If fg + threept + ft = 0 statement in the Contribution function.
   c. Click Debug on the menu bar, then click the Toggle Breakpoint option to set a breakpoint at the If fg + threept + ft = 0 statement in the Contribution function.
   d. Save and close the Code window and return to Microsoft Access.
   e. Click Queries on the Objects bar, then double-click the Rankings query. This action should call the Contribution function, which will stop and highlight the statement where you set a breakpoint.
   f. Click View on the menu bar, click Immediate Window, type "?fg", then press [Enter].
   g. Type ?offreb, then press [Enter].
   h. View the results in the Immediate window, close the Immediate window, click Debug on the menu bar, click Clear All Breakpoints, click the Continue button on the Standard toolbar, then close the Code window and return to Access.
   i. Close the Rankings query, close the Basketball-O database, then exit Access.

Independent Challenges

1. As the manager of a doctor's clinic, you have created an Access database called Patients-O to track insurance claim reimbursements and general patient health. You wish to modify an existing function within this database.

To complete this independent challenge:

a. Start Access and open the database Patients-O from your Project Disk.
b. Open the Code window for the BMI Function, then record your answers to the following questions on another sheet of paper:
   - What is the name of the function?
   - What are the function arguments?
   - How many comments are in the function?
c. Edit the BMI Function by adding a comment at the end of the code with your name and today's date.
d. Edit the BMI Function by adding a comment above the Function statement with the following information: 'A healthy BMI is in the range of 21-24.
e. Edit the BMI Function by adding the following If statement between the Function and BMI statements: If height = 0 Then BMI = 0 Else
f. Edit the BMI Function by adding an End If statement between the BMI and End Function statements.
g. The final BMI function code should look as follows:

```
Function BMI(weight, height)
    If height = 0 Then
        BMI = 0
    Else
        BMI = (weight * 0.4536) / (height * 0.0254)^ 2
    End If
End Function
```

h. Save, print, and close the Code window.
i. Double-click the BMI Query to open its datasheet, and test the If statement by entering 0 in the Height field for the first record for Sara Johnson.
j. Edit the first record to contain your first and last names, then print, save, and close the BMI query datasheet.
k. Close the Patients-O database then exit Access.

2. As the manager of a doctor's clinic, you have created an Access database called Patients-O to track insurance claim reimbursements. You wish to study the existing sub procedures stored as class modules in the Claim Entry Form.

To complete this independent challenge:

a. Start Access and open the database Patients-O from your Project Disk.
b. Click the Forms button on the Objects bar, click the Claim Entry Form, then click the Design button in the database window.
c. Click the Code button on the Form Design toolbar, then record your answers to the following questions on another sheet of paper:
   - What are the names of the Sub procedures that exist in this class module?
   - What event triggers each Sub procedure?
   - What Access function is used in the PtFirstName_AfterUpdate() sub, how many arguments does it have, and what does it do? (*Hint*: You may have to use the Help documentation if you are not familiar with this function. In the Code window, click Help on the menu bar, then click Microsoft Visual Basic Help.)

- What is the purpose of the On Error command? (*Hint*: Use the Visual Basic Help documentation to find information on this command.)

d. Close the Code window, close the Claim Entry Form, and close the Patients-O database.
e. Exit Access.

3. As the manager of a doctor's clinic, you have created an Access database called Patients-O to track insurance claim reimbursements that are fixed (paid at a predetermined fixed rate) or denied (not paid by the insurance company). You wish to enhance the database with a class module.

To complete this independent challenge:

a. Start Access and open the database Patients-O database from your Project Disk.
b. Open the CPT Form in Design view.
c. Expand the width of the CPT Form to about the 5" mark on the horizontal ruler.
d. Use the Command Button Wizard to add a command button in the Form Header section. Choose the Add New Record action from the Record Operations category.
e. Choose the text Add Record for the button and name it "AddRecordButton".
f. Use the Command Button Wizard to add a command button in the Form Header section to the right of the existing Add New Record button. (*Hint*: Move and resize controls as necessary to put two command buttons in the Form Header section.)
g. Choose the Delete Record action from the Record Operations category.
h. Choose the text Delete Record for the button and name it "DeleteRecordButton".
i. Save and view the CPT Form in Form view and click the Add Record command button.
j. Add a new record (it will be record number 65) with a CPTCode value of 999 and an RBRVS value of 1.5.
k. Click the new record you just entered, and then click the Delete Record command button to make sure it works.
l. Click the Design View button, click the Delete Record command button, then press [Delete] on the keyboard.
m. Click the Code button on the Standard toolbar to examine the class module associated with this form, then record your answers to the following questions on another sheet of paper:

- How many subs exist in this class module and what are their names?
- What was the effect of deleting the command button in Form Design view on the associated Visual Basic code?

n. Add a comment as the last line of code in the Code window with your name and the current date, then save, print, and close the Code window.
o. Save and close the CPT Form, close the Patients-O database; then exit Access.

4. MediaLoft has developed a Web site that provides internal information to their employees. In this independent challenge, you'll surf the Internet to find Web pages that present information about how Modules are used in Access databases.

a. Connect to the Internet, go to the MediaLoft intranet site at http://www.course.com/illustrated/MediaLoft
b. Click the link for the Research center, then click the link for Microsoft Access Information.
c. Find the Search This Site text box and enter "Visual Basic" to request information on this subject. (*Hint*: Web sites change often, and you may need to find and click a Search button before you are able to enter your search criteria).
d. Refine your search as necessary, then find and print two support articles with the words "Visual Basic" in the summary line.
e. Close your browser window.

▶ Visual Workshop

As the manager of a college basketball team, you are helping the coach build meaningful statistics to compare the relative value of the players in each game. The coach has stated that one offensive rebound is worth as much to the team as two defensive rebounds, and would like you to use this rule to develop a "rebounding impact statistic" for each game. Open the Basketball-O database and use Figure O-21 to develop a function called ReboundImpact in a module called Rebound Statistic to calculate this statistic. Be sure to put your own name and date as a comment in the last row. Print the function.

FIGURE O-21

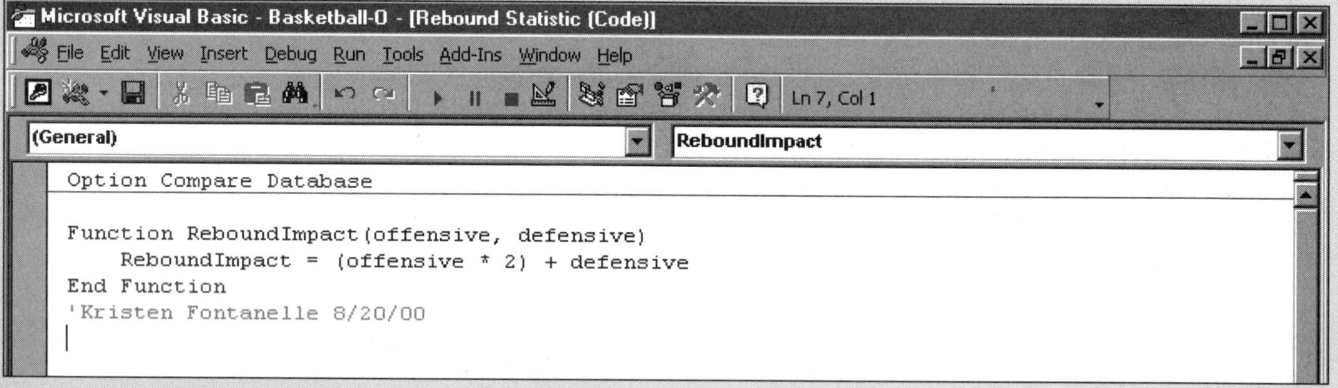

Access 2000

Unit P

Managing the Database

Objectives

- MOUS ► Convert databases
- MOUS ► Set Passwords
- MOUS ► Change Startup Options
- MOUS ► Encrypt and Decrypt a database
- MOUS ► Analyze Performance
- MOUS ► Split a Database
- MOUS ► Replicate Using the Briefcase
- ► Synchronize Using the Briefcase

After you have invested months of effort into developing an Access database, spending a few hours protecting the database, analyzing its use, and improving its performance is a practical and wise investment. As more and more users become dependent on the database, any effort you take to make the database faster, easier, and more secure will provide tremendous benefits. Proper administration of a database is an important responsibility. Kristen examines several administrative issues such as setting passwords, changing startup options, and analyzing database performance to protect, improve, and enhance the Technology database.

Unit P

Access 2000

Converting databases

When you **convert** a database you change the file into one that can be opened in another version of Access. For example, it would be necessary to convert an Access 97 database to an Access 2000 database if your company upgraded from the Office 97 suite to the Office 2000 suite of Microsoft software. In Access 2000, you can convert an Access 2000 database to an Access 97 database with only a few conversion exceptions (links to data access pages are lost, for example). Access 2000 is the first Access database version that has supported this downward conversion capability. Kristen has been asked by the Training Department to convert the Technology-P database to a version that can be opened and used in Access 97 for use in their training classes. She uses the conversion capability of Access 2000 to accomplish this.

Steps

1. Start Access, then open the **Technology-P database** on your Project Disk
   To convert a database, you must make sure that no other users have it open. Because you are the sole user of this database, you can start the conversion process.
2. Click **Tools** on the menu bar, point to **Database Utilities**, point to **Convert Database**, then click **To Prior Access Database Version**
   The Convert Database Into dialog box opens, prompting you for the name of the database.
3. Make sure the Save In list references your Project Disk, then type **Technology97** in the File name text box
   Your screen should look like Figure P-1. Because both Access 2000 and Access 97 databases have the same **.mdb** file extension, it is helpful to identify the version of Access in the filename if you are going to be working with both file types on the same computer.
4. Click **Save** in the Convert Database Into dialog box
   Access starts the conversion process; you can follow the progress on the status bar. Access creates a database file Technology97 in an Access 97 format on your Project Disk. There are no prompts indicating that the process is finished. Rather, you are returned to your original Access 2000 file, Technology-P.
5. Right-click the **Start button** on the taskbar, click **Explore**, locate your Project Disk, then view the contents on your Project Disk
6. Click the **Views button list arrow** on the Explorer Standard Buttons toolbar, then click **Details**
   Your screen should look similar to Figure P-2. You can see a column of information for file types. Notice that the list includes Technology97, the database that was just created by converting the Technology-P Access 2000 database to an Access 97 version database. The filename Technology-P appears twice, as an .mdb and .ldb file. The **.ldb** file is a temporary file that keeps track of record-locking information when the database is open. It helps coordinate the multiuser capabilities of an Access database so that several people can read and update the same database at the same time. If you had Access 97 on your computer, you could open the Technology97 database into that application window without any conversion or error messages.
7. Click **File** on the menu bar, then click **Close**
   The Technology-P database window appears on your screen.

Trouble?

You may need to click expand buttons (they appear as plus signs) in the Folders list to view all of the folders on the Project Disk.

FIGURE P-1: Convert Database Into dialog box

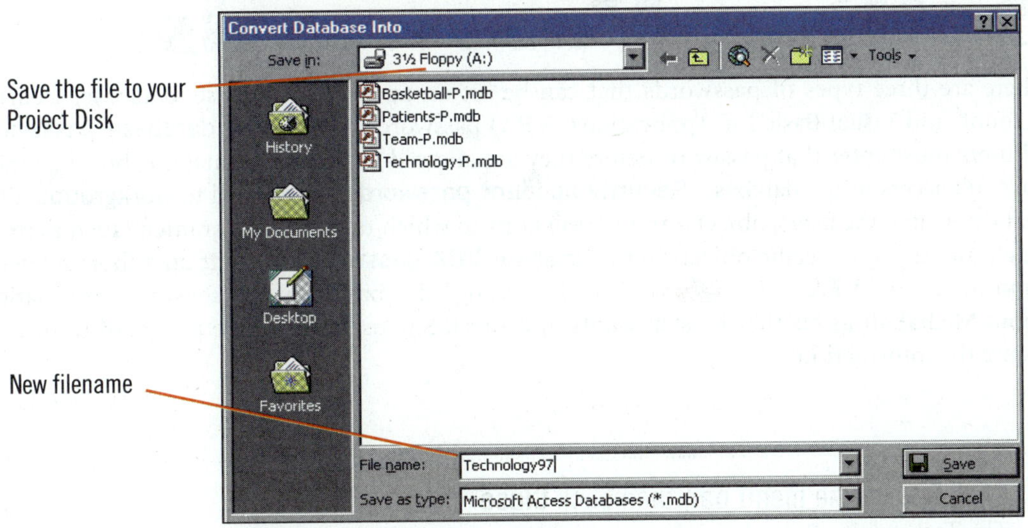

FIGURE P-2: Exploring the Project Disk

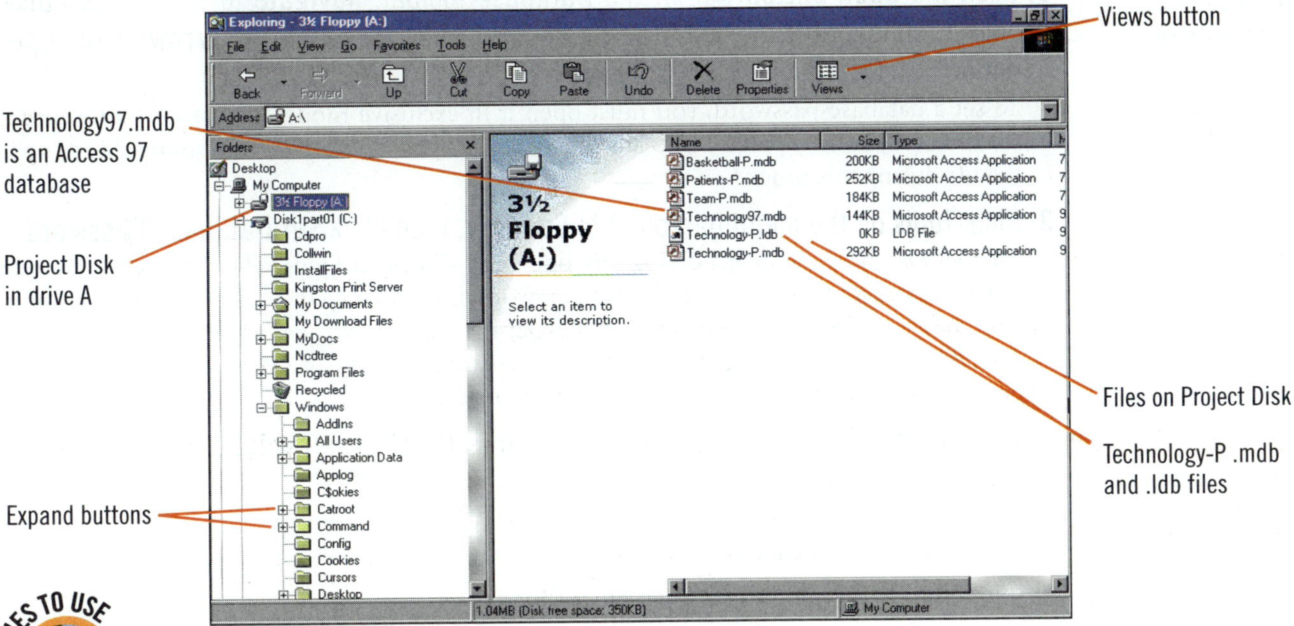

Clues to Use: Converting from Access 97 to Access 2000

If you open an Access 97 database file in Access 2000, the dialog box shown in Figure P-3 will appear, enabling you to convert the database to an Access 2000 version as you open it or to just open it without converting it. If you open it without converting it, you will be able to view all objects and change data, but you will not be able to modify any of the objects in Access 2000. In this way, both Access 97 and Access 2000 users can share the same database.

FIGURE P-3: Convert/Open Database dialog box

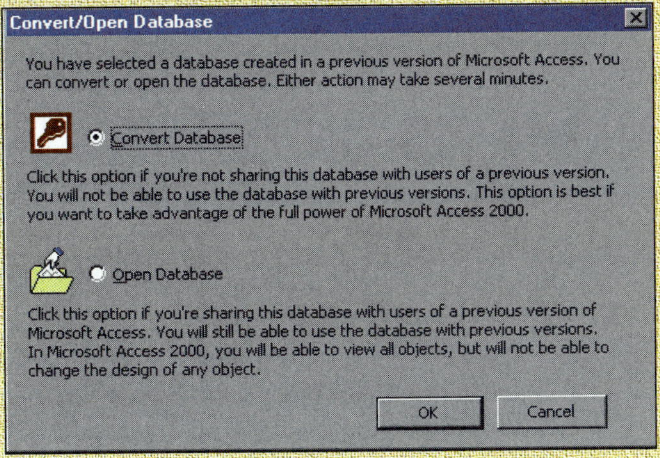

Unit P

Access 2000

Setting Passwords

There are three types of passwords that can be set on an Access database: database, security account, and Visual Basic for Applications (VBA) passwords. If you set a **database password**, all users must enter that password before they are allowed to open the database, but they then have full access to the database. **Security account passwords** are applied to **workgroups**, files that determine the users, objects, and permissions to which the users are granted (such as read, delete, or edit) for specific objects in the database. **VBA passwords** prevent unauthorized users from modifying VBA code. The Technology database contains sensitive information about MediaLoft assets that Kristen wants to protect. She uses a database password to further secure the information.

Steps

QuickTip

It's always a good idea to back up a database on another disk before creating a database password.

QuickTip

Check to make sure the Caps Lock light is not on if your password is lowercase letters.

1. Click **File** on the menu bar, then click **Close**
   The Technology-P database closes, and the Access window remains open.
2. Click the **Open button** on the Database toolbar, navigate to your Project Disk, click **Technology-P** in the database window, click the **Open list arrow** in the Open dialog box, then click **Open Exclusive**
   To set a database password, you must open it in exclusive mode. **Exclusive mode** means that you are the only person who has the database open, and others will not be able to open the file during this time.
3. Click **Tools** on the menu bar, point to **Security**, then click **Set Database Password**
   The Set Database Password dialog box opens, as shown in Figure P-4. Passwords are case sensitive, and if you lose or forget your password, it can't be recovered. For security reasons, your password will not appear as you type; for each keystroke, an asterisk will appear. Therefore, you must enter the exact same password in both the Password and Verify text boxes to make sure that you didn't make a typing error.
4. Type **cyclone** in the Password text box, press **[Tab]**, type **cyclone** in the Verify text box, then click **OK**
   Passwords should be easy enough to remember, but not obvious—such as your name, the word "password," the name of the database, or the name of the company.
5. Click **File** on the menu bar, then click **Close**
   You closed the Technology-P database, but left the Access window open. An important part of database administration is testing a new database password.
6. Click on the Database toolbar, navigate to your Project Disk, then double-click **Technology-P** in the database window
   The Password Required dialog box opens, as shown in Figure P-5.
7. Type **cyclone**, then click **OK**
   The Technology-P database opens, giving you full access to all of the objects. You must exclusively open a database to remove a database password, as was required to set a database password.
8. Click **File** on the menu bar, click **Close**, click on the Database toolbar, navigate to your Project Disk, click **Technology-P** in the database window, click the **Open list arrow** in the Open dialog box, click **Open Exclusive**, type **cyclone** in the Password Required dialog box, then click **OK**
9. Click **Tools** on the menu bar, point to **Security**, click **Unset Database Password**, type **cyclone**, then click **OK**

FIGURE P-4: Set Database Password dialog box

FIGURE P-5: Password Required dialog box

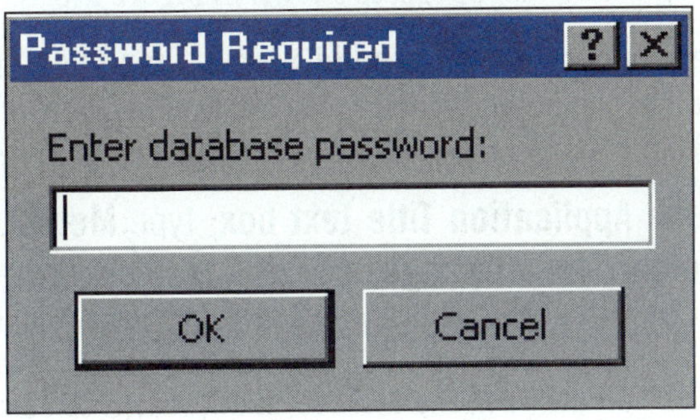

CLUES TO USE

Creating workgroups

To create workgroups that define the specific users and object permissions to which the users have access, use a program called **Workgroup Administrator**. Workgroup Administrator is started by double-clicking the Wrkgadm.exe file found in the C:\Program Files\Microsoft Office\Office folder of a typical installation. If you lose or forget any of the entries you make to workgroup information files, however, there is no way to recover them. Also, all entries in the workgroup information files are case sensitive, just like the database password.

Unit P

Access 2000

Changing Startup Options

Startup options are a series of commands that execute when the database is opened. Many common startup options can be defined through the Startup dialog box, such as which form and menu bar to display when the database opens. Other startup options require that a **command-line option**, a special series of characters that starts with a forward slash added to the end of the path to the file (for example, C:\My Documents\MediaLoft.mdb /excl), execute a command when the file is opened. See Table P-1 for more information on several startup command-line options. Because she knows that most users immediately open the Employees form as soon as they open the Technology-P database, Kristen uses the Startup dialog box to specify that the Employees form opens as soon as the Technology-P database opens.

Steps

1. Click **Tools** on the menu bar, then click **Startup**
   The Startup dialog box opens, as shown in Figure P-6.
2. Click the **Display Form/Page list arrow**, then click **Employees**
   In addition to specifying which form will open when the Technology-P database opens, the Startup dialog box provides several other options as well.
3. Click in the **Application Title text box**, type **MediaLoft Computer Assets**, click the **Allow Toolbar/Menu Changes check box** to clear the check box, then click **OK**
   Clearing the Allow Toolbar/Menu Changes check box will not allow users to customize or change the view of toolbars or menus in any way. Provided the correct toolbars appear on each screen, not allowing the users to change them can simplify and improve the usability of the database. The text entered in the Application Title text box appears in the Access window title bar.
4. Close the Technology-P database, click the **Open button** on the Database toolbar, navigate to your Project Disk, then double-click **Technology-P** in the database window
   The Technology-P database, followed by the Employees form, opens, as shown in Figure P-7. You can press and hold [Shift] while opening a database to bypass the startup options. If the database is also password protected, you would have to remove the password before you could bypass the startup options.
5. Close the Employees form, then click **View** on the menu bar
   The Toolbars option is no longer available because you disabled toolbar changes in the Startup dialog box.
6. Right-click the **database toolbar**
   There are no shortcut menus available from any toolbars because you disabled toolbar changes in the Startup dialog box.

FIGURE P-6: Startup dialog box

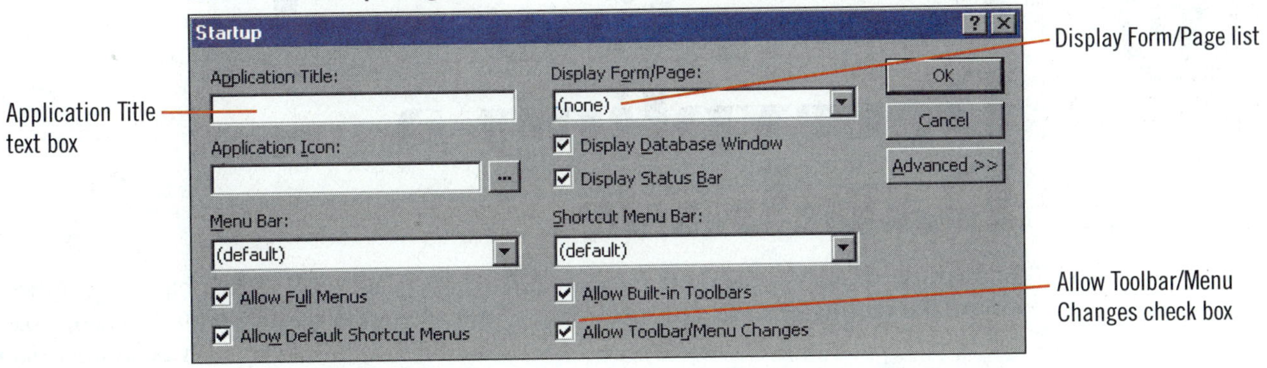

FIGURE P-7: Employees form automatically opens

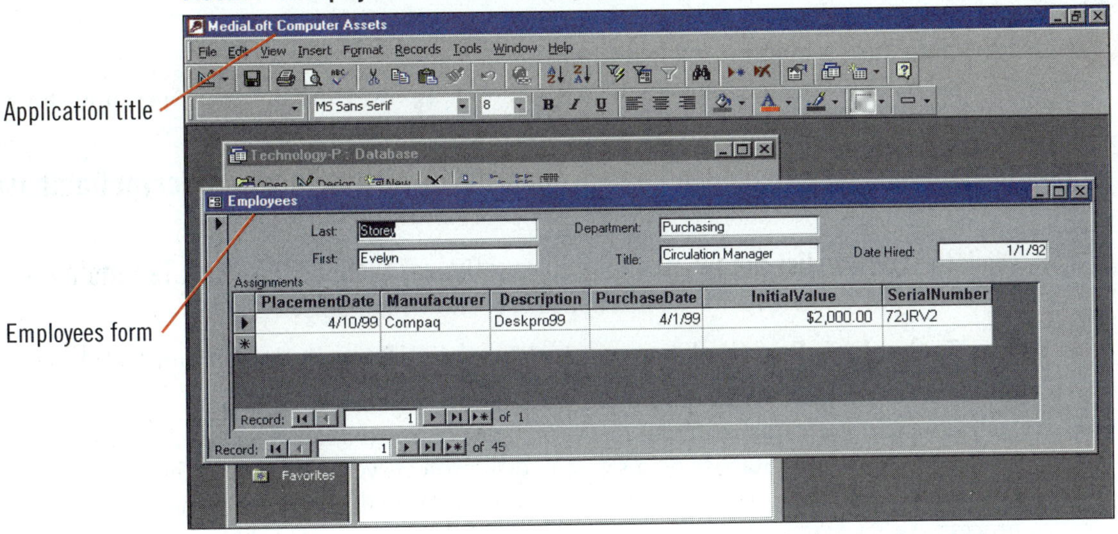

TABLE P-1: Startup command-line options

option	effect
/excl	Opens the database for exclusive access
/ro	Opens the database for read-only access
/pwd *password*	Opens the database using the specified *password*
/repair	Repairs the database (In Access 2000, compacting the database also repairs it. So if the Compact on Close feature is chosen, the /repair option is not needed.)
/convert *target database*	Converts a previous version of a database to an Access 2000 database with the *target database* name
/x *macro*	Starts Access and runs specified *macro*
/nostartup	Starts Access without displaying the startup dialog box
/wrkgrp *workgroup information file*	Starts Access using the specified *workgroup information file*

Unit P

Access 2000

Encrypting and Decrypting a Database

Encrypting means to make the database objects and data itself indecipherable to other programs. **Decrypting** reverses the encryption. If you are concerned that your Access database file might be stolen and the data stripped from it by another program (such as another database program, a word processor, or a utility program), encryption may be warranted. Other potential threats to the security of your database are described in Table P-2. MediaLoft has recently connected their corporate file servers to the Internet, so Kristen is more concerned about securing corporate data than ever before. She uses Access encryption and decryption to learn how to secure the data within the Technology-P database.

Steps

QuickTip

It's always a good idea to back up a database on another disk before encrypting it.

1. Click **File** on the menu bar, click **Close**

   The Technology-P database window closes, but the Access window is still open. You cannot encrypt an open database.

2. Click **Tools** on the menu bar, point to **Security**, then click **Encrypt/Decrypt Database**

   The Encrypt/Decrypt Database dialog box opens, as shown in Figure P-8.

3. Click the **Look in list arrow**, navigate to your Project Disk, double-click **Technology-P**

   The Encrypt Database As dialog box appears, as shown in Figure P-9.

4. Type **Technology-P** in the File name text box, click **Save** in the Encrypt Database As dialog box, then click **Yes** to replace the existing file

   You can encrypt a database file to the same filename or to a new filename. In either case, a back-up copy of the database on a separate disk protects your file should the encryption be unsuccessful (unlikely but possible) or the equipment malfunctions during the encryption process. An encrypted database works in exactly the same way as the original file to users authorized to open the file. Encryption helps protect the data as it is being sent over network connections. You decrypt a database using the same steps.

5. Click **Tools** on the menu bar, point to **Security**, then click **Encrypt/Decrypt Database**

6. Click the **Look in: list arrow**, navigate to your Project Disk, then double-click **Technology-P**

   The Decrypt Database As dialog box opens, because Technology-P is currently encrypted. For now, decrypt the database back to its original state.

7. Double-click **Technology-P** in the Decrypt Database As dialog box, then click **Yes** when prompted to replace the existing file

FIGURE P-8: Encrypt/Decrypt Database dialog box

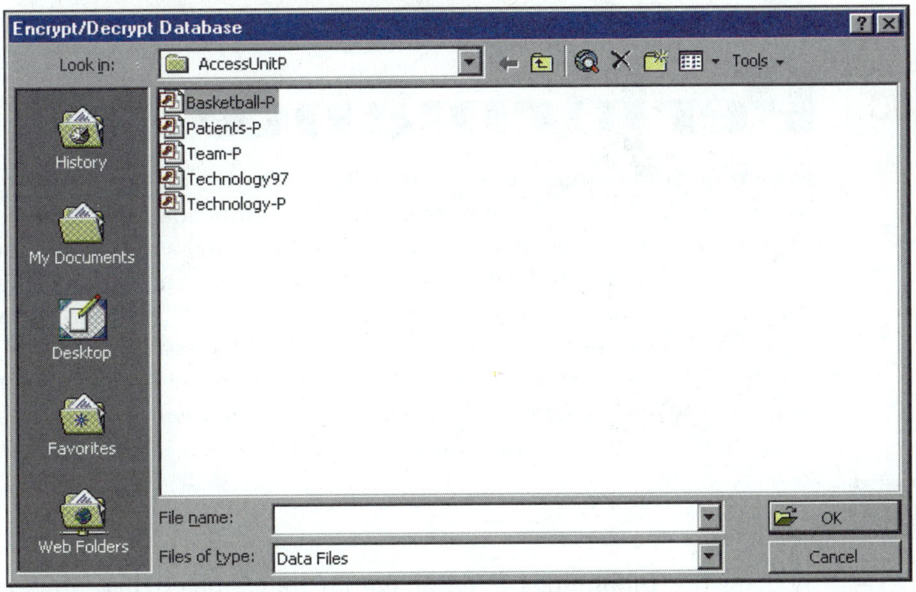

FIGURE P-9: Encrypt Database As dialog box

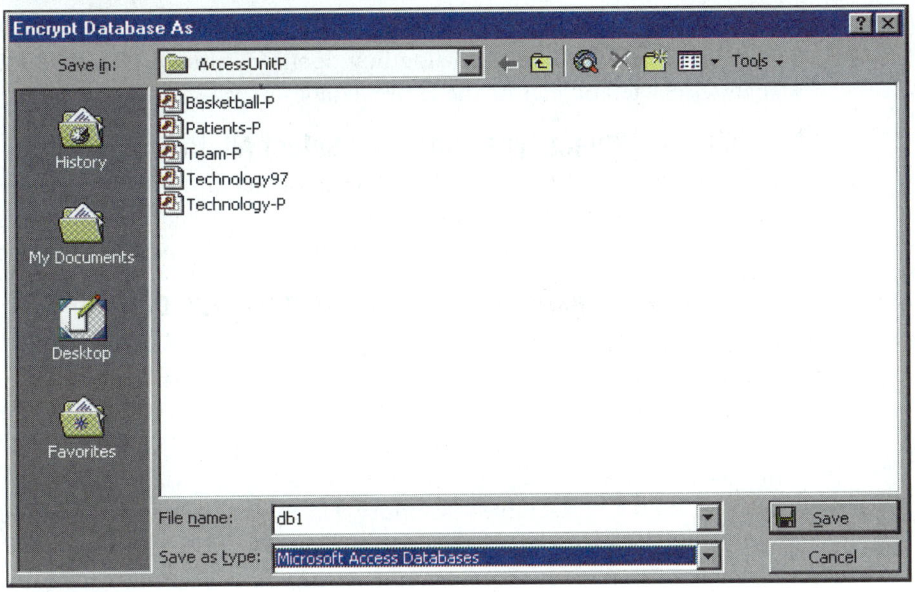

TABLE P-2: Database threats

incident	what can happen	appropriate action
Virus	Viruses can cause a vast number of damaging actions, ranging from profane messages to destruction of files.	Purchase the leading virus-checking software for each machine, and regularly update it.
Power outage	Power problems such as **brown-outs** (dips in power often causing lights to dim) and **spikes** (surges in power) can cause damage to the hardware, which may render the computer useless.	Purchase a **UPS** (Uninterruptible Power Supply) to maintain constant power to the file server (if networked); purchase a **surge protector** (power strip with surge protection) for each end user.
Theft or intentional damage	Computer thieves or other scoundrels steal or vandalize computer equipment.	Place the file server in a room that can be locked after hours; use network drives for end user data files that are backed up on a daily basis; use off-site storage for backups; set database passwords and encryption so that files that are stolen cannot be used; use computer locks for equipment that is at risk, especially laptops.

Analyzing Performance

Access provides a powerful tool called the **Performance Analyzer** that studies the structure and size of your database and makes a variety of recommendations on how you could improve its performance. Usually, the decision whether to fix a database that runs too slowly boils down to two choices: time and money. With adequate time and knowledge of Access, you can alleviate many performance bottlenecks by using software tools and additional programming techniques. With extra money, however, you can purchase faster processors and more memory to accomplish the same thing. See Table P-3 for more tips on optimizing the performance of your computer. Kristen uses the Performance Analyzer to see whether Access has any easy recommendations on how to maintain peak performance of the Technology-P database.

Steps

1. Open the **Technology-P database** on your Project Disk, then close the **Employees form** that automatically opens
2. Click **Tools** on the menu bar, point to **Analyze**, then click **Performance**
   The Performance Analyzer dialog box opens, as shown in Figure P-10. You can choose to analyze selected objects or the entire database.
3. Click the **All Object Types tab**, click **Select All**, then click **OK**
   The Performance Analyzer examines each object and presents the results in a dialog box as shown in Figure P-11. The key shows that the analyzer gives four levels of advice regarding performance: recommendations, suggestions, ideas, and items that were fixed.
4. Click the **Table 'Assignments': Change data type of field 'SSN' from 'Text' to 'Long Integer'** in the Analysis Results list
   The icon tells you that this is an idea. The Analysis Notes section of the Performance Analyzer dialog box gives you additional information regarding that specific item. In this case, the idea is to change the data type of the field SSN from Text to Number (with a Long Integer field size). While this might not be an appropriate action for an SSN field, the three fields in the PCSpecs table—Memory, HardDisk, and MHz—all represent numeric values that could be changed from Text to Number with the suggested field size. All of the Performance Analyzer's ideas should be considered, but they are not as important as recommendations and suggestions.
5. Click **Close** to close the Performance Analyzer dialog box

FIGURE P-10: Performance Analyzer dialog box

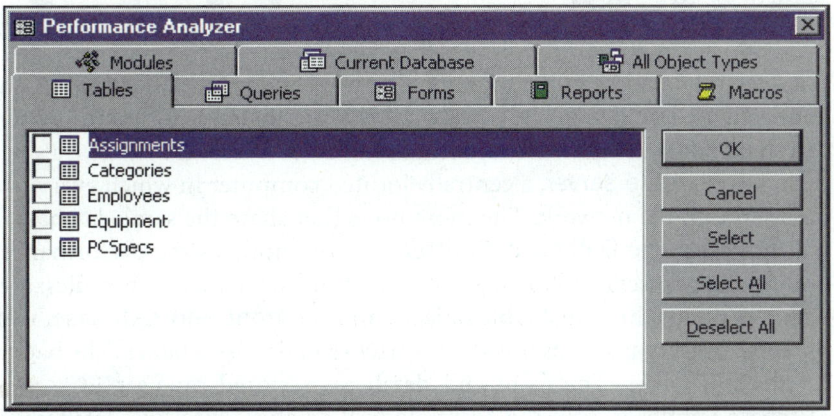

FIGURE P-11: Performance Analyzer results

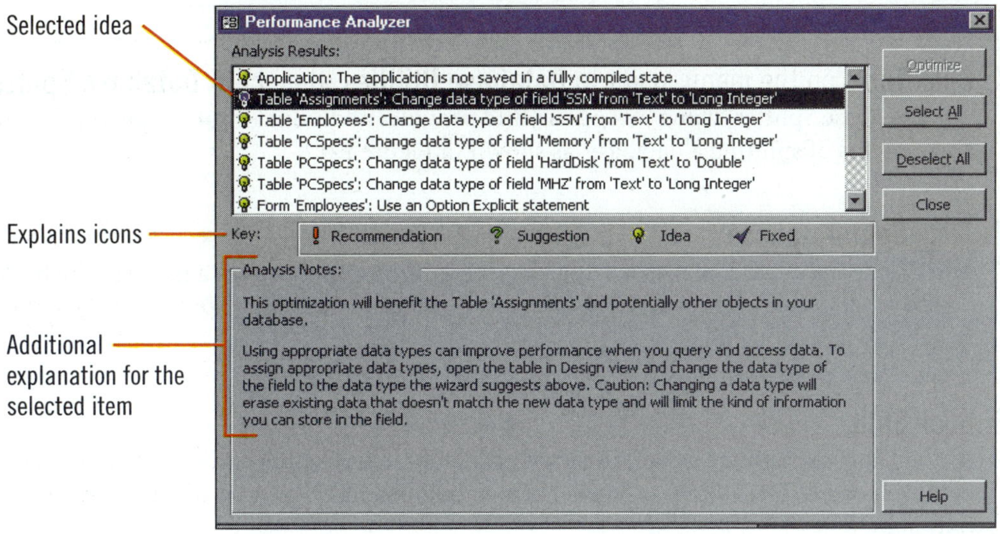

TABLE P-3: Tips for optimizing performance

degree of difficulty	tip
Easy	Close all applications that you don't currently need to free up memory and other computer resources.
Easy	Eliminate memory-resident programs such as complex screen savers, e-mail alert programs, and virus checkers if they can be run safely on an "as-needed" basis.
Easy	If you are the only person using a database, open it in exclusive mode.
Easy	Use the Compact on Close feature to regularly compact and repair your database.
Moderate	Add more memory to your computer; once the database is open, memory is the single most important determinant of overall performance.
Moderate	If others don't need to share the database, load it on your local hard drive instead of the network's file server (but be sure to back up local drives regularly, too).
Moderate	**Split** the database so that the data is stored on the file server, but other database objects are stored on your local, faster hard drive.
moderate to difficult	If using disk compression software, stop doing so or move the database to an uncompressed drive.
moderate to difficult	Run Performance Analyzer on a regular basis, examining and appropriately acting on each recommendation, suggestion, and idea.
moderate to difficult	Make sure that all PCs are running the latest versions of Windows and Access; this may involve purchasing more software or upgrading hardware to properly support these robust software products.

Unit P

Access 2000

Splitting a Database

A successful database grows in many new ways and creates the need for higher levels of database connectivity. **Local area networks** (**LANs**) are installed to link multiple PCs together so they can share hardware and software resources. Once a LAN is installed, a shared database will often be moved to a **file server**, a centrally located computer in which every user can access the database through the network. The more users that share the same database, however, the slower it will respond. The **Database Splitter** feature improves the performance of a database shared among several users by allowing you to split the database into two files: the **back-end database**, which contains the actual table objects, and the **front-end database**, which contains the other database objects as well as links to the back-end database tables. The back-end database is stored on the file server. The front-end database is stored on user PCs. Kristen uses the Database Splitter to split the Technology-P database into two databases in preparation for the new LAN being installed in the Information Systems Department.

Steps

QuickTip

It's always a good idea to back up a database on another disk before splitting it.

Trouble?

Verify that the file's path is to your Project Disk.

1. **Click Tools on the menu, point to Database Utilities, then click Database Splitter**
   The Database Splitter dialog box opens, and provides additional information on the process and benefits of splitting a database, as shown in Figure P-12.

2. **Click Split Database**
   The Create Back-end Database dialog box opens, prompting you for a name of the back-end database, the one that will hold the table objects. The suggested name Technology-P_be.mdb is acceptable.

3. **Click Split**
   As the Database Splitter is working on your database, the status bar indicates that tables are being exported. The Database Splitter dialog box prompts you that the database is successfully split.

4. **Click OK**
   The Technology-P database has become the front-end database, with all database objects intact except for the table objects. Technology-P no longer contains any table objects, but rather links to the Technology-P_be database that stores the actual data. See Figure P-13.

5. **Click File on the menu bar, then click Exit**
   You closed the Technology-P database and exited Access. In a LAN environment, splitting a database then storing the back-end on the file server and the front-end on the **client** (the user's PC) dramatically improves performance when compared to using a database that is completely stored on the file server. On a split database, the only traffic that travels through the network is the actual data. All of the other objects that users need are stored on their local hard drives. (As many copies of the front-end database can be made as are needed so that each user has a copy of the front-end database on his or her own machine). Storing the actual tables in the back-end database on the file server maintains data integrity because all users update the same database file.

FIGURE P-12: Database Splitter dialog box

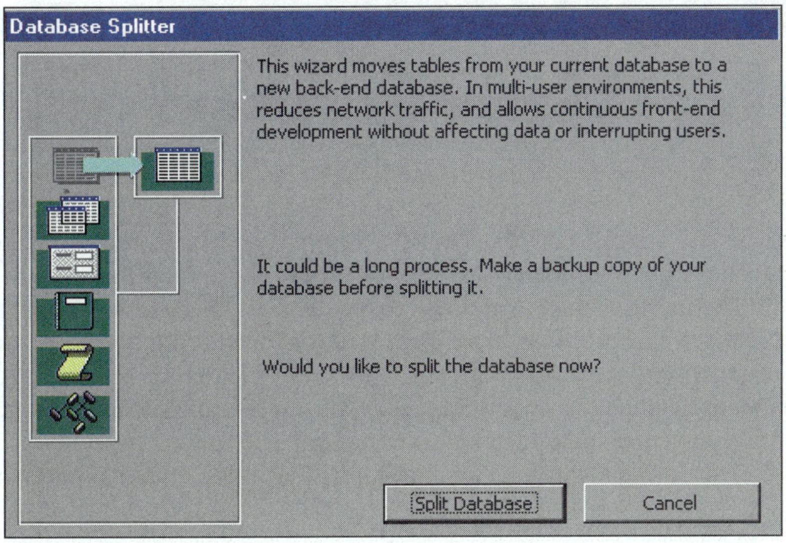

FIGURE P-13: Tables are linked in the front-end database

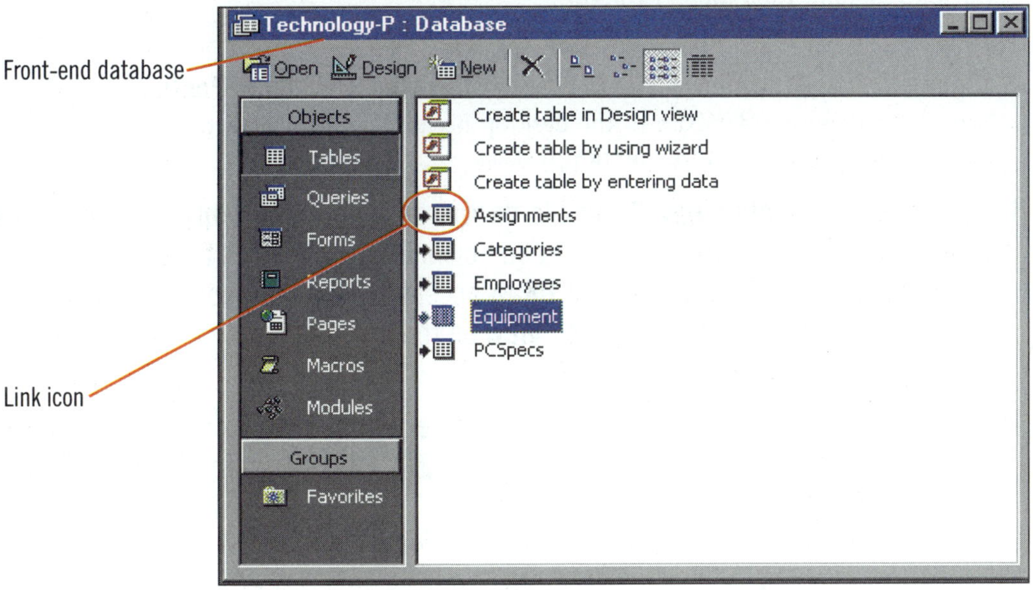

Access 2000

CLUES TO USE

Defining Client/Server computing

Splitting a database into a front-end and back-end database that work together is an excellent example of client/server computing. **Client/server computing** can be defined as two or more information systems cooperatively processing to solve a problem. In most implementations, the **client** is defined as the user's PC and the server is defined as the shared file server, mini-, or mainframe computer. The **server** usually handles corporate-wide computing activities such as data storage and management, security, and connectivity to other networks. Within Access, client computers generally handle those tasks specific to each user such as storing all of the objects (other than table objects) used by that particular user. Effectively managing a vast client/server network in which many front-end databases link to a single back-end database is a tremendous task, but the performance and security benefits are worth the effort.

Unit P

Access 2000

Replicating Using the Briefcase

If you want to copy a database to another computer, such as a home or laptop computer that you use on the road, the Windows Briefcase feature can help you. The **Briefcase** makes a special copy of the original database (called a **replica**) and keeps track of changes made in either the original database (called the **master**) or the replica so that they can be resynchronized at a later date. The master database and all replica database files created from the master are called the **replica set**. The process of making the copy is called **replication**, and the process of reconciling and updating changes between the replica and the master is called **synchronization**. Kristen is heading to a conference and wants to take the Technology-P_be database with her so that she can enter and update information in the Employee table. She uses the Briefcase program to keep the original database and the copy she will put on her laptop synchronized.

Steps

QuickTip

It's always a good idea to back up a database on another disk before replicating it.

Trouble?

To install Briefcase: open Control Panel, double-click Add/Remove Programs, click Windows Setup tab, double-click Accessories, click Briefcase check box, click OK.

Trouble?

The My Briefcase window may look different due to the Windows 98 settings on your computer.

Trouble?

If the My Briefcase wizard is open on the desk top, click Finish to continue.

1. Right-click the **Start button**, click **Explore**, locate your Project Disk in the Folders list, click **Technology-P_be** in the list of files, click the **Copy button** on the Standard Buttons toolbar, then close Explorer
   You placed the Technology-P_be.mdb file on the Windows Clipboard.
2. Minimize all open windows, right-click the **Desktop**, then click **Paste**
   You copy the master database to the desktop because you can't create a replica set with a master and replica both stored on floppy disks.
3. Right-click the **Technology-P_be** file on the desktop, click **Copy**, double-click **My Briefcase**, click **Edit** on the menu bar, click **Paste**, click **Yes** to continue, click **No** to not backup your database, click **OK** to accept the Original copy as the database that will allow design changes, click **View** on the menu bar, then click **Details**
   Your screen should look like Figure P-14.
4. Close the My Briefcase window, remove any existing disks from **drive A**, insert a blank formatted disk into **drive A**, right-click on the Desktop, point to **Send To**, then click **3½ Floppy (A)**
   For this lesson, you will update the replica on the floppy disk using your existing machine.
5. Double-click the **My Computer icon**, double-click **3½ Floppy (A)**, double-click in the 3½ Floppy (A:) window, double-click **Technology-P_be** in the My Briefcase window, then double-click the **Employees table**
   The Replicated Employees table opens. You can add a new record to the table.
6. Click the **New Record button**, then add yourself as a new record using the following information:

last	first	Department	title	location	e-mail	DateHired	SSN
Your Last Name	Your First Name	Information Systems	CIO	Corporate	yourname@ medialoft.com	1/1/00	444-33-2222

7. Close the Employees table datasheet
   Your screen should look like Figure P-15. Both the title bar of the database and the table icons indicate that you are working with a replica. The replica contains the record you just added, but the master does not.
8. Click **File** on the menu bar, then click **Exit**

FIGURE P-14: My Briefcase

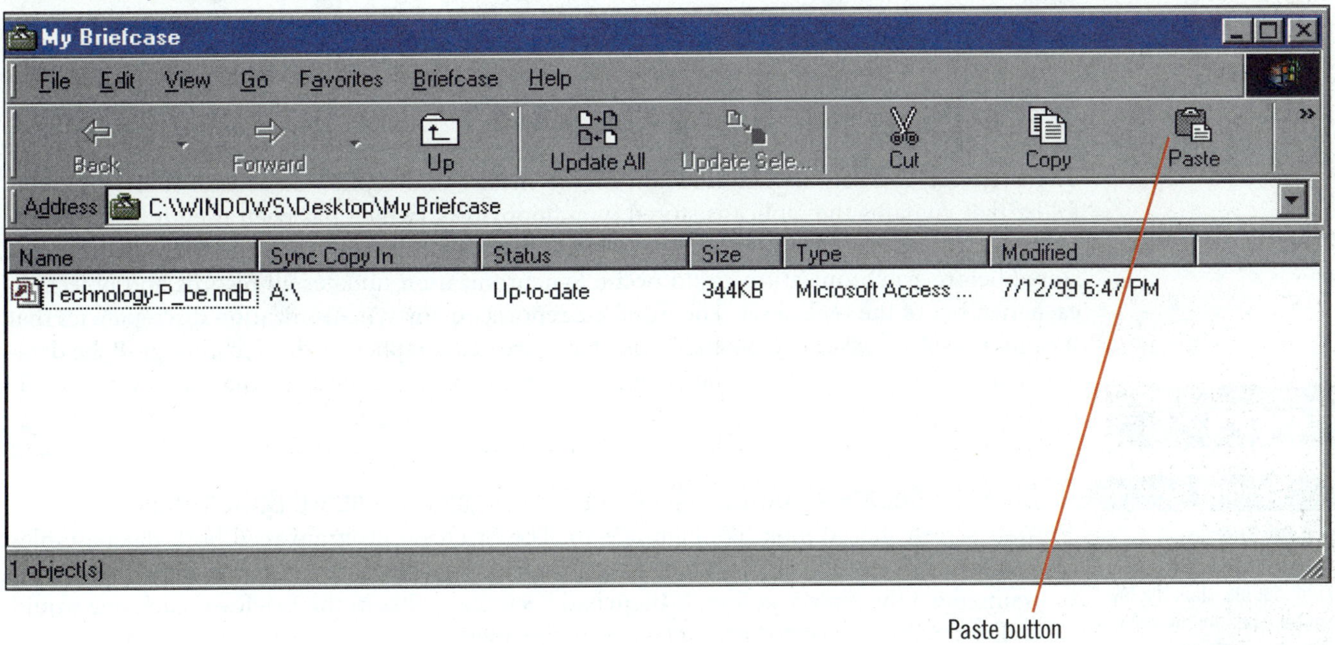

FIGURE P-15: Replica database

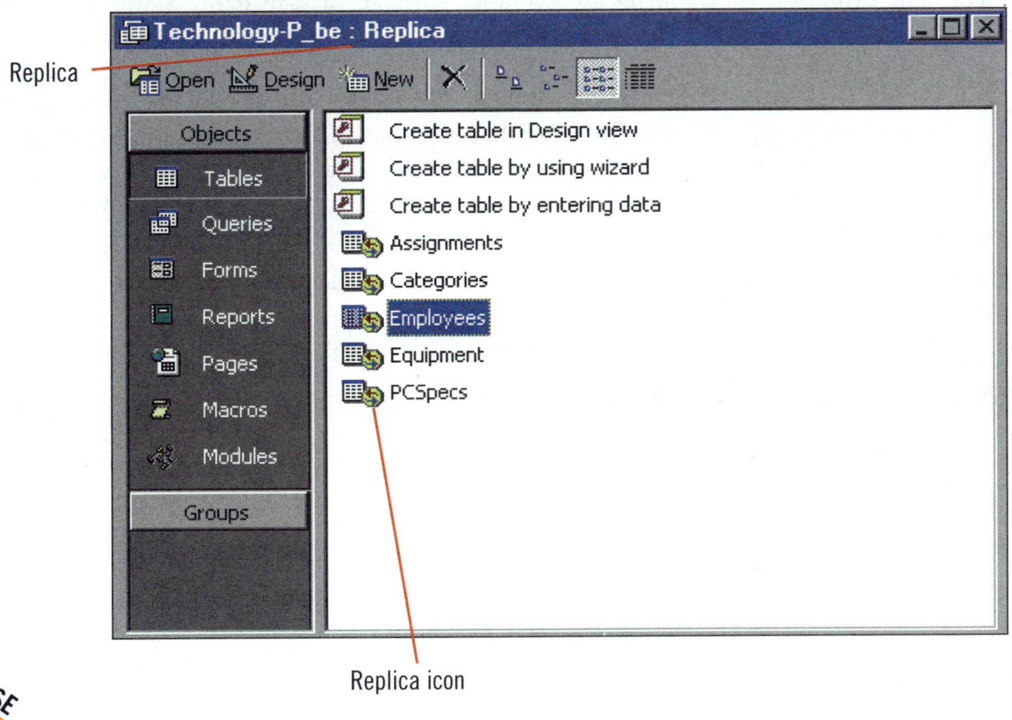

CLUES TO USE

Creating a Briefcase folder

By default, the desktop displays a single Briefcase icon called "My Briefcase." Briefcase icons are actually a special type of folder designed to help users with two computers keep the files that are used on both computers updated. If you open the My Briefcase folder and find other files in it, or if there is no Briefcase on the desktop, you can easily create as many new Briefcase folders as you need. You create, delete, copy, and move a Briefcase folder in exactly the same manner as with a regular folder in Windows Explorer. For example, if you want to create a new Briefcase folder on the Desktop, you can right-click the Desktop, point to New, then click Briefcase.

Access 2000

Unit P
Access 2000

Synchronizing Using the Briefcase

The Briefcase controls synchronization of the master and replica databases. If the Briefcase folder that contains the replica is stored on a floppy disk (which has been used in a secondary computer), the floppy disk would have to be inserted into the computer on which the master is stored before synchronization could occur. Synchronization updates all records and objects in each member of the replica set. The Briefcase reports on any synchronization discrepancies that it cannot resolve. Now that Kristen has created a replica of the Technology-P_be database and added a record to it, she is anxious to synchronize it with the master to see how the Briefcase keeps the replica set up-to-date.

Steps

Trouble?

If the A:/My Briefcase window is not open on the desktop, double-click the My Computer icon, double-click 3½ Floppy (A:), then double-click My Briefcase in the 3½ Floppy (A:) window

1. Click the **Update All button** on the My Briefcase Standard Buttons toolbar
   Your screen should look like Figure P-16. The Briefcase program read both database files and determined that the replica had been updated but the master had not. Therefore, it recommended the replace action. If there had been many files in the Briefcase, each one would be listed with a suggested action (replace, skip, merge).
2. Click **Update**
   The Briefcase replaces the master file on your desktop with the replica file on your floppy and displays the My Briefcase window with an "Up-to-date" Status message for the Technology-P_be.mdb file, as shown in Figure P-17. Had you made changes to both the master and the replica, the Briefcase window would have recommended a more complex action (merge), as shown in Figure P-18. The **merge** action evaluates the changes in each object and applies them to the other. For example, the merge action will resynchronize the two databases if you edit or add records in both the master and replica. You also can add new objects to both. You can make design changes only to existing objects, however, in the master database.
3. Close the My Briefcase window
4. Close the 3½ Floppy (A:) window, then close the My Computer window
5. Delete the Technology-P_be Design Master from the desktop

Trouble?

If you created a new Briefcase folder for this unit, delete it.

CLUES TO USE

Using the Briefcase with a laptop computer

A common scenario in which Briefcase folders have tremendous value is when a master database is stored on a file server and the replica is stored on the hard drive of a laptop computer. When you are in the office, your laptop computer is connected to the network through a docking station so you can use the master database just like all of the other users. When you are in the field, however, your laptop computer is disconnected from the corporate database and you work on the replica stored in a Briefcase folder on the laptop's hard drive. When you return to the office, you use the Briefcase update features to resynchronize the two copies.

FIGURE P-16: Update My Briefcase window–Replace action

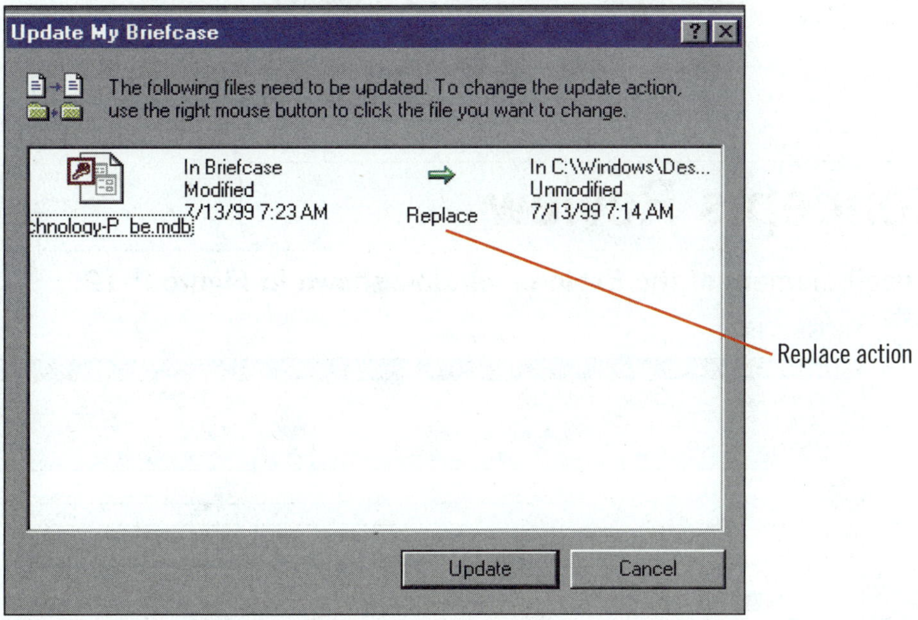

FIGURE P-17: My Briefcase window showing an up-to-date file

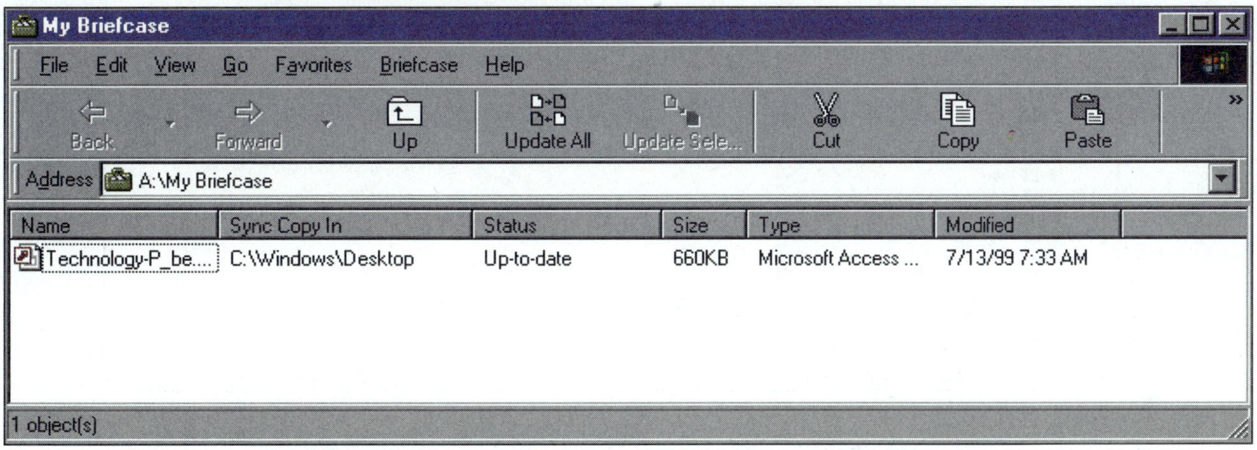

FIGURE P-18: Update My Briefcase window–Merge action

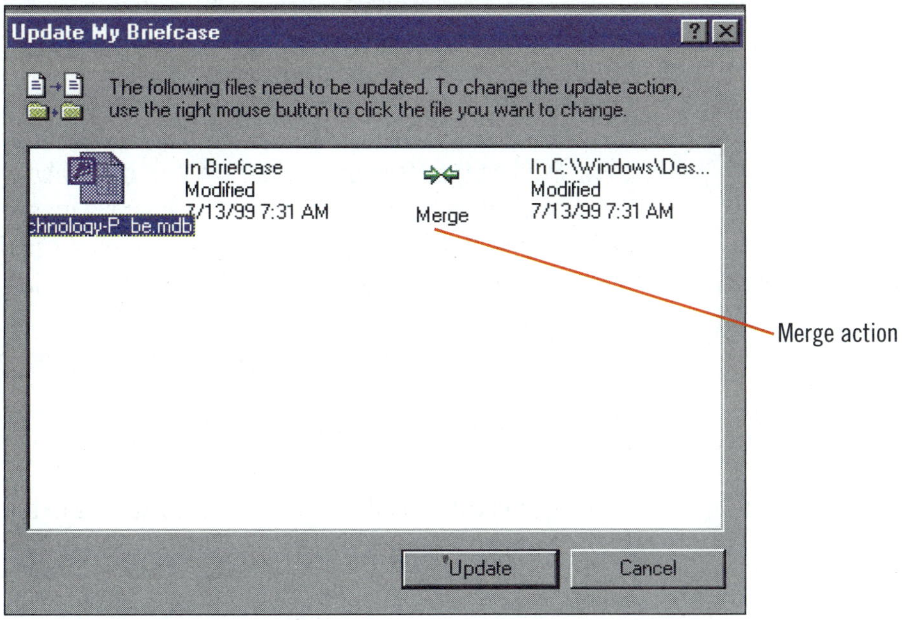

Practice

► Concepts Review

Identify each element of the Explorer window shown in Figure P-19.

FIGURE P-19

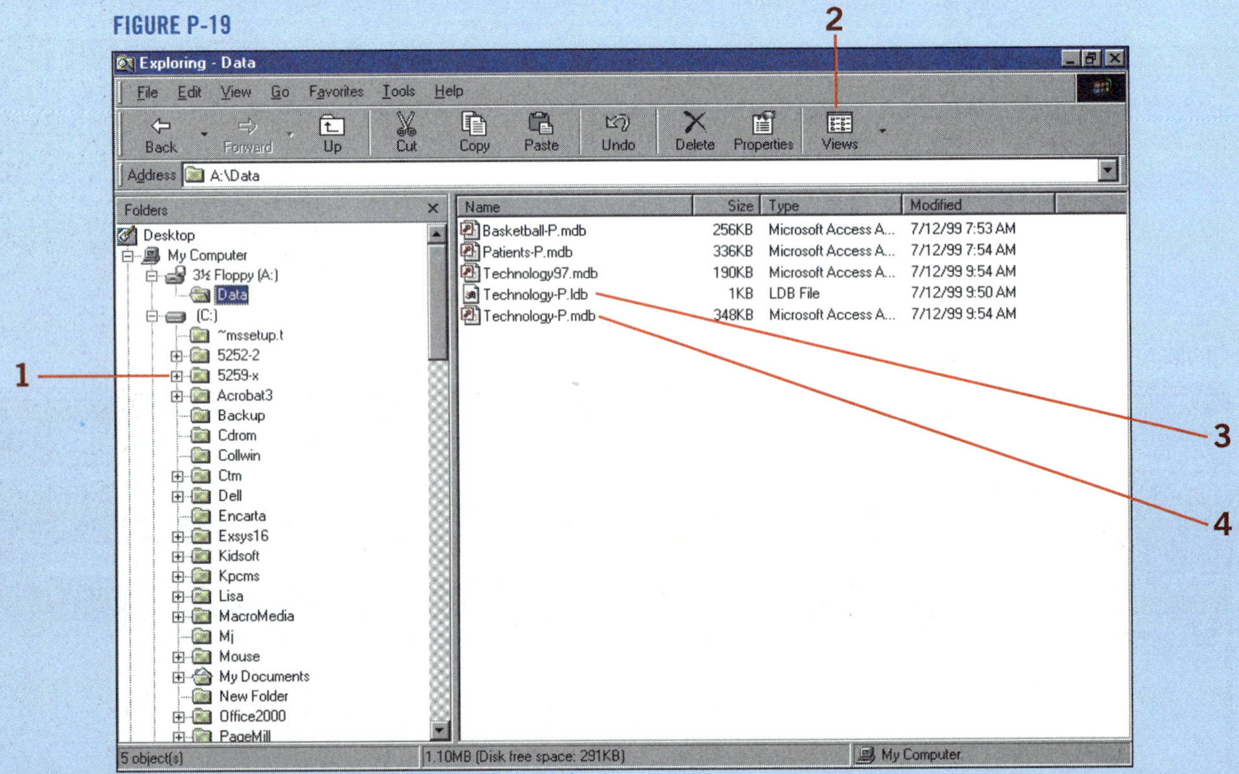

Match each term with the statement that describes its function.

5. Exclusive mode
6. Database Splitter
7. Encrypting
8. Performance Analyzer
9. Synchronization

a. Studies the structure and size of your database and makes a variety of recommendations on how you can improve its speed.
b. Breaks the database into two files to improve performance. One database contains the table objects and the other contains the rest of the objects with links to the table objects.
c. Updates the files in a replica set so that they all have the same information.
d. Scrambles a database so that it is indecipherable when opened by another program.
e. Means that no other users will have access to the database file while it's open.

Select the best answer from the list of choices.

10. Changing a database file into one that can be opened in another version of Access is called
- **a.** Splitting.
- **b.** Analyzing.
- **c.** Converting.
- **d.** Encrypting.

11. Which is NOT a type of password that can be set on an Access database?
- **a.** Database
- **b.** Security account
- **c.** Object
- **d.** Visual Basic for Applications

12. Which of the following determines the users, objects, and permissions to which the users are granted?
- **a.** Passwords
- **b.** Workgroups
- **c.** Permission logs
- **d.** Briefcase names

13. Which character precedes a command-line option?
- **a.** !
- **b.** @
- **c.** /
- **d.** ^

14. Which of the following is NOT an advantage of splitting the database using the Database Splitter?
- **a.** It keeps the data centralized in the back-end database for all users to access.
- **b.** It gives the users local control over form and report objects.
- **c.** It helps increase the overall performance of a LAN.
- **d.** It creates replica sets that can be used to synchronize files on laptops.

15. Startup command line options are:
- **a.** A special series of characters added to the end of the path to the file that start with a forward slash.
- **b.** Entered in the Startup dialog box.
- **c.** Used to automate the synchronization of a replica set.
- **d.** Special objects that execute first when the database is opened.

16. Client/server computing can be defined as:
- **a.** Two or more information systems cooperatively processing to solve a problem.
- **b.** A process to resynchronize a replica set.
- **c.** A LAN, WAN, or the Internet.
- **d.** A way to study the structure and size of your database to make a variety of recommendations on how you could improve its performance.

17. If you want to copy a database to another computer, such as a home or laptop computer you'll use on the road, which of the following features would keep the databases up-to-date?
- **a.** Database Splitter
- **b.** Performance Analyzer
- **c.** Startup Options
- **d.** Briefcase

Skills Review

1. **Converting databases.**
   - **a.** Start Access and open the Basketball-P database.
   - **b.** Click Tools on the menu bar, point to Database Utilities, point to Convert Database, then click To Prior Access Version.
   - **c.** Navigate to your Project Disk in the Convert Database Into dialog box, type "Basketball97" as the filename, then click Save.
   - **d.** Open Windows Explorer, open your Project Disk, and check to make sure that both the Basketball-P and Basketball97 databases are stored on the Project Disk. You also will see a Basketball-P.ldb file, because Basketball-P.mdb is currently open.
   - **e.** Close Explorer.

2. **Setting Passwords.**
   - **a.** Close Basketball-P, but leave Access open.
   - **b.** Click the Open button on the Database toolbar, navigate to your Project Disk, then click Basketball-P.
   - **c.** Click the Open list arrow, then click Open Exclusive.
   - **d.** Click Tools on the menu bar, point to Security, then click Set Database Password.
   - **e.** Check to make sure the Caps Lock light is not on, type the word "colonial" in the Password text box, tab, type "colonial" in the Verify text box, then click OK. (Remember that passwords are case sensitive.)
   - **f.** Close the Basketball-P database, but leave Access open.
   - **g.** Open the Basketball-P database, type "colonial" in the Password Required dialog box, then click OK.
   - **h.** Close the database, then open the Basketball-P database in Exclusive mode.
   - **i.** Click Tools on the menu bar, point to Security, click Unset Database Password, type "colonial", then click OK.

3. **Changing Startup Options.**
   - **a.** Click Tools on the menu bar, then click Startup to open the Startup dialog box.
   - **b.** Type "SUNY Binghamton Women" in the Application Title text box, click the Display Form/Page list arrow, click the Player Entry Form, clear the Allow Toolbar/Menu Changes check box, then click OK. Notice the change in the title bar.
   - **c.** Close the Basketball-P database, but leave Access open.
   - **d.** Open the Basketball-P database.
   - **e.** Close the Player Entry Form that automatically opened when the database was opened.
   - **f.** Check the Access title bar to make sure it displays "SUNY Binghamton Women."
   - **g.** Right-click the Database toolbar to make sure that you are unable to change or modify any of the toolbars.
   - **h.** On a piece of paper, identify one reason for changing each of the three startup options modified in steps b, c, and d.
   - **i.** Close the Basketball-P database, but leave Access open.

4. **Encrypting and Decrypting a Database.**
   - **a.** To encrypt the database, click Tools on the menu bar, point to Security, then click Encrypt/Decrypt Database.
   - **b.** Navigate to your Project Disk, click Basketball-P, then click OK.
   - **c.** In the Encrypt Database As dialog box, click Basketball-P, then click Save.
   - **d.** Click Yes when asked to replace the existing Basketball-P file.
   - **e.** To decrypt the database, click Tools on the menu bar, point to Security, then click Encrypt/Decrypt Database.
   - **f.** In the Decrypt Database dialog box, click Basketball-P, then click OK.

g. In the Decrypt Database As dialog box, click Basketball-P, click Save, then click Yes.
h. On a piece of paper, identify two database threats for which encryption could be used to protect the database.

5. **Analyzing Performance.**
   a. Open Basketball-P, then close the Player Entry Form.
   b. Click Tools on the menu bar, point to Analyze, then click Performance.
   c. Click the All Object Types tab, click Select All, then click OK.
   d. Click each of the Analysis Results and read the Analysis notes.
   e. On a piece of paper, record the analysis results (there should be three entries), and identify whether they are recommendations, suggestions, ideas, or items that were fixed.
   f. Close the Performance Analyzer dialog box.

6. **Splitting a Database.**
   a. Click Tools on the menu, point to Database Utilities, then click Database Splitter.
   b. Click Split Database, make sure that the Save in: list points to your Project Disk, then click Split to accept the default name of Basketball-P_be as the filename.
   c. Click OK when prompted that the database was successfully split.
   d. On a sheet of paper, identify two reasons for splitting a database.
   e. On the paper, identify the back-end and front-end database filenames, and explain what these databases contain.
   f. On the paper, explain what the table icons in the front-end database look like and what they represent.
   g. Close the Basketball-P database.

7. **Replicating Using the Briefcase.**
   a. Copy the Team-P database from your Project Disk, then paste it to the Desktop of your computer.
   b. Copy the Team-P database from your Desktop, then paste it to an empty Briefcase folder. Click Yes when asked to continue, click No when asked to make a back-up copy, then click OK to choose the Original File.
   c. Double-click the Team-P database in the New Briefcase window, double-click the Players table, then modify the record for PlayerNo 21 with your own First and Last names, HomeTown, and HomeState. (*Hint*: If no empty Briefcase window exists on your Desktop, create one by right-clicking the Desktop, pointing to New, then clicking Briefcase.)
   d. Close the Players table, then close the Team-P Replica database and exit Access. Close the Briefcase window.
   e. Open the Team-P Design Master database from your Desktop, then open the Players table. PlayerNo 21 will not be modified.
   f. Change PlayerNo 22 so that a friend's First and Last names, HomeTown, and HomeState are entered.
   g. Close the Players table, then close the Team-P Design Master database and Access window.

8. **Synchronizing Using the Briefcase.**
   a. Open the Briefcase on the Desktop where the replicated Team-P database exists, click the Update All button, then click the Update button to merge the databases.
   b. Double-click the Team-P entry in the Briefcase window to open the replica database, double-click the Players table, then print the Players datasheet. Both PlayerNo 21 and 22 should show the changes you made.
   c. Close the Players datasheet, close the Team-P Replica, and close the Briefcase window.
   d. Delete any files you created in the desktop.

Independent Challenges

1. As the manager of a doctor's clinic, you have created an Access database called Patients-P to track insurance claims. You wish to set a database password on this file and also encrypt the database.

To complete this independent challenge:

a. Start Access.
b. Click the Open button on the Database toolbar, navigate to your Project Disk, click Patients-P, click the Open list arrow, then click Open Exclusive.
c. Click Tools, point to Security, then click Set Database Password.
d. Enter "health" in the Password text box as well as the Verify text box, then click OK.
e. Close the Patients-P database.
f. Open the Patients-P database, enter "health" in the Password Required dialog box.
g. Close the Patients-P database.
h. To encrypt the database, click Tools, point to Security, then click Encrypt/Decrypt Database.
i. In the Encrypt/Decrypt dialog box, click Patients-P, then click OK.
j. Enter "health" as the password, then click OK.
k. In the Encrypt Database As dialog box, click Patients-P, click Save, then click Yes to replace the existing file.
l. Exit Access.

2. As the manager of a doctor's clinic, you have created an Access database called Patients-P to track insurance claims. You wish to change the startup options.

To complete this independent challenge:

a. Start Access and open the database Patients-P from your Project Disk.
b. If prompted for a password (if you completed Independent Challenge 1, the file will be password protected), enter "health" and click OK.
c. To set startup options, click Tools on the menu, then click Startup.
d. In the Startup dialog box, enter "Dr. Biheller and Dr. Langguth" in the Application Title text box, choose the Claim Entry Form as the choice for the Display Form/Page option, clear the Allow Toolbar/Menu Changes check box, then click OK.
e. Close the Patients-P database.
f. Open the Patients-P database to test the Startup options. Enter the "health" password if prompted.
g. Close the Claim Entry Form, then right-click the Database toolbar to make sure that toolbars cannot be modified. Check to make sure that "Dr. Biheller and Dr. Langguth" appears in the title bar of the Access window.
h. Close the Patients-P database, then exit Access.

3. As the manager of a doctor's clinic, you have created an Access database called Patients-P to track insurance claims. You wish to use the Briefcase to synchronize a replica set.

To complete this independent challenge:

a. Open Windows Explorer, locate then copy the Patients-P database from your Project Disk, close Explorer, then paste the Patients-P database to your Desktop. (*Hint*: You can also use My Computer to find and copy the Patients-P database.)
b. If a password is set on the Patients-P database, you must remove it before you can use the database to create a replica set. If a password is not set on the Patients-P database, skip to step d. Open Access, then open the Patients-P database stored on your Desktop by using the Open Exclusive option.

c. Enter "health" as the password, close the Claim Entry Form if it automatically opened, click Tools, point to Security, click Unset Database Password, enter "health", click OK, then close the Patients-P database and Access window.
d. Copy the Patients-P database on your Desktop, then paste it into an empty Briefcase window. (*Hint*: If there is no empty Briefcase window on the Desktop, create one by right-clicking the Desktop, pointing to New, then clicking Briefcase.)
e. Click Yes to continue, click No about making a backup copy, and OK to choose the Original Copy as the one that will allow changes to the design of the database.
f. Double-click the Patients-P database in the Briefcase window, close the Claims Entry Form if it is opened, double-click the Doctors table, then enter your own information as a new record in the PodFirstName (your first name initial), PodLastName (your last name), and PodCode (your first and last name initials, which must be unique from the other records because it is the key field) fields.
g. Close the Doctors datasheet, then close the Patients-P Replica database.
h. Open the Patients-P database Design Master, which is stored on the Desktop.
i. Close the Claim Entry Form if it is opened, then double-click the Doctors table to open its datasheet.
j. Add a friend's name as a new record in the table, making sure that you enter unique initials in the PodCode field.
k. Close the Doctors datasheet, then close the Patients-P Design Master.
l. Open the Briefcase folder that contains the Patients-P replica, click the Update All button, then click Update to merge the changes in the Replica and Design Master.
m. Double-click either the Patients-P Replica or Design Master file to open it, close the Claim Entry Form as necessary, double-click the Doctors table, then print the datasheet. You should see both your name and your friend's name entered as records in the datasheet.
n. Close the Doctors datasheet, close the Patients-P database, and close Access.
o. Delete any files you created on the desktop.

WEB WORK

4. MediaLoft has developed a Web site that provides internal information to their employees. In this independent challenge, you'll surf the Internet to find Web pages that present information on how to create a secure Access database and how to work with the Briefcase.

a. Connect to the Internet, and go to the MediaLoft intranet site at http://www.course.com/ illustrated/MediaLoft
b. Click the link for Research center, then click the link for Microsoft Windows Information.
c. Find the Search This Site text box and enter "Briefcase" to request information on this subject. (*Hint*: Web sites change often, and you may need to find and click a Search button before you are able to enter your search criteria.)
d. Refine your search as necessary, then find and print two articles with the word "Briefcase" in the summary line.
e. Find the Search This Site text box and enter "Security" to request information on this subject. (*Hint*: Web sites change often, and you may need to find and click a Search button before you are able to enter your search criteria.)
f. Refine your search as necessary, then find and print two articles that discuss security options available in Access.
g. Close your browser window.

Visual Workshop

As the manager of a doctor's clinic, you have created an Access database called Patients-P to track insurance claims. Use the Performance Analyzer to generate the results shown in Figure P-20 by analyzing all object types.

FIGURE P-20

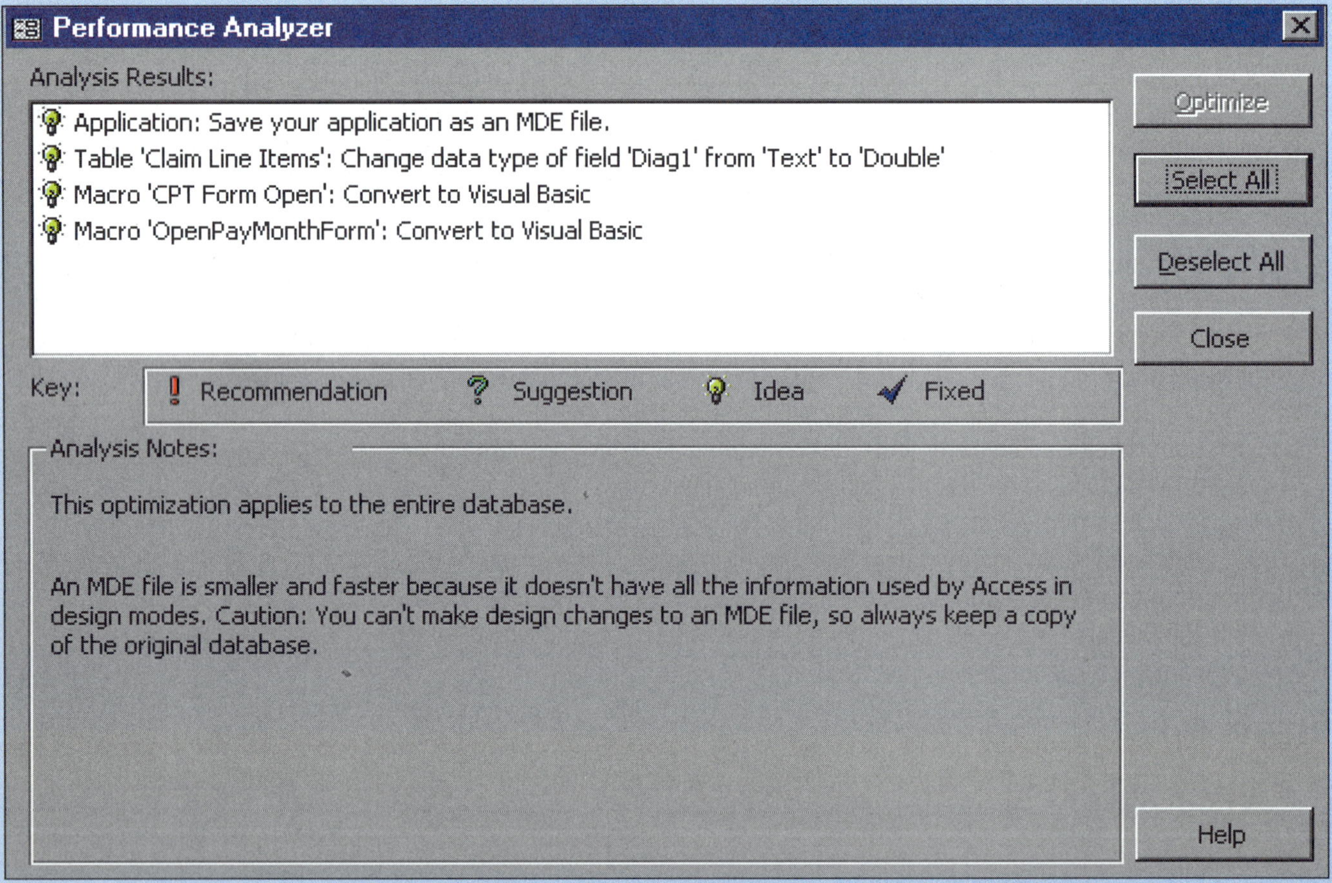

Access 2000 MOUS Certification Objectives

Below is a list of the Microsoft Office User Specialist program objectives for Core and Expert Access 2000 skills showing where each MOUS objective is covered in the Lessons and Practice. This table lists the Core and Expert MOUS certification skills covered in the units in this book and in *Microsoft Access 2000 – Illustrated Introductory* (Units A–H). For more information on which Illustrated titles meet MOUS certification, please see the inside cover of this book.

MOUS standardized coding number	Activity	Lesson page where skill is covered	Location in lesson where skill is covered	Practice
AC2000.1	**Planning and designing databases**			
AC2000.1.1	Determine appropriate data inputs for your database	Access B-2 Access E-2	Details, Table B-1 Details	Skills Review, Independent Challenges 1–4, Visual Workshop
AC2000.1.2	Determine appropriate data outputs for your database	Access A-4 Access E-4	Table A-2 Details	Skills Review, Independent Challenges 1–4
AC2000.1.3	Create table structure	Access B-4 Access E-6	Steps 2–7 Steps 2–5	Skills Review, Independent Challenges 1–4
AC2000.1.4	Establish table relationships	Access E-16	Steps 1–5	Skills Review, Independent Challenges 1–4
AC2000.2	**Working with Access**			
AC2000.2.1	Use the Office Assistant	Access A-18	Steps 3–6	Skills Review
AC2000.2.2	Select an object using the Objects Bar	Access A-8 Access B-8	Steps 5–6 Steps 1–2	Skills Review, Independent Challenges 1–4
AC2000.2.3	Print database objects (tables, forms, reports, queries)	Access A-16 Access C-14 Access C-16	Steps 1–7 Step 7 Step 8	Skills Review, Independent Challenges 1–4
AC2000.2.4	Navigate through records in a table, query, or form	Access A-10 Access C-14	Steps 2–6 Steps 3–5	Skills Review, Independent Challenges 1–4
AC2000.2.5	Create a database (using a Wizard or in Design View)	Access H-2	Steps 1–6	Skills Review
AC2000.3	**Building and modifying tables**			
AC2000.3.1	Create tables by using the Table Wizard	Access B-4	Step 1	Skills Review, Independent Challenges 1–2
AC2000.3.2	Set primary keys	Access B-4 Access E-6	Steps 6–7 Step 6	Skills Review, Independent Challenges 1–4
AC2000.3.3	Modify field properties	Access B-6 Access E-6	Steps 5–6 Step 5	Skills Review, Independent Challenges 1–4
AC2000.3.4	Use multiple data types	Access B-6 Access E-6	Step 2 Steps 3–5	Skills Review, Independent Challenges 1–4
AC2000.3.5	Modify tables using Design View	Access B-6 Access E-6	Steps 1–8 Steps 3–6	Skills Review, Independent Challenges 1–4
AC2000.3.6	Use the Lookup Wizard	Access H-2	Steps 7–9	Skills Review
AC2000.3.7	Use the Input Mask wizard	Access E-8	Steps 4–8	Skills Review
AC2000.4	**Building and modifying forms**			
AC2000.4.1	Create a form with the Form Wizard	Access C-4	Steps 1–3	Skills Review, Independent Challenges 1–3

MOUS standardized coding number	Activity	Lesson page where skill is covered	Location in lesson where skill is covered	Practice
AC2000.4.2	Use the Control Toolbox to add controls	Access C-10 Access C-16	Steps 1–7 Steps 2–5	Skills Review, Independent Challenges 2–3
AC2000.4.3	Modify Format Properties (font, style, font size, color, caption, etc.) of controls	Access C-8 Access C-10	Steps 2–5 Steps 5–6	Skills Review, Independent Challenge 2–3
AC2000.4.4	Use form sections (headers, footers, detail)	Access C-6 Access C-12 Access C-16	Steps 1–6 Steps 2–5 Steps 2–5	Skills Review, Independent Challenges 2–3
AC2000.4.5	Use a Calculated Control on a form	Access C-10	Steps 2–7	Skills Review, Independent Challenge 2
AC2000.5	**Viewing and organizing information**			
AC2000.5.1	Use the Office Clipboard	Access D-10	Clues to Use	Skills Review, Independent Challenges 2–3
AC2000.5.2	Switch between object Views	Access B-6 Access B-18	Step 7 Step 6	Skills Review, Independent Challenges 1–4, Visual Workshop
AC2000.5.3	Enter records using a datasheet	Access A-12 Access E-12	Steps 2–4 Step 7	Skills Review, Independent Challenges 3–4, Visual Workshop
AC2000.5.4	Enter records using a form	Access C-14 Access G-16	Step 2 Steps 2–4	Skills Review, Independent Challenge 1, Visual Workshop
AC2000.5.5	Delete records from a table	Access A-14	Step 9	Skills Review
AC2000.5.6	Find a record	Access B-10 Access B-12 Access B-14	Details Steps 4–7 Steps 4–8	Skills Review, Independent Challenge 1, Visual Workshop
AC2000.5.7	Sort records	Access B-10 Access B-12	Steps 1–3 Details	Skills Review, Independent Challenges 1–4
AC2000.5.8	Apply and remove filters (filter by form and filter by selection)	Access B-10 Access B-14	Details Steps 1–6	Skills Review
AC2000.5.9	Specify criteria in a query	Access B-16 Access B-18	Step 6 Step 4	Skills Review, Independent Challenges 1–4, Visual Workshop
AC2000.5.10	Display related records in a subdatasheet	Access E-16 Access H-22	Step 8	Independent Challenge 2
AC2000.5.11	Create a calculated field	Access C-10 Access F-10	Steps 1–6 Steps 2–3	Skills Review, Independent Challenge 3
AC2000.5.12	Create and modify a multi-table select query	Access F-2 Access F-6	Steps 2–6 Steps 2–4	Skills Review, Independent Challenges 1–4, Visual Workshop
AC2000.6	**Defining relationships**			
AC2000.6.1	Establish relationships	Access E-16	Steps 1–8	Skills Review, Independent Challenges 1–4, Visual Workshop
AC2000.6.2	Enforce referential integrity	Access E-16	Step 4	Skills Review, Independent Challenges 1–4
AC2000.7	**Producing reports**			
AC2000.7.1	Create a report with the Report Wizard	Access D-4 Access H-6 Access H-14	Steps 2–5 Steps 5–6 Step 1	Skills Review, Independent Challenges 1–4, Visual Workshop

MOUS standardized coding number	Activity	Lesson page where skill is covered	Location in lesson where skill is covered	Practice
AC2000.7.2	Preview and print a report	Access D-6 Access H-14	Step 7 Step 8	Skills Review, Independent Challenges 1–4, Visual Workshop
AC2000.7.3	Move and resize a control	Access D-12 Access H-14	Steps 2–5 Steps 4–6	Skills Review, Independent Challenges 1–4, Visual Workshop
AC2000.7.4	Modify format properties (font, style, font size, color, caption, etc.)	Access D-14 Access H-10	Steps 2–7 Steps 3–6	Skills Review, Independent Challenges 1–4, Visual Workshop
AC2000.7.5	Use the Control Toolbox to add controls	Access D-6 Access H-10 Access H-14	Steps 3–6 Step 6 Step 5	Skills Review, Independent Challenges 1–4, Visual Workshop
AC2000.7.6	Use report sections (headers, footers, detail)	Access D-3 Access D-6 Access H-14	Table D-1 Steps 1–7 Steps 3–6	Skills Review, Independent Challenges 1–4, Visual Workshop
AC2000.7.7	Use a Calculated Control in a report	Access D-12	Step 4	Skills Review, Independent Challenge 1
AC2000.8	**Integrating with other applications**			
AC2000.8.1	Import data to a new table	Access H-4	Steps 6–7	Skills Review
AC2000.8.2	Save a table, query, form as a Web page	Access G-17	Clues to Use	Skills Review, Independent Challenge 4
AC2000.8.3	Add Hyperlinks	Access C-17	Clues to Use	
AC2000.9	**Using Access Tools**			
AC2000.9.1	Print Database Relationships	Access E-16	Step 6	Skills Review, Independent Challenge 1
AC2000.9.2	Backup and Restore a database	Access H-16	Steps 4–6	Skills Review
AC2000.9.3	Compact and Repair a database	Access H-16	Steps 1–2	Skills Review
AC2000E.1.	**Building and modifying tables**			
AC2000E.1.1	Set validation text	Access E-14	Step 2	Skills Review, Independent Challenge 1
AC2000E.1.2	Define data validation criteria	Access E-14	Step 1	Skills Review, Independent Challenge 1
AC2000E.1.3	Modify an input mask	Access E-8 Access E-9	Steps 4–7 Clues to Use	Skills Review
AC2000E.1.4	Create and modify Lookup Fields	Access H-2	Steps 7–9	Skills Review
AC2000E.1.5	Optimize data type usage (double, long, int, byte, etc.)	Access E-10 Access E-11	Steps 2–6 Table E-4	Skills Review, Independent Challenges 2–3
AC2000E.2	**Building and modifying forms**			
AC2000E.2.1	Create a form in Design View	Access G-6	Steps 1–8	Skills Review
AC2000E.2.2	Insert a graphic on a form	Access C-16	Steps 2–4	Skills Review, Independent Challenge 3, Visual Workshop
AC2000E.2.3	Modify control properties	Access C-8 Access G-10 Access G-14 Access L-2 Access L-4	Steps 2–3 Steps 4–7 Steps 2–3 Step 5 Steps 2–4	Skills Review, Independent Challenges 1–4

MOUS standardized coding number	Activity	Lesson page where skill is covered	Location in lesson where skill is covered	Practice
AC2000E.2.4	Customize form sections (headers, footers, detail)	Access G-8 Access G-14	Step 3 Step 6	Skills Review, Independent Challenges 1–4, Visual Workshop
AC2000E.2.5	Modify form properties	Access G-6 Access G-14 Access L-2 Access L-8	Step 6 Steps 1–6 Step 3 Steps 1–6	Skills Review, Independent Challenges 1–4, Visual Workshop
AC2000E.2.6	Use the Subform Control and synchronize forms	Access G-6 Access G-7 Access G-8	Steps 7–8 Clues to Use Steps 1–5	Skills Review, Independent Challenges 1–4, Visual Workshop
AC2000E.2.7	Create a Switchboard	Access M-14	Steps 1–8	Skills Review, Independent Challenge 4, Visual Workshop
AC2000E.3	**Refining queries**			
AC2000E.3.1	Apply filters (filter by form and filter by selection) in a query's recordset	Access B-14 Access K-2 Access K-16	Steps 1–5 Step 6 Steps 6–7	Skills Review, Independent Challenge 2, Skills Review, Independent Challenges 3–4
AC2000E.3.2	Create a totals query	Access K-2	Steps 4–7	Skills Review, Independent Challenge 2
AC2000E.3.3	Create a parameter query	Access K-4 Access K-5	Steps 1–3 Clues to Use	Skills Review, Independent Challenges 1–4
AC2000E.3.4	Specify criteria in multiple fields (AND vs. OR)	Access F-6 Access F-8	Steps 2–4 Steps 2–4	Skills Review, Independent Challenges 1–3
AC2000E.3.5	Modify query properties (field formats, caption, input masks, etc.)	Access F-10 Access K-6	Steps 5–6 Steps 1–7	Skills Review, Independent Challenges 1–4, Visual Workshop
AC2000E.3.6	Create an action query (update, delete, insert)	Access K-8 Access K-10 Access K-12 Access K-14	Steps 1–6 Steps 1–6 Steps 1–6 Steps 1–6	Skills Review, Independent Challenges 1–4, Visual Workshop
AC2000E.3.7	Optimize queries using indexes	Access K-7	Clues to Use	
AC2000E.3.8	Specify join properties for relationships	Access K-16	Steps 2–4	Skills Review, Independent Challenges 3–4
AC2000E.4	**Producing reports**			
AC2000E.4.1	Insert a graphic on a report	Access H-10 Access H-14	Step 5 Steps 4–7	Skills Review, Independent Challenges 1–4
AC2000E.4.2	Modify report properties	Access D-8 Access H-8 Access L-2	Step 2 Step 2 Step 3	Skills Review, Independent Challenges 1–4, Visual Workshop
AC2000E.4.3	Create and modify a report in Design View	Access D-6 Access H-6	Steps 1–6 Steps 1–3	Skills Review, Independent Challenges 1–4, Visual Workshop
AC2000E.4.4	Modify control properties	Access H-8 Access H-10 Access L-16	Steps 1–7 Step 5 Step 5	Skills Review, Independent Challenges 1–4, Visual Workshop
AC2000E.4.5	Set section properties	Access H-8 Access L-16	Step 2 Steps 1–5	Skills Review, Independent Challenges 1–4
AC2000E.4.6	Use the Subreport Control and synchronize reports	Access L-14	Steps 1–4	Skills Review, Independent Challenges 1–4, Visual Workshop

MOUS standardized coding number	Activity	Lesson page where skill is covered	Location in lesson where skill is covered	Practice
AC2000E.5	**Defining relationships**			
AC2000E.5.1	Establish one-to-one relationships	Access I-4 Access I-5	Steps 2–6 Table I-2	Skills Review, Independent Challenges 1–3
AC2000E.5.2	Establish many-to-many relationships	Access I-5	Table I-2	
AC2000E.5.3	Set Cascade Update and Cascade Delete options	Access I-4	Steps 6	
AC2000E.6	**Utilizing web capabilities**			
AC2000E.6.1	Create hyperlinks	Access I-10 Access J-4	Steps 2–8 Steps 2–6	Skills Review, Skills Review, Independent Challenge 1
AC2000E.6.2	Use the group and sort features of data access pages	Access J-6 Access J-12	Steps 3–6 Steps 1–4	Skills Review, Independent Challenge 2
AC2000E.6.3	Create a data access page	Access J-6	Steps 1–3	Skills Review, Independent Challenges 1–3, Visual Workshop
AC2000E.7	**Using Access tools**			
AC2000E.7.1	Set and modify a database password	Access P-4	Steps 1–9	Skills Review, Independent Challenges 1–3
AC2000E.7.2	Set startup options	Access P-6	Steps 1–6	Skills Review, Independent Challenge 2
AC2000E.7.3	Use Add-ins (Database Splitter, Analyzer, Link Table Manager)	Access M-4 Access P-10 Access P-12	Steps 2–5 Steps 2–5 Steps 1–5	Skills Review, Independent Challenge 1, Skills Review, Independent Challenge 3, Visual Workshop
AC2000E.7.4	Encrypt and Decrypt a database	Access P-8	Steps 2–7	Skills Review, Independent Challenge 1
AC2000E.7.5	Use simple replication (copy for a mobile user)	Access P-14 Access P-15 Access P-16	Steps 1–8 Clues to Use Steps 1–4	Skills Review, Independent Challenges 3–4
AC2000E.7.6	Run macros using controls	Access N-12 Access N-13	Steps 1–5 Clues to Use	Skills Review, Independent Challenges 1–3, Visual Workshop
AC2000E.7.7	Create a macro using the Macro Builder	Access N-4	Steps 1–5	Skills Review, Independent Challenges 1–3, Visual Workshop
AC2000E.7.8	Convert database to a previous version	Access P-2	Steps 1–7	Skills Review
AC2000E.8	**Data Integration (New Skill Set)**			
AC2000E.8.1	Export database records to Excel	Access I-16	Steps 1–6	Skills Review, Visual Workshop
AC2000E.8.2	Drag and drop tables and queries to Excel	Access I-16	Step 5	Skills Review, Visual Workshop
AC2000E.8.3	Present information as a chart (MS Graph)	Access L-10 Access L-12	Steps 1–5 Steps 2–6	Skills Review, Independent Challenge 3
AC2000E.8.4	Link to existing data	Access I-8	Steps 1–6	Skills Review, Independent Challenges 1–3

Project Files List

To complete many of the lessons and practice exercises in this book, students need to use a Project File that is supplied by Course Technology and stored on a Project Disk. Below is a list of the files that are supplied, and the unit or practice exercise to which the files correspond. For information on how to obtain Project Files, please see the inside cover of this book. The following list only includes Project Files that are supplied; it does not include the files students create from scratch or the files students create by revising the supplied files.

Unit	File supplied on Project Disk	Location file is used in unit
Access Unit I	Training-I.mdb New Courses.xls Course Materials.xls Directions to MediaLoft.doc Final Attendance Log Report.xls	Lessons
	Machinery-I.mdb Machinery Employees.xls Machinery Vendors.xls Product Contacts.doc	Skills Review
	Basketball-I.mdb BB Stats.xls Course Load.xls BB Player Information.doc	Independent Challenges 1–3
	Training-I.mdb	Independent Challenge 4
	Basketball-I.mdb	Visual Workshop
Access Unit J	Training-J.mdb	Lessons Independent Challenge 4
	Machinery-J.mdb	Skills Review
	Basketball-J.mdb	Independent Challenges 1–3 Visual Workshop
Access Unit K	Training-K.mdb	Lessons Independent Challenge 4
	Seminar-K.mdb	Skills Review
	Basketball-K.mdb	Independent Challenges 1–3 Visual Workshop
Access Unit L	Training-L.mdb	Lessons
	Seminar-L.mdb	Skills Review
	Basketball-L.mdb	Independent Challenges 1–3 Visual Workshop
Access Unit M	Technology-M.mdb *(Disk 1)*	Lessons
	Basketball-M.mdb *(Disk 2)*	Skills Review
	Patients-M.mdb *(Disk 2)*	Independent Challenges 1–3 Visual Workshop
Access Unit N	Technology-N.mdb	Lessons
	Basketball-N.mdb	Skills Review
	Patients-N.mdb	Independent Challenges 1–3 Visual Workshop

Unit	File supplied on Project Disk	Location file is used in unit
Access Unit O	Technology-O.mdb	Lessons 1–8
	Basketball-O.mdb	Skills Review Visual Workshop
	Patients-O.mdb	Independent Challenges 1–3 Visual Workshop
Access Unit P	Technology-P.mdb	Lessons 1–8
	Basketball-P.mdb Team-P.mdb	Skills Review
	Patients-P.mdb	Independent Challenges 1–3 Visual Workshop

Access 2000

Glossary

.ldb The file extension for a temporary file that exists when an Access database is open that keeps track of record locking information when the database is opened.

.mdb The file extension for Access databases.

Action A task that you want a macro to perform. Each macro action occupies a single row in the macro window.

Action query A query that makes changes to underlying data. There are four types of action queries: delete, update, append, and make-table.

Add-In An extra Access feature that extends the functionality of Access but is not part of the core program. Some add-ins are available through Microsoft and some by third parties. They are "added in" when the user chooses to install them.

Aggregate functions Special functions used in a summary query that calculate information about a group of records rather than a new field of information about each record.

Ampersand (&) The character used to concatenate items in an expression.

Analyze It with MS Excel An Access feature that quickly copies Access data to a blank Excel workbook.

And criteria Criteria placed in the same row of the query design grid. All criteria on the same row must be true in order for a record to appear on the resulting datasheet.

AND query A query which contains AND criteria (two or more criteria present on the same row of the query design grid. Both criteria must be true for the record to appear on the resulting datasheet).

Append query An action query that appends records to another table.

Argument For a macro, arguments are additional information for each action of a macro that further clarifies how the action is to execute. For a module, arguments are constants, variables, or expressions that are passed to a procedure and are required for it to execute.

Arguments The pieces of information a function needs to create the final answer. In an expression, multiple arguments are separated by commas. All of the arguments are surrounded by a single set of parentheses.

Arithmetic operators Plus (+), minus (-), multiply (*), divide (/), and exponentiation (^) characters used in a mathematical calculation.

Ascending order A sequence in which information is placed in alphabetical order or from smallest to largest. For a text field, numbers sort first, then letters.

Text ascending order: 123, 3H, 455, 98, 98B, animal, Iowa, New Jersey
Date ascending order: 1/1/57, 1/1/61, 12/25/61, 5/5/98, 8/20/98, 8/20/99
Number ascending order: 1, 10, 15, 120, 140, 500, 1200, 1500

AutoFormats Predefined formats provided by Access that contain background pictures and font, color, and alignment choices that can quickly be applied to an existing form or report.

AutoKeys A special name reserved for the macro group object that contains key combinations (such as Ctrl+L) that are used to run associated macros.

AutoNumber A data type in which Access enters a sequential integer for each record added into the datasheet. Numbers cannot be reused even if the record is deleted.

Back-end database When a database has been split using the Database Splitter, a back-end database is created which contains all of the data and is stored on a computer that is accessible by all users (which is usually the file server in a LAN).

Bang notation Syntax used to separate parts of an object (the parts are separated by an exclamation point, hence "bang") in the Visual Basic programming language.

Between . . . And operator Used when specifying limiting criteria between two values in a query; it is equivalent to >= (greater than or equal to) and <= (less than or equal to).

Body The basic design surface of the data access page that displays text, controls, and sections.

Bookmark A specific location within a Word document marked by an invisible code. Hyperlinks within Access can be created to open a Word document and display the text at a particular bookmark.

Bound control A control used in either a form or report to display data from the underlying record source; also used to edit and enter new data in a form.

Bound image control A bound control used to show OLE data such as a picture on a form or report.

Break mode Temporary suspension of program execution in which you can examine, debug, reset, step-through, or continue program execution.

Breakpoint A bookmark set in VBA code that temporarily suspends execution of the procedure at that point in time so that the user can examine what is happening.

Briefcase A Windows program used to help synchronize two computers that regularly use the same files.

Brown-out Dip in the level of electrical current causing the lights to dim or "brown-out."

Browser Software loaded on a microcomputer such as Microsoft's Internet Explorer (IE) or Netscape Navigator used to find and display Web pages.

Calculated control A control that uses information from existing controls to calculate new data such as subtotals, dates, or page numbers; used in either a form or report.

Calculated field A field created in Query Design view that results from an expression of existing fields, Access functions, and arithmetic operators. For example the entry Profit: [RetailPrice]-[WholesalePrice] in the field cell of the query design grid creates a calculated field called Profit that is the difference between the RetailPrice and WholesalePrice fields.

Caption property A field property used to override the technical field name with an easy-to-read caption entry when the field name appears on datasheets, forms, and reports.

Caption section A section available in the Design view of a page object used to display text.

Cascade Delete Related Records An option available when enforce referential integrity is applied that automatically deletes all records in the "many" table if the record with the matching key field in the "one" table is deleted.

Cascade Update Related Fields An option available when enforce referential integrity is applied that automatically updates the data in the foreign key field if the matching key field is changed.

Chart Graph: Visual representation of numeric data that helps a user see comparisons, patterns, and trends in data.

Chart placeholder A picture of a chart that represents the chart control within Report Design view. You must double-click the chart placeholder to edit the chart.

Chart Wizard Access Wizard that steps you through the process of creating charts within forms and reports.

Check box Bound control used to display "yes" or "no" answers for a field. If the box is "checked" it indicates "yes" information in a form or report.

Class modules Modules used only within a particular form or report object and therefore stored within the form or report object.

Client In client-server computer architectures, the client computer is generally the user's computer.

Client/server computing Two or more information systems cooperatively processing to solve a problem. In Access, a back-end and front-end database participate in client/server computing, each assigned to the tasks to which it is best suited.

Clipboard The temporary location that can store up to 12 items that are copied. When you paste, you paste information that is stored on the Clipboard.

Clipboard toolbar A toolbar that shows the contents of the Office Clipboard; contains buttons for copying and pasting items to and from the Office Clipboard.

Code window See *Visual Basic Code window.*

Collapse button A "minus sign" to the left of a record displayed in a datasheet that when clicked on, collapses the subdatasheet that is displayed. When you click a Collapse button on a page, less detail about the item being collapsed will appear.

Combo box A bound control used to display a list of possible entries for a field in which you can also type an entry from the keyboard. It is a "combination" of the list box and text box controls.

Command button An unbound control used to provide an easy way to initiate an action or run a macro.

Command Button Wizard A Wizard that steps you through the process of creating a command button.

Command-line option A special series of characters added to the end of the path to the database file that start with a forward slash and modify the way that the database is opened.

Comment line A VBA statement that does not execute any actions but is used to clarify or document other statements. Comment lines appear in green in the Code window and start with a single apostrophe.

Compacting Rearranging the data and objects on the storage medium so that space formerly occupied by deleted objects is eliminated. Compacting a database doesn't change the data, but it generally reduces the overall size of the database.

Compile time The period during which source code is translated to executable code.

Compile time error A VBA error that occurs because of incorrectly constructed VBA code.

Conditional expression An expression that results in either a "true" or "false" answer that determines whether a macro action will execute or not.

Conditional formatting Formatting applied to a control on a form or report that changes depending upon a value in a field, an expression, or on which field has the focus. For example, a text box may be conditionally formatted to display its value in red if the value is a negative number.

Constant In VBA, a constant is an item that retains a constant value throughout the execution of the code.

Control Source property The most important property of a bound control on a form or report because it etermines which field the bound control will display.

Control Any element on a form or report such as a label, text box, line, or combo box. Controls can be bound, unbound, or calculated.

ControlTip Text property Property of a control that determines what text displays in tip that pops up when you point to that control with the mouse.

Converting Changing a database file into one that can be opened by an earlier version of Access.

Criteria The entry that determines which records are displayed when finding or filtering records in a datasheet or form, or when building a query.

Crosstab query A query that presents data in a cross-tabular layout (fields are used for both column and row headings), similar to pivot tables in other database and spreadsheet products.

Crosstab Query Wizard A wizard used to create crosstab queries that helps identify which fields will be used for row and column headings, and which fields will be summarized within the datasheet.

Currency A data type used for monetary values.

Current record symbol A black triangle symbol that appears in the record select box to the left of the record that has the focus in either a datasheet or a form.

Data The unique entries of information that you enter into the fields of the records.

Data Access Page See *Page.*

Database A collection of data associated with a topic (for example, sales of products to customers).

Database password A password that is required to open a database.

Database software Software used to manage data that can be organized into lists of things such as customers, products, vendors, employees, projects, or sales.

Database Splitter An Access feature that improves the performance of a shared database by allowing you to split it into multiple files.

Database window The window that includes common elements such as the Access title bar, menu bar, and toolbar. It also contains an Objects bar to quickly work with the seven different types of objects within the database by clicking the appropriate object button.

Database Wizard A powerful Access wizard that creates a sample database file for a general purpose such as inventory control, event tracking, or expenses. The objects created by the Database Wizard can be used and modified.

Datasheet A spreadsheet-like grid that shows fields as columns and records as rows.

Datasheet view A view that lists the records of the object in a datasheet. Table, query, and most form objects have a Datasheet view.

Data type A required property for each field that defines the type of data that can be entered in each field. Valid data types include AutoNumber, Text, Number, Currency, Date/Time, OLE Object, Memo, Yes/No, and Hyperlink.

Date/Time A data type used for date and time fields.

Debug To determine why a macro doesn't run properly.

Declaration statements VBA statements that precede procedure statements and help set rules for how the statements in the module are processed.

Decrypt To reverse the encryption process.

Delete query An action query that deletes records based on an expression.

Delimited text file A file that contains one record on each line with the fields separated by a common character such as a comma, tab, or dash.

Descending order A sequence in which information is placed in reverse alphabetical order or from largest to smallest. For a text field, letters sort first, then numbers.

Text descending order: Zebra, Victory, Langguth, Bunin, 99A, 9854, 77, 740, 29, 270, 23500, 1

Date descending order: 1/1/99, 1/1/98, 12/25/97, 5/5/97, 8/20/61, 8/20/57

Number descending order: 1500, 1400, 1200, 140, 120, 15, 10, 1

Design view A view in which the structure of the object can be manipulated. Every Access object has a Design view.

Detail section The section of the form or report that contains the controls that are printed for each record in the underlying query or table.

Dialer Software that helps you dial-up to connect you to your ISP.

Dialog box A special form that is used to display information or to prompt a user for a choice.

Documenter An Access feature that creates reports on the properties and relationships between the objects in your database.

Domain Name The middle part of a URL such as www.course.com where "course" is the domain name.

Dot notation Syntax used to separate parts of an object (the parts are separated by a period, hence "dot") in the Visual Basic programming language.

Drag and drop A process which involves dragging an Access icon from the database window to another application window (the target window) in order to quickly copy and paste information. The target window is usually a Word document or Excel workbook window.

Dynamic HTML file An HTML file (Web page) that is tied to an underlying database and therefore displays current information and data.

Dynaset A type of recordset displayed within a query's datasheet that allows you to update all fields except for those on the "one" side of a one-to-many relationship.

Dynaset (inconsistent updates) A type of recordset displayed within a query's datasheet that allows you to update all fields.

E-mail Electronic mail sent and received without printed paper by using computers.

Edit mode The mode in which Access assumes you are trying to edit that particular field, so keystrokes such as [Ctrl][End], [Ctrl][Home], [←]and [→] move the insertion point within the field.

Edit record symbol A pencil-like symbol that appears in the record selector box to the left of the record that is currently being edited in either a datasheet or a form.

Embedded Refers to the relationship between a chart created within Access and the database itself. Although the chart is created through the MS Chart program, it is embedded and stored within the Access database. Sometimes embedded is compared to linked data. Linked data is physically stored outside the Access database file. Embedded data is stored within the file.

Encrypt To make the database objects and data within the database indecipherable to other programs.

Enforce referential integrity An option applied to a one-to-many relationship between two tables that does not allow a value to be entered into the foreign key field that is not first entered into the primary key field. It also does not allow records to be deleted in the "one" table if related records exist in the "many" table.

Event Something that happens within a database (such as the click of a command button or the entry of a field) that can be used to initiate the execution of a macro. Events are associated with toolbars, objects, and controls, and can be viewed by examining that item's property sheet.

Excel The spreadsheet software application within the Microsoft Office Suite.

Exclusive mode If you open an Access database in exclusive mode, others cannot open the file. You must open a database in exclusive mode before you can set a database password.

Expand button A "plus sign" to the left of a record that is displayed in datasheet view that when clicked, will show related records in a subdatasheet. When you click an Expand button, more detail about the item being expanded will appear.

Explorer A Windows program used to manage files, folders, and disk drives.

Exporting A process that copies data from Access into a different Access database or file format.

Expression A combination of values, functions, and operators that calculates to a single value. Access expressions start with an equal sign and are placed in a text box in either Form or Report Design view.

Field The smallest piece or category of information in a database such as the customer's name, city, state, or phone number.

Field list A list of the available fields in the table or query that it represents.

Field names The names given each field in Table Design or Table Datasheet view. Field names can be up to 64 characters long.

Field Property See *Properties.*

File server A centrally-located computer to which every user has access on the network. The function of the file server is to store and serve application and data files to the individual client computers on the LAN.

File transfer Uploading and downloading of files through computing networks.

Filter A temporary view of a subset of records. A filter can be saved as a query object if you wish to apply the same filter later without recreating it.

Filter window A window that appears when you click the Filter by Form button when viewing data in a datasheet or in a form window. The Filter window allows you to define the filter criteria.

Find Duplicates Query Wizard A wizard used to create a query that determines whether a table contains duplicate values in one or more fields.

Find Unmatched Query Wizard A wizard used to create a query that finds records in one table that doesn't have related records in another table.

Focus The property that refers to which field would be edited if you started typing.

Footer Information that prints at the bottom of every printed page (or section when using forms and reports).

Foreign key field The field added to the "many" table involved in a one-to-many relationship.

Form An Access object that provides an easy-to-use data entry screen that generally shows only one record at a time.

Form Design toolbar The toolbar that appears when working in Form Design View with buttons that help you modify a form's controls.

Form Footer A section that appears at the bottom of screen in Form View for each record, but prints only once at the end of all records when the form is printed.

Form Header A section that appears at the top of the screen in Form View for each record, but prints only once at the top of all records when the form is printed.

Form View toolbar The toolbar that appears when working in Form View with buttons that help you print, edit, find, filter, and edit records.

Format Painter A tool used within Form and Report Design view to copy formatting characteristic from one control, and paint them on another.

Formatting Enhancing the appearance of the information in a form, report or datasheet.

Front-end database When a database has been split using the Database Splitter, a front-end database is created which contains links back to the data stored in the back-end database as well as any objects needed by the user. The front-end database is stored on the user's computer, which is also called the client computer.

Function Special, predefined formula such as Sum, Count, Date, Left, and Avg that are part of an expression and perform a specific calculation that returns a value. Access supplies many built-in functions. VBA allows you to create your own unique functions as well.

Functions A special, predefined formula that provides a shortcut for a commonly used calculation, for example, SUM

Graphic See *Image.*

Group Footer section The section of the report that contains controls that print once at the end of each group of records.

Group Header section The section of the report that contains controls that print once at the beginning of each group of records.

Grouping controls Specifying that several controls in the Design view of a form or report are in a "group" so that you can more productively format, move, and change them.

Grouping records In a report, grouping records means to sort them based on the contents of a field, plus provide a group header section that precedes the group of records as well as a group footer section that follows the group of records.

Groups bar Located just below the Objects bar in the database window, the Groups bar displays the Favorites and any user-created groups, which in turn contain shortcuts to objects. Groups are used to organize the database objects into logical sets.

GUI (Graphical User Interface) A characteristic of the design of the screens of a computer program. If GUI, the user interacts with the computer program using point-and-click, click-and-drag, and double-click techniques as well as graphical symbols such as icons, command buttons, and list arrows. Non-GUI screens use text-based menu options or command lines to prompt for user input.

Handles See *Sizing handles.*

Header Information that prints at the top of every printed page (or section when using forms and reports).

Help system Pages of documentation and examples that are available through the Help menu option, the Microsoft Access Help button on the Database toolbar, or the Office Assistant.

Home page The first page displayed on a Web server.

HTML (Hypertext Markup Language) A programming language used to create Web pages.

Hyperlink A data type that stores World Wide Web addresses.

If . . . Then . . . Else A series of VBA statements that allow you to test for a logical condition and execute one set of commands if the condition is true and another if the condition is false.

Image A nontextual piece of information such as a picture, piece of clip art, drawn object, or graph. Because images are graphical (not numbers or letters), they are sometimes referred to as graphical images.

Imported table A table created in another database product or application such as Excel, that is copied and pasted within the Access database through the import process.

Importing A process to quickly convert data from an external source, such as Excel or another database application, into an Access database

Index A field property used to speed up queries that are often sorted or grouped by that field.

Input mask A field property that controls both the values that the users can enter into a text box, as well as provides a visual guide for users as they enter data.

Input mask wizard A wizard that helps you determine the three parts of the input mask property.

Internet A worldwide network of computer networks that send and receive information through a common protocol called TCP/IP.

Intranet A WAN that is built with the same technologies as those used to support the Internet, yet is secured for the internal purposes of a business.

ISP (Internet Service Provider) A company that provides Internet access. To access the Internet from a home computer, your computer must first dial an ISP that in turn connects your computer with the Internet.

Junction table A table that links two other tables with a many-to-many relationship. The junction table holds two foreign key fields that create separate links to the original tables in separate one-to-many relationships.

Key field A field that contains unique information for each record. Also known as *Primary key field.* A key field cannot contain a null entry.

Key field combination Two or more fields that as a group, contain unique information for each record.

Key field symbol In a table's Design view, the symbol that appears as a miniature key in the field indicator box to the left of the field name. It identifies the field that contains unique information for each record.

Label An unbound control that displays static text on forms and reports.

LAN (Local Area Network) A computer network of local resources connected by a direct cable. LANs do not cross public thoroughfares such as streets or rivers.

Layout The general arrangement in which a form will display the fields in the underlying recordset. Layout types include Columnar, Tabular, Datasheet, Chart, and PivotTable. Columnar is most popular for a form, and Datasheet is most popular for a subform.

Leszynski Naming Convention A naming convention in which each object or field is preceded by a three-character tag to help identify it. For example, tables are named starting with the tag "tbl" as in "tblEmployees."

Line control An unbound control used to draw lines on a form or report that divide it into logical groupings.

Link Childs field A subform property that determines which field will serve as the "many" link between the subform and main form.

Link Masters fields A subform property that determines which field will serve as the "one" link between the main form and the subform.

Linked table A table created in another database product or application such as Excel, that is stored outside of the open database, but which can still be used within Access to modify and use its data.

Linking A way to connect data in an external source to an Access database in a way that does not copy or move the original data yet allows it to be manipulated within the Access database.

List box A bound control that displays a list of possible choices from which the user can choose. Used mainly on forms.

Logic error A VBA error that occurs because the code runs without problems, but the procedure still doesn't produce the desired results.

Lookup Wizard A wizard used in Table Design view that allows one field to "lookup" values from another table or query. For example, you might use the Lookup Wizard to specify that the CustomerNumber field in the Sales table display the CustomerName field entry from the Customers table.

Macro An Access object that stores a collection of keystrokes or commands such as printing several reports in a row or providing a toolbar when a form opens.

Macro group An Access macro object that contains more than one macro.

Macro window The Design View of a macro in which you specify which actions and the order in which they will run.

Main form A form that contains a subform control.

Main report A report that contains a subreport control is called the main report.

Make-table query An action query that creates a new table.

Many-to-many relationship The relationship between two tables in an Access database in which one field value in each table can have more than one matching record in the other. You cannot directly create a many-to-many relationship between two tables in an Access database. A junction table is used to connect two tables with this relationship.

Master The original Access database file that is copied to the Briefcase.

Memo A data type used for lengthy text such as comments or notes. It can hold up to 64,000 characters of information.

Merge An action that may occur during the synchronization of a replica and master database in which changes in each database are analyzed and applied to the other.

Merge It with MS Word An Access feature that begins the process of connecting Access data to a Word document for the purpose of creating merged letters, envelopes, or labels.

Method An action that an object can perform.

Microsoft Office Premium Edition The Microsoft software products of Word, Excel, Access, PowerPoint, and Outlook that are sold as an integrated set.

Modem Short for modulate-demodulate; hardware that converts digital computer signals to analog telephone signals to allow a computer to send and receive information across ordinary telephone lines.

Module An Access object that stores Visual Basic programming code that extends the functions and automated processes of Access.

MsgBox A macro action that displays an informational message.

Multimedia controls Non-textual controls such as those that display picture, sound, or motion information.

Multi-user The characteristic that allows multiple people to use the same file or resource at the same time.

My Computer A icon on the Windows desktop that gives the user access to the drives, folders, and files within the computer.

Name AutoCorrect An Access feature that fixes discrepancies between references to field names, controls, and objects when you rename them.

Navigation buttons Buttons in the lower-left corner of a datasheet or form that allow you to quickly navigate between the records in the underlying object as well as add a new record.

Navigation mode A mode in which Access assumes that you are trying to move between the fields and records of the datasheet (rather than edit a specific field's contents), so keystrokes such as [Ctrl][Home] and [Ctrl][End] move you to the first and last field of the datasheet, respectively.

Network administrator A person who builds or manages a networking infrastructure.

New Record button A button that, when clicked, presents a new record for data entry. It is found on both the Form View and Datasheet toolbars as well as part of the Navigation buttons.

Newsgroups Groups with a common interest that provide public mailboxes (accessible only by computers) in which members can send and read messages. Messages posted to a newsgroup are intended for anyone who cares to read the messages in that newsgroup.

Normalization The process of designing a relational database, which involves determining the appropriate fields, tables, and table relationships.

Null The term that refers to a state of "nothingness" in a field. Any entry such as 0 in a numeric field or an invisible space in a text field is *not* null. It is common to search for empty fields by using the criteria "Is Null" in a filter or query. "Is Not Null" criteria finds all records where there is an entry of any kind.

Number A data type used for numeric information used in calculations, such as quantities.

Object A table, query, form, report, page, macro, or module.

Objects bar In the opening database window, the toolbar that presents the seven Access objects. When you click an object button on the Objects bar, options and wizards to create an object of that type as well as existing objects of that type appear in the main portion of the database window.

Object Browser A window that lists the defined modules and procedures as well as available methods, properties, events, constants, and other items that you can use in the code.

ODBC (Open Database Connectivity) A protocol for accessing data in SQL database servers.

Office Assistant An animated character that appears to offer tips, answer questions, and provide access to the program's Help system.

Office Clipboard A temporary storage area shared by all Office programs that can be used to cut, copy and paste multiple items within and between Office programs. The Office Clipboard can hold up to 12 items collected from any Office program. See also *Clipboard* and *Clipboard toolbar.*

OfficeLinks buttons The set of three buttons on the Database toolbar that are used to quickly copy Access data to the Word or Excel programs.

OLE Object A data type that stores pointers that tie files created in other programs to a record such as pictures, sound clips, word-processing documents, or spreadsheets.

One-to-many line The line that appears in the Relationships window that shows which field is duplicated between two tables to serve as the linking field. The one-to-many line displays a "1" next to the field that serves as the "one" side of the relationship and an infinity symbol next to the field that serves as the "many" side of the relationship when referential integrity is specified for the relationship. Also called one-to-many join line.

One-to-many relationship The relationship between two tables in an Access database in which a common field links the tables together The field is a key field in the "one" table of the relationship, but can be listed "many" times in the "many" table of the relationship.

One-to-one relationship The relationship between two tables in an Access database in which a common field links the tables together. The same field value can be entered only one time in each of the tables. One-to-one relationships are rare, and tables linked in this way can be combined into one table.

Option Button A bound control used to display a limited list of mutually exclusive choices for a field such as "female" or "male" for a gender field in a form or report. Also called a radio button.

Option Group A bound control placed on a form that is used to group together several option buttons that provide a limited number of values for a field.

Or criteria Criteria placed on different rows of the query design grid. A record will appear in the resulting datasheet if it is true for any single row.

OR query A query that contains OR criteria (two or more criteria present on different rows in the query design grid. A record will appear on the resulting datasheet if it is true for either criteria.)

Orphan record A record in the "many" table of a one-to-many relationship between two tables that has no matching record in the "one" table. If referential integrity is enforced, it is not possible to create orphan records.

Page An Access object that creates Web pages from Access objects as well as provides Web page connectivity features to an Access database. Also called Data Access Page.

Page Design view The window in which you develop page objects by adding, moving, and manipulating controls.

Page Footer section The section of the form or report that contains controls that print once at the bottom of each page.

Page Header section The section of the form or report that contains controls that print once at the top of each page. On the first page of the report, the Page Header section prints below the Report Header section.

Parameter query A query that displays a dialog box prompting you for criteria each time you run it.

Parent/Child relationship The relationship between the main form and subform. The main form acts as the parent, displaying the information about the "one" side of a one-to-many relationship between the forms. The subform acts as the "child" displaying as many records as exist in the "many" side of the one-to-many relationship.

Password A combination of characters required to gain access to the user's computer or files. See also *Database password, Security account password,* and *VBA password.*

Performance Analyzer An Access feature that studies the size and structure of your database and makes a variety of recommendations on how you could improve its performance.

PivotTable list A bound control used with the page object that helps you reorganize data into summarized columns and rows similar to a crosstabular datasheet.

Pop-up form A special type of form that stays on top of other open forms, even when another form is active.

Positioning The relative space between the text, sections, and other elements on the body of a data access page.

Primary key field See *Key field.*

Primary sort field In a query grid, the left-most field that includes sort criteria. It determines the order in which the records will appear and can be specified "ascending" or "descending."

Print Preview A window that displays how the physical printout will appear if the current object is printed.

Procedure A series of VBA programming statements that perform an operation or calculate an answer. There are two types of procedures: functions and subs.

Properties Characteristics that further define the field (if field properties), control (if control properties), section (if section properties), or object (if object properties).

Property sheet A window that displays an exhaustive list of properties for the chosen control, section, or object within the form or report Design view.

Protocol A set of rules.

Publish It with MS Word An Access feature that quickly copies Access data to a blank Word document.

Publishing Sending (uploading) Web page files to a Web server.

Query An Access object which provides a spreadsheet-like view of the data similar to tables. It may provide the user with a subset of fields and/or records from one or more tables. Queries are created when the user has a "question" about the data in the database.

Query design grid The bottom pane of the Query Design view window in which you specify the fields, sort order, and limiting criteria for the query.

Query Design view The window in which you develop queries by specifying the fields, sort order, and limiting criteria that determine which fields and records are displayed in the resulting datasheet.

Raw data The individual pieces of information stored in the database in individual fields.

Record A group of related fields, such as all demographic information for one customer.

Record locking An Access feature that prevents two people from changing the same record at the same time.

Record Navigation section A section available in the Design view of a page object used to display the navigation toolbar.

Record selector box The small square to left of a record in a datasheet that marks the current record or edit record symbol when the record has focus or is being edited. Clicking the record selector box selects the entire record. In Form view, the record selector box expands to the entire height of the form because only one record is viewed at a time.

Record source In a form or report, either a table or query object that contains the fields and records that the form will display. It is the most important property of the form or report object. A bound control on a form or report also has a record source property. In this case, the record source property identifies the field to which the control is bound.

Record source property The most important property of a form or report because it determines the recordset that the form or report will display.

Recordset The fields and records that are displayed by the object.

Rectangle control An unbound control used to draw rectangles on the form that divide the other form controls into logical groupings.

Referential integrity Ensures that no orphaned records are entered or created in the database by making sure that the "one" side of a linking relationship (CustomerNumber in a Customer table) is entered before that same value can be entered in the "many" side of the relationship (CustomerNumber in a Sales table).

Relational database A database in which more than one table, such as the customer, sales, and inventory tables, can share information. The term "relational database" comes from the fact that the tables are linked or "related" with a common field of information. An Access database is relational.

Replica The copy of the Access database file that is stored in the Briefcase.

Replica set Both the original (master) and replicated (replica) database file. There may be more than one replica in a replica set, but there is only one master.

Replication The process of making replicas of a master database file using the Briefcase.

Report An Access object that creates a professional printout of data that may contain such enhancements as headers, footers, and calculations on groups of records

Report Footer section On a report, a section that contains controls that print once at the end of the last page of the report.

Report Header section On a report, a section that contains controls that print once at the top of the first page of the report.

Row selector The small square to the left of a field in Table Design view.

RTF (Rich Text Format) A document file format that retains many basic formatting embellishments such as fonts and colors but does not support advanced features such as bookmarks and clip art. The RTF format is commonly used when more than one word processing program needs to share a file, because an RTF file can be opened in most of the leading word processing software packages.

Run Executing actions. For example, you run an action query to change data and you run a macro to execute the actions contained therein.

Run-time error A VBA error which occurs because you are attempting an illegal or impossible operation; such as dividing by zero or moving focus to a control that doesn't exist.

ScreenTip A pop-up label that appears when you point to a button. It provides descriptive information about the button.

Secondary sort field In a query grid, the second field from the left that includes sort criteria. It determines the order in which the records will appear if there is a "tie" on the primary sort field. (For example, the primary sort field might be the State field. If two records both contained the data "IA" in that field, the secondary sort field, which might be the City field, would determine the order of the IA records in the resulting datasheet.)

Section A location of a form or report that contains controls. The section in which a control is placed determines where and how often the control prints.

Section properties Properties associated with form, report, or page sections that control how the sections will display and print.

Security account password A password applied to workgroups used to determine which objects each workgroup has access to and at what level.

Select query The most common type of query that retrieves data from one or more linked tables and displays the results in a datasheet.

Server In client-server computer architectures, the server computer is generally the one that serves files.

Server-generated HTML files Web pages created by the Web server. They are dynamic, and therefore show current data, but are read-only.

Shared network folder A folder on a computer network to which multiple people have access.

Shortcuts Pointers to objects placed in the Favorites or user-created groups in the Groups bar.

Show Check Box A check box in Query Design View that determines whether the chosen field will be displayed on the datasheet or not.

Simple Query Wizard A wizard used to create a select query.

Single stepping Running a macro one line at a time, and observing the effect of each line as it is executed.

Sizing handles Small squares at each corner of a selected control. Dragging a handle resizes the control. Also known as *handles*.

Snapshot A type of recordset displayed within a query's datasheet that does not allow you to update any field.

Sort To place records in an order (ascending or descending) based on the values of a particular field.

Source document The original paper document that records raw data such as an employment application. In some databases, there is no source document because raw data is entered directly into the computer.

Specific record box Part of the Navigation buttons that indicates the current record number. You can also click in the specific record box and type a record number to quickly move to that record.

Spike A surge in electricity that can cause damage to a computer.

SQL (structured query language) statement, A standard programming language for selecting and manipulating data stored in a relational database.

Standard modules Modules stored as objects within the database window. Standard modules can be executed from anywhere within the database.

Startup options A series of commands that execute when a database is opened.

Statement A line of VBA code.

Static HTML file An HTML file (Web page) that is current only as of the moment that the Web page was created. It is not linked to an underlying Access database.

Status bar The bar at the bottom of the Access window that provides informational messages and other status information (such as whether the Num Lock is active or not).

Status Bar Text property Property of a control that determines what text displays in the status bar when that control has the focus.

Sub A procedure that performs a series of VBA statements but does not return a value nor can it be used in an expression. You create subs to manipulate controls and objects.

Sub procedure See *Sub*.

Subdatasheet A datasheet that shows related records. It appears when the user clicks a record's expand button.

Subform A form placed within a form that shows related records from another table or query. A subform generally displays many records at a time in a datasheet arrangement.

Subreport A report placed as a control within another report.

Summary query A query used to calculate and display information about records grouped together.

Surge protector Equipment that protects computers in the event of surges or spikes in electricity.

Switchboard A special type of form that uses command buttons to simplify and secure access to database objects.

Switchboard Manager An Access feature that simplifies the creation and maintenance of switchboard forms.

Synchronization The process of reconciling and updating changes between the master and replicas of a replica set.

Syntax error A VBA error which occurs because of a typing error or misspelling. Syntax errors are highlighted in the Code window in red.

Tab control An unbound control used to create a three-dimensional aspect to a form so that other controls can be organized and shown in Form view by clicking the "tabs."

Tab order The sequence in which the controls on the form receive the focus when pressing [Tab] or [Enter] in Form view.

Table An Access object which is a collection of records for a single subject, such as all of the customer records. Tables can be linked with a common field to share information and therefore minimize data redundancy.

Table Datasheet toolbar The toolbar that appears when you are viewing a table's datasheet.

TCP/IP (Transmission Control Protocol/Internet Protocol) The communications protocol by which the Internet routes messages and Web pages through the Internet network.

Text A data type that allows text information or combinations of text and numbers such as a street address. By default, it is 50 characters but can be changed to 50 characters. The maximum length of a text field is 255 characters.

Text box A common control used on forms and reports to display data bound to an underlying field. A text box can also show calculated controls such as subtotals and dates.

Toggle button A bound control used to indicate "yes" or "no" answers for a field. If the button is "pressed" it displays "yes" information.

Toolbox toolbar The toolbar that has common controls that you can add to a report or form when working in the report or form's Design view.

Top Values feature A feature within Query Design view that allows you to limit the number of records in the resulting datasheet to a value or percentage of the total.

Unbound controls Controls that do not change from record to record and exist only to clarify or enhance the appearance of the form, such as labels, lines, and clip art.

Unbound image control An unbound control used to display clip art that doesn't change as you navigate from record to record on a form or report.

UNC (Universal Naming Convention) A convention used to locate a file on a network. The structure of a UNC is \\server\sharedfoldername\filename and it is commonly used to locate files stored on a local area network.

Update query An action query that updates data based on an expression.

UPS (Uninterruptible Power Supply) Equipment that maintains constant electricity to a computer over a period of time in the event of brownouts, power surges, or power outages.

URL (Uniform Resource Locator) Each resource on the Internet (including Web pages) has an address so that other computers can accurately and consistently locate and view them.

Validation rule A field property that establishes criteria for an entry to be accepted into the database.

Validation text A field property that determines what message will appear if a user attempts to make a field entry that does not pass the validation rule for that field.

Variable A named storage location that can contain data that can be modified during program execution.

VBA (Visual Basic for Applications) The Access programming language that is very similar to Visual Basic and which is stored within module objects.

VBA password A password that prevents unauthorized users from modifying VBA code.

View buttons Four buttons in the database window that determines how the object icons are displayed (as Large Icons, Small Icons, List, and Details).

Visual Basic Code window The Design View of a module in which you write Visual Basic for Applications programming code.

Visual Basic for Applications See *VBA*.

WAN (Wide Area Network) A computer network that connects computers and LANs across public thoroughfares. WANs must use existing telecommunications networks (usually telephone lines) to accomplish this.

Web folder Special folders dedicated to storing and organizing Web pages on a Web server.

Web page A special type of file created with HTML code that contains hyperlinks to other files.

Web server A file server (large microcomputer) that stores, downloads, and routes Web pages.

Webmaster A person who works with Web servers, Web folders, and supporting Internet technologies.

What if analysis A process in which a user interactively applies assumptions to a set of numbers in an Excel spreadsheet to watch the resulting formulas recalculate automatically.

Wildcard characters Special characters used in criteria to find, filter, and query data. The asterisk (*) stands for any group of characters. For example, the criteria I* in a State field criteria cell would find all records where the state entry was IA, ID, IL, IN, or Iowa. The question mark (?) wildcard stands for only one character. The pound sign (#) can only be used as a wildcard in a numeric field and stands for a single number.

Wizard An interactive set of dialog boxes that guides you through an Access process such as creating a query, form, or report.

Word The word processing application within the Microsoft Office Suite.

Workgroup A description of users, objects, and permissions to which those users have access to the objects stored as a file.

Workgroup administrator A program used to create workgroups.

World Wide Web page A hyperlinked document that makes the Internet easy to navigate.

WorldWide Web See *WWW*.

WWW (World Wide Web) A vast number of linked documents stored on thousands of different Web servers.

Yes/No A data type that stores only one of two values (Yes/No, On/Off, True/False).

Zoom dialog box A dialog box that allows you to enter and view a large expression in a query or property text box.

Index

Index

Index

Index

Index